*Hungarian Religion,
Romanian Blood*

Hungarian Religion, Romanian Blood

A Minority's Struggle for National Belonging, 1920–1945

R. Chris Davis

The University of Wisconsin Press

Publication of this book was made possible, in part,
by a grant from the First Book Subvention Program
of the **Association for Slavic, East European, and Eurasian Studies**.

The University of Wisconsin Press
728 State Street, Suite 443
Madison, Wisconsin 53706
uwpress.wisc.edu

3 Henrietta Street, Covent Garden
London WC2E 8LU, United Kingdom
eurospanbookstore.com

Copyright © 2019
The Board of Regents of the University of Wisconsin System
All rights reserved. Except in the case of brief quotations embedded in critical articles and reviews, no part of this publication may be reproduced, stored in a retrieval system, transmitted in any format or by any means—digital, electronic, mechanical, photocopying, recording, or otherwise—or conveyed via the Internet or a website without written permission of the University of Wisconsin Press. Rights inquiries should be directed to rights@uwpress.wisc.edu.

Printed in the United States of America

This book may be available in a digital edition.

Library of Congress Cataloging-in-Publication Data
Names: Davis, R. Chris (Robert Chris), 1975– author.
Title: Hungarian religion, Romanian blood: a minority's struggle for national belonging, 1920–1945 / R. Chris Davis.
Description: Madison, Wisconsin: The University of Wisconsin Press, [2018] | Includes bibliographical references and index.
Identifiers: LCCN 2017051213 | ISBN 9780299316402 (cloth: alk. paper)
Subjects: LCSH: Csangos—Romania—Moldavia—History—20th century. | Moldavia (Romania)—Ethnic relations—20th century.
Classification: LCC DR214.C73 D38 2018 | DDC 305.894/511047609041—dc23
LC record available at https://lccn.loc.gov/2017051213

ISBN 978-0-299-31644-0 (pbk.: alk. paper)

For

Maria, Sofi, and **Sebi**

Cain said to Abel his brother, "Let us go out to the field." And when they were in the field, Cain rose up against his brother Abel, and killed him. Then the LORD said to Cain, "Where is Abel your brother?" He said, "I do not know; am I my brother's keeper?" And the LORD said, "What have you done? The voice of your brother's blood is crying to me from the ground. And now you are cursed from the ground, which has opened its mouth to receive your brother's blood from your hand."

Genesis 4:9–12

Contents

List of Illustrations		ix
Preface		xi
Dramatis Personae		xvii
Introduction		3
1	Demography Is Destiny: People, Space, and Nation	22
2	The Sacred: Religion, Kulturkampf, and Catholic-Orthodox Polemics	36
3	The Profane: A True Science of the Nation and People	65
4	Certifiably Romanian: Codifying National Belonging	87
5	Resettlement "Home": Solving Demographic Crises	115
6	The Cry of Blood: The Csangos Recertified	139
Conclusion		164
Glossary		171
Notes		183
Bibliography		217
Index		239

Illustrations

István Györffy's ethnographic map of the Csango land, 1899–1902	2
Csango region demarcated inside a map of Romania	5
Csangos in front of the village church in Sabaoani/Szabófalva, 1918	8
Csangos in the village of Sabaoani/Szabófalva, 1931	9
Bishop Mihai Robu with faculty and students at the Seminary of Iaşi, 1934	40
Cover of the Catholic journal *Viaţa* (The life), 1941	50
Csango men in the village of Şumuleu-Ciuc/Csíksomlyó, 1934	85
Hungarian ethnographer Pál Péter Domokos recording folk songs, 1932	86
Nationality certificate, 1942	96
Nationality certificate, 1942	97
Nationality certificate, 1944	98
Blood-group frequency chart of the Moldavian Csangos	150

Preface

This book explores the limits or, at any rate, the elasticity of ethnic and national identities, of belonging to one or another group, community, people, nation, or state. After more than a decade researching this topic and writing this book, I am convinced that we can no longer say someone is "ethnically" Hungarian or Romanian or even Csango—the minority community whose contested identity is at the heart of this book—but, rather, that they are "ethnographically" one thing or the other (or both), since it is usually the science (and scientism) and always the *graphos*, the writing, that tells us so. The term "ethnic" may well go the way of "race" as an inherently faulty or fleeting attempt to concretize something nebular and usually ascriptive. Still, as categories of analysis, concepts such as race, ethnicity, and nationhood remain important to historical understandings and discussions of east-central Europe, especially during the interwar and World War II periods. Historians and others are justified in their efforts to seek new ways to write about twentieth-century European history by focusing on different aspects of the historical experience, especially among nonelites, since pinning down something as indefinite as ethnicity or nationality is always subjective and frequently contentious. For many communities and individuals in east-central Europe in the 1930s and 1940s, questions of national belonging, ethnic origin, and race were seminal and omnipresent, a part of lived reality. This was true especially for minorities, including peasants and ethnically ambiguous (if also ambivalent) communities, such as the Hungarian- and Romanian-speaking Roman Catholics of eastern Romania, dubbed the Moldavian Csangos. By the start of World War II, picking a side, so to speak, as either Hungarian or Romanian, could mean the difference between keeping a home that had been in your family for centuries or else relocating, at the point of a gun, to a foreign country—or worse, ending up in a concentration camp. If uprooted in the early years of the war, the best alternative for some of these Csangos was landing on a plot of mud in Hungarian-occupied Serbia, in Vojvodina, taking over a recently "evacuated" Jew's house or a Serb's farm, with the Serbian Army and Serbian neighbors poised to win back their own legacies, memories, and properties, of which the Hungarian and German armies had relieved them through Blitzkrieg.

I have tried to situate my history of the Csangos and their dilemma within more recent transnational and comparative historiography on twentieth-century Romania and Hungary, specifically as a case study on how minorities can exemplify—by way of analogy or anomaly—any number of larger national, ideological, and historical trends. In this respect, the Csangos also provide a good case study of recent themes in contemporary scholarship on Romania, especially work done on population policies and sociological and anthropological research in interwar and World War II Romania. From these broader thematic and methodological vantage points we can more easily disentangle the ethnocentrism from competing historical narratives on contested minority communities and examine them in relation to one another. By examining the interplay between these narratives and the web of meanings within these discursive battles on inclusivity and exclusivity, we can better understand how these texts and discourses were received, interpreted, and in some cases internalized or else rejected.

What I do hope to demonstrate in this book are not only the manifold ways in which minorities or putative "Others" have negotiated the shifting definitions of race, ethnicity, and nationality but also the ways in which family, community, and religion mediated or transcended these and other social and cultural categories that predominated in twentieth-century European and global history (and persist to this day). Did some minorities readily commute or conceal their nationality and ethnicity in order to preserve their religion? Was religion, for some, a more salient marker of identity and a more meaningful social practice? The letters of these individuals and families to both the Romanian and Hungarian governments reveal a community in distress, exploring and utilizing the nationalist idiom in an effort to rescue or remove themselves from wartime, nationalist politics. Their actions and testimonies suggest they were constructing new identities *against* the world rather than *within* it. I sometimes imagine a man in his early forties, a brother, a husband, a father—like me. His connections to home and family at this time would have been perilous, and the choices he would have faced seem impossible. What must he have told himself? Perhaps something like the following:

> In this my modest house my father was born, as was I, as were my children. That creek down there is where I learned to swim with the boys who would

later become my brothers in arms, fighting with me against bygone empires in foreign lands during the Great War. Many never returned to that creek. Over here, under that tree, is where I kissed my future wife for the first time. Over there, on that hill, is where I buried two of my daughters, who lay next to my parents, watching over me. All this, I must leave behind, because I make the sign of the cross from right to left, as a Catholic, rather than left to right, as Eastern Orthodox? Because in my home I speak Hungarian? And because I cannot demonstrate something called my Romanian ethnicity to the satisfaction of that corrupt prefect of police, who was sent from Bucharest last year? I will otherwise be "returned" to what these ethnographers and doctors tell me is my ancestral homeland, in a marsh called Vojvodina, full of Serbs, Germans, and Jews.

People like stories. It helps them make sense of things. History, as I have painstakingly learned, is as much storytelling as anything else. I have become ever more self-reflective as a writer and teacher of history, as someone who has now created his own narrative of a people who are not my own. The individuals I write about in the pages that follow, from the racial anthropologists and the intrepid ethnographers to the priests entering the world of the profane, were doing much the same thing—telling a story for one purpose or another. Their purposes, whether Romanian or Hungarian, Csango, Oxthodox, Protestant, or Catholic, may have been to reclaim or reject the Catholic community in Moldavia, as the case may be, or to curry favor with a political or religious faction. Many of the Hungarian ethnographers, political activists, and priests endeavored to "save" the Csangos from "Romanianization" by the nationalizing, homogenizing Romanian state and its surrogates, the Romanian Orthodoxists. Many of their Romanian counterparts, including a number of very important and committed priests, with the backing of the Vatican, likewise endeavored to "save" the Romanian Catholics of Moldavia from the centuries-old onslaught of Hungarianization or "denationalization." Or maybe some of them, like me, just found meaning in writing about a curious historical problem.

I am a part of all that I have met," reflected Tennyson's Ulysses upon returning home to Ithaca, having completed his arduous, decade-long journey after the Trojan War. Never has this line rung truer than in the waning days of my own long and arduous journey that has been the making of this book. Foremost I would like to thank Robert J. W. Evans and Marius Turda in Oxford for their mentorship and friendship. My friend and colleague Eric Beckett Weaver likewise deserves special mention, especially for his critical feedback at various stages of the manuscript. I am grateful moreover for his help in reviewing many of my translations from Hungarian into English. Any mistakes are, of course, my own.

I have had the great fortune of working with many fine academics and friends in Romania, Hungary, the United Kingdom, and the United States. Roland Clark, Valentin Săndulescu, Călin Cotoi, Cristian Vasile, Ionuț Florin Biliuță, Răzvan Pârâianu, and James Kapalo have all imparted a great deal of knowledge, not only through their scholarship but also in their discussions or correspondence with me on a range of topics, especially on locating sources. Claudiu Crăciun gave much support and encouragement, both personally and professionally. Dennis Deletant has also been most generous with his time and support over the years. Ferenc Pozsony, Vilmos Tánczos, and Lehel Peti have likewise been extremely generous with their time and resources. I am also grateful to Gwen Walker, Peter Kracht, Andrzej Kamiński, and the organizers of the fifteenth annual "Recovering Forgotten History" summer workshop in Poland for selecting my book project for discussion and review at the conference. Thanks to Adam Burakowski, Agniezska Barszczewska, and my dear friend and colleague Rigels Halili for their critical feedback of my text that summer in Krakow. Deserving special mention for providing or helping me locate materials in Romania over the years are Alina Ilinca, George Vișan, and the staff at the Archive of the National Council for the Study of the Securitate Archives; the archivists at the National Historical Archive in Bucharest; Anton Coșa at the Dumitru Mărtinaș Association of Roman Catholics in Bacău; and Father Cornel Cadar and Father Cristian Bîrnat at the Archive of the Roman Catholic Episcopate in Iași. In Hungary, I am grateful to the librarians and archivists at the National Széchényi Library, Central European University Library, the Hungarian National Archive, and particularly to Hanga Gebauer at the Ethnographic Museum in Budapest.

Funding for research was made possible by the Fulbright Commission, the American Council of Learned Societies, the International Research and Exchanges Board, and the Romanian Cultural Institute. I am also grateful to New Europe College in Bucharest and the Centre for Advanced Study in Sofia, whose research fellowships and intellectual community of scholars nurtured the early stages of this book, and to the Association for Slavic, East European, and Eurasian Studies for the first book subvention award. I would not have been able to complete this project back in the United States had it not been for the steadfast support of the faculty, administration, and students at my home institution, Lone Star College-Kingwood. Before all this research came to fruition, I was fortunate to have experienced firsthand, as a Peace Corps volunteer

Preface

in Sfântu-Gheorghe/Sepsiszentgyörgy, Transylvania, so much of the culture and history I write about in this book. Without the wonderful administration, teachers, and students at the Hungarian-language high school Székely Mikó Kollégium, where I taught English, and all the great people at the former Peace Corps office in Bucharest, I would never have embarked on this journey. But for the support of my family and friends, both in the United States and in Europe, I would never have completed it.

Dramatis Personae

My purpose for including this Dramatis Personae is, first, to serve as a reference point for some of these otherwise obscure individuals who recur throughout the book; and, second, to serve as a kind of biographical survey of the individuals (and their professions) who shaped the history of this era, this place. For geographical and linguistic terms unfamiliar to the reader, I advise the reader to consult the Glossary at the back of the book.

Descriptions of the men below pertain mainly to their activities during the interwar years and especially World War II. The fact that the protagonists and antagonists of this story are all men is not lost on me. Alas, these are who wrote about and politicized the identity of the so-called Csango community, the main subject of this book. To be sure, women began to play quite important roles in the emergent sociological, ethnographic, and youth movements, including fascist and communist movements, in interwar Romania and Hungary. However, the debates over the Csangos, at this time, emanated from male-dominated social and professional milieus in Romania and Hungary, including the Roman Catholic and Eastern Orthodox priesthoods, the various historical and scientific academies, and the offices (both high and low) of military and state.

Roman Catholic Theologians in Moldavia and Bucharest

The Roman Catholic clergy in Moldavia and Bucharest was an eclectic group of men. Although most hailed from villages within the Roman Catholic–inhabited region in eastern Romania, they had varied familial lineages, as, over the previous centuries, the missionaries and appointed hierarchy came from the Catholic states and kingdoms of central and western Europe. But by the twentieth century many of the higher-positioned clergy from this milieu traveled and studied abroad, including in Italy, France, and Germany. They wrote and taught history, philosophy, literature, and philology and served not only as the spiritual but also the intellectual and political guides of the Csango communities. During the interwar period and World War II, most of these priests endorsed the Romanianization agenda of the state, and a few, like their Romanian Orthodoxist counterparts (below), joined ultranationalist organizations in interwar Romania, including the Legion of the Archangel Michael. They encouraged their Hungarian-speaking parishioners to abandon their Hungarian identity (including names and language), due either to a genuine fidelity to Romanian nationalist ideals or else a strategic response to the antiminority politics of the Romanian state and society, including involuntary loss of citizenship and coerced expatriation.

Cassulo, Andrea (1869–1952) was an Italian archbishop and diplomat who served as apostolic nuncio to Romania during World War II. He is perhaps most famous for his efforts to rescue Romanian Jews (especially baptized Jews) during the Holocaust. His main diplomatic mission, however, was to intervene on behalf of persecuted and imprisoned Romanian Catholics.

Cisar, Alexandru (1888–1954) was a native of Bucharest (though of Czech family origins) and the Bishop of Iași from 1920 to 1924. In 1924, Cisar became the first Romanian-born Archbishop of Bucharest after a new Romanian law stipulated the clerical hierarchy must be Romanian citizens.

Frollo, Iosif (1886–1966) was a Catholic lay theologian, linguist, and professor. He was a major writer on Catholic issues in Romania's interwar years and led the Romanian branch of Catholic Action (Acțiunea Catolică). Frollo's writings on the ethnic and religious belonging of Catholics to the Romanian nation provided a template for subsequent writings on the history and nationality of the Csangos.

Ghiuzan, Iosif (1898–1932) was a parish priest outside Băcau and taught at the seminary in Iași. He contributed numerous articles in Catholic journals in the late 1920s, anticipating the decisive factor in later debates on the Csangos' national belonging during World War II, namely that the Csangos were Romanian by origin and blood.

Mărtinaș, Ioan (1925–1986) was a parish priest in the village of Gherăești, professor at the seminary in Iași, and historian of Roman Catholicism in Romania and eastern Europe. He was also a high-ranking member of the Romanian fascist movement the Legion of the Archangel Michael (also known as the Iron Guard).

Dramatis Personae

Pal, Iosif Petru (1889–1947) was the head of the Franciscan order in Romania, taught theology and philosophy at Catholic seminaries in Moldavia, and wrote on the history of Roman Catholicism in Romania. Educated and ordained in Rome, he became one of the most influential members in the hierarchy of the Iași diocese.

Robu, Mihai (1884–1944) was the first Moldavian-born Bishop of Iași. During the 1930s and 1940s, he promoted the Romanianization of the Roman Catholic Church in Romania and resisted Hungarian efforts to portray the Csango community as ethnically Hungarian.

Romanian Orthodox Theologians (Lay and Clerical)

The Romanian Orthodox theologians and philosophers of religion below synthesized their theologies with variant strains of nationalist thinking and discourse (for more on Romanian Orthodoxism, consult the Glossary at the back of the book). To one degree or another, they believed that Romanian Orthodoxy was inseparable from the Romanian national character. The implication here is that Romanians of the Roman Catholic rite (a minority in the country) could never truly be Romanian. Some of these theologians (clerical as well lay) took part in the various fascist movements in interwar Romania, including the Legion of the Archangel Michael. Most of the men below were advocates for removal of Romania's minorities (both ethnic and religious) and took very public and often hostile positions against the Roman Catholic Church.

Bălan, Nicolae (1882–1955) was the Transylvanian-born Metropolitan of Transylvania from 1920 until his death. A major theologian of his day and a frequent supporter of the Legion and other ultranationalist causes, Bălan opposed the Romanian-Vatican Concordat and warned against the dangers of denationalization via the growth of Catholicism in Romania and the need to resist it through the agency of the Orthodox Church.

Crainic, Nichifor (1889–1972) was a theologian, publicist, politician, and among the most prominent Romanian intellectuals of the radical right. An avowed anti-Semite, Crainic promoted a nationalist if also mystical theology. As minister of propaganda between 1940 and 1943, he became a leading advocate for the forced removal of Romania's ethnic and religious minorities.

Ionescu, Nae (1890–1940) was, like Crainic, a right-wing theologian, publicist, politician, and among the most influential intellectuals in interwar Romania.

He propagated racist policy prescriptions for the removal of Romania's minority populations. In 1930, he stoked the interwar period's famous "A fi bun român" (To be a good Romanian) polemic with the Catholic theologian Frollo (above).

Scriban, Iuliu (1878–1949) was a professor of theology, reputed polemicist, and one-time member of A. C. Cuza's virulently anti-Semitic National-Christian Defense League. He held the title of archimandrite and was one of the highest-ranking members of the Romanian Orthodox Church.

Stăniloae, Dumitru (1903–1993) was a young cleric and very much under the sway of Crainic and Ionescu (above) who in the 1930s harbored anti-Catholic sentiments. He subsequently became one of the most important Orthodox theologians of the twentieth century and certainly the most prominent in Romania.

Romanian Politicians, Military, Royalty

Antonescu, Ion (1882–1946) was a Romanian general who, shortly after Romania joined the Axis Powers and entered World War II, rose to the rank of marshal and then prime minister and conducător (or "leader") of Romania. A fervent anti-Semite, he governed Romania as a military dictatorship and ally of Nazi Germany during the war. He targeted minorities for various population relocations and exchanges and advocated the ethnic cleansing of Romania, which led to the murder of hundreds of thousands of Jews and Roma in Romanian-controlled territory. He was executed in Romania for war crimes.

Antonescu, Mihai (1904–1946) was a vice president of the Council of Ministers, deputy prime minister, and minister of foreign affairs during World War II (though no familial relation to Ion Antonescu, above). Mihai Antonescu was the second most powerful man in World War II Romania, overseeing the wartime bureaucracy that permitted the deportation and killing of Romanian Jews and Roma. He was executed in Romania for war crimes.

Carol I, King of Romania (1839–1914; r. 1866–1914) was the first king of the unified, independent Kingdom of Romania. A Roman Catholic, he hailed from the Hohenzollern-Sigmaringen dynasty of Germany.

Carol II, King of Romania (1893–1953; r. 1930–1940) was the son of Ferdinand I and the first Romanian monarch born in Romania and raised in the Romanian Orthodox faith. He aligned Romania with Nazi Germany, passed the first in a series of anti-Semitic "blood laws," and at the end of his reign established a royal dictatorship before abdicating in 1940.

Dramatis Personae

Ferdinand I, King of Romania (1865–1927; r. 1914–1927) succeeded his uncle Carol I and ruled the much-enlarged "Greater Romania" during the first half of the interwar period. A German and Roman Catholic by birth, Ferdinand helped establish the Romanian-Vatican Concordat of 1927.

Ghibu, Onisifor (1883–1972) was a Transylvanian regionalist and a prominent education reformer and politician during the interwar period. He led the ostensibly secular charge for the nullification of the Romanian-Vatican Concordat.

Goga, Octavian (1881–1938) was a politician, poet, and journalist and one of Romania's leading anti-Semites and Nazi sympathizers. During the short-lived Goga-Cuza government (1937–38), Goga and the law professor A. C. Cuza served as prime minister and minister of state, respectively, and oversaw Romania's first wave of anti-Jewish laws. Both men publicly advocated Romania's minority populations.

Gruia, Ion V. (1895–1952) was one of the most important Romanian jurists of the 1930s and early 1940s. As minister of justice in 1940, his legal writings codified the distinction between citizens of "Romanian blood" and citizens of "non-Romanian blood," effectively establishing a *numerus clausus* in Romania during World War II.

Ionescu, Constantin S. (dates unknown) was a general in the Romanian Army and, at various times, the county prefect of Iași and Bacău as well as the mayor of Iași. In 1941 he instructed regional bureaucrats to deny citizenship rights to the Roman Catholics of the region (Romanian citizens all) on the pretense that they were Hungarians and thus foreigners.

Petit, Eugen Dimitrie (1882–1959) was a jurist, magistrate, and counselor in the Court of Cassation in Bucharest. Born in Iași but of French descent, he was attuned to the discrimination faced by fellow Roman Catholics in the region. Petit used his expertise and position to challenge Romania's blood laws during World War II, writing a seminal text on inherent problems of legislating ethnic origin.

Romanian (including Transylvanian) Writers, Historians, and Scientists

Many of Romania's leading population scientists and racial anthropologists hailed from Greek Catholic families from Transylvania and thus were former subjects of the Hungarian crown (and thus subject to Hungarianization policies in the late nineteenth and early twentieth centuries, especially in churches and schools). Unsurprisingly, after the unification of Transylvania with Romania in

1920 they pioneered much of the research into the ethnic origins of supposedly denationalized Romanian populations. Many of the men below were true polymaths and thus difficult to categorize professionally. Some, like Meteş, Vâlsan, and Opreanu, published literary works of their own. Like their Hungarian counterparts, they were genuinely interdisciplinary before the term was even coined. Most were academicians, educators, or technocrats in the government bureaucracy, yet were nationalists of one stripe or another.

Chindea, Teodor (1895–1982) was a Romanian schoolteacher and amateur historian from the Szeklerland who wrote on the plight of ethnic Romanians there. He was among the first to popularize the denationalization theories that preoccupied Romanian historians and social scientists during the interwar period.

Golopenţia, Anton (1909–1951) was a sociologist, statistician, geopolitician, and among the most important scientists writing on minority populations in interwar and wartime Romania. During World War II, he investigated the ethnic basis of the Csangos and led expeditions in Romanian-controlled Transnistria to identify ethnic Romanians across the border.

Gusti, Dimitrie (1880–1955) was a sociologist and, along with Nicolae Iorga (below), the most prominent Romanian academic of his day. His sociological approach to village research—in which teams of village researchers collected ethnographic data and produced village monographs—endeavored to create for Romania a "science of the nation." The Gusti School directly and indirectly inspired some of the most important ethnographical works (by Romanians and Hungarians) on the Csangos, then and since.

Iorga, Nicolae (1871–1940) was Romania's leading historian and public intellectual, as well as a committed nationalist and politician who served as a member of parliament, cabinet minister, and, for one year, prime minister. Iorga and other prominent Romanian historians had long accepted that the Csangos were, by ethnic origin and settlement history, isolated communities of Hungarians. By the mid-1930s, however, Iorga accepted new historical theories of the Csangos as denationalized Romanians, lending much credibility to revisionist historical narratives about the ethnic origins of large swathes of peoples inhabiting Romanian territory.

Manuilă, Sabin (1894–1964) was Romania's leading statistician and demographer throughout this period. He coordinated Romania's national censuses and formulated many of its population policies, including the government's racial projects aiming at a systematic demographic reordering of the country through population transfers. Manuilă supported the coup against

Dramatis Personae

Antonescu in 1944. In 1947/8 he immigrated to the United States, where he continued to hold respected academic positions, including at Stanford University and the US Census Bureau.

Meteș, Ștefan (1887/8?-1977) was a prominent historian and theologian from Transylvania who popularized a number of denationalization theories during the interwar period, including the Szeklerization of Orthodox Romanians in eastern Transylvania.

Opreanu, Sabin (1888-1978) was a geographer and mentee of Gheorghe Vâlsan (below) and head of the Institute of Geography at the University of Cluj. He was among the first to suggest the mass of Szeklers were none other than denationalized Romanians who had been Szeklerized by the Hungarian churches, specifically the Catholic Church.

Popa-Lisseanu, Gheorghe (1886-1945) was a noted philologist, classicist, and member of the Romanian Academy. An influential figure in academic and policy circles in Bucharest, he championed the denationalization theories first developed by Chindea and Opreanu (above).

Vâlsan, Gheorghe (1885-1935) was one of Romania's foremost geographers. He intermingled ethnography and folklore in his research and writing and inspired everyone from professional social scientists to amateur historians to schoolteachers to embark on a "true science of the Nation and its people" and to rewrite its history from multifarious local perspectives.

Hungarian Politicians, Military

Bárdossy, László (1890-1946) was a pro-German politician who served as prime minister of Hungary in 1941-42. The Bárdossy government ordered the Hungarian Army's invasion of Yugoslavia and Russia alongside the German Army, promulgated anti-Jewish laws in Hungary, and devised a series of plans to resettle into Hungarian territory hundreds of thousands of (purported) ethnic Hungarians from across eastern Europe. He was executed in Hungary for war crimes.

Besenyő, Sándor (1905-?; a.k.a. Siculus) was an activist, writer, translator, and attaché for the Hungarian consulate in Romania, aiding the Hungarian government's effort to relocate the Csangos to Hungary during World War II. He taught theology in the seminary in Iași in the 1930s and published some highly charged works depicting the plight of the Csangos in the early 1940s.

Bonczos, Miklós (1897-1971) was a Transylvanian-born lawyer, writer, extreme right politician, and member of parliament, as well as the minister of interior for a brief stint in 1944 before fleeing to Argentina. As head of the Foreign Hungarians Repatriation Committee, he played a key role in the development and implementation of Hungary's wartime population policies.

Sztójay, Döme (1883–1946) was a pro-German politician and general in the Hungarian Army. He served as ambassador in Berlin during the war and, in 1944, became the Hitler-backed prime minister of Hungary after Germany occupied the country. Under Sztójay, the Hungarian government legalized the fascist Arrow Cross Party, resumed the deportation of Hungarian Jews to Germany, and restarted talks with Romania about relocating the Csangos to Hungary. He was executed in Hungary for war crimes.

Teleki, Pál (1879–1941) was a noted geographer and professor and major political figure in Hungary, serving twice as prime minister. As prime minister in 1940, he indicated to local Hungarians living in Romanian Bukovina and Moldavia that he would approve plans to resettle them into Hungary. With and without formal agreements in place, many from among these communities sold their belongings, renounced their Romanian citizenship, and prepared to emigrate.

Werth, Henrik (1881–1952) was the pro-German chief of general staff of the Hungarian Army during World War II and led Hungary's invasion of the Soviet Union and Yugoslavia. Himself of German ancestry, he advocated the wholesale removal of minorities from Hungary and resettlement of ethnic Hungarians in their stead. He was found guilty in Hungary for war crimes and sentenced to death.

Hungarian (including Transylvanian) Writers, Historians, and Scientists

The sociographical, historiographical, and even the political youth movements in interwar Hungary and Transylvania produced a wide range of history, ethnography, and literature that spanned the ideological spectrums of the time and cut across class lines. Most of the writing either consciously or unconsciously attempted to reckon with Hungary's defeat in World War I and the resulting loss of territory as per the Treaty of Trianon in 1920. Much of this writing explored the plight of Hungarian minorities in the newly formed (or expanded) states bordering Hungary, and many of these writers were themselves from the borderlands of the now-dissolved Dual Monarchy (Austria-Hungary). They explored Hungarianness in new and curious ways and meditated on the fate not only of Hungarian minorities but also on the broader

Dramatis Personae

Hungarian nation and race. During the war, some of these men became exponents of the Hungarian government's population-transfer schemes to resettle these minorities in Hungarian territory.

Domokos, Pál Péter (1901–1992) was an ethnographer, historian, and educator who hailed from the Szekler land. He published a major ethnography on the Csangos and was a social activist in interwar Transylvania. As a wartime diplomat in the Hungarian Embassy in Bucharest, he aided the Hungarian government's effort to resettle the Csangos in Hungary.

Lükő, Gábor (1901–2001) was an ethnographer, folklorist, museumologist, and social psychologist who studied under Romanian sociologist Dimitrie Gusti (above). He contributed a major ethnography on the Csangos during the interwar period, identifying within the Csango land two distinct communities of Hungarians based on dialect and material culture.

Mályusz, Elemér (1898–1989) was one of Hungary's major historians of the twentieth century, publishing widely on demographic, settlement, and local history. A self-styled "ethnohistorian" who established the Institute of Settlement and Ethnohistory in Budapest, Mályusz was a countervailing force against Western and especially German influences in Hungarian historiography in the 1930s and 1940s and committed himself and his students to rather ethnocentric interpretations of Hungarian national history. His approach to local and interdisciplinary history inspired several of the most important works on the Csangos.

Mikecs, László (1917–1944) was a young intellectual and somewhat Romantic "ethnohistorian" who moved in Hungarian and Romanian circles in Transylvania, Moldavia, and Bucharest and studied under some of the most important academics of the time. While based in Cluj during the war, he published several major studies on the Csangos. Mikecs was captured by the Red Army and deported east, where he died in a Soviet detention camp.

Németh, Kálmán (1897–1966) was a medical doctor and parson in Bukovina who spearheaded propaganda efforts to convince the Bukovinan Szeklers and the Moldavian Csangos to relocate *en bloc* to Hungary. Romanian authorities arrested him in 1940 for suspected irredentist activities.

Veress, Endre (1868–1953; pseud. John [János] Tatrosi) was a widely educated and well-traveled historian, archivist, teacher, and translator. Born and raised in Bucharest, he wrote extensively on the Hungarian minorities in east-central Europe, including the Csangos. Veress was an early influence on the new generation of Hungarian intellectuals writing in interwar Romania.

*Hungarian Religion,
Romanian Blood*

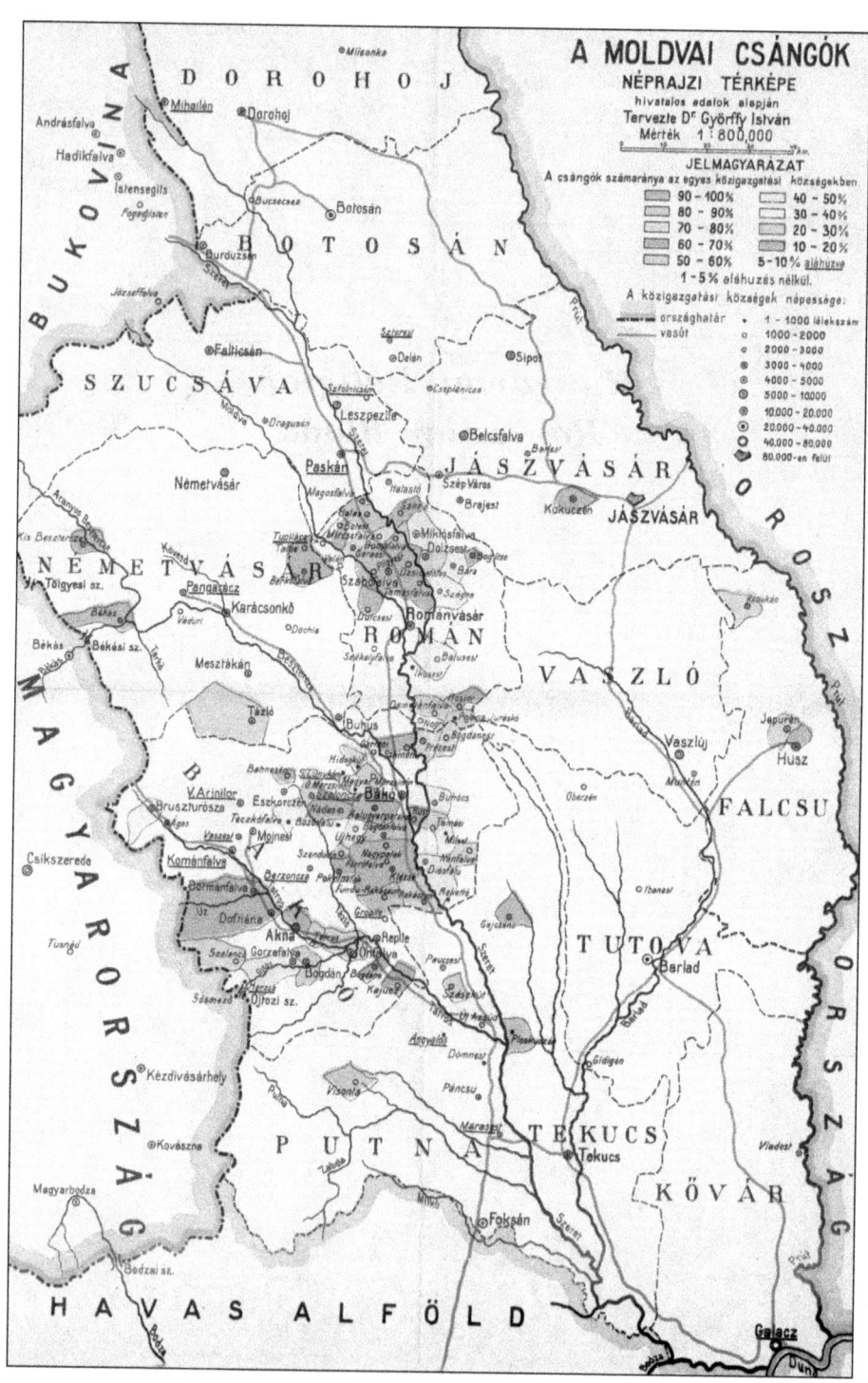

István Györffy's ethnographic map of the Csango land, 1899-1902. Hungary (Magyarország) on the left, and Russia (Oroszország) on the right. (courtesy of the National Széchényi Library of Hungary, Budapest [call. nr. T 3 749])

Introduction

In the summer of 1942, amid the welter of world war, Axis-allied states Romania and Hungary considered expatriating the Catholic population from Moldavia, in eastern Romania, to Hungarian-occupied Yugoslavia, which the Hungarian Army had recently "cleansed" of Jews, Serbs, and Roma in the wake of the German *Blitzkrieg*. Catholicism, as everyone in Romania knew, was a Hungarian religion. Indeed, many of these two hundred thousand or so Catholics, known as Csangos, spoke an archaic mix of Hungarian and Romanian. Romanian intelligence reports depicted the community as a threat to national integrity, as "a state within a state" and "the gangrene of the national body." By contrast, Hungarian writings on the Csangos portrayed them as "lost Hungarians" of "good Hungarian stock" and, thus, a source of great biological and demographic potential. With their interests seemingly aligned, the two states agreed to strip the Csangos of their Romanian citizenship and forcibly colonize them in the marshy lowlands of war-torn Vojvodina, some seven hundred kilometers away from their homeland in the foothills and river valleys of the Eastern Carpathians. However, a recalcitrant, inner circle of priests from among the Csangos had other plans.

With Vatican support, this coterie of priests contrived the arrest and imprisonment of several clergymen within their ranks suspected as Hungarian spies and propagandists. In hopes of demonstrating the "true" origin of the community, they enlisted the unlikely support of Romania's leading racial anthropologist, compelling parishioners from a string of Catholic villages to submit blood samples for a comprehensive racial study. Finally, and perhaps most audaciously, they rewrote the entire history of Roman Catholicism in the borderlands of Transylvania and Moldavia, disputing the widely held view of the community as the Christianized descendants of the original Hungarian tribes from central Asia. In doing so, they claimed that the putative "Hungarianness" of the Hungarian-speaking Roman Catholics of Moldavia was, essentially, a seven-hundred-year-old case of mistaken identity: the so-called Csangos were in point of fact "lost" Romanians and not Hungarians, even if their language, their creed, and nearly a millennium of recorded history suggested otherwise.

The case of the Csangos reveals a war within the war. For Romania and Hungary some of the most important battles were waged between one another over ledgers and indexes, through the production of legitimizing papers certifying large swathes of people as "ours" and not "theirs." Already by 1940, the governments of Romania and Hungary had created bureaus and committees staffed with leading specialists across the sociological, geographical, and biomedical sciences. Their task was to establish, scientifically, the ethnic origin and racial composition of the hopelessly mixed populations inside the territories they occupied and coveted, laying the foundation for a future peace settlement. This was a war led not by field marshals in the mud and snow on the eastern battlefront or atop the rubble of Stalingrad but by technocrats in the dusty, smoke-filled institutes for demographic and sociological research, whose foot soldiers were dedicated teams of anthropologists, sociologists, demographers, and historians.

As part of a broader agenda to legitimize territorial claims in contested multiethnic borderlands after World War I, Romanians and Hungarians competed over the identification and belonging of otherwise marginalized peoples. To fit communities such as the Csangos inside new paradigms of European national states and communities, a new generation of historians, scientists, politicians, and even clergy on all sides attempted to trace the ethnic genealogies of forgotten or neglected populations to establish once and for all their national belonging, thereby bolstering claims over the territories they inhabited. The state-sponsored population policies, discriminatory legislation, and sociological and biomedical research generated in pursuit of this goal offered new ways to analyze, represent, and regulate these populations. Racial anthropology, in particular, helped determine whether populations with ambiguous or disputed ethnonational identities could be integrated into, or excluded from, the majority population or else used to colonize lands recently cleansed of other, nationally mismatched populations.

But the categorization of minority populations and their subjection to coercive population policies is only one side of this story. The other side tells how the savvy group of priests in a Romanian backwater resisted this categorization and manipulated, to their own advantage, the powerful mechanisms of state rule, showing how some religious, linguistic, and ethnically obscure minorities were able to escape the fate and victimhood of so many less-fortunate others.

Introduction

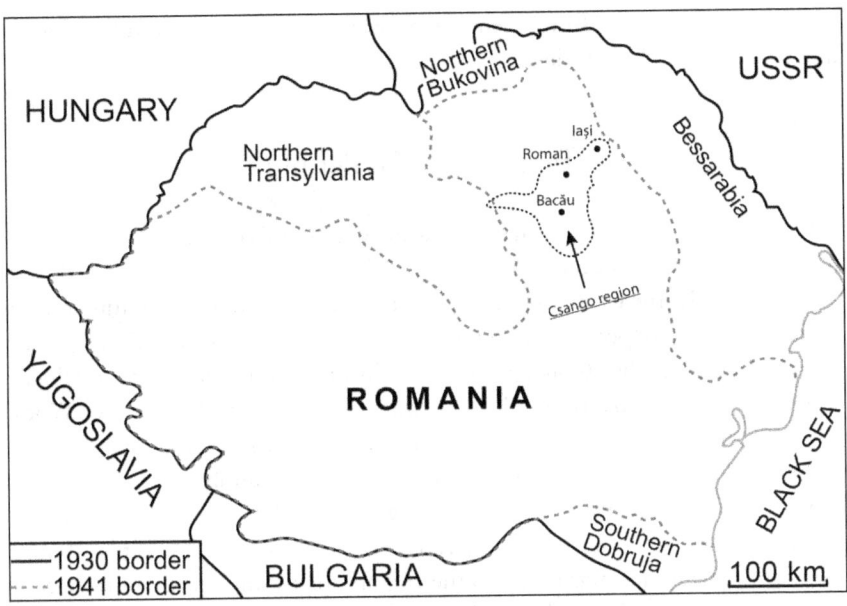

Csango region demarcated inside a map of Romania showing the 1930 and 1941 borders. Roman Catholics in Moldavia inhabit villages clustered around the cities of Bacău, Roman, and to a lesser extent Iași. (image created by Pamela Clarke and R. Chris Davis, with support of the Lone Star College-Kingwood Graphic Design Department)

By engaging in the most pressing historiographical and anthropological debates of the day, this clerical elite secured for the Csangos the coveted certificates of Romanian nationality and ethnic origin, exempting them from the discriminatory policies and violence that targeted so many of Romania's Jews, Roma, Slavs, and other minorities.

National and ethnic imagining has long been a two-way process between majorities and minorities. And as this story demonstrates, minorities in east-central Europe were not, merely, uniform and conspicuous blocks of people, unable to influence or counter the prevailing historical and political forces shaping the lives of every other member of society. Rather, in all their manifold contradictions, peculiarities, and ambiguities, they were active participants in their own fate and in the fate of others and sometimes had a say in how ethnicity, race, and national belonging were constructed and interpreted, not only at the local levels but also at the highest levels of, and between, states. In their efforts to establish and assert their own identities, minorities likewise shaped the politics and history of nations, states, and churches and, in doing so, shaped the history and future of Europe. In this sense, the Csangos offer a lesson in the rigidity and malleability of identities under pressure.

Biography of a People

"Who, precisely, are the Csangos?" The answers to this question are as numerous as they are contentious.

Historically, the Csangos were a rural people engaged in agriculture, raising crops such as corn, potatoes, and hemp. They also raised cows and sheep, with cowherds and shepherds taking care of family and communal herds and flocks. Up to the Communist period in Romania, which began shortly after World War II, and especially prior to collectivization in 1962, they maintained a rather archaic or traditional society based strongly on family, church, and local bonds. In previous centuries, many among this population lived in free villages (*răzeși* in Romanian, *részes* in Hungarian), with common landholdings, though later settlers who immigrated into the region, for example from elsewhere in Moldavia or from Transylvania in the west, became serfs tied to the lands owned by Moldavian boyars. Prior to the introduction of civil law, the communities were self-governed by male-dominated village councils. Village elders, who commanded a great deal of respect and advised the elected justices and appointed village guards, wore their hair long in the back and were distinguished by their beards.[1] Hungarian historians, ethnographers, linguists, and musicologists have, over the last century and a half, discerned a material culture and patrimony unique to the Csangos: an oral folk tradition, notably in song as well as dance; an archaic dialect; and textiles and costumes that distinguished the community in Moldavia, but with variations from one village to the next. From the way babies are swaddled to the way homes and villages are constructed, to the iconic Csango pipes that accompany soulful ballads, the Csangos can rightly claim a cultural heritage both distinct from and proximate to other Hungarians and Romanians. However, in terms of everyday life, as peasants their lives were likely not so different from any other peasant communities in that part of eastern Europe. The Csangos joined the 1907 Romanian Peasants' Revolt and fought for Romania in all of its major wars, including World War I and World War II.

Like everywhere else in the Roman Catholic world, in Catholic Moldavia the bishops appointed parish priests. Prior to the twentieth century, these priests were more often Italian missionaries of the Franciscan order as well as Polish Jesuits. In smaller numbers were Swiss, French, Belgian, and Hungarian priests. All but the Hungarians supported the primacy of the Romanian language in the region (Italian and Hungarian missionaries were regularly at odds over the church's language policy in the Hungarian-speaking regions of Moldavia). Romanian, like Italian, is an Indo-European, Romance language, whereas Hungarian is a non-Indo-European, Finno-Ugric language and, thus, comparatively more difficult for western and northern Europeans to learn. Historically, the bishoprics founded here, though frequently vacated and overrun, were the farthest outposts of Roman Catholicism in eastern Europe. The goal of the Catholic missions in Moldavia was not only to protect the existing Catholics there but also to convert the mostly Romanian Orthodox population, who formed the religious majority in the principality. This latter goal could be achieved only by engaging the "schismatics" in their mother tongue. By the latter half of the nineteenth century, and certainly during the first half of the twentieth, Romania's modern nation builders increasingly sought to impose the Romanian language and culture on its existing and would-be citizens, regardless of any historical ties to nations and churches outside Romanian territory. The Catholic Church, for the most part, abided, viewing the propagation of the faith as far more important than promoting foreign-language use among its flock or else preserving some notion of ethnic or national kinship with Hungary.

From a Romanian state-building viewpoint, even well into the twentieth century, the Hungarian-speaking Roman Catholic population in Moldavia seemed an odd and alien population. By the late nineteenth and early twentieth century, only a few Romanian historians had even bothered to mention them in one or another of the burgeoning national histories being written after the unification of the Principalities of Moldavia and Wallachia in 1859 and then the kingdom's independence from Ottoman suzerainty in 1878. Informal education, such that it existed, was provided by the Catholic churches in the local parishes.

By the end of World War I, however, the Catholic Church had established a number of educational institutions in the larger towns in Moldavia, such as seminaries, elementary schools for both girls and boys, and a school of cantors. Initially, the seminary was taught in both Romanian and Hungarian. By the start of the twentieth century, however, the Romanian government insisted the language of instruction be exclusively in Romanian. By the early twentieth century, more and more Roman Catholics migrated to urban centers in search of work. By the interwar period, Roman Catholics in towns like Iași and Bacău worked in nascent industries, as railways operators, bakers, or as shopkeepers. Many joined the Romanian Army. One owned a cinema. And there had always

Csangos in front of the village church in Sabaoani/Szabófalva, Neamț County, 1918. (courtesy of the Archive of the Episcopate of Iași)

been a foreign lineage of Roman Catholics among the city elite—lawyers, professors, and the clerical hierarchy—whose families had emigrated from Catholic countries in western Europe such as France or Italy.

In contrast to the secular state, the local Romanian Orthodox Church viewed the Catholic population—especially the proselytism of the Catholic religious orders—as subversive to the religious stability and preeminence of Romanian Orthodoxy, which viewed itself as a national church. As in other Eastern Orthodox nations in eastern Europe, and as the name suggests, the autocephalous churches of the eastern Christian rite developed alongside or even as precursors to the various national movements in the region. The Romanian Orthodox hierarchy saw itself and its church as inextricably linked to the Romanian nation state. By the interwar period, an increasingly nationalist group of Orthodox theologians and philosophers had cultivated an ideology of national and religious synonymity: to be authentically Romanian was necessarily to be Romanian Orthodox, and vice versa. And with the drafting of the first Romanian Constitution in 1923, the church had won for itself the designation "the dominant church" (*biserica dominantă*). In this new era, in the new Greater Romania, Catholics in Moldavia had very little place.

Introduction

Csangos in the village of Sabaoani/Szabófalva, Neamţ County. Ethnographic photo by Veress Sándor, 1931. (courtesy of the Ethnographic Museum, Budapest)

The Csangos had lived for centuries in the various iterations of the Moldavian principality and, later, in the unified Romanian kingdom and nation state. Nevertheless, they maintained relationships with the Hungarian Kingdom and, especially, with the Hungarians on the other side of the Carpathians in Transylvania. These links could be stronger or weaker depending on events at given times, such as invasions from the east, mistreatment by a particular ruler, religious persecution, or famine or drought on either side of the Carpathians. For instance, it was a common practice in the Transylvanian Szekler villages for a widower to travel the Ghimeş pass to Moldavia to find a new bride, a Csango bride, among the Hungarian-speaking Catholic villages. In the latter half of the nineteenth century the Society of Saint Ladislas (Szent László Társulat) and other Hungarian organizations, including advocates in the Hungarian Archdiocese, promoted greater ties between the Hungarian national movement and the Csangos living in Romania, mostly by providing funding and other materials for education in the Hungarian language and by sending priests from Hungary. These initiatives had limited success. Habsburg and Vatican authorities impeded these efforts, as the forays into Romanian territory to influence the sensibilities of Romanian citizens, even if they were Catholics and Hungarian speakers, smacked of meddling in another country's internal affairs. Complicating matters were the ever-present tensions over the "Transylvanian Question": To which nation did the territory rightly belong, Hungary or Romania?

Still, the Csangos and other Hungarian-speaking communities across the historic borders of Hungary attracted more and more interest inside Hungary during the lead-up to Hungary's millennial celebrations in 1896, which celebrated the thousand-year presence of the Magyars in central Europe. This event marked a national self-examination into what it meant to be Hungarian. Who were they, where were they? This included a search for origins and the settlement history of the early Magyars, imbued with a kind of romantic fascination with Hungarian archaicity. In the early years of the new century, the world-famous Hungarian composers Béla Bartók and Zoltán Kodály traveled to Csango villages to record folk ballads, paving the way for a new generation of Hungarian village researchers, "sociographers," "ethnohistorians," and political activists to follow. After Hungary's defeat in World War I and the subsequent national humiliation of the postwar Treaty of Trianon in 1920, this search took on existential dimensions. Precisely who the Csangos were, and to whose nation they belonged, took on greater saliency during the next world war.

Not "Who" but "What"?

Clearly there are many ways of counting the Csangos and describing them as a subject (or object) of historical inquiry, for example, by declared identity, linguistic or ethnographic traits and divisions, or purported "ethnic origin."[2] A 2001 Committee on Culture, Science and Education report to the Parliamentary Assembly of the Council of Europe declared that "the Csangos are a non-homogeneous group of Roman Catholic people of Hungarian origin."[3] Miklós Kontra states that "from an ethnic historical point of view, there is no doubt that the Csángós are Hungarians who migrated from Hungary to Moldavia."[4] A likewise representative view of Hungarian historians, ethnographers, and demographers writing on the Csangos might be that of ethnographer Vilmos Tánczos, who writes, "Both Hungarian and international scholars unanimously agree that the Moldavian Catholic population, called Csángós, apart from a small number of Romanian, German, Polish, and Italian and Gypsy groups who became fully assimilated, is Hungarian by origin," adding moreover that "this fact is accepted even by prominent Romanian scholars."[5] A genetic study of the Hungarian population specified the following: "The group

Introduction

of some 120,000 ethnic Hungarians who live in Rumanian Moldavia are most commonly referred to as 'Csángó' (Chango). These Moldavian Hungarians are rather dispersed over the area."[6] Another genetic study represented the Csangos as "an isolated subpopulation among the Hungarians" who have remained separated from the rest of the Romanian population because of their language and their Catholic religion.[7]

If one or another theory on the origins of these settlements is accepted, then the Csango population can be seen as the descendants of the waves of Hungarian migrations into the region over the last half millennium or so.[8] As the majority of present-day Catholics in the region do not speak Hungarian but Romanian, it might stand to reason that the greater part of this population had in due course been Romanianized. Thus, one broad and seemingly inclusive definition might be "the Catholics of Moldavia," namely those who live clustered around the towns of Bacău and Roman and extending along the Siret and Trotuş River valleys, the so-called Csango land. Understood as such, the designation or ethnonym "Csango(s)" serves as a catchall for the entire Catholic population of Moldavia, a number that would total about 230,000.[9]

The term Csango has long connoted ethnic, linguistic, and historical affiliations to Hungary or to being "Hungarian." Consequently, many Romanian-speaking Catholics of Moldavia reject being included or dubbed as "Csangos," for to be cast as such is, more often than not, also to be cast as "Hungarian."[10] The ethnonym and associated identities are therefore incompatible with—and in some cases an affront to—their specifically Romanian ethnic, national, and linguistic identities and heritage and, hence, their Romanian ethnic origin. A more exclusivist way of circumscribing the Csangos is to count them as those Catholics residing in the Csango land who still regularly use one or another Csango or Szekler dialect of Hungarian.

When viewed as a Hungarian ethnic and religious minority in Romania, the community exemplifies what Rogers Brubaker identifies as "nationally mismatched" persons with "structurally ambivalent membership status, belonging by residence and (in most cases) by formal citizenship to one state and by putative ethnonational affinity to another."[11] In Brubaker's schematic, a "triadic nexus" became more apparent after the breakup of the Habsburg Monarchy and the formation of Greater Romania after World War I, a nexus that linked the Csangos as the national minority (if an ambiguous or contested one), Romania as the nationalizing state, and Hungary as the external nationalizing homeland. To this I might also add the role of the Vatican in evangelizing or missionizing Roman Catholicism in the region, and in doing so creating a "quadratic nexus" linking the two national states, the minority, and religion.

Since the Middle Ages, Moldavia was an important point of entry for Catholic missionaries in an eastern Europe dominated by the Eastern Orthodox Church, a region referred to as *partibus infidelium*. Maintaining a Catholic toehold in Orthodox lands was a priority for the Congregation of the Propaganda Fide. Protecting and nurturing a Catholic identity among practitioners of the faith in Eastern Orthodox lands superseded any other linguistic or national identity.[12] Since the mid-nineteenth century, when Europe's national movements began to swell, Vatican policy has generally favored the assimilation of the Csangos as Romanians.

According to some (mainly Hungarian) ethnographers and historians who accept and use the Hungarian language criterion to define the Csangos, the Csango population ranges from 60,000 to 100,000.[13] However, a much lower number, anywhere from 5,000 to 25,000, is arrived at when counting the community according to those who have self-declared as "Csango," or "Hungarian," or else as a "Hungarian speaker" in successive Romanian censuses since 1930.[14] The reasons and motivations for such low numbers and discrepancies—from the forces of assimilation and modernization, ethnic politicization and nationalization, clericalism, bureaucratization, and not least, war—will be illuminated in the following chapters.

The paltry numbers of self-identified Csangos, both presently and historically, further complicate any discussion of the community's contested identity and national belonging. Nevertheless, I do employ the term Csango primarily for reasons of economy and convention. While I use it to refer to the Hungarian- *and* Romanian-speaking Catholics of Moldavia, more often than not I am simply referring to those who were imagined or "othered" as Csangos, whether they self-identified as Romanian, Hungarian, Csango, or even eschewed a hard and fast ethnic identification in favor of a religious one, such as "a Catholic" from one village or another in Moldavia. I readily acknowledge the many problems associated with my rather broad use of the term, not the least of which is that many people regard it as pejorative or else reject the term altogether. Yet the term Csango was *ascriptive* from the very beginning of its usage in the eighteenth century. Ethnographers, historians, political leaders, and even local actors ascribed the Csango ethnonym to the Catholics of Moldavia, whether they liked it or not.[15]

As a result of the nationalization and centralization projects in both Hungary and Romania at the start of the twentieth century—and the attendant state and local bureaucratization devised to account for and manage their diverse and growing populations—the Hungarian *Csángó* and the Romanian *Ceangău* also became *inscriptive* markers of identity. In Hungary, Romania, and elsewhere

Introduction

in Europe the term "Csango" was deployed not only in historical and ethnographical texts but also in official government documents and even personal identity papers, which by World War II indicated proof of the bearer's ethnic origin.[16] To the extent that I concern myself about the provenance of the Csangos, I prefer a much less reductionist approach to discussions and theories on the question of the Csangos' ethnic origin. I favor instead the notion of "origins," plural, supposing that a multiplex set of historical, demographic, linguistic, and migratory forces and processes over the centuries produced the ethnogenealogies of the Catholic communities in Moldavia.

The inherent difficulties in naming and counting the Csangos at the very outset of any discussion on the community indicate the many problems one encounters when writing about the contested, if also "enigmatic," history and identity of the Csangos. As Joseph Rothschild has remarked about ethnopolitics and "ethnopolitical entrepreneurs" in modern societies, any number of ethnic or ethnonational "cutting edges" are always available for mobilization; the politicization of ethnicity furthermore "stresses, ideologizes, reifies, modifies, and sometimes virtually re-creates the putatively distinctive and unique cultural heritages of the ethnic groups that it mobilizes."[17] The contested if also fragmented history, identity, and belonging of the Csangos give much credence to Rothschild's and later Brubaker's insights about potentialities for evoking and reifying ethnic "groups," not least by the historians and social scientists who write about the Csangos even today.[18]

A set of criteria used to frame the Csangos prior to the 1920s, when ethnicity was either less relevant or else relevant in different ways (for example, to determine national belonging), produces an understanding or image of the Csangos that in many ways became obsolete during the 1930s. During World War II, especially, the more salient identity markers of race and ethnic origin transcended the more traditional markers of language and religion. These newly ascribed identities, moreover, often determined whether an individual, a village, or even an entire community could be forcibly relocated or deported. Later, the onset of Communism in east-central Europe reshaped the "minority question" in manifold ways. Industrialization, collectivization, restrictions on religious practice, and the conceit that Stalinist-Leninist precepts and class consciousness had solved the region's ethnic divisions and national antagonisms, created new contexts and conditions in which the Csangos could view themselves (as an *ethnie* or an ethnic community) and be viewed by others (as an ethnic category).[19]

For these and other reasons I have taken a different methodological approach to my own inquiry into the history of the Csangos, proposing first of all to replace the interrogative pronoun "who" with "what," thereby posing a much different question, namely, "*What* are the Csangos?" This convenient but no less challenging reframing of the Csango problem allows me to explore the topic in ways that are less contingent on some *a priori* definition or understanding of the Csangos, avoiding especially any assertions or conclusions about their ethnic origin(s) or national belonging. The Csangos never really produced a secular intelligentsia. There is no tale of the enterprising young Csango autodidact who fled village life, travelled abroad, and came back to write and publish the great Csango novel or book of poems. The inquiry then becomes much less about the putative self-identity (or identities) of the Csangos and much more about the historians, ethnographers, politicians, scientists, and clergy who wrote about Csangos; the historiographies and historical narratives about the Csangos; the institutions that supported these authors and their agendas; and, in turn, the ideological, intellectual, and social-scientific contexts in which these authors lived, researched, and wrote.

That these biographies and lifeworlds were often in direct contact and competition with one another opens up an array of analytical possibilities. Consequently, I have abandoned any search for the essence of the Csangos and any pretense for discovering and knowing their origin, choosing instead to search for the ways in which the Csangos were ethnically categorized and historicized in Romania and Hungary over the better part of the twentieth century. Having spent many years on this topic, I have consciously stepped away from efforts to speak for the Csangos, partly because it is an impossible task, as individuals in this community now claim an array of identities and affiliations, and partly because I have concluded it is neither my job nor my place, as individuals and communities tagged with the Csango label (whether they embrace it, reject it, or are simply indifferent to it) are capable of speaking for themselves. At any rate, there are plenty of historians, ethnographers, activists, research and cultural institutes, and NGOs in both Hungary and Romania who are more than willing to speak on behalf of the community. Instead, I am telling a larger story about the agency of minorities in determining their place within nation-states, the role of minorities in constructing the ethnic identities of majorities, and the place of religious voices and clerical activism in public debates about nationhood and citizenship. In short, this is not just a book about the Csangos but about European nationalisms, state building, and religion in the first half of the twentieth century.

My approach is emboldened by a new and innovative body of scholarship on the Csangos and other ethnic and religious minorities in east-central Europe. In attempting to wrest the Csangos from the very same analytical dilemmas

Introduction

described above, Călin Cotoi has proposed examining the "figures of Csangoness," specifically the different ways of shaping and inscribing the Csangos and, moreover, of "choosing" and "being" Csango (or not). From this perspective, the Csango identity can be analyzed "not as a self-centered one but as a set of cultural, socio-economic and confessional projects unfolding in history."[20] What emerges is a much more diverse and interesting way of constituting and analyzing the Csangos. Sándor Ilyés likewise approaches "the image of the Csangos" and their symbolic value to the Hungarian nation by exploring the power of Hungarian ethnography's colonizing character in narratives and representations of the Csangos, especially in the contemporary Hungarian and Romanian press.[21]

Central to the investigation into how the historical narrative and ethnonational identity of the Csangos were transferred from the Hungarian national metanarrative to the Romanian one are the concepts of Romanianization, Hungarianization, and denationalization. At a theoretical level, Marius Turda's description of the "biologization of national belonging" in the interwar period and Balázs Trencsényi's study on the construction of national characterologies in Romania, Hungary, and Bulgaria provide useful frameworks for the Csango topic.[22] These approaches offer insight into the mechanisms through which ethnic majorities and minorities were constructed, essentialized, and then linked to the survival of the nation. Such approaches, moreover, provide contextualization for similar processes in twentieth-century Europe, lending a useful comparative dimension to the Csango case study.

Through "clerical agency"—an approach borrowed from James Kapalo's study on the history of the Gagauz community (a Turkic-speaking community of Eastern Orthodox Christians living mainly in Moldova)—we witness the Csango priests as partisans, as historians, as instruments of national policy, and as arbiters of a collective national consciousness.[23] As agents of the Csangos' ethnic-identity formation and national consciousness, they absorbed Hungarian and Romanian national historiographies in order to extricate the Csangos from the former and insert them into the latter. These priests-cum-historians created and published counternarratives to the Hungarian historiography on the Moldavian Catholics and defended their communities against discrimination by the Romanian state. At the height of World War II, these clergymen served as informal politicians and diplomats, as liaisons between the Antonescu regime and the Vatican, often in conjunction with the apostolic nuncio, Andrea Cassulo. One priest even became a sector chief in Romania's largest fascist movement, the Legion of the Archangel Michael, so as to ingratiate the Catholics with this predominantly Orthodox nationalist movement should it prove lasting. Another priest cooperated with a Romanian racial anthropologist's blood sampling in Csango villages in an effort to find whatever means possible to demonstrate the community's national belonging to the ethnic Romanian body.

Interest in these figures lies not so much in the scientific or historical merits of their works or activities but rather in the major impact they had on the ethnic and national identity formation of the Csango community as well as in their contributions to the much larger story about the struggle of ethnic and religious minorities for national belonging in twentieth-century Romania. The "representative biographies" of these otherwise minor figures elucidate shared patterns of experience and recontextualize the formative social and cultural conditions in which these individuals lived and worked, thus reconciling the particular with the general.[24] This approach enables a closer look at the individuals, ideologies, and policies that transformed the identities and external representations of the Csango community in Moldavia.

The Nation as Subject and Object

For centuries, the Csangos had resided in the historical principality of Moldavia. Their settlements and churches in the region were as old as any others. Their men had fought and died in every major Romanian war. Nevertheless, by the outbreak of World War II the community was asked to justify its existence within the Romanian nation (*neam*) by proving its credentials as a member of the ethnic Romanian body (*etnicul*) or otherwise meeting the standards of Romanian national specificity.

By "nation" I employ a basic understanding of the term, namely, "the ethnic idea of *people*, who may or may not have a state."[25] As applied to the Romanian case and explored in this book, I find particularly useful the complementary frameworks on the inner (*subjective*) and exterior or biological (*objective*) character of Romanian identity described by Katherine Verdery and Marius Turda, respectively. Verdery discusses "The Nation as Subject," in which Romanian national identity and symbols became internalized as a meaningful element of the social person: "At issue is the process whereby a national ideology comes to be experienced as part of a sense of *self as ethnic*; that is, how it constitutes ideological subjects who regard themselves as *national*."[26] This, argues Verdery, involved creating "a subjectivity of the national kind" that could respond emotionally to the propagation of external national symbols that were created by Romanian elites, whether in the form of national heroes or the assemblage of the national historiographical canon. As Verdery observes, these debates were attempts to construct a "Romanian inner self" or "inner state of being." Consequently, they concerned themselves with notions of Romanian spirituality and psychology, displaying an overriding preoccupation with interiority and "an inward migration of identity into a form of subjective consciousness." It is no surprise, therefore, that these interwar-era debates on the origin and essence of the Romanian soul and collective psyche were argued most stringently by theologians, both lay and clerical.

In these debates on national specificity, what has been lacking is an understanding of the central role played by the ethnic and religious Other—and specifically the Catholic Church. For instance, Nae Ionescu's famous disquisition on "the individuation" of the ethnic and the confessional was the outcome of a polemic with the Roman Catholic theologian Iosif Frollo. Ionescu's ideas on the subject shaped a nationalist discourse that helped define an era, and consequently Ionescu's "A fi bun român" (To be a good Romanian) is discussed in every major work on the Orthodoxists.[27] However, only rarely is Frollo mentioned, and thus the history of this all-important dialectic is sorely lacking its antithesis. Who was Iosif Frollo? Would Ionescu's now famous (or infamous) articulation and synthesis of Orthodoxy and Romanianness have been penned without Frollo's willingness to engage in the polemic? The point is to show how these events and interactions between individuals, from majorities and minorities alike, had a bearing on the way discourses and policies were shaped.

Marius Turda, by contrast, discusses "The Nation as Object," in which Romanian scientists argued that national identity and symbols adhered to biological laws and were transmitted from one generation to the next. Viewed as such, a proper understanding of the nation required a specific, scientific form of knowledge: "Eugenics and racial anthropology aimed at creating a national ontology, wherein the nation as object was deemed paramount." The seemingly objective incursions into the ethnic fabric of society through physical analysis (especially by way of anthropometry, craniology, and serology) allowed these intellectuals to represent the nation as an idealized Romanian *Volksgemeinschaft*.[28] Discourses on Romanian "ethnic ontology"[29] were also used to demonstrate the national belonging of the Csangos to the Romanian nation, effectively trumping the more subjective understandings of Romanianness and providing a template for putative minorities to recast themselves as majorities through the "uncovering" of their true (that is, biological) ethnic being.

Of course, Romanian terms and concepts such as *etnicul* or *specificul național*, roughly translated as "national specific" or "national essence," were sometimes ambiguous and always contested. They were, moreover, predicated on various "inherent" or "essential" qualities of the Romanian people (*popor*), qualities that ranged from the psychological to the spiritual to the biological. We should bear in mind that these terms and concepts—including notions of race and national belonging—were not only understood and instrumentalized differently between Romania and Hungary but also within Romania and Hungary, sometimes with vastly different applications, motivations, and outcomes. Such categorizations were formulated not only in discourses and ideologies but also put into practice. The multifarious notions of race, nationality, or "ethnic origin" were incorporated into policy decisions and applications by the state, which could have enormous impacts on communities that did or did not conform to this or that categorization—categorizations that were, in any case, changing with the exigencies of domestic and international politics as well as war.

Often overlooked or underresearched are the ways in which these concepts were put into practice by minority communities themselves, especially by their elites. In the case of the Csangos, a number of their priests borrowed the language of Romanian nationalism—replete with its emphasis on religion as a marker of Romanian national identity and belonging—so as to refashion the ethnic identity of the community as Romanian. In doing so, they hoped to secure a place for the Csangos as "good Romanians" within a Romanian state and national body that was being reconfigured on the ethnic principle.

Inscribing Identity

Romanian research into the Csangos must also be seen in the broader context of racial research and the research on ethnic origins elsewhere in central and eastern Europe, especially the increasing importance of the East European Research discipline or *Ostforschung* carried out in Nazi Germany, particularly on the contested ethnic and racial identities of communities in occupied Poland and Ukraine.[30] Key to the development of population policies and colonization projects was research undertaken by the *Ostforscher* on populations such as the Masures and the so-called "Lodzer Mensch" (the ethnic Germans of the cosmopolitan Polish city of Łódź) in Poland; the Sorbs inside Germany; and the Karaite Jews in Ukraine. This kind of research certainly had its corollary in Romania, especially in the contested territories of Transylvania, Bukovina, and Bessarabia, and even farther east in parts of Romanian-controlled Ukraine during World War II.

Though the influences on Romanian and Hungarian ethnographic and demographic research came mainly from Germany, it should also be noted that similar efforts had long been underway in the Soviet Union. As detailed in the work of Francine Hirsch, the Soviets' quest for ethnographic knowledge to inform its own ability to colonize and to rule its vast, multiethnic empire was accelerated after the emergence of national socialism and the consolidation of the Nazi state in the mid-1930s. Though Soviet ethnographic and sociological research lacked the overtly racist and biological frameworks undertaken in the Third Reich, it nevertheless sought to categorize its diverse population according to nationality in order to pursue the regime's goal of state-sponsored evolutionism. Of course, Soviet colonial policies were designed ostensibly to integrate disparate, non-Russian populations into a unified Soviet state.[31] However different the policy ends—whether to excise certain categories of people in the name of "purifying the nation" and creating *Lebensraum* or else to do so in the name of spreading the "Soviet 'national idea'" and consolidating the "Soviet whole"—demographic restructuring and redrawing of borders along the ethnic principle were predicated on the historical, ethnographic, and sociological knowledge of populations. Between the historical Lithuanian, Polish, German, and Czech lands existed any number of communities that spoke different languages, practiced different religions, or held different customs than the majority of their immediate neighbors or the kingdom or nation in which they lived.[32]

The *Ostforschung* in the Third Reich enabled professional historians to turn their sources into "weapons" in the struggle for national survival and superiority. It further enabled the collusion between, on the one hand, the familiar and more traditional historical discipline and, on the other, the more scientifically minded sociological, anthropological, and biomedical sciences, lending an air of legitimacy to the otherwise ahistorical "realities" of race and psychology.[33] The seeming ambiguity of some minority populations threatened the nation-making project, especially in the heterogeneous border zones that existed between and even within states. As Winson Chu points out in his study on the Lodzer Mensch, the "not-quite-German[ness]" of these and other such communities posed a danger to the idea and mythology of unitary Germanness, threatening the very concept of *Volksgemeinschaft* (German anthropologists even referred to them as "amphibians").[34] The inhabitants who occupied these "middlegrounds" threatened not only the respective nation-building projects in east-central Europe but also the very foundational myths so essential to legitimizing the newly recognized states in the region: in the age of ethnically based nationhood and statehood, how were multiethnic and multiconfessional upstart nations to portray themselves as unitary and homogeneous since time immemorial?[35]

Much of the legislation revising nationality and citizenship in late 1930s and wartime Romania were copied from Germany. As with the racial laws in Nazi Germany, the blood laws in Romania sharpened the dividing lines between the minority and majority populations. At the same time, however, this legislation unwittingly created numerous bureaucratic hindrances to the everyday workings of both local economies and the national economy and placed additional stresses on the interactions between individuals and the state during the war. It also created numerous agencies and go-betweens as well as a flurry of new stamps, documents, paperwork, local interests, corruption, and power relationships, both within the state bureaucracy and civil service and between these agencies and the individual citizens they were to serve. As Chad Bryant has noted, "The ascription of nationality had become the plaything of the polycratic state."[36]

In Romania, the shaping of the national community around sound methodological and ideological principles was not the exclusive domain of state agencies, legislators, and the army of social and biomedical scientists working in Bucharest and other major cities. During the interwar period and World War II, the ascription and inscription of nationality through the production and issuance of nationality certificates occurred within a diffuse and rather ad hoc system of personal and local interests. Often this led to corruption or else hindered the mobilization of populations and economic resources, having disastrous effects on the war effort. Confiscated property could not be efficiently redistributed because bidders at auctions lacked "proof" of their Romanian ethnic origins or because one or another prefecture refused to validate someone's paperwork. For similar reasons, preferential credits for goods that were supposed to be available to ethnic Romanians were unable to be distributed and therefore sat useless in warehouses. Thus, the proliferation of documents and the thickening of the bureaucracy for the purposes of individual and collective identification often created conditions that made control over the population more rather than less difficult.

As Jane Caplan and John Torpey have discussed, this state-sponsored process of identification and registration—of creating, in the words of James C. Scott, a "legible people"—was a reciprocal force driving the categorization of collective identities. The state created an ongoing "project of legibility" that could increase its capacity for discriminating intervention, rendering a synoptic and schematic view of the population it ruled.[37] Through mapping, census taking, and the issuance of nationality certificates, these forms of enumeration became, in the parlance of colonialism studies, "cultural technologies of rule." These powerful disciplining mechanisms facilitated administrative consolidation and centralization, aided the work of state building, and enabled coercion and control over the population even at the local levels of state power and authority such as the village hall or county prefecture.[38]

For both the Romanian and Hungarian states, communities such as the Csangos ultimately posed a counting problem. During World War II, for all the rhetoric and ideological bluster, these two states were run by military dictatorships, technocratic and bureaucratic. Ultimately, the critical importance attached to ethnicity and race at the very top levels of government was a means to an end, namely territory and borders, which could only be bolstered and legitimated by countable warm bodies. Statistics and demography mattered most; by the end of the war, numbers in a column meant more than all the treatises on the ethnic substance that defines a nation, or a nation's soul or character, which both Romanian and Hungarian ideologues peddled in the interwar period.

The attempt to make political and ethnic boundaries congruent, and the attempt to homogenize national states within these boundaries, had enormous impacts on the ways in which individuals could assert their own identities or else *name* themselves as a member of one or another ethnonational community. Two phenomena occurred simultaneously through the modernization and homogenization of these multiethnic and confessional states in east-central Europe: individuals increasingly lost control over the ascription of their own nationality and therefore lost control over their own destiny as conationals of a given state or national community; and state officials—including historians and social scientists but also lower-level functionaries—gained and wielded increasing power to establish and mark nationality. These were enormous undertakings that not only reshaped European borders but also reshaped the compositions and identities of the populations within these borders.[39]

Demography Is Destiny
People, Space, and Nation

What became known as Greater Romania during the interwar period started with the territorial addition of Bukovina, Bessarabia, and Transylvania (including the Banat, Crişana, and Maramureş) to the Romanian Old Kingdom beginning in 1918, nearly doubling its size and population. Unification of these provinces to the Romanian Old Kingdom was recognized internationally through the ratification of the Treaty of Saint Germain in 1919 and the Treaties of Paris and Trianon in 1920. The new Romanian Constitution of 1923 expanded civil and political rights for men in Romania. Legislation passed between 1929 and 1932 granted women civic and political emancipation, including limited rights to vote in national elections.[1] Within this expanded territory resided large numbers of ethnic and religious minorities. Many among the Hungarians of Transylvania, the Germans of Bukovina, and the Slavs of Bessarabia had no desire to live under a Romanian national state yet did not want to abandon their property and homelands to opt for citizenship elsewhere. For its part, the Romanian ethnic majority had to reconcile the presence of large numbers of non-Romanians or non-Orthodox, especially the Jews and Hungarians.

New visions of the ethnically homogeneous nation-state left little room for ethnic, religious, or linguistic minorities in either Hungary or Romania. Romanian policy makers sought to reduce the proportion of ethnic minorities within the national space lest their numbers justify any future territorial revision favoring Romania's neighbors. By June 1940, less than a year after the Ribbentrop-Molotov Pact, Stalin was in a strong enough position to demand that Romania cede back to the Soviet Union the territories of northern Bukovina and Bessarabia or else face invasion. As the Red Army advanced that summer, the Romanian government was forced to evacuate much of its population from the region and relinquish the territories. The Soviet Union occupied northern Bukovina and Bessarabia until the Romanian Army, now allied with Nazi

Germany, pushed out the Soviets the following summer. By then, the Soviet Union had deported or repatriated tens of thousands of Germans, Romanians, Hungarians, Poles, and Jews. The Soviet Union completed its plans for ethnically reordering the region after the Red Army regained control of Northern Bukovina and Bessarabia in 1944.

In contrast to neighboring Romania, Hungary during the interwar period was a fraction of its former size. As a result of the peace settlement after World War I the country lost over 60 percent of its prewar population and over 70 percent of its former territory, including large Hungarian-inhabited territories such as Transylvania. Almost two decades later, however, Hungary regained large swaths of these former territories through a new round of international awards (or dictates, depending on one's view), especially the First and Second Vienna Awards of 1938 and 1940. After the partitioning of Czechoslovakia, Hungary regained lands from the Slovak Republic as well as Carpatho-Ruthenia. From Romania, it acquired Northern Transylvania. Hungary annexed yet more of its former territories after its invasion of Yugoslavia in spring 1941, thereby acquiring part of the Vojvodina. The Hungarian government used ethnic Hungarians from throughout the Carpathian basin to repopulate its recent territorial gains, especially the southern region bordering Yugoslavia. Many in the Hungarian government viewed the Szeklers and Csangos as "authentic" Hungarians suitable for recolonizing the Hungarian state along ethnic and racial lines. Even before the start of World War II, influential members within the Hungarian government, the Catholic and Reformed churches, and secular institutions began advocating the *hazatelepítés*—"the resettlement home"—of the Szeklers of Bukovina and the Csangos of Moldavia. This was not merely the issuance of repatriation papers. Rather, it was a systematic attempt to relocate thousands of Hungarian-speaking Catholic and Protestant villagers from Romania, induced by promises of reallocated property within southern Hungary and financial assistance from the Hungarian government.

Back in Moldavia, around the counties of Bacău and Roman, the Csangos became scapegoats in a nationwide climate of xenophobia and resentment toward Hungary and the Hungarians, a climate generated in response to Hungary's long-standing revisionist policies and finally Romania's cession of Northern Transylvania to Hungary on 30 August 1940. Fervent anti-Hungarian discourse in Romania penetrated not only the Catholic intellectual circles in Bucharest and Iași but also the rural Csango communities throughout Moldavia. Typically this was manifest in the Catholics' interaction with their Orthodox neighbors and Romanian public officials, including the county prefects, town mayors, local police, and schoolteachers.[2] Like the Jews, the Roman Catholics represented a relatively large minority in Moldavia.[3] At the turn of the twentieth century, over 64,000 Roman Catholics populated the province, the great majority being the Romanian- and Hungarian-speaking Csangos (there were also small numbers of Polish, German, and Ruthenian Catholics). The Romanian census in 1930 recorded 109,953 Roman Catholics in the region, and the 1941 census listed 126,456. Thus, there was an enormous increase in the number of Roman Catholics in Moldavia, a 70 percent rise over the first three decades of the century and nearly a doubling by the end of the fourth (by contrast, the overall population increase in Moldavia was 37 percent from 1902 to 1930). Between the years 1912 and 1930, the Catholic population had increased 42 percent, while over the same period the rest of the population increased by just 14 percent. Though one Romanian anthropologist at the time would see this as clear evidence of the force of Catholicization in the region, naturally coming at the expense of Orthodox Romanians, it was also the case that the Catholics here had much higher birthrates and that the immigration of Szeklers into Moldavia added to the Hungarian-speaking Catholic population in the region.[4]

During the interwar period, the Hungarians of Transylvania and the Csangos of Moldavia were no longer separated by political boundaries. The two provinces—one historically part of the Hungarian Kingdom, the other historically part of the Romanian Old Kingdom—were now adjacent provinces within the same country, Greater Romania. Consequently, economic and cultural ties grew stronger with the ability to move unhindered between the provinces. While large numbers of Szeklers migrated south to Bucharest to escape their economically depressed homeland in eastern Transylvania, many other Szeklers, mainly craftsmen and traders, migrated eastward across the Carpathians and into the Csango land in search of work, bolstering the numbers of Hungarian-speaking Catholics there.[5] In addition, a large influx of Jews from the contested region of Galicia arrived in Moldavia between 1918 and 1924. These Jews had fled Galicia after the rise in anti-Semitic violence, drought, disease, and famine that accompanied the Russian Revolution, Russian Civil War, the Red and White Terrors, the Polish-Ukrainian War, and the Polish-Soviet War. These were yet more waves in a succession of waves of Jewish immigration into Romanian territory (mainly Moldavia, Bukovina, and Bessarabia) since the latter half of the nineteenth century, when Jews fled en masse the deprivations and pogroms in the Pale of Settlement in western Russia. After Hitler's invasion of Poland in 1939, thousands more Jews (alongside Catholic Poles) fled south into Romania via Bukovina, many of whom sought safe haven in Bacău. The population surge in Moldavia was therefore attributable mainly to high minority birthrates and immigration, combined with the fact that

Romanian birthrates and overall annual population increase were Europe's highest.[6]

Given this rapid change in the demographic composition of Moldavia—a major grievance underlying the new nationalist paradigm of "Romania to the Romanians"—the region, despite its historical ethnic and religious diversity, became an inhospitable place for many foreigners. Xenophobia, chauvinism, anti-Semitism, and racism would characterize the region by the outbreak of World War II. As early as the mid-1920s, the city of Iași, the historical capital of the principality of Moldavia, turned into a hotbed of anti-Semitism. Subsequently, new and increasingly accepted forms of racism were introduced by the writings and actions of the extreme right, which was spearheaded by A. C. Cuza's National-Christian Defense League (LANC) and Corneliu Codreanu's Legion of the Archangel Michael, whose political arm is better known as the Iron Guard.[7] Indeed, both literally and figuratively, the "road to extermination," paved by decades of incitement and hostilities against foreigners, ran straight through Moldavia. In the summers of 1940 and 1941, the Moldavian towns of Dorohoi and Iași become sites of two of Romania's most notorious pogroms. In other localities in northern Moldavia, Romanian military personnel shot Jews in the streets and threw others from trains. In June 1941 Antonescu issued an order directing all Jews between eighteen and sixty years of age living in villages between the Siret and Prut Rivers be rounded up within forty-eight hours, packed into trains, and "evacuated" to the south of Romania in advance of the German-Romanian invasion of the Soviet Union. In May 1942 the same fate befell thousands of Romania's Roma population. The subsequent pogroms, shootings, ghettoization, and internment inside Romania, followed by the deportation of Jews and Roma to concentration camps in Romanian-controlled Transnistria, would make up a constellation of violence resulting in the systematic destruction of Romanian Jewry during World War II.[8] The Csangos, whose villages dotted the Siret River valley and extended eastward toward and around Iași, lived amidst all of this, sometimes witnessing firsthand what happens to populations deemed insufficiently Romanian, inimical to nation and state.

Romania and Its Others

After centuries of Turkish suzerainty, culminating in heavy-handed Greek-Phanariot rule from the early eighteenth century to the mid-nineteenth century, Romania emerged into the modern period as a hodgepodge of ethnicities, languages, confessions, and foreign and domestic allegiances. Greek was the lingua franca in most cities, and thus the culture of its officialdom and elites was as much Greek or French as it was Romanian. As well, Russian had long been the lingua franca of the Army officer corps. Old Church Slavonic persisted as the language of liturgy in the Orthodox Church until gradually replaced by Romanian during the eighteenth century (the Romanian language itself was written in the Cyrillic alphabet until 1860). It was only in the mid-nineteenth century, after the unification of the principalities of Wallachia and Moldavia, that the appellation "Romanian" became widely used. Prior to unification, the Romanian aristocracy was mainly of Greek origin. Greeks and Armenians dominated the lucrative merchant and civil-service positions, while Albanian Muslim troops, the *arbănaşi* or *arnăuţi*, were garrisoned throughout the principalities or used as bodyguards for the boyars.[9] Hungarians had long dominated the Romanians in Transylvania and had even introduced Greek Catholicism there, winning numerous converts from Eastern Orthodoxy.

Even after the Romanian national movement dashed headlong into the twentieth century, no real consensus emerged on what precisely it meant to be Romanian. In the post–World War I nation-building project, Romanian intellectuals attempted to cultivate national aspirations among the Romanian peasantry and to craft an ethnic Romanian majority from its heterogeneous population. To convince Romanians that they were, indeed, *Romanian*, required new understandings about what constituted Romanian identity.

Of course, this effort by Romanian elites to generate and popularize a sense of national belonging was part of the broader process of nation building in Europe and elsewhere. As Eugen Weber has shown, the making of the modern French nation and state was, essentially, the story of how an undeveloped, multilingual France became "integrated into the modern world and the official culture—of Paris, of the cities."[10] The Romanian peasantry was no different from other disparate, rural communities that populated central and eastern Europe, or for that matter western Europe at an earlier time. Their identities were tied to locality, profession, class, or religion rather than to nationality, ethnicity, or race, designations few villagers in such a milieu would have understood. To the extent that they did characterize something akin to a national identity, it was, for them, something mutable—something that could change with marriage, education, or military service.[11] Historian Vejas Gabriel Liulevicius has asserted that in lands such as these—at the crossroads of culture, ethnicity, language, religion, and history—national identity was very much a conscious choice, and ethnicity sometimes elective, as many possible identifications were available to individuals: "Radical contingency, not clear and inexorable fatality, ruled ethnicity."[12]

After World War I, Romanian perceptions of minority communities changed radically. In an attempt to reconcile the fact that millions of ethnic Others[13] now resided in the much larger Romanian national space, Romanian nation builders began to generate increasingly ethnicized and confessional notions of national belonging. The fact that a number of Romania's historical and political leaders—especially those from Transylvania—were Greek and Roman Catholics (or possessed some semblance of "foreign" ethnic or religious heritage) was not lost on the new generation of Romanian nationalists, whose conception of national belonging linked Orthodoxy to ethnicity.

Yet, undeniably, the Romanian national past was forged in large part by those categories of peoples now deemed Others, from the Greek Catholics Samuil Micu-Klein and Petru Maior of the Enlightenment-era Transylvanian School (Şcoala Ardeleană); to the Catholic Hohenzollern-Sigmaringen dynasty of Romanian kings;[14] to the more recent converts to Catholicism such as Prime Minister Ion C. Brătianu, one of the leading political figures of the nineteenth century who converted to Roman Catholicism on his deathbed; and to Prince Vladimir Ghika, the grandson of the last ruler of Moldova (Ghika was beatified in 2013).[15] Andrei Şaguna (b. Anastasiu Şaguna), the great nineteenth-century metropolitan of the Romanian Orthodox Church and one of the leaders of the Romanian national movement, was born in Miskolc, Hungary, of Macedo-Romanian parents from Albania who were themselves Catholic converts. Even the purported Germano-Slavic ancestry of Corneliu Codreanu, the leading figure of Romania's extreme right, became the subject of much controversy at his trial in 1938.[16]

But for nationalist Orthodox theologians in the 1930s, it was not simply that ethnic and religious Others posed threats to the Romanian national body, a charge that was, in any case, symptomatic of the pervasive xenophobia at the time. Rather, they went to great lengths to deny such communities the ontological possibility of even *being* Romanian. In fact, it was over the course of his vituperative polemic against Catholicism that one of the most influential Romanian intellectuals and nationalists of the period, Nae Ionescu, would crystalize his theological and philosophical ideas on the "individuation" of the ethnic and the confessional, in which ethnicity and Orthodoxy formed coequal, constituent parts of Romanian national specificity. By the mid-1930s and the beginning of World War II, the reconceptualization of Romania's national specificity took on biopolitical and racial forms. From these discourses emerged a number of theories on the denationalization of autochthonous, ethnically Romanian communities in highly contested, multiethnic regions such as Transylvania, Bukovina, and the Timoc valley. Denationalization theories posited that many of the non-Orthodox, non-Romanian-speaking communities residing in Greater

Romania were originally ethnic Romanians who had been assimilated to other nationalities. Because Romanian nationality was now seen as an embedded cultural and biological feature of these "lost" Romanians, it was presumably recoverable through reassimilation or "re-Romanianization" projects. The denationalization theories developed by Gheorghe Popa-Lisseanu were further legitimized by the racial and serological research undertaken by anthropologists such as Iordache Făcăoaru and Petru Râmneanțu in the 1930s.

The synthesis between history and science—and in some cases, religion—offered a new template for explaining the historical presence of large numbers of putative ethnic Others in Romania's symbolic geography. This Othering process took place not only inside the internationally recognized borders of Romania, such as in Transylvania and Bukovina, but also outside Romania's frontiers, such as in the Timoc valley that straddled Yugoslavia and Bulgaria and across the Bug River in Transnistria, Soviet Ukraine.

The Csangos were likewise placed into the category of Other. For centuries living in the east Carpathian space, the Csangos long remained outside the historical and cultural bounds of the Hungarian nation. Even their "ethnonym"—the Hungarian word *csángó* being derived from a verb meaning to "wander" away from a herd or flock—attests to the inherent alterity of the Csangos, even in the mental mapping of Hungarians. But it was not until the mid-twentieth century that this took on radical dimensions and had a major impact on the shift in their historical narrative as well as the collective self-perceptions of their ethnonational identity (as ethnic Romanians). At this point, they moved from being merely *strâine*, or "foreigner," in the Romanian cultural and political context to that of alien invader, despite the fact that the Csangos had lived in Moldavia for centuries (indeed, Roman Catholics were among the earliest Christian settlers in the region and were key to repopulating the region after the Tatar invasions of the thirteenth century).

The question remains, how were these multiethnic communities disaggregated in the social and national consciousness of what was to become "the Romanians"? One way in which minority populations such as the Csangos could transcend or escape the status of stranger and scapegoat was to recast themselves as "authentic" members of the *Volk*, typically as a hidden, persecuted, and misunderstood kin. Unlike the Jews, the Csangos could (re-)represent themselves as indigenous Christians in the eastern Romanian space who had withstood the pressures of the Romanians' arch enemy, the Hungarians. In doing so, the Csango clergy attempted to demonstrate that a long-standing Romanian ethnos lay buried in their Hungarian ethnic, cultural, and linguistic attributes.

In 1938 King Carol II decreed a royal dictatorship in Romania and with it, the abolition of the 1923 Constitution that had enshrined into law the liberalizing terms of the Minority Treaties from the Versailles postwar settlement. The 1938 Constitution and the laws passed by King Carol II would alter the relationship of minorities with the Romanian state, as would the legislation passed during the wartime Antonescu military dictatorship. Such laws abrogated the civic and political rights of many nonethnic Romanians, redefining Romanian citizenship and curtailing the participation of minorities in the civic and public life of the nation. Retroactively, many Romanian citizens who were not ethnically Romanian were now codified as "foreigners" and forced to apply (or reapply) for Romanian citizenship; suspect individuals and entire categories of the population were also forced to apply for certificates showing proof of ethnic Romanian origin. These laws also introduced "Romanian blood" and "Romanian origin" as prerequisites for entry into a number of public institutions such as the Romanian civil service and the military's officer corps. Ultimately, this obsession with ethnic origins, national characterology, and the desire to live in an ethnically homogeneous national state culminated in policies aimed at purifying the nation by physically reorganizing the Romanian state according to the "ethnic principle," a euphemism for exclusionary legislation and forced relocations of minority populations.

Pursuing many of these aims was a widening circle of Romanian demographers, geographers, and anthropologists. They applied seemingly objectifying scientific knowledge in their efforts to realize a new vision of a nation, one that could be reorganized politically and socially along ethnic Romanian lines. They were active in forging a sociological and biopolitical agenda for research and policy, much of which was dedicated to the question of the ethnic origins of Romanians and the minorities living in Greater Romania and in adjacent territories. These figures rose to prominence in the late 1930s and during World War II, as demography and the policy of Romanianization became organizing principles of the Romanian state. Such policies and principles were embodied in one of the most important Romanian institutions during the war, the State Undersecretariat of Romanianization, Colonization, and Inventory (Subsecretariatul de Stat al Romanizării, Colonizării și Inventarului; SSRI).[17]

Romanian research into ethnic or racial origins and composition of its populace had parallels with the *Ostforschung* in Nazi Germany around the same time, for example in the latter's investigation into the so-called Goralenvolk (highland folk), a community of Polish highlanders in the Podhale region in southern Poland, near the Slovak border. The Nazi regime persuaded many of these Polish-speaking citizens that they were not, in fact, Slavs but rather descendants of ancient Germanic tribes and, consequently, that they should collaborate with the SS. As Michael Burleigh has noted, the *Ostforscher* was not part of a radicalized, lunatic fringe but was included within the established educated elite. Moreover, the emergence of a regime that sought a massive territorial and demographic reordering of Europe provided such researchers, scientists, and historians unprecedented opportunities "to translate the labors of the study into present political fact."[18] In Antonescu's dictatorship, figures such as statistician Sabin Manuilă and sociologist Anton Golopenţia became indispensable technocrats who worked on population policies in an effort to recapitalize the ethnic potential of the Romanian nation. These men of science became all the more important as Romania reoccupied parts of Bessarabia in the east (including Transnistria) and planned for a final settlement over Transylvania in the west.

Hungary and Its *határon túli magyarok*

In contrast to interwar Romania's nation builders, interwar Hungary's nation builders had to reconcile themselves to Hungary's extensive territorial and population losses following the Treaty of Trianon. One of their main goals was to bolster the ethnic Hungarian diaspora—often referred to as *határon túli magyarok*, or "Hungarians across the border"—in the successor states, with eyes cast to the day greater Hungary would be reconstituted through territorial revision.[19] The Transylvanian-Hungarian researcher and writer Ödön Nagy expressed the fears in Hungary regarding the loss and diminution of Hungary's "internal diaspora" in Romania: "Members of the internal diasporas do not position themselves according to the focus of the main ethnic group . . . but function outside the main lines of the main ethnic group and thus take no part in its nation-building process. They are nothing but a virtual number, a disorganized mass within the body of the ethnic community . . . and can be regarded as a channel letting thousands of members of the ethnic group leak out from the body of the nation into the powerful stream of another nation every year."[20]

In the wake of Austria-Hungary's dissolution, new groups of Hungarian social scientists, historians, and literati emerged in the successor states. In Transylvania, where the largest Hungarian ethnic minority remained, a spirit was rekindled for research in ethnography, anthropology, and social-political activism. Though these groups splintered into various ideological and political factions, they were united in their efforts to raise awareness about the fate of

Hungarian villages and the threat of assimilation.[21] Most of these young intellectuals were social and political critics, journalists, historians, and ethnographers. From this milieu emerged the Erdélyi Fiatalok (Transylvanian Youth) and Hitel (credit) movements and their eponymous journals. As successors to a lost generation—a generation of Hungarian intellectuals killed in the First World War or repatriated to Hungary after Trianon—this "Transylvania Youth" conducted research in Hungarian villages and wrote on political, social, and religious topics concerning the plight of the Hungarian minority. Such movements and personalities produced within Romania an intellectual and political milieu of Hungarians who also wrote on the Csangos, including Pál Péter Domokos, T. Attila Szabó, László Mikecs, and Gábor Lükő. Their historiographical production and political advocacy were among the few sources of resistance against the Romanianization efforts of the Csango clergy in Moldavia during the 1930s and early 1940s.

Hungarian ethnographers and historians, from Hungary proper and from Transylvania, increased their historical production on the Csangos in the 1930s. Nearly half a century before Anthony D. Smith wrote about the concept of "ethnohistory," the Hungarian historian Elemér Mályusz had championed *népiségtörténet* (ethnohistory) as a way to understand the communal past of the Hungarian nation by going directly to the *ethnie*, eschewing the more fashionable Hungarian variant of German *Geistesgeschichte* philosophy and historiographical method practiced by a number of leading Hungarian historians of the day, notably Gyula Szekfű. Mályusz's "ethnohistorical" approach had a major influence on those seeking to rediscover the "orphaned" Hungarian diaspora left behind in the successor states.[22]

Equally important were the influences of the *szociográfia* (sociography) and *falukutatók* (village explorers) movements in Hungary, which encouraged enterprising young researchers to explore the countryside, experience life in impoverished villages, and document the grinding poverty and social conditions of the peasantry. In the minds of many Hungarian nationalists who lamented the decay of the Hungarian nation, the peasantry was seen as the last remnant of Hungarian tradition and cultural authenticity. As a reservoir of ethnic and even racial strength, the Hungarian peasant represented the greatest potential for Hungary's national rebirth, for prevailing against the country's cosmopolitanism, urbanization, falling birthrates, and "foreign elements" proliferating in its growing cities.

In Romania, a number of personal and transnational networks connected the Hungarian-styled village research and folk populism to the famed sociological school of Dimitrie Gusti, whose sociological approach to village research—in which teams of village researchers collected ethnographic data and produced village monographs—endeavored to create for Romania a "science of the nation." These scientific and historiographical currents directly and indirectly inspired some of the most important ethnographical work on the Csangos, then and since.

National and Ethnic Imagining

In Romania, historiography on the Csangos prior to the 1940s was minimal. Dimitrie Cantemir's brief account of the community in his *Descriptio Moldavie* (1714) depicted the community as an enclave of ethnic Hungarians of the Roman Catholic rite who had separated from the larger body of the Hungarians. Most of the early twentieth-century Romanian historiography on the Csangos echoed Cantemir and mirrored Hungarian historiography, which asserted the community was Hungarian by origin and identity. In 1905 historian Radu Rosetti wrote a profile of the church life of Moldavian Catholics, which included descriptions of their settlements. Gheorghe I. Nastase followed up on this in 1934 with a portrait of the Moldavian Catholic community during the compilation of the *Codex Bandinus* in the seventeenth century. Renowned historians Nicolae Iorga and Constantin Giurescu likewise reproduced descriptions of the Csangos as Hungarians.

However, a seismic ideological and historiographical shift was already underway by the 1920s. After the signing of the Paris Treaties after World War I, these respective national-historiographical traditions became locked in competition over historical and territorial rights. Through this process, the Romanian and Hungarian national communities were increasingly ethnicized, cast as organic and homogeneous national communities, as the living embodiment and the lifeblood of the national body. Added to this was the increasing significance of religion in the postwar ideations of national belonging and national characterology: to be a good citizen-soldier defending Christian Hungary was to be either Calvinist or Catholic; while to be "authentically" Romanian was to be Eastern Orthodox.[23] This marked a break from the Enlightened, French-inspired understandings of nationhood as something universalist, cosmopolitan, contractual, and thus primarily civic. From the end of the nineteenth century through the beginning of the twentieth, Romanian nation builders modeled their state's relationship with its citizens increasingly along the German model of nationhood, as something irreducibly particular and ethnocultural or even racial; in this conception, to be Romanian was to share a common origin, language, and history and, moreover, to have a specific spirituality, namely Eastern Orthodoxy.[24]

Despite attempts to bind the nation's multiethnic and multiconfessional inhabitants together on a more civic and contractual basis through the 1923 Constitution and the 1924 naturalization and citizenship laws, the politics and ideologies of the interwar period soon became dominated by more radical and exclusivist definitions of nationality and national belonging.[25] Much as in Germany since the late nineteenth century, in Romania the Jews and other minorities—however patriotic, cultured, and educated—were not a part of the romantic or mystical *Volk*. This concept of the *Volk*, in which the nation state and national belonging were derived through shared blood and culture, exceeded the universal Enlightenment principles of organization through shared civic values and revered institutions.[26]

The influence of German *Volksgeschichte* revealed the national community as something organic and integrally linked, historicized through time, space, blood, and soil. From this emerged both a physical and metaphysical competition between Romania and Hungary over claims to putative minority communities such as the Csangos. For both Romanian and Hungarian historians, the nation's soul or spirit, its psychology and its destiny, were at the very core of national identity. This promoted a new way of thinking about the nation, one that was conceptual and idea oriented.[27] Led by Gyula Szekfű's adaptation of German *Geistesgeschichte*, Hungarian historians offered interpretations of their national history as manifestations of the "eternal and moral forces" operating in the Hungarian *lélek* (soul).[28] In Szekfű's most influential work, *Harom nemzedék: Egy hanyatló kor története* (Three generations: The history of a declining age), published in 1920, he argued that to survive the social and political crisis Hungary now faced, its leaders would have to formulate a new ideology of the state and society, one that consolidated and extolled the cultural and spiritual values of the Hungarian soul and asserted Hungarian cultural superiority.[29]

Though this *Geistesgeschichte* movement would ultimately splinter, the notion of the Hungarian soul as a driving force in the history of the Hungarian nation and people remained a central theme of the works and thinking of historians in Hungary, especially those writing on the Csangos. Gábor Lükő, one of the most important writers on the Csangos in the 1930s, would incorporate these ideas not only in his work on the Csangos but also in his subsequent works on symbolism, the manifestations of the Hungarian soul, and the historical, cultural, and linguistic relationship of Hungarians with the other Finno-Ugric and Turkish peoples. In his 1942 monograph *A magyar lélek formái* (The forms of the Hungarian soul), a culmination of his life's work, Lükő mapped out what he saw as uniquely Hungarian conceptualizations of space and time, explaining how these phenomena operated deep within the subconscious of the Hungarian psyche but were nevertheless evident in Hungarian folk culture.[30]

Ideas on writing national histories from cultural, ethnic, and psychological viewpoints circulated as transnational scientific paradigms throughout east-central Europe and took hold in both Romania and in Hungary. Vogueish concepts of culture, nation, ethnicity, and race challenged traditional consensuses about community, belonging, and history. The *Volksgeschichte*, *Kulturgeschichte*, and *Völkerpsychologie* trends emanating from Germany, and to a lesser extent the Annales School in France, likewise had a major influence on Romanian history writing during the interwar period. Gheorghe I. Brătianu, Petre P. Panaitescu (who joined the Iron Guard), and Constantin C. Giurescu as well as other young historians of their generation formed the so-called Şcoala Nouă (New School) and clustered around *Revista istorică română* in the early 1930s, promoting a less romantic and methodologically more rigorous pursuit of history. In their investigations into the formation of the Romanian people, these historians wrote on the existence of a permanent ethnic Romanian substratum embedded within the national community.[31] Also in Romania, the literary critic Eugen Lovinescu proposed a "synchronism" between Western ideas and Romanian conditions as a pathway both to modernization and to a reinterpretation of Romania's past. Lovinescu had a major influence on the young crop of historians, who responded to Lovinescu's call for a new national narrative. Together, they challenged the historians of the pre–World War I generation over methodology and the direction of national history, especially over Nicolae Iorga and Vasile Pârvan's emphasis on peasantism, the sociopolitical integration of the state, and the unity of Romanian civilization from the earliest times to the present. History was to move beyond the description of ancient institutions, the deeds of prominent individuals, and past politics; it would now incorporate the culture and deeds of the social collective.[32]

Romanian philosopher and psychologist Constantin Rădulescu-Motru had profound influence on the notion of *românismul* (Romanianism) in the 1930s and 1940s, advocating scientific and secularist approaches to understanding metaphysicality of Romanian nationality, connecting the collective psychology and ethnic composition of the nation with its soul and destiny. Taking a more subjective and mystical view of all of this was philosopher Lucian Blaga's concept of the "Mioritic space," in which Romanian national identity should be understood as a "special constellation of spiritual determinants" that belong to it exclusively. He spoke of Romanianness as the product of a cultural and environmental "stylistic matrix" that included landscape, folklore, history, and destiny.[33]

This kind of thinking dominated both countries and was conveyed in the writings not just of professional historians, ethnographers, and philosophers but also an increasing number of poets, novelists, journalists, and even theologians. These men were some of the most influential writers in the two countries, from Dezső Szabó, László Németh, and Gyula Illyés in Hungary, to Mircea Eliade, Emil Cioran, Nae Ionescu, and Nichifor Crainic in Romania. They captured the popular imagination in their respective countries. In many ways, these groups of intellectuals had greater sway over national discourse and sentiment than their historian counterparts in the national academies. Men such as Szabó in Hungary and Ionescu and Crainic in Romania tapped into public fears about the "centrifugal tendencies" of minorities, the decay and contamination of the once-pure ethnic community, and the revisionist designs of hostile neighboring states. They inspired student and youth movements, harnessing to their respective causes many of the alienated post–World War I generation.

Although the writings, ideas, and mindsets of these men were often in competition with one another—even when they agreed on broader general points or shared a common nationalist political agenda—a fertile intercourse nevertheless took place between popular writing and historical writings, between literature, sociology, psychology, philosophy, and theology. By the 1930s and 1940s, the biomedical sciences would be integrated into this discursive mix, adding race, blood, and an obsession with ethnic origin and genealogy to the discussions on national character and national destiny.

2

The Sacred

Religion, Kulturkampf, and Catholic-Orthodox Polemics

Religion has long played a role in shaping Romanian national politics. Never was this more evident than during the interwar period, when the Romanian state struggled to unify its new territories, centralize its bureaucracy, develop a national school system, and implement land reform. All of these issues affected the churches to varying degrees. In regions inhabited by large numbers of minorities, such as in Transylvania, traditions of confessional autonomy ran deep, and thus religious and ethnic affiliations corresponded closely to one another.[1] School systems in many parts of Romania and Hungary remained largely the domain of the churches. As such, religion was often subsumed into the idea of nationality and was thus seen as an expression of the national or ethnic principle. Quarrels over specifically religious questions frequently turned into political questions and became part of the broader struggle between the nationalities.[2] In Romania, Germans primarily practiced Roman Catholicism or Lutheranism; Hungarians adhered to Roman Catholicism, Calvinism, or, in fewer numbers, Unitarianism or Greek Catholicism; Romanians meanwhile followed Eastern Orthodoxy or Greek Catholicism; and Jews practiced Judaism.

That language, nationality, and religion had prescribed relationships in Transylvania and Moldavia mirrored similar "contact zones" elsewhere in east-central Europe up to World War II. In the heterogeneous region of Kashubia in northwestern Poland (the historic Eastern Pomerania), for instance, a proverb had long held that "what is Catholic is Cassubian, what is Protestant is German."[3] In Moldavia the adage might well have been "what is Hungarian is Catholic, what is Romanian is Orthodox." Religious differences thus reinforced ethnic and national differences. While ethnicity could sometimes be "elective" or "amphibious" in these parts, religion rarely was. "Creed," observed British historian C. A. Macartney about multiconfessional Transylvania in 1937, "is a mark as distinctive and by tradition almost as immutable as color might be, and there is in the eyes of everyone something unnatural about a person whose language or other national attributes are at variance with the creed with which those attributes are usually identified."[4] The idea that a community of Roman Catholics with significant numbers of Hungarians speakers among them could be anything but ethnically Hungarian defied historical experience and common sense.

The Churches in the New Romania

Prior to the formation of Greater Romania in 1918, the non-Orthodox confessions in the Romanian Old Kingdom (the first independent Romanian nation state, 1881–1913, known colloquially as Vechiul Regat or just Regat) were effectively autonomous within the Romanian state, regulated and administered by an archdiocese or ecclesiastical center from abroad.[5] After World War I, in order to meet its obligations under the Minority Treaties, the Romanian government passed new legislation establishing criteria for Romanian citizenship and nationality. As part of a Romanianization agenda to incorporate its new territories and centralize its bureaucracy, the government also formulated new policies on nationwide education, language use, and administration of the churches.

Alongside the flurry of nationality and citizenship legislation in the early 1920s, the new Romanian Constitution of 1923 redefined the centuries-old relationships between the individual, the state, and religion, placing all the nation's churches under state regulation apart from canon law and dogma. This new document proclaimed Romania a "unitary and indivisible national state" and stipulated that the royal family be raised in the Orthodox faith and that the heads of all churches in the country be Romanian citizens.

Most significantly, the Constitution of 1923 established the primacy of the Orthodox Church, codifying it as, literally, the nation's "dominant church" (*biserică dominant*). It also designated the Greek Catholic Church as the only other "national" one. These two national churches formally took precedence over all other minority religions, known as *culte* or "denominations," including the Jewish, Roman Catholic, Protestant, and Islamic ones. As set forth in Article 22 of the new constitution, "The Orthodox and Greek Catholic Christian Churches are Romanian churches. The Romanian Orthodox Church, being the religion of the great majority of Romanians, is the dominant church in the State of Romania; and the Greek Catholic faith has primacy over the other faiths." Minority churches were henceforth placed under the authority and administrative structure of the Romanian state. Curricula in seminaries had to incorporate national standards such as training in the Romanian language. And the clergies of the minority churches were, effectively, made into government employees. Like all government employees in the new Romania, they were required to take loyalty oaths to the state, which now paid their salaries.

In 1925 the Romanian Orthodox Church was finally elevated to the rank of Patriarchy, a recognition that successive Romanian governments and leaders of the Romanian Orthodox Church had solicited from the Patriarchate of Constantinople since the Romanian Constitution of 1866 declared the church independent of any foreign hierarchy. Thus, during the first half of the 1920s, few Romanian institutions benefited more from the unification of Greater Romania than the Romanian Orthodox Church. After the incorporation of Transylvania into Greater Romania in 1920, many Orthodox Romanian nationalists relished the possibility that Greek Catholics—many of whom were self-identified ethnic Romanians living in Transylvania—and, not least, their physical churches and land holdings, might soon return to the Orthodox Church.

However, a number of events presaged a reversal of these fortunes. It soon became evident that the Romanian state's assimilation policies during the early 1920s had failed to integrate the four million new Romanian citizens of varying ethnic, national, linguistic, and confessional identifications. The modernization of state apparatuses and the relative liberalization of the Romanian political elite since the mid-nineteenth century—and with this the import of western European ideas into Romanian cultural and political life—divided Romanian intellectuals into what scholars of Romania have dubbed either Europeanist or Traditionalist.[6] Many Romanian nationalists, especially those who viewed the Romanian Orthodox Church as an anchor of Romanian nationality, spurned the modern, western European "forms" of life. Located squarely in this Traditionalist camp was an increasingly influential and radical group of theologians, philosophers, and other literati ascendant on the Romanian cultural and political scene, known collectively as the "Orthodoxists," a moniker assumed from their ideology of "Orthodoxism," which was at once theological, philosophical, and political.[7]

Though by no means a uniform group or movement, they viewed the "Europeanist" and "internationalist" encroachments from the West as alien to the psychology of the Romanian people, incompatible with the various notions of "Romanianism" and other national-specific forms of traditionalism. They integrated religion and theology into their concept (and glorification) of the Romanian national community. In this way, the Orthodoxists superimposed

Romanian Orthodoxy onto the specific ethnonational character of the Romanian people, making national belonging coterminous with religious belonging. For these increasingly influential clerics, politicians, and public intellectuals, a minority confessional community, by virtue of their non-Romanian-Orthodox faith, could not be regarded as truly Romanian. Even if members of such communities were Romanian citizens, spoke Romanian, and had lived in Romanian territory for generations, they could not "truly" be Romanian, for to be a Romanian was, perforce, to be a Romanian Orthodox.

The Catholic Church in Romania likewise experienced substantial change during the interwar period. In national and religious politics, the visibility and importance of the Roman Catholic hierarchy in the Moldavian city of Iași increased significantly. Prior to the 1920s, the Catholic leadership in Romania consisted mainly of foreign-born bishops and missionaries from Germany, Austria, Hungary, Italy, Poland, or elsewhere in central Europe. During the interwar period, however, Romanian-born priests were elevated to top positions in the archdiocese and elsewhere so as to put a "Romanian face" on the church.

Archbishop Raymund Netzhammer criticized the nationalization program of the Romanian government, especially those measures intended to limit the use of Hungarian in the Iași diocese, which naturally affected the Hungarian-speaking Csangos (whom Netzhammer considered to be of Hungarian nationality). The German-born Netzhammer, who had served as archbishop of Bucharest since 1905 and been a close advisor to, and confident of, Romania's previous king, the German-born Carol I (r. 1881–1914), openly complained about the hardships of Hungarian schools in Bucharest, the confiscation of church properties in the guise of land reform, and the Romanian government's mistreatment of Hungarians in the Transylvanian diocese. He also voiced concerns about the anti-Catholic resentment harbored by the Orthodox clergy, who, according to Netzhammer, considered the Catholic prelates a "foreign body, insidious, a permanent threat."[8] In addition, both Netzhammer and the papal nuncio Francesco Marmaggi publicly opposed the subordination of the Transylvanian dioceses to the archdiocese in Bucharest. Since both Netzhammer and Marmaggi were at odds with the new alliance between the Holy See and the Romanian state, and since heads of churches were now required to be Romanian citizens, the Vatican relieved the two men of their positions in 1923 and 1924, respectively.[9]

Netzhammer's replacement as archbishop of Romania was the current bishop of Iași, Alexandru Cisar, the first Romanian-born bishop ever to hold either title (he was from Bucharest, though of Czech family origins). Cisar, in turn, appointed Mihai Robu as the new bishop of Iași, the first Moldavian ever

Bishop Mihai Robu with faculty and students at the Seminary of Iași, 1934. (courtesy of the Archive of the Episcopate of Iași)

to hold that position.[10] Robu, in fact, came from the traditional northern Csango village of Săbăoani.[11]

The Vatican-Romanian Concordat: "The Origin of Evil Itself"

Looming over this increasingly fraught relationship between, on the one hand, the Roman Catholic hierarchies in Iași and Bucharest and, on the other, Romanian state authorities and the Romanian Orthodox hierarchy was the controversial signing of a Concordat between the Holy See and the Romanian state in 1927 (ratified by the Romanian Senate in 1929). In the history of interwar Romania, 1927 proved a watershed year that also witnessed the founding of Corneliu Codreanu's fascistic Legion of the Archangel Michael (Legiunea Arhanghelului Mihail), perhaps better known as the Iron Guard (Garda de fier), which was the movement's paramilitary political arm established in 1930, and then the serialization of Mircea Eliade's *Itinerar spiritual* (Spiritual itinerary), a manifesto for the young Romanian intellectuals who would later be dubbed the "Generation of 1927" or simply the "Young Generation." Broadly speaking, the Concordat affirmed the rights and liberties of Roman Catholics as confessional minorities in Greater Romania. It provided a legal framework for the life and operations of the Catholic Church in Romania, with provisions governing the hierarchies of the Greek, Latin, and Armenian rites, as well as the Ruthenian congregations. The treaty also rearranged the bishoprics in Romania, most notably the Latin rite bishoprics in Transylvania, and subordinated the nine-hundred-year-old Transylvanian diocese to the existing archdiocese in Bucharest.

Ostensibly, the Romanian state signed and ratified the Concordat to strengthen its prestige abroad and to enhance its relations with the Catholic countries of Europe. Vasile Goldiş, the minister who represented Romania at the signing of the Concordat, proclaimed that by agreeing to the treaty, "the Great Pontiff of Rome" had confirmed the statehood and legality of the new Romanian state, "acknowledging to the entire world that 2.5 million Catholics have found in Romania the conditions for progress and spiritual contentment." In light of this, "any slander or calumny [against Romania] must be silenced."[12] For its supporters, the Concordat achieved two main objectives: one was internal, namely the regulation of the Catholic Church within Romania; the other was external, namely, recognition and legitimization of Romania as a sovereign state capable of conducting affairs with other states on the European stage.

The signing of the Concordat was contentious from the outset, as many Orthodox Romanians viewed the treaty as a flagrant violation of recently enshrined national principles. This set off a wave of protest from both secular Romanian nationalists and the Romanian Orthodox Church. They viewed such favorable terms for the Vatican and the practicing Catholics in Romania as proof the Catholic Church, through the zealous clericalism of its hierarchy, was a force for "the infiltration of Hungarianization and Catholicization" in Romania.[13] As Marmaggi remarked to Netzhammer at the beginning of negotiations, "You'll see what happens when one day ten million Romanians shall accept the authority of the Pope."[14] While a somewhat naïve and offhanded remark, it nevertheless betrayed the long-term strategy and aspirations of Vatican policy in the Orthodox lands of eastern Europe. That the Concordat was initiated a decade earlier by Romania's now-deceased Catholic king and negotiated by its German-born archbishop of Bucharest, who was not a Romanian citizen, was equally abhorrent.[15] Most vexing to Romanian nationalists and Orthodoxists was the Concordat's explicit guarantee of "equality" of all churches before Romanian law, a guarantee that exacerbated tensions between the Christian confessions and further politicized religion in the country.

The Romanian Orthodox Church opposed the treaty because it challenged the church's recently enshrined national preeminence. The granting of special rights to the Roman Catholic Church in Romania and the recognition of the Archdiocese of Romania threatened to undermine not only the Orthodox Church's position as a leading institution atop Romanian society but also its efforts to return Romania's Greek Catholics to the bosom of Orthodoxy. Though Orthodox fears about the Hungarianization and Catholicization of Romanian society were mostly exaggerated, they were not entirely unfounded. The Concordat moved the Greek Catholics closer to the Vatican by regularizing the status of Greek Catholics in both state and canon law.[16] Clearly, the Vatican wanted to bolster the Greek Catholic Church as a distinctly *Catholic* presence in Orthodox lands and, simultaneously, to prevent the Orthodox Church from acting on its own designs for the reunification of the Orthodox and Greek Catholic churches.[17] Even the terminology of the Concordat was considered an affront to the Orthodox Church and the Romanian Constitution. In using the Romanian terms *religia catolică* (Catholic religion) and *Biserica catolică* (Catholic Church) rather than *cultul catolic* (the Catholic denomination), Romanian nationalists and Orthodoxists felt the Concordat flagrantly undermined the Constitution and the subsequent 1928 Law on Religious Denominations, which specified the existence of only two Romanian churches (*biserici românești*), namely the Romanian Orthodox and the Greek Catholic churches. All other churches were to be regarded as denominations (*culte*).

Led by patriarch of Romania Miron Cristea and the metropolitan of Transylvania Nicolae Bălan, the Romanian Orthodox Church spearheaded opposition to the treaty. In the Romanian Senate, Bălan engaged in a series of debates against his clerical counterpart, the outspoken Greek Catholic bishop of the Cluj-Gherla Diocese, Iuliu Hossu, who had not only promoted the signing of the Concordat but also participated in its negotiations.[18] Specifically, Bălan claimed the Concordat undermined the principle of *biserica dominantă* and threatened to unleash the rampant, subversive "clericalism" and "proselytizing" of the Catholic hierarchy. He therefore appealed to his fellow senators: "I know the papacy, I know its past, its doctrine and trends. I do not want to be unfair, but I know that when you let the papacy set foot in your country, especially through a Concordat, you take your country into such continual turmoil and unrest that it cannot resolve its national problems."

The Concordat, therefore, challenged the ascendency of the Orthodox Church in Romania. Worse, according to Bălan, the treaty "furthered the goals of the Hungarian state for the infiltration of Hungarianization and Catholicization among our people."[19] In addition to this, he raised grave concerns over the fate of the Greek Catholic Church and the role that Hungarians (both in Hungary and in Transylvania) had played in negotiating and signing the Concordat.

Considering all of this, Bălan called for the nullification of the treaty, as it was both "anti-constitutional" and "anti-patriotic."[20]

Discord between proponents and opponents of the Concordat only heightened existing concerns over the jurisdictional rights of the Catholic and Lutheran churches—especially in light of an increased presence of neo-Protestant groups—exacerbating fears of sectarianism and foreign influence within the country. The increasing visibility of other religions led many Romanian politicians and intellectuals to conclude that the minority religions represented "Trojan horses" from other states, whose goal was to destabilize Romanian politics and sow cultural and social disunity.[21]

Opposition to the treaty was not limited to the Orthodox Church hierarchy. Onisifor Ghibu, a Transylvanian regionalist and a prominent education reformer and politician during the interwar period, led the ostensibly secular charge for the nullification of the Concordat. Ghibu agreed with the majority of Romanian Orthodox intellectuals when expressing his indignation at this special treatment the Catholics had conferred upon themselves: "In avoiding the term 'denomination,' the Vatican has from the outset situated itself apart from the other denominations and created, therefore, a state of privilege before all the other minority denominations." Like Metropolitan Bălan, who was also a Transylvanian and a regionalist, Ghibu surmised that the Concordat with Romania was the product of collusion between Hungary and the Holy See, whose aim was to advance the cause of Hungarian revisionism over Transylvania. Ghibu sounded the alarm that "dozens of Hungarian propagandists in religious guise" had spread numerous pamphlets from Budapest and Rome claiming Hungary had been "unjustly mutilated" in the Treaty of Trianon. "To the ends of the earth," this propaganda was "filling the minds and hearts of their readers with lies and hatred against Romania." Ghibu argued for the nullification of the Concordat through any means necessary: "*Kulturkampf*? Yes, if necessary. *Kulturkampf* or any other means of fighting against those who would mock Christ and seek the abolition of the Romanian State and the Romanian people! . . . Will we meet resistance from the Greek Catholics? Possibly—but only from those who accede to the secret calculations between the papacy and the Hungarians. But these Greek Catholics are thus Hungarian, not Romanian."[22]

Kulturkampf was a reference to the discriminatory policies enacted by Bismarck against the Roman Catholic Church in Prussia during the 1870s, policies that sought to bring the church under state control and to suppress nationalist tendencies among the Catholic clergy there. Just as the Catholicism of national minorities represented an internal enemy threatening the cohesion of the predominantly Protestant Prussian state some fifty years earlier, so too did Catholicism in Romania represent a "Hungarian national force inside the country." For Ghibu, the refortification of Roman Catholicism in Romania was not a religious problem but rather "a problem of national politics," specifically the politics of Hungarian revisionism.[23]

The philosopher and ultranationalist Nae Ionescu was even more militant in his opposition to the Concordat, which he referred to as "the origin of evil itself." Ionescu was one of the most influential Orthodoxists and, for that matter, one of the most influential writers and ideologues in interwar Romania, serving as mentor and spiritual guide to many of the leading figures of the Young Generation. In his typical hyperbolic style, he proclaimed the Concordat symptomatic of the Greek Catholics' erroneous belief in a "hybrid character" of the "structure of [the Romanians'] spiritual race." For Ionescu, the Romanian state was a modern political organism whose "structure, laws of evolution and the decisive elements of its evolution" had become estranged from the religious factor—namely Romanian Orthodoxy—"so essential to the life of this organism."[24]

Opposition to the Concordat must also be seen as central to the politics of Romanian integration after 1920. As proponents of a more regionalist approach to the integration of the Romanian provinces, both Ghibu and Bălan were engaged in a parallel struggle against the Bucharest Liberals' centralization policies, which they believed threatened the autonomy of the Orthodox and Greek Catholic churches as institutional stakeholders in Romanian society, especially in Transylvania.[25] Bălan, moreover, was separately engaged in an ecclesiastical battle against the synod in Bucharest. Ionescu had no shortage of personal and political scores to settle. For him, character assassination and religious polemics were a form of art he regularly employed to discredit his opponents, even in his most philosophical of expositions.

The Orthodoxist Offensive

During the interwar period a prominent group of theologians and philosophers of religion imbued their respective theologies with emergent discourses about nation and even race. Opposition to the Concordat, alongside the increasing anti-Catholic sentiment, contributed to and was symptomatic of an influential but disparate set of ideas about the mystical nature of the Romanian Orthodox Church and its essential role in the life of the ethnic nation. While anti-Catholicism was a facet of Orthodoxist and nationalist thinking in interwar

Romania, it was neither a central tenet nor espoused by all Orthodoxists at all times. In fact, most of Romania's nationalist ideologues embraced Romania's Latin heritage, blending an Occidental civilizational and even biological identity with an Oriental or Byzantine spiritual one. For these men, the Romanian nation occupied a unique historical position at the confluence of European east and west. Despite this rather selective connection to both east and west, heated and sometimes vicious polemics between Orthodoxists and Catholics emerged during this time. The discourse fused Christian theology and dogma to national politics, nationalized the debate on the belonging and identity of Catholics in Romania, and sparked an unprecedented historiographical production by the Catholic clergy in Moldavia.

A brief description of how an increasingly vocal and influential coterie of Orthodox intellectuals and theologians ethnicized a mystical and highly nationalistic variant of Romanian Orthodoxy is necessary to understanding the context in which these debates took place. Within this group of Orthodoxists, contemporary historians count some of the most notable Romanian thinkers and writers of the interwar period, including Mircea Eliade, Lucian Blaga, Ion Gh. Savin, Nichifor Crainic, Dumitru Stăniloae, and the aforementioned Nae Ionescu (among whom only Crainic, Savin, and Stăniloae were professional theologians). Ionescu and Stăniloae viewed Romanian ethnicity and Romanian Orthodoxy as indivisible, thus excluding millions of non-Orthodox Romanian citizens from their claims of Romanian national belonging. Likewise, Crainic promoted a national theology and was a leading advocate for the forced removal of Romania's ethnic and religious minorities, a position that Stăniloae also endorsed. Many of the Orthodoxists took very public and often hostile positions against the Roman Catholic Church, especially after the signing of the Concordat.[26]

Both Crainic and Stăniloae subsumed into Eastern Orthodoxy the "Latin elements" that had been transmitted through the Romanian people over the ages. For Stăniloae, "Orthodoxy presents itself to us, especially following the experiences over the last century of fierce imitation of the West, as the single supporting and creating factor of ethnic originality in our Latin background." For it was Orthodoxy that represented in the Romanian's nature "the mystic river of existence" while Latinity, like Catholicism, represented the positivist, rationalist pole of existence. Romanians had reinforced this Latinity over the ages through borrowing and had absorbed these elements not for their spiritual but rather for their positivist content: "Without Orthodoxy, we have a Latinity (*latinitate*) that is devoid of soul."[27] Stăniloae wrote on the harmony that Orthodoxy facilitated between the individual and society and the "equilibrium" Romanian spirituality provided between God's activity and that of man. Calvinism and Lutheranism ruined this equilibrium in favor of God, "considering man as carried by superhuman or subhuman forces and falling into sickly prophecies and messianism." Catholicism, meanwhile, ruined this equilibrium in favor of man, leading foolhardily to utopianism and a luring of heaven down to earth.[28]

Crainic argued that Romania's Latinity did not in itself require an orientation toward the West. Romanians were geographically located in the Orient and, through their Eastern Orthodox religion, were the "guardians of truth of the Oriental world." Thus, he believed, Romania's orientation could only be toward itself, embracing its own legacy: "Our own culture can only develop organically in the environment provided by our land and our spirit. Westernization means the denial of our oriental character; the nihilism of pro-European trends means the denial of our creative potential. This, consequently, means the denial of a genuinely Romanian culture."[29]

During the 1930s, the ethnically grounded theologies of the lay Orthodoxist intellectuals greatly influenced Stăniloae, who later in life would become one of the most important Orthodox theologians of the twentieth century and certainly the most prominent in Romania. During the interwar period, however, Stăniloae was a young man and very much under the sway of ultranationalists Crainic and Ionescu. To be sure, Stăniloae harbored some anti-Catholic sentiments at this time; furthermore, he endorsed both Crainic and Ionescu's radical and even racist policy prescriptions for the removal of Romania's minority populations. Nevertheless, his thinking and writing on the Catholic Church were complex and, in any case, evolved over his lifetime.

Crainic skillfully navigated the cultural and political currents of his day, and indeed lived a diverse public life as a poet, professor, journalist, speechwriter, and theologian as well as a government minister and parliamentarian. He had evolved ideologically from a poet rooted in the traditionalism of the 1910s and 1920s into a radical, racist, and fascist ideologue by the 1930s and 1940s.[30] Like most of the Orthodoxists, he maintained deep reservations if not antipathy toward the papacy and those elements of Catholic theology at odds with Orthodoxy, elements he believed corruptive to Romanian society and culture. In particular, he saw the universalizing and proselytizing mission of the Catholic Church as threatening Romania's Byzantine Orthodox culture. Crainic saw in the Catholic Church the embodiment of everything Western—bourgeois, urbane, inorganic—that was so antithetical to Romania's natural course of historical development.

Though Crainic was a staunch Orthodoxist and wrote critically of Catholicism and the pope, his antiminority politics never explicitly called for the expulsion of Romanian Catholics on religious grounds. In fact, Crainic had a wide array of friendships and personal connections with Catholics. He cofounded the Bucharest-based ecumenical journal *Farul nou* (New lighthouse) with the Roman Catholic priest Anton Durcovici and the leftist Orthodox theologian and writer Grigore Pişcuiescu (Gala Galaction, pseudonym).[31] The editor and a regular contributor to the journal, which by the mid-1930s took a decidedly Catholic turn, was the prominent Roman Catholic theologian Iosif Frollo. In addition to drawing on Eastern writers as sources of mysticism, especially nineteenth- and twentieth-century Russian Orthodox theologians, Crainic drew on a number of Western and Catholic writers, from the German poet Rainer Maria Rilke to the early neoplatonists and church Fathers.[32]

Politically, Crainic allied himself with many Catholic members of other European fascist movements, including the Ustaše in Croatia (European fascist movements emerged mainly from Catholic countries, notably Italy, Spain, Croatia, and France as well as the partly Catholic countries Germany and Hungary). From these movements Crainic drew inspiration. He praised Mussolini and "the Catholic character of fascism" in Italy. He viewed the role of Catholicism, "this traditional religion of the Italian people," in the development of Italian fascism as crucial. Italian fascism had been embraced without restriction or modification: "From the religious point of view, fascism [in Italy] is a restoration; not a restoration of the medieval Ceasaro-papism but a restoration of a Catholicism as a fundamental spiritual function of Italian life."[33] Thus corporatist, fascist Catholic Italy became an authoritarian political model for Orthodox Romania, especially as Catholic Italians and Orthodox Romanians were "spiritually linked" through blood and history: "The spirit of old Rome determined the forms of the brilliant civilization of Dacia Felix. The spirit of new Rome indicates the form of history that nationalist Romania is destined to create. Today the colonization of old Roman legions is no longer needed: Rome is in our blood."[34]

While indeed Crainic saw Orthodoxy as a mark of Romanianness, he, for one, did not deny *Romanianness* to ethnic Romanians of differing Christian confessions, only subordinating them to ethnic Romanians of the Orthodox faith. This idea is encapsulated in the title of his most famous work, *Ortodoxie şi etnocraţie* (Orthodoxy and ethnocracy), published in 1938, in which he laid out an unapologetic and discriminatory system of rule within a Romanian "ethnocratic state." By contrast, Nae Ionescu placed Orthodoxy within the very ontology of the Romanian people, thereby explicitly denying Catholics the possibility of *being* Romanian.[35]

The anti-Catholicism in the works and politics of Nae Ionescu requires a great deal of unpacking. Ionescu's animus to Catholicism had its roots in his formative years in Germany where he studied philosophy in Munich, the intellectual heart of the German Catholic world. Ionescu had spent many years engaging leading Catholic intellectuals such as Cardinal Eugenio Pacelli (the future Vatican secretary of state who later became Pope Pius XII) and the Romanian convert to Catholicism, Prince Vladimir Ghika. These experiences contributed to Ionescu's lifelong antipathy to Catholicism and to the revival of its scholasticism, which Ionescu saw as the embodiment of the Western European tradition—its rationalism, positivism, "Caesaropapism," Roman centralization, and Thomist devotion to reason and Aristotelianism.[36]

Through Orthodoxism (the sacred) and its corollary, Romanianism (the profane), these intellectuals envisioned a pathway to God through the nation. The Orthodoxists believed the national character of the Romanian people, or their specific Romanianness, was rooted in Romania's Eastern Orthodox spirituality and its peasant heritage.[37] Their concept of the nation combined religion and ethnicity—exclusively Romanian Orthodoxy and Romanian ethnicity—as essential components of the national-spiritual body. Necessarily, this excluded a large portion of the Romanian citizenry (according to the census in 1930, about 30 percent of the Romanians self-declared as something other than ethnic Romanian or Eastern Orthodox). As institutional pillars of the nation, the Romanian Orthodox Church and the greater Romanian state worked together to foster national identity and induce national cohesion. In reaction to the encroachments of westernism, internationalism, Catholicism, and rationalism into Romanian national life, some Orthodoxists claimed the Orthodox Church possessed an "indissoluble relation to nationality," that there existed a "sacred unity" between the Romanian nation and the Romanian Orthodox Church.[38] For them, the minority churches in Romania were not simply excluded from theological underpinnings of the nation but inimical to its life and well-being.

These attitudes toward ethnic and religious minorities had an enormous impact on the way the Catholics negotiated their relationship with the Romanian state, whose nation-building elite had proved increasingly inept at solving the state's minority problem. The source of this problem lay in the government's inability to integrate, culturally and economically, the millions of non-Romanians populating the country's newly added territories. The government failed to raise the Romanians' standard of living in comparison with the Hungarians, Germans, and Jews, who often dominated the cities, universities, and industries and were generally wealthier (or perceived as wealthier). The elevation of the cultural, political, and legal status of the confessions in Romania as a result of measures such as the Concordat produced within the nationalist discourse the question as to whether Romanianism (*românismul*) and Catholicism were compatible. In the new model of the nationalizing and homogenizing state, could Catholics of either the Greek or Latin rites be considered "good" Romanians?

Catholic Counteroffensives

It is clear from their journals and other publications that the Catholic intelligentsia in Romania was acutely aware of the nationalist currents shaping Romanian politics in the 1930s.[39] In fact, these authors mounted intellectual and theological counteroffensives by openly engaging the Orthodoxists in the pages of Catholic journals. Though most Catholic publications out of Iaşi and Bucharest were not widely read in Romania, they were nevertheless circulated throughout the Catholic-inhabited areas in Moldavia. The readership of these publications consisted mainly of the Catholic clergy but also included the literate Catholic public in villages and towns. Moreover, these publications were useful for disseminating the Roman Catholic Church's positions on both religious and secular matters.[40] Catholic theologians wrote on some of the most pressing social, political, and religious issues of the day, discussing topics such as nationality and Christianity, ethnicity and race, Nazism and fascism, democracy, the communist threat, *numerus clausus*, and especially the strained relations between the Orthodox and Catholic Churches in Romania.

The voices in the Catholic journals responded not only to the verbal salvos of Ionescu and others but also to the general anti-Catholicism and anti-Hungarianism growing in Moldavia, generated mainly by local Orthodox priests. Many Orthodoxists, including Stăniloae, had described the Catholic Church as an international organization akin to the League of Nations. In interwar Romania, characterization of the church as "internationalist" conjured up images of Jews, freemasons, and communists. Catholic writers were attuned to this and made every effort to refute what they saw as the vilification of their church: "Our church does not represent a 'black' international, as portrayed by those who have slandered her behind the guise of these kinds of attacks, which have justified establishing all 'internationals' as socialist, communist, etc. The church is supranational—concerning chiefly the human soul."[41]

The Roman Catholic clergy lamented that the "general orientation of the press in Moldavia insists on the element of Romanian ethnic autochthony." The Orthodox clergy, who influenced the general mentality in Moldavia, regarded Catholics as "something foreign, as some partly ethnic and partly religious

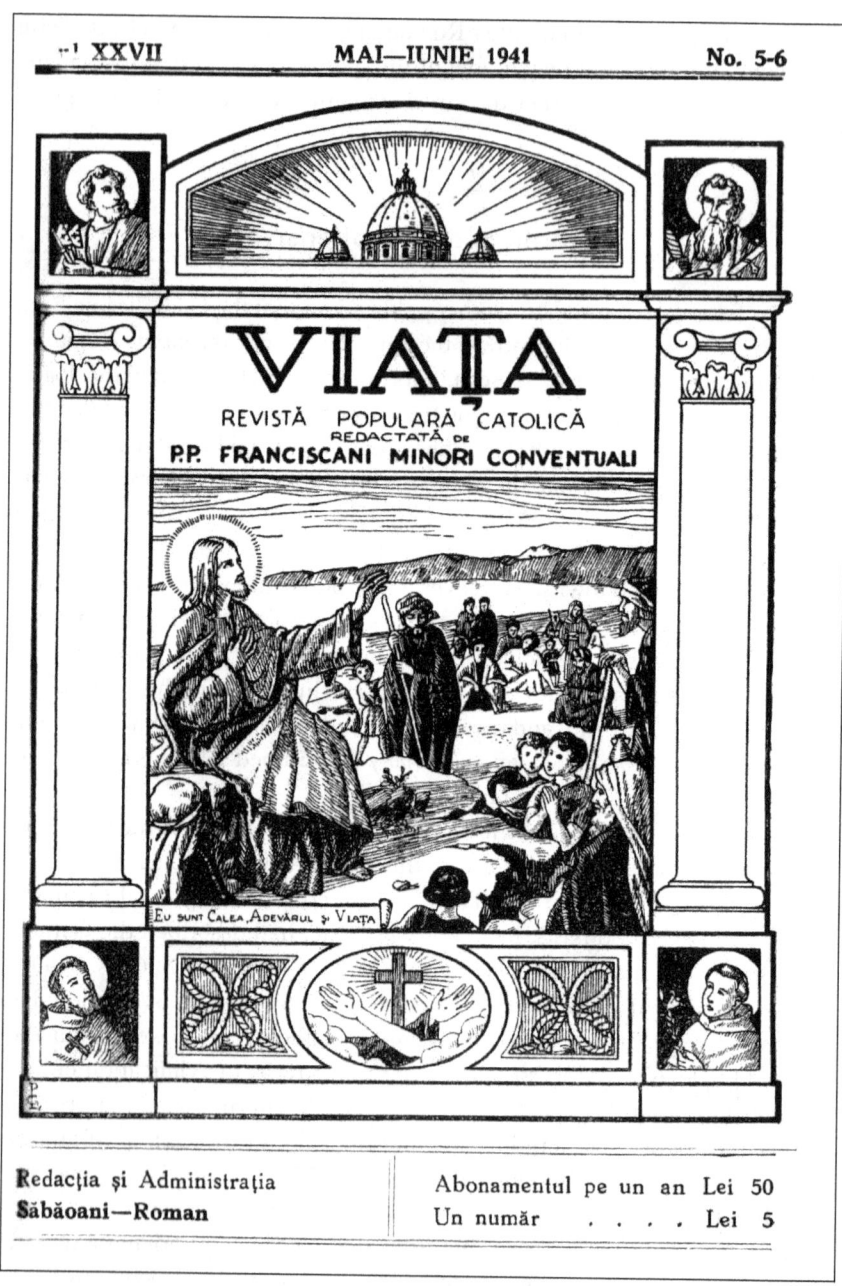

Cover of the Catholic journal *Viaţa* (The life), 1941. Published by the Franciscan Order in Romania. (Romanian Academy Library)

minority who are destined to cause local problems and, as such, are somehow harmful to the country."[42]

Catholic writers challenged the Orthodoxists' claim of a synonymity between Orthodoxy and Romanianness, which precluded Catholics from being "true" Romanians. As early as 1928, the Roman Catholic priest Iosif Ghiuzan refuted these ideas in his defense of the Csangos. Born in the Csango village of Adjudeni/Dzsidafalva, Ghiuzan studied philosophy and theology in Italy, taught at the seminary in Iași, and served as a parish priest in a village outside Bacău, in the heart of Catholic Moldavia.[43] He contributed numerous articles in Catholic journals in the late 1920s, anticipating the decisive factor in subsequent debates on the Csangos' national belonging during World War II, namely that the Csangos were Romanian by origin and blood.

Though Ghiuzan acknowledged that, indeed, one could be a Romanian citizen yet have a different nationality—as was the case with the Romanian Poles, Germans, Hungarians, and Italians—this was assuredly not the case with the Csangos. For Ghiuzan, "the nationality of a man is in blood and soul; religion and faith is in the mind and will of a man, in his conviction." Blood and soul were thus determinative factors: "Someone can have Romanian blood and soul, and in his mind be convinced of the truth of the Catholic religion and embrace it. If for instance a Romanian becomes convinced that the Catholic Church is the true one of Jesus Christ and becomes Catholic, does the blood in his veins actually change? Certainly not." In the late 1920s, the signifier "Romanian Catholics" (*român catolic*) began to appear frequently in the writings of the Catholic intelligentsia in Moldavia and Bucharest (the term is even used as a title of one of Ghiuzan's articles). The qualifier *Romanian* almost always appeared in italics to emphasize the community's national belonging as Catholics to the Romanian nation. Thus, their Catholic blood was also Romanian blood, and Roman Catholics were now *Romanian* Catholics: "We are *Romanian Catholics*. A Romanian may very well be Catholic, because he can have a Romanian heart and blood and a mind convinced of the truth of the Catholic religion. Let us protest vigorously both in public and in private, on any occasion, particularly when faced with authorities, against our being considered foreigners because we are Catholic. Nationality is one thing, religion another."[44]

Ghiuzan noted that in the Moldavian counties of Roman and Bacău, many Catholic-inhabited villages were said to be "Hungarian, Ciangăi." He acknowledged that some in these villages spoke "a kind of Hungarian language" and that historians had speculated the community was descendant from the Cuman tribes that entered Moldova in the Middle Ages. Regardless of their settlement history, he contended, these inhabitants had for centuries lived in these villages, worked these lands, paid taxes, and fought for the country alongside their Orthodox neighbors.

Was Romania specifically an Orthodox country? According to Ghiuzan, the country was neither Orthodox nor Catholic, nor any other religion—"rather, the country is Romanian," simply put. Going one step further, Ghiuzan suggested Orthodoxy was not even the true ancestral Christian religion of Romania. Latin priests had first brought Christianity to Romanian territory, and for centuries the Romanian nation had long held tight to "old Mother Rome." Only much later, after years of tribulation and victimization, did the Romanians become dependent on the patriarchs of Byzantium, who, Ghiuzan claimed, led them away from the Roman Church: "Thus, the true ancestral religion [of Romania] is Catholicism."[45] However, if the "ancestral religion" was also to be the national religion, then, he pointed out, Romanians should revert to paganism!

Though Catholic writers emphasized the important role of spirituality and religion in the life of the nation, they also stressed that reason and rationality were an important aspect in the communion with the divine. In this respect, the Orthodoxist characterization of Catholic thinking as rationalist and positivist was near the mark. For these Catholic theologians, religion revealed the supernatural world, which admittedly could not be understood through reason alone but also through faith: "On the contrary, the relation between [reason and faith] is complementary, as reason goes together with faith up to a point, namely the limit between the natural and the supernatural."[46]

No one embodied this rationalist spirit more than the Catholic lay theologian, linguist, and professor Iosif Frollo.[47] Without a doubt, Frollo was the most important and most prolific writer on Catholic issues in Romania's interwar years, and a strong voice in defense of its Catholic congregations in 1930s' Romania. He was "the right-hand man" of Archbishop Cisar and an ally to the Catholic hierarchy and intelligentsia in Bucharest.[48] Frollo contributed to and edited a number of Catholic journals and taught French, Romanian, and Latin in some of Bucharest's most prestigious lyceums. He even taught French and Latin to the young Mircea Eliade, one of the leading intellectuals of the Young Generation.

Frollo was also leader of the Romanian branch of Catholic Action (Acțiunea Catolică), an organization of the Roman Catholic Church whose mission, in the words of Pope Pius XI in 1927, was to encourage "the participation of the laity in the hierarchical apostolate of the Church, transcending party politics." Catholic Action was, in many ways, a nonclerical extension of the church hierarchy used to activate Catholic populations "for the diffusion and exercise of Catholic principles" in their respective societies.[49] The Romanian branch of

Catholic Action formed shortly after the signing of the Romanian-Vatican Concordat in 1927. By supporting the activity of its laity, the Catholic Church in Romania could provide cover for its clergymen who were, according to the Law on Religious Denominations, forbidden to engage in politics. Through the layman Frollo and his activity in Catholic Action, the Catholic Church could maintain some level of distance from national politics and the highly charged and very public debates with the Orthodoxists.

Frollo's writings on the ethnic and religious belonging of Catholics to the Romanian nation would provide a template for subsequent writings on the history and nationality of the Csangos. However, Frollo's discussion of these topics—and more importantly, his political activities during the tumultuous interwar years—were, like his Orthodoxist counterparts, a product of the rising nationalist tide sweeping the region. Unsurprisingly, during the 1930s Frollo and a small number of Catholics became involved with the Legion of the Archangel Michael, Romania's largest and most prolific fascist movement.

In contrast to the mystical, anti-Western, and antirationalist tenets of the Orthodoxists, Catholic intellectuals such as Guizan and Frollo defended reason as an important means to Christian spiritual transcendence. Frollo linked reason to the virtue of self-sacrifice for the communal good and to the virtue of patriotism, which he argued was not something inherent but rather formed in individuals and communities through education: "For the country has a material aspect, which one cannot apprehend without the aid of reflection, and a spiritual aspect, which illuminates and deepens it. . . . Without the intervention of human reason and voluntary effort, man is egotistical and unable to sacrifice for others." These virtues were continually being cultivated yet were susceptible to augmentation and decline. They were not predicated on some mystical force within individuals and communities owing simply to confession: "We can find—and in fact we do find—examples of supreme sacrifice and the highest forms of patriotism even where there is no sign of the Christian spirit. But love of country that is based on Christianism is egocentric in gigantic proportions."[50]

Frollo took aim at those "inept" ideologues "making their religion of the nation from this Orthodoxism" by professing the synonymity between Orthodoxism and Romanianism. He accused the Orthodoxists of exploiting the gospels and the Christian Orthodox faith to perpetuate their own, narrow political agendas and aspirations for power. This Orthodoxists' attempt "to monopolize patriotism" and to cast themselves as the only authorized representatives of Romanianism was "sheer impertinence" to the many non-Orthodox Romanians who had "demonstrated not through words but by their deeds and patriotism that they are Romanian in every fiber of their structure, from father to son of countless generations."[51]

The "Good Romanian"

The polemic on the "antinomy" between Romanianism and Catholicism pitted the Orthodoxists Ionescu, Stăniloae, and Iuliu Scriban against the Catholic theologian Iosif Frollo. At issue were competing ideas about what it meant "to be a good Romanian" (*a fi bun român*), as the polemic would be referred to in a number of articles at the time. This notion of a "good Romanian" harkened back to the coronation speech of King Ferdinand (r. 1914–27)—who, like his father and predecessor Carol I, was a German belonging to the Roman Catholic branch of the Hohenzollern family—during which he vowed before the nation to be "a good Romanian."

An offhanded remark in 1930 about the sister of well-known novelist and journalist Cezar Petrescu sparked a controversy and subsequent debate that would shape the contours of Romanian identity then and since. The sister, Ștefania Petrescu, had recently converted to Catholicism and joined a nunnery. Since then, she had been labeled an *unguriancă* (Hungarian woman) for having converted to the "Hungarian" religion.[52] Incensed at Ștefania's transgression against the Orthodox Church and the Romanian nation, Scriban—a priest at the honorific rank of archimandrite, a professor of theology, a polemicist, and a one-time member of A. C. Cuza's virulently anti-Semitic National-Christian Defense League—penned a scathing article titled "Catholic nuns do not give up their vices" in the pages of *Cuvântul*, one of Romania's leading dailies. In the article, Scriban excoriated poor Ștefania as a "wicked woman" and traitor to her country for joining the Sisters of Sion, who had "deceived the girl into turning away from her parents, her home, her country, and the law." For Scriban, Ștefania's conversion to Catholicism was anathema. She was a "beast," "wicked," "defiled," to be "banished to the wilderness." Scriban's rebuke was merciless: "Whoever turns to Catholicism ceases to be a good Romanian, and if one enters the monastic life, then one becomes perverted to the highest degree so as to become the most dangerous enemy of the Romanian nation."[53] This, from one of the highest-ranking members of the Romanian Orthodox Church.

Frollo responded to Scriban a week later in the pages of *Cuvântul*, questioning the source of such bitterness within Orthodox circles against Romania's

Catholics, insisting Catholicism was not antithetical to Romanianism. As a case in point, Frollo noted that some of Romania's most revered national historical figures were Greek Catholics, including the nineteenth-century prime minister and founder of the National Liberal Party Ion C. Brătianu and Enlightenment-era theologian, historian, and member of the famed Transylvanian School Samuel Micu-Klein, who, more than anyone before him, nurtured ideas about the Roman origins of the Romanians. Considering these two outstanding examples in the Romanian's pantheon of national heroes, Frollo asked, rhetorically, "Can a Catholic, therefore, not be a 'good Romanian'?"[54] A few days later, in a column of his own, Ionescu retorted, "Good Romanians you can be—surely, you are. But are you Romanian?" By this Ionescu implied that indeed it was possible for Catholics to be "good Romanians," by which he meant good citizens, possessing good intentions toward the Romanian state—yet never could they be authentic Romanians, like Orthodox Romanians.

While Ionescu acknowledged Micu-Klein as "one of the founders of Romanian consciousness" and credited Brătianu for helping to create the modern Romanian state, he nevertheless questioned whether the state that Brătianu created was ever "truly Romanian." If so, then surely Brătianu could be regarded and remembered as a true Romanian. But Ionescu's insinuation was that Romania was not, truly, a *Romanian* state, and therefore Brătianu was a "good Romanian" only in the sense that he had the best intentions for the Romanian people and state—"but 'Romanian' he was not." And what of the great Samuel Micu-Klein, celebrated as the progenitor of Romania's national awakening and consciousness? Could his Romanianism likewise be called into question simply because he did not belong to the Romanian Orthodox rite? Indeed, it could, according to Ionescu: "Being Romanian is a natural state, a poised formula of one's existence from which certain forms unfold in life. To be Romanian means to have a certain mettle from which certain attitudes and gestures necessarily devolve. One's will has nothing to say in this situation because one cannot normally outdo oneself other than by ceasing to be oneself. . . . No one can be Romanian, for instance, unless one achieves concretely, individually, the organizing spiritual structure on the basis of which is the essence of the Romanian nation."[55]

For Ionescu, being Romanian was something ontological. Romanian Orthodoxy was not extrinsic to Romanian ethnicity but, rather, integral to it. In this way, fellow Romanian Christians such as Greek and Roman Catholics, to say nothing of Romanian Jews, could never count themselves as authentic members of the Romanian national body, however much their patriotic will and good deeds might qualify them as decent citizens of Romania.[56] Ionescu and other Orthodoxists now began to assert that people's attitude toward God, and the ways in which they experience divinity, were interwoven in the nation's fabric.

No doubt exasperated by the dogmatism and growing fanaticism of his interlocutors, Frollo spent the next year penning a monograph addressing Ionescu and Scriban's diatribe against Romania's Catholics. In his *Romînism și catolicism* (Romanianism and Catholicism), published in 1931, Frollo attempted to extricate religion from the Orthodoxist conception of Romanian ethnicity. He rejected Scriban's contention that conversion to Catholicism perverted the Romanian, that a Romanian could somehow become "denationalized" through religious conviction: "Becoming Catholic, far from denationalizing a Romanian, is fulfilling his ethnic being and thus, far from diminishing patriotism, increases it. . . . To say 'good Romanian' is a pleonasm, when it is sufficient to say and mean 'Romanian' pure and simple. Using this expression, you leave the concept of Romanian with a very vague meaning, because you have stripped it of its very core, namely its ethnic meaning, removing from it even the value of the notion of citizenship."[57]

Frollo defined a Romanian as "any man originating from Romania who speaks Romanian and has no known ancestors who spoke another maternal language." Accordingly, ethnicity represented the "eminent form" of Romanianism. The nation, meanwhile, functioned as an organism that, over the course of its life, assimilated and eliminated any number of traits. Frollo identified two essential traits from which the Romanian national character arose: language and homeland. These two alone represented what was essential to the Romanian national character. They were, not coincidentally, two qualities that Catholics such as the Csangos possessed: a centuries-old homeland in the heart of Moldavia and some claim as a community of Romanian speakers, if not in whole then in part.

For Frollo, to regard Orthodoxy as a third "essential" element was erroneous; unlike territory and language, Orthodoxy as a trait was not specific to Romania. Were Bulgarians, Serbians, and Russians also somehow Romanian because they were Orthodox, he asked? Was a Catholic in Germany any less of a German than his Protestant brother? Frollo nevertheless acknowledged that one could not be Romanian simply by willing oneself to be Romanian. However, unlike nationality, religion was a matter of will: "I am or I am not Romanian because I was made or not made by Romanian parents. However, I am Orthodox or Catholic because I want to be Orthodox or Catholic; indeed, I can say I am Orthodox or I am Catholic only because I want to be so."[58]

Romanian *Kulturkampf* in Context

This polemic against the Roman and Greek Catholics led by Ionescu and others, and more generally the ideas and discourses on the mysticization and ethnicization of Romanian Orthodoxy, must be seen within the context of the fickle nature of Romanian politics in the 1930s, which frequently involved intrigue, collusion, and the shifting of allegiances in an ongoing battle between parties, personalities, and the Crown for political power. Nationalist politicians, theologians, and intellectuals often conflated Romanianness with Orthodoxy as a rhetorical and polemical device simply to attack opponents who happened not to be Romanian Orthodox, thus casting doubts as to their opponents' legitimacy as leaders of the nation. For many Orthodoxists and other Romanian nationalists, linking religion to ethnicity was an ardent ideological and philosophical position. Nevertheless, these and other polemics should be understood in their proper historical and political (and even personal) contexts. Many of the ideological and even theological expositions of Ionescu and Crainic were a product of the political machinations endemic to interwar Romania. Political feuds, especially between Orthodoxists from the Regat and Greek Catholics from Transylvania, were often couched in theological polemics.[59]

These discourses were also the product of self-valorization. Ionescu, in particular, whose ideas radiated from the columns of his daily *Cuvântul* and his lectures at the University of Bucharest, was never at a loss to deploy invectives against minorities and his political foes. A polemicist and gadfly, Ionescu sought to discredit and undermine his opponents in both subtle and overt ways and to politicize religion to these ends. From 1930 to 1933 he was part of King Carol II's *camarilla*, promoting the king's efforts to weaken Romania's major political parties, especially the Liberals and the National Peasant Party. Carol used Machiavels such as Ionescu—whose daily, *Cuvântul*, was one of the most widely read in Romania—in thinly veiled attacks on the main political parties and their respective leaders, often pitting one against the other. By the end of the 1930s, Carol and his allies aimed to subvert the democratic parliamentary system and to consolidate power in the Crown. Ionescu endorsed Carol's antidemocratic agenda and supported his restoration to the throne on the basis of nationalist principles, as Carol was the rightful heir.[60] Crainic's writings on Orthodoxism and "ethnocracy," which were more elaborate and certainly more prolific than Ionescu's, should be viewed in tandem with his career as a politician and propagandist in the Antonescu regime. Crainic's mystical theology should also be seen within the highly politicized context of university theology faculties in the interwar period.[61]

Reactionary and exclusionary discourses of the kinds described in this chapter suffused and targeted any number of agendas, debates, groups, and individuals in interwar Romania. Often the vituperative polemics, scurrilous accusations, and scaremongering were as much personal as political, a matter of rivalry and prestige, as in the case of Nichifor Crainic and Nae Ionescu. Both men competed for symbolic leadership of the swelling radical youth movement and to be the doyen of the Iron Guard. Their respective publications also competed for readership and relevancy in public debates, especially in creating a nationalist idiom and in framing the nationalist discourse. This dialectic between confession and ethnicity—between the sacred and profane—worked out in the Catholic-Orthodox polemics of interwar Romania, would presage the reconstruction of the Csangos' historical narrative by Catholic priests-cum-historians a decade later. The religious criterion for national belonging would continue to pose obstacles for communities such as the Jews, Gagauz, Hungarians, and especially the Moldavian Csangos. For even if the Csangos could refashion themselves as ethnic Romanians, their Catholic religion—both as a practice and as a marker of identity—was for them something immutable.

Catholics and the Iron Guard

The nexus of Orthodox clergy, Orthodoxist intellectuals (both lay and clerical), and the Legion has a historiography all its own. However, the relationship of the Legionary movement to Romania's non-Orthodox Christians—and to Romania's Catholics in particular—is rarely highlighted. Recent scholarship on the Legionary movement has emphasized not only its palingenetic character but also the heterogeneous religious sources (including pre-Christian ones) from which its ideology and dogma drew. This analysis of the movement suggests that the Legion in fact subordinated the Orthodox Church to its ideal of national salvation and worldwide "national ecumenicity."[62] Echoing Roger Griffin's work on the palingenetic character of fascist movements, historian Constantin Iordachi has argued that the ideological foundations of the Guard rested not on the Orthodox Church but rather on a Romantic palingenetic project that employed a kind of religious, patriotic, and charismatic syncretism that was enriched by—rather than predicated on—specific Eastern Orthodox religious themes. The movement was informed more generally by Christian traditions, such as sacrifice and the expiation of sins, and in this respect, it included a number of Catholic and Protestant dogmas. From Catholic fascist Italy and Spain, Codreanu and the Legion borrowed elements such as an overtly militant and crusading spirit, the sanctification of the movement's martyrs, and the cult of Saint Anthony of Padua (Codreanu's personal patron and protector).⁶³

The syncretic and quasi-ecumenical character of the Legion broadened the movement's appeal beyond the strictly Orthodox Romanian population. In fact, the Legion counted among its membership Roman Catholics and even Protestants, albeit in very small numbers. In addition, Greek Catholics, especially the clergy, made up a relatively large portion of the Legion's membership. The Aromanians—a disparate community of Romanophile Vlachs who spoke a Latinate language akin to Romanian—also joined in large numbers relative to the size of their population. While Aromanians were Eastern Orthodox by religion, they were nevertheless newcomers to Romanian territory, having been resettled from Greek Macedonia (with some from Albania and Bulgaria) into a new homeland in Romanian Southern Dobrudja in the first decades of the twentieth century. Many of these Aromanians were first-generation Romanian citizens. In Bessarabia, small numbers of ethnic Slavs and even Gagauz joined the Legion. For these minorities, there was no better way to demonstrate loyalty to the Romanian nation than by joining its most ardent nationalist movement.

While non-Orthodox membership in the Legion should not be overstated, it is fairly evident that the Guard was far more dynamic (if not opportunistic) in terms of its membership, especially after it became a more prominent force in national politics by the mid-1930s. As a political party, it also aimed to play a role in electoral politics and, as such, gradually became more inclusive of other Christians. Thus, at the height of its power and appeal, adherence to Romanian Orthodoxy was clearly not a prerequisite: the organization was, foremost, a Christian nationalist-fascistic movement, in which the Romanian national character mattered more to the Legion's sense of belonging (to both the nation and the Legion itself). As self-sacrificing, patriotic *Romanian* members of the most radical and nationalist political force in the country, Greek and Roman Catholics could affirm their loyalty to the nation and support of its national ideals in spite of their non-Orthodox faiths.

For Codreanu, Romanian ethnicity—however broadly understood—remained a precondition for national belonging. Yet from what can be gleaned from his writings and actions, his understanding of what constituted an "authentic Romanian" was less biologized than in other racist-nationalist programs in interwar Romania, such as those proposed in Crainic's "ethnocracy" and Iuliu Moldovan's "Biopolitical State," or for that matter in Nazi Germany. Instead, Codreanu's conception of the authentic Romanian was something more territorialized and mythologized, connoting something archetypal that embraced all Romanians—past, present, and future—who hailed from the ancestral land (*pământul strămoşesc*): "When we say the Romanian nation, we mean not only all Romanians living in the same territory, sharing the same past and the same future, the same dress, but all Romanians, alive and dead, who have lived on this land from the beginning of history and will live here also in the future."[64]

Moreover, Codreanu's program for the regeneration of the nation was more often couched in spiritual and nonrational or nonscientific terms. This is not to overlook a central component of the Legionary program, namely anti-Semitism, which it pursued with violent zeal. Though the movement lacked the ideological underpinnings of Nazi-inspired racial theories, individual members nevertheless invoked the language of biological racism when characterizing as "parasitic" the millions of "foreigners" who populated the nation.[65] Certainly, Codreanu was no friend of the Hungarians, the Russians, or any others considered Romania's present and historical enemies. But a special hatred was reserved for Jews. In a rather strange anecdote, Codreanu drew a distinction between, on the one hand, those "poisoners of the soul," the Jews, and, on the other, the marginalized and less perfidious Christian others, such as the Csangos. In his autobiographical manifesto, *Pentru legionari* (For the legionaries), published in 1936, Codreanu described his student days in Berlin in 1922. He recounted the willful blindness of European Jewry to the implications of Mussolini's March on Rome and the coup d'état, in considering the Jewish "problem" in Mussolini's Italy minor by comparison with Germany and Romania. Nevertheless, the coming to power of Italy's National Fascist Party showed the potential for some of Europe's most radical and violent anti-Semites to seize power in their own countries. It was this merging of radical nationalism and violent anti-Semitism that would distinguish the fascist movements in central and eastern Europe (such as in Germany, Hungary, and Romania) from their Italian forerunner: "In Italy, there are as many Jews as there are Csangos in the Siret valley in Romania. An Italian anti-Semitic movement in Italy would be as if we Romanians had started a movement against the Csangos. But if Mussolini would have lived in Romania he could not but be anti-Semitic, for Fascism means, first of all, defending your nation against the dangers that lie in wait for it. It means the destruction of these dangers and the clearing of the way toward life and glory for your nation."[66]

Shortly after this writing there did emerge a virulent anti-Semitic movement in Italy, including the passage of race laws in 1938 and the internment of Jews in concentration camps after Italy entered the war in 1940. Moreover, local officials and Orthodox priests in the Catholic-inhabited villages in Moldavia, spearheaded by the prefect of Bacău County, General Constantin S. Ionescu, did start a movement against the Csangos. Codreanu evidently did not consider the Csangos to be ethnically Romanian. As Christians, however, the Csangos could have a role in a Codreanu-led fascist Romania, provided they supported the Legion's larger political and electoral goals, even if a majority of the Catholics had little interest in the violent anti-Semitism, Orthodox mysticism, targeted political assassinations, and cult of death and personality that became hallmarks of the Legion.

The Csangos, however, failed to support the Legion in any meaningful numbers, despite the fact that the movement began in Moldavia, in the city of Iași (it moved its headquarters to Bucharest in 1932), and attracted young men from a variety of backgrounds. Still, some prominent Roman Catholics from the region joined the Legion and other right-wing movements. The previously discussed Iosif Frollo was a follower of one of Romania's leading anti-Semites, the politician and racist A. C. Cuza. According to his secret police files, Frollo became involved with a number of right-wing groups beginning in the 1930s, including Cultul Patriei (Cult of the fatherland) and Cruciada Românismul (Crusade of Romanianism).[67] Though Frollo denied some of these connections, it is a matter of record that he was a member of the Legion and a sympathizer and admirer of Codreanu. In fact, Frollo was a personal friend of Codreanu's father, the ultranationalist and anti-Semite Ion Zelea (Zieliński) Codreanu, who was active in the pre–World War I nationalist movement launched in Iași by A. C. Cuza (with whom Codreanu *père* was a close friend and compatriot) and famed historian and politician Nicolae Iorga.[68] Frollo was apparently quite impressed by the younger Codreanu's booklets *Cărticica șefului de cuib* (The nest leader's manual), published in 1933, and *Pentru legionari*, which Frollo claimed to have studied closely.[69] After reading an article by Frollow in *Farul nou* praising *Pentru legionari*, Corneliu Codreanu asked for a meeting with the widely respected Catholic theologian, who only a few years earlier had publicly wrangled with the likes of Nae Ionescu. In their two meetings together, Codreanu and Frollo discussed the Legion's composition and needs.[70] Codreanu then convinced Frollo to run on the Legion's Totul pentru Țară (All for the fatherland) party ticket in the 1937 parliamentary election (the party was the political and electoral wing of the movement, which aimed to legitimize the Legion in local and national government). Frollo accepted and ran for the Senate in Bacău and Roman Counties, where the majority of Csangos lived.[71] Clearly the nomination of this prominent Catholic, theologian, journalist, and professor was an attempt to win votes in the predominantly Catholic regions.

However, Totul pentru Țară had a dismal showing in Bacău and Roman Counties.[72] In a circular dated 14 January 1938, Codreanu assailed the Catholics' lack of support in the election, especially considering the martyrdom of the Legionaries Ion Moța and Vasile Marin, who had "died defending the

Catholic Church" in the Spanish Civil War. As retribution, Codreanu instructed the Legionary nests in Bacău and Roman to ban all Catholics from joining the movement for the next three years.[73] That Codreanu saw fit to ban the Catholics of Bacău and Roman Counties suggests that, indeed, the Legion counted some of the community within its ranks. It should be noted, however, that "excommunication" of this sort was a typical response from Codreanu for even the smallest of transgressions.

In 1938 Frollo testified in defense of Codreanu during the latter's sensational trial, which was orchestrated by King Carol and which ultimately led to Codreanu's conviction, imprisonment, and assassination later that year. Frollo described the Legion as a movement of "high morality" and "extreme honor" and vouched for Codreanu's character as a patriot, incapable of rebellion or treason.[74] The Legion lived on, however. It finally acquired national power in late 1940, after Romania was pressured by Germany to cede back territory to Hungary, the Soviet Union, and Bulgaria. From November 1940 to January 1941, the National Legionary State ruled Romania under an uneasy alliance between Codreanu's successor Horia Sima and general Ion Antonescu. The Legionary government forced Carol to abdicate the throne in favor of his powerless, nineteen-year-old son Michael. When Sima and the Legionaries attempted to oust Antonescu and seize total power over the country in a coup d'etat (which was accompanied by massacres of political opponents such as Nicolae Iorga and a Jewish pogrom in Bucharest), Antonescu put down the coup and crushed the Legion. He elevated himself to the rank of marshal and established a military dictatorship that ruled Romania for the duration of the war.

Frollo served as inspector general in the Ministry of Education in this extremely violent and corrupt but short-lived government, the National Legionary State. His son and lawyer Vladimir Anton Frollo, also a Catholic, was a well-known and high-ranking member of the Legion. Antonescu later imprisoned Vladimir Frollo for his activities in the Legion.[75] There is little documentary evidence indicating that upper levels of the Roman Catholic hierarchy were involved with the Iron Guard, with only a handful of exceptions, one of them quite significant. Securitate archives also reveal that Father Ioan Mărtinaş, the parish priest of Gherăeşti and professor at the seminary in Iaşi, was a sector chief (*şef de sector*) and instructor in the Legion, evidently a prominent one in Roman County.[76] It appears Mărtinaş acted as a liaison of sorts between the young Moldavian Catholics in the Pregătirea Premilitară (the premilitary training for Romanian men between the ages of eighteen and twenty-one years, which lasted about eight months) and their Romanian military commanders. In the Gherăeşti-Roman unit of the Premilitară, forty-two of these Catholic cadets wrote a letter of complaint in mid-December 1940 to their superiors, accusing their unit commander of verbal abuse: "He humiliates us in front of everyone, calling us 'Hungarians.' He said that we do not perform our duties because we are Hungarian, that the Country [Romania] protects us in vain."[77]

The cadets appealed to their superiors to end the abuse, to no avail. Less than a month later, another sixteen Catholic cadets protested their treatment by the unit's commander and the other Romanians in their unit, complaining the latter regularly referred to the Catholics as "aliens, disgusting, worthless": "[The commander] says that when we go to Father Mărtinaş to complain against him [the commander], we are acting as spies and traitors against the unit; and traitors to the cause of the war must be punished by death."

In their letter, they further complained that the commander had misappropriated the money (some 35 lei) that every recruit from Gherăeşti and Pildeşti had donated to the unit to purchase trumpets. After three years, the trumpets never arrived and the commander refused to reimburse the cadets: "We ask that this money be returned to us so that we can give it to the Legionary Aid (ajutorul legionar)."[78] The Legionary Aid was a Legionary organization that promoted volunteerism, aid to the poor modeled on Christian charity, social work, and assistance to Romanian refugees from the territories Romania ceded in 1940.[79] It seems natural that such an organization appealed to these disaffected Catholic cadets. Alongside the Legionary Workers' Corps (corpul muncitoresc legionar), the Legionary Aid targeted the support of disaffected rank-and-file military in an attempt to draw support away from their officers—who in the main supported Antonescu over the Legion—and to remedy the social problems faced by soldiers in the Romanian army.[80] These letters suggest that Father Mărtinaş was indeed a significant player in the regional hierarchy of the Legion. Whether under his influence or of their own accord, some Catholics did support the movement. Under duress, these young Catholics turned first to their Legionary sector chief, who happened to be their local priest; and of all the charity organizations to support, including ones that were supported by the church, they found it desirable (or expedient) to donate to a Legionary one.

In the aftermath of Antonescu's suppression of the Legion's rebellion, Mărtinaş was likewise imprisoned alongside thousands of Legionary members. He was interned in Târgu Jiu prison on 8 July 1941, though released soon thereafter on the intervention of Andrea Cassulo, the apostolic nuncio to Romania. It was during this stint in prison that Mărtinaş developed tuberculosis, a malady he would suffer the rest of his life. He returned to Iaşi where he continued to write and to publish, including a monograph on the Romanian origins of the Csangos, titled *Cine sunt catolicii moldoveni?* (Who are the Catholics of Moldova?)

in 1942. Mărtinaș later confessed that his motivation for joining the movement was to protect the Catholic Church in Romania and, by extension, his fellow Moldavian Catholics. By having a representative of the Catholic clergy within the Legion, the church was likely safeguarding itself against the most violent political force in the country. Such fears were not entirely unfounded. During one of his interrogations after again being arrested and imprisoned, this time by the Romanian Communists, Mărtinaș recalled his involvement in the Legion. In many ways, his activities in the Legion were motivated by a sort of ad hoc "concordat" between the movement and the Catholic Church in Moldavia:

> When I agreed to support the Legionaries, I carried out negotiations with Codreanu and I put conditions on this, not for my personal favor but for the advantage of the church. I asked some favors for the church—not for me. Codreanu realized that if we Catholic priests supported him, all the Catholics would support him. I had guarantees on his part that our word would be decisive when the issue of our church was discussed. When I agreed to support the politics of the Legionaries, I did it not because I wanted to be a minister [in the government] but to help the church, and if I was punished for these politics then I suffered for a holy cause and therefore have all the right to think about a divine reward.... The Legionary movement was a dream, and they thought that this dream could become a reality but it remained a dream and is destined to remain a dream. We ourselves [Moldavian Catholics], we have our own way. We do not walk along their way, nor in any other way. It is because of this we are persecuted—because we have our own way.[81]

From the episcopate and seminary in Iași, and in parishes across Moldavia, the Catholic hierarchy would have been all too familiar with the rhetoric and political violence of the Legion. In these circumstances, having Mărtinaș or Frollo as intercessors between the church and the Legion—whether they joined on their own initiatives, with or without the blessing of church superiors—was not imprudent given the political circumstances at the time. In this way, the Catholic Church would not be seen as wholly uncommitted or ill-disposed to the Legionary State or any other nationalist dictatorship, should one prove lasting.

3

The Profane
A True Science of the Nation and People

The "trick of historiographic nationalism," notes Kate Brown, has been to turn history into a tool of conquest: "After armies physically take an area, historians work to justify the occupation. By negating the experience of everyone defined outside the national community, national histories can make it seem that only a given national group belongs to a given place."[1] The World War I peace settlement and the spread of new ideas about national and ethnic belonging radically changed the context in which even small, relatively isolated communities such as the Csangos were forced to reevaluate their historical connection to both Romania's and Hungary's pasts—as well as these countries' respective presents and futures. Twentieth-century discourses of identity and national belonging in Romania, Hungary, and elsewhere in east-central Europe worked to reify the ethnic identities of minorities. In both Romania and Hungary, population transfers, nationality registers, and race laws attempted to reconfigure the state along ethnic lines, forcing minority communities such as the Csangos to stake an ethnic claim as either "good Romanians" alongside the ethnic majority or else as second-class minority citizens alongside the other Hungarians of Romania.

Discourses of Identity and Belonging

A major shift in thinking (and speaking) about the ethnic and national dimensions of identity, both individual and collective, took place in east-central Europe following World War I, and Romania was no exception. Inside the newly expanded, postwar Romania, the country's leading intellectuals (including theologians) and politicians began reconceiving and redefining along ethnic lines the relationship between nation, state, church, and citizen.² Influenced especially by German ideas of nationhood, new concepts about Romanian national belonging were now predicated on shared origins and even an ethnically imbued sense of religion and spirituality, as espoused by the Romanian Orthodoxists.

In both Romania and Hungary, historians and others were influenced by ideas circulating throughout east-central Europe, prompting a rewriting of national histories from newly discerned ethnic and even psychological viewpoints.³ The influence of German *Volksgeschichte*, for example, revealed the national community as something organic and integrally linked, historicized through time, space, blood, and soil. That such *völkisch* discourses and histories found fertile ground in Hungary and Romania was perhaps inevitable. As Manfred Hettling has observed, use of the *Volk* could provide a stabilizing factor in weakly developed (or weakened) states and societies, such as those in interwar east-central Europe. A newly enlarged (at the expense of its neighbors), multiethnic Romania and a beaten, truncated Hungary were certainly no exception. "The people" themselves—whether German *Volk*, Hungarian *nép*, or Romanian *popor* or *neam*—were politicized and historicized in order to connect them to a common origin and past as well as a common fate, thereby establishing the continuity of the "summoned people," usually bounded within a specific territory.⁴ From this "summoning" of the people through the twin forces of ethnicization and historicization emerged both a physical and a metaphysical competition between Romania and Hungary over claims to putative minority communities such as the Csangos. In addition, for many Romanian and Hungarian historians, the nation's soul or spirit, its psychology, and its destiny were entwined in national identity. This promoted a new way of thinking about the nation as a whole, one that was conceptual and idea oriented.⁵

During the interwar period, new discourses on race marked a dramatic break from culturalist and civic understandings of national belonging to more salient ethnicized and biologized ones. By the late 1930s, these ideas and discourses became linked to the very destiny of the nation and, consequently, informed policy prescriptions for dealing with ethnic minorities. In Romania, a scientific or objectified understanding of national and ethnic belonging could be measured and manifested in, for example, blood indices and physical anthropology; as a result, national character and belonging could be codified, certified, and legitimized on nationality certificates, which attested to the ethnic origin of the individual or community who possessed them.

Romanian and Hungarian ethnographic, sociological, and anthropological research into the Csangos must also be seen in the broader context of such research elsewhere in central and eastern Europe, especially the increasing importance of the East European Research discipline, or Ostforschung, in Germany, particularly on the contested ethnic and racial identities of communities in Poland and Ukraine.[6] The Ostforschung and its corollaries in Romania and Hungary enabled professional historians, sociologists, and ethnographers to turn their sources into "weapons" in the struggle for national survival and superiority. It further enabled the collusion between the familiar and more traditional historical discipline, on the one hand, and on the other, the more scientifically minded sociological, anthropological, and biomedical sciences, lending an air of legitimacy to the otherwise ahistorical "realities" of race and psychology. In Nazi Germany, the research of the Ostforscher strengthened belief in the indivisibility of the ethnonational community and fed existing *"völkisch* fantasies" that might someday be realized through empire building and massive colonization, both internally and externally.[7]

Jews and Roma were almost always excluded from the ethnic nation. However, the ethnic origins and national belonging of some minority communities were dubious or contested. Especially in the heterogeneous border zones that existed between and even within states, this seeming ambiguity threatened the nation-making project.[8] Any number of ethnically "amphibious" communities or otherwise diverse peoples challenged the myth of cultural and biological unity of Germans, Hungarians, or Romanians, as the case may be.[9] In Romania, the nation-building intelligentsia increasingly put into question the "Hungarianness" of the Csangos in western Moldavia and the Szeklers[10] in eastern Transylvania, two minority communities in the geographical heart of the nation. Whether Csangos or Szeklers in Romania, Masures in Poland, or Sorbs in Germany, the inhabitants who occupied these "middlegrounds" threatened not only the respective nation-building projects in east-central Europe but also the very foundational myths so essential to legitimizing the newly recognized states in the region. In the age of ethnically based nationhood and statehood, how were multiethnic and multiconfessional upstart nations to portray themselves as unitary and homogeneous since time immemorial?[11]

Ethnographic, demographic, and historical data, when analyzed within the modernizing frameworks of disciplines such as geopolitics, geohistory, or biopolitics, could validate and sustain ideological interpretations of the historical and political legitimacy of the ethnic majority's supremacy over its minorities. Conversely, this kind of research could be used to oppose the exercise of any meaningful control over what adjacent nations—and their national minorities who remained in Romania—regarded as homeland, thereby frustrating claims for territorial revision, cultural and political autonomy, and greater minority rights. As Chu has characterized similar undertakings by German scholars in search of an ever-widening *Volksgemeinschaft* in eastern Europe, "the collusion of demography with ideology and scholarship with opportunism" led to enormous changes in perceptions of minorities at home and abroad.[12]

The sociological, anthropological, and demographic research undertaken by scientists and culture warriors in interwar Romania and Hungary, as well as the "ethnocratic" and biopolitical discourses that accompanied it, would later inform the demographic reordering undertaken by the Romanian and Hungarian governments during World War II, including internal and external colonization, ghettoization, internment, deportation, and population transfers. Both the serological and ethnographic research on the ethnic origins of the Transylvanian Hungarians from the 1920s and 1930s, for instance, would be replicated and imposed on the Moldavian Csangos in the 1940s. Understanding the contexts in which many of these studies were undertaken and published is important, as they created a radical new vernacular that informed major policy decisions, from education to sterilization to population transfers. As Irina Livezeanu noted about interwar discussions on the denationalization processes concerning Szeklers, "It is not so much whether and to what extent 'Szeklerization' [of ethnic Romanians in Transylvania] happened, but that it was noticed, theorized, and 'deconstructed' by Romanians unwilling to simply accept a Szekler presence in eastern Transylvania."[13]

The disarray that characterized Hungarian politics and society after the trauma of Trianon and the White Terror created opportunities for a new camp of Hungarian historians, social scientists, and literati to reassess the decline of the nation over previous generations and to chart a new course for Hungary's revitalization. As in Romania, these intellectuals and activists reconceptualized the idea of the nation, redefined the parameters of national belonging, and generated new discourses on politics and ethnicity to meet the challenges of the new era. In doing so, young Hungarian ethnographers and historians also constructed new historical narratives and transmitted knowledge about Hungarian minorities living outside Hungarian territory since the breakup of the Habsburg Monarchy or even earlier. In interwar Hungary, policy makers and the broader public were increasingly attuned to accounts of "lost" or "pure" ethnic Hungarian kin across the borders, dislocated and suffering at the social and economic margins of hostile neighboring states.

A New Mission for Romanian Sciences

Telling the story of the quest for ethnic or national origins is also telling the history of science. The interwar period in Romania witnessed a growing disenchantment with more positivist and empiricist modes of social analysis and history writing, stoked by fears about the future of European and Western civilization. This disenchantment found its greatest expression in Spengler, who influenced many young Romanian intellectuals studying in Germany. The sense of decline and the need for "regeneration" or "transfiguration" was the purview not just of Romanian philosophers and intelligentsia, including well-known figures Emil Cioran and Mircea Eliade, but also of the growing ranks of Romanian scientists who had been studying abroad, notably in Germany, Austria, and Hungary.[14]

Disillusioned with the results of traditional science and the sense of backwardness and inconsequentiality of the Romanian nation—a sense cultivated from years studying abroad for a specialized higher education they could not attain at home in Romania—this new cadre of experts in sociology, geography, anthropology, and the biomedical sciences advocated in all disciplines a paradigmatic shift for the role of science within the nation. This shift, they hoped, would complement if not accelerate the political, cultural, and spiritual regeneration of the Romanian nation.

It is at this time in Romania we see the marriage of historically distinct branches of physical, natural, and social sciences: under the tutelage of Simion Mehedinți and Gheorghe Vâlsan, geographers created or imported new subsets of scientific knowledge, such as biogeography, human geography and anthropogeography, and geohistory. Within Dimitrie Gusti's network, sociology became a nation-building science, a "militant sociology" or *sociologia militans*. Gusti's impact on Romanian social sciences and national politics cannot be overstated. He established Romanian sociology as a coherent (and, to his mind, superior) discursive field for advancing social reforms, defining national specificity, and building the nation. His approach was as undertaken by a myriad of practitioners, mostly leftists of all stripes but also some rightists, such as Traian Herseni, as well as some notable Hungarian and American researchers.[15] In this respect, Gustian sociology had an international and, in some cases, transnational flare. It was also a highly interdisciplinary endeavor, drawing together not only sociologists, ethnographers, and anthropologists but also geographers, musicologists, economists, lawyers, agronomists, and other specialists into rather eclectic teams of researchers. Centered around the production of a village monograph, these teams descended on the Romanian countryside to survey every aspect of village life in large-scale, mostly empirical investigations, attempting to elucidate the "social reality" of the places and peoples they studied.

A Romanian variant of geopolitics, led by Anton Golopenția and Ion Conea, emerged from the confluence of these new trends in sociology and geography. And under the influence of eugenicists Iuliu Moldovan, Gheorghe Banu, and Francisc Rainer, Romanian biomedical and social scientists began writing on racial anthropology, ethnobiology, and biopolitics. Soon, nearly all the sciences in Romania became nation-building sciences.

The discourses generated by social and biomedical scientists facilitated a new type of social engineering through population policies, including public health and social hygiene, as well as the encouragement of population growth and the alteration of the population's ethnic composition via migration control and population exchanges with neighboring countries.[16] In significant ways, professional and amateur historians, linguists, journalists, educators, and politicians appropriated the languages of ethnography, anthropology, and the racial and biomedical sciences, investing the very notion of nationality and community with biological and geographical significance. This scientific self-reflection had implications for the larger national polity and the future viability of the nation, leading to radical interpretations of national belonging and a more focused attention on the Romanian ethnogenesis. Prominent Romanian geographer Gheorghe Vâlsan, who intermingled ethnography and folklore into his research and writing, spoke of "ethnic organicity" and "geographical organicity," arguing that ethnicity and geography were coterminous. He perceived the "ethnic factor" as being the only one capable of transforming the physical characteristics of the earth in useful and significant ways for human communities.[17]

As with the philosophers and literati who made up Romania's famed "Young Generation" of intellectuals, many of the younger sociologists-turned-geopoliticians likewise had studied abroad, especially in Germany. They brought back to Romania new perspectives, influenced not only by their German and French mentors but also by their interactions with Hungarian, Bulgarian, and Ukrainian peers. Through these revelatory experiences, they could now perceive Romania in a larger geopolitical context. Anton Golopenția's education abroad impressed upon him the urgency of Romania's national struggle against equally determined and hostile neighbors in a battle over finite national spaces. A self-styled geopolitician who would, during World War II, lead ethnographic expeditions into Transnistria on behalf of the Antonescu regime, likened each nation-state to an army, maneuvering through hostile territory, reliant on its own strength. At the vanguard of these army-states would be the "spies and scouts formed by complex research teams."[18] Romanian sciences therefore needed to examine the national body and develop a new epistemology of the nation, to document "scientifically" Romania's elusive ethnonational specificity.[19]

As Maria Bucur has noted, this new scientific paradigm employed rationalist and empirical methods to explain social problems, linking moral and political crises to biology and heredity.[20] Science in the service of the national majority would have major consequences for the ethnic minorities, notably the Jews, Roma, Hungarians, and Slavs.[21] Its unleashing from the laboratory to the more humanistic and sociological fields produced in many historians, politicians, and literati an almost mystical belief in science, which in turn fed a neurosis about ethnic origins and purity. Disciplines such as racial anthropology, eugenics, and social hygiene transferred the language of hereditary and biological determinism into the nationalist idiom. A number of state-sponsored organizations and institutions provided a platform and funding for Romanian scientists to promote the health of ethnic Romanians and to take stock of the national body. Their goal, as Marius Turda has argued, was the creation of a racial utopia, the Romanian ethnic state.[22]

"Denationalization"

The assumption that many Hungarians in Romania were actually denationalized Romanians who could be "re-Romanianized" formed the basis of a number of policies targeting minorities.[23] Article 8 of the Primary Education Act of 1924, for instance, stipulated that "citizens of Romanian origin who have lost their mother tongue may not send their children to any school, public or private, other than a school in which instruction is given exclusively in Romanian."[24] During the interwar period, as historians and scientists traveled across the nation to investigate firsthand more and more of the Romanian population, it soon became clear that demography was destiny. Seen in these terms, one of the greatest threats to the integrity of the ethnic Romanian nation was the Szekler community, the relatively large community of Hungarian-speaking Catholics and Protestants in eastern Transylvania. Though historically on the periphery of Habsburg/Dualist Hungary, the Szeklers had long enjoyed a privileged status and had carved out a distinct cultural, economic, and political space for themselves. As a result of the Treaty of Trianon, however, Transylvania—and with it, the Szekler land and its inhabitants—belonged to the Romanians. The Transylvanian Hungarian population in general, and the Szeklers in particular, proved problematic for the inchoate Greater Romanian state, as the Szeklers formed a sizeable population of ethnic, linguistic, and religious minorities living in a compact mass deep in Transylvania, geographically in the very center of the new state.

For Romania's nation builders, the initial solution to the Szekler problem—namely that they were too many, living too close together, in a region far too important—was not one of aggression but rather of bureaucratic and institutional assimilation, primarily through education policy and tighter economic and infrastructural links to Bucharest.[25] The Romanian government embarked on a massive educational reform agenda in the 1920s. It established new Romanian-language schools and new Orthodox and Greek Catholic churches and parishes in the region, passed new laws forcing state schools whose language of instruction was Hungarian to switch to Romanian, brought into the diverse new territories Romanian teachers from the Regat, and implemented an affirmative action policy that guaranteed job preferences to ethnic Romanians. By the end of the decade, however, most Romanian politicians and nationalists regarded these Romanianization policies in the newly added territories as utter failures.[26]

The Szekler land was also home to small numbers of Romanians, including Hungarian-speaking persons of the Romanian Orthodox faith. As Romanian historians and scientists undertook research in the Szekler land, they began to raise questions about the ethnic composition of the region and the "true" ethnic origins of the Szeklers. Were the Szeklers actually ethnic Hungarians? If not, what, then, was their origin, and to which nation or ethnic community did they belong? Other communities in peripheral regions such as the Timoc valley, Bukovina, parts of Moldavia, and Bessarabia soon became the object of similar questions and studies. According to a new cadre of historians and ethnographers, many of these communities were originally ethnically Romanian but had long been linguistically assimilated or denationalized by other nationalities. Throughout the interwar period and into the 1940s, a number of studies and monographs promoted the idea that many if not all of the Szeklers possessed a separate ethnic genealogy or "ethnogenealogy" from the body of Hungarians who entered Europe from Asia. According to this reinterpretation of the settlement and presence of Hungarian speakers in eastern Transylvania, the modern-day Szeklers were in point of fact denationalized Romanians from Transylvania, having been subjected to centuries of forced assimilation by Hungarian overlords, Hungarian administrative policies, and especially the Hungarian Catholic and Calvinist churches.

In a nation eager to document the character and plight of ethnic Romanians who had long survived foreign dominion, new avenues for research and publication opened up for Romanian historians and social scientists, particularly those from Transylvania. One of Romania's foremost geographers, the aforementioned Gheorghe Vâlsan, sounded a clarion call for professionals and amateurs alike to rewrite and invigorate the nation's history: "In every corner of the Romanian land there needs to be found a priest, a teacher, an enlightened man, to attempt to draw upon the unknown ways distinctive to the life of his region. Gradually, research on the regions will multiply and fill gaps. We are at the most significant moment of our national history, and a faithful image of the land and people of Romania in this epoch will be uniquely documented. For our efforts, future researchers will acknowledge us."

Vâlsan proposed a massive undertaking to take stock of the country down to the smallest region, to achieve a "true knowledge" that the researcher would glean from a careful study of each corner of his region, "welded together from birth through to death, from which he understands all of its secrets." Following a "singular" and "unitary plan," a "true science of the Nation and the people" would take root: "The rest is only a science of transition, from which nothing but a few happy fragments will remain."[27] This vanguard of Romanian historians and scientists sought to go beyond the mere chronicling of history or the collecting of material culture of the people inhabiting the newly unified provinces. They sought to locate, quantify, and, in some cases, recover the Romanianness of these inhabitants.

The scientific mission described by Vâlsan was also meant to inspire research outside the formal academies, to be conducted by locals who had a more intimate knowledge of their regions and localities. One such researcher was Teodor Chindea, a Romanian schoolteacher who had been raised in the Szekler region as a minority Romanian in a village and region dominated by Hungarians.[28] Chindea maintained that Hungarian authorities had, for generations, forced young Romanian men of the region to attend Hungarians schools and to be conscripted into Hungarian regiments so as to be more easily assimilated: "Little by little, year after year, the echo of his own past was fading away, turning into a remote memory, hidden somewhere in his blood, like an ancient instinct." In this way, the Romanians of the region "perish, generation after generation, and become absorbed into the mass of the Szeklers." Chindea's explicit aim was to popularize this kind of research and knowledge, to highlight the "suffering" of the Romanian inhabitants, and to combat the "Hungarian propaganda" that prevailed in the region.[29] Most important, the process of the denationalization of the Romanians in Transylvania had to be arrested: "The problem of Szeklerization of the Romanian elements is no longer a problem with a local character; it is in point of fact a national problem. It is not our intention to sow the seeds of dissension, for we only claim the right to be regarded as a Romanian population, which by the hostility of time was torn off the common root. . . . We need to stave the process of Szeklerization and bring back to the original source (*matcă*) the Hungarianized Romanians of today. Otherwise, we risk in a few short decades having a demographic map with fatal consequences to our national interest."[30]

Even Romania's most ardent fascist movement chimed in. Legionaire Horațiu Comaniciu wrote his "Hymn of the Szeklerized Romanians" to attract Romanians and Hungarians in the Szekler land to the Iron Guard:

> We have waited for you with thirst, Căpitan / Let the ancestral feelings come into us
> For we have lost language and faith / Under the cruel whip of foreign domination
> O, come to us, Căpitan / We strive in labor and suffering
> We have lost language and law / O, come to a higher altar.
> From our tormented souls, / The apostasy of so many traitors,
> You alone can eradicate this despair, / And ease in us the sadness of the Nicadors.[31]

Eventually, denationalization theories speculated that the entire body of Hungarians in eastern Transylvania, not just smaller populations of ethnic Romanians within the Szekler land, possessed a Romanian ethnogenesis. Geographer Sabin Opreanu, a mentee of Vâlsan, was among the first to suggest that the mass of Szeklers were none other than denationalized Romanians who had been Szeklerized by the Hungarian churches, specifically the Catholic Church.[32] He characterized the Szekler land as a "stratified space of confessions," in which younger Hungarian ethnic and religious elements lay atop much older Romanian Orthodox ones. These older Romanian elements formed the basis of this population, making it Romanian, not Hungarian. By peeling away these linguistic and confessional layers, he claimed, one could uncover the latent existence of a Romanian ethnic and racial continuity within the region.[33]

Those like Opreanu who theorized on the ethnic origins of the Szeklers aimed not simply to explain the presence of Hungarian-speaking Catholics and Protestants in the eastern Carpathian space. What had to be examined and adduced were the implications of the Szekler presence for the survival of Romanians in Transylvania. The twin forces of Szeklerization and Catholicization had to be resisted and, if possible, reversed. Opreanu, for one, tasked himself with identifying the failures of the Romanian government and the Romanian Orthodox Church due to these institutions' "great lack of interest and solicitude" and poor organization.

Opreanu and others who wrote on the denationalization of Transylvanian Romanians were not content with overturning the Hungarian historical narratives that had chronicled the settlement of Hungarians and the spread of Catholicism and Calvinism in Transylvania. More important, they felt the imperative to demonstrate the victimization of the Romanian people at the hands of foreigners, many of whom were comprised of ethnic Romanians corrupted by centuries of forced assimilation by the Szekler "barbarians": "It is difficult to specify today the percentage of Romanians who have disappeared into Szeklers, except to say this number is large. It is probable that over half of the blood that flows in the veins of these people is Romanian blood, sucked dry over the centuries through the Szeklerization of Romanian elements."[34] For Opreanu, the evidence was irrefutable: "The inevitable conclusion one reaches after the analysis of all historical, statistical, philological, physical, and ethnological evidence, is that the majority of today's Szeklers are denationalized Romanians."[35]

Research and publications of this type intensified in the years preceding the 1940 border revisions and the subsequent entry of Hungary and Romania into World War II. In 1939, Octavian M. Dobrotă published *Români Secuizați și Regiune Secuizată* (Szeklerized Romanians and Szeklerized region).[36] Rather wistfully, he dedicated his study to his "Szeklerized brothers," the "scattered ashes on the Romanian embers, who flicker in the Szeklerized counties, waiting to catch the raising Romanian flames." To continue mistaking the Szeklers for Hungarians rather than denationalized Romanians was, for him, criminal. The inhabitants of the region were in the majority Romanians by origin, "native Romanians, Szeklerized by force, disinherited of their Romanian custom, faith, and language."[37]

Several prominent members of the Orthodox Church hierarchy, including Protopop Aurel Nistor and historian and theologian Ștefan Meteș, also raised alarms about the Szeklerization of the Orthodox Romanians in eastern Transylvania.[38] In a speech at the opening of the Diocesan Assembly on 16 April 1939, the metropolitan of Transylvania Nicolae Bălan warned his fellow clergymen against the dangers of denationalization and the need to resist it through the agency of the Orthodox Church: "[In Transylvania] we have lost many sons of our nation, under foreign domination, masters and oppressors of the Romanian element. Estrangement (*înstrăinare*) was achieved by breaking these sons away from their ancestral church; this is proof moreover that only through the church is it possible to rekindle the national soul in Szeklerized Romanians."[39] For Bălan and other clerics and Orthodoxists, the Romanian souls lost as a result of denationalization at the hands of Hungarian authorities and the Catholic Church not only diminished the Romanian Orthodox Church as an arbiter of Romanian national consciousness but also posed economic and political threats to the Orthodox Church: fewer Romanians in the region meant weaker claims on parishes, churches, and other properties, which in turn reduced the Orthodox Church's share of the state budget.

As the threat of denationalization became part of a national cause linked to the very health and survival of the nation, the theories and discourses on the problem soon became invested with racial and biopolitical tropes. Much of the research on the topic incorporated contemporaneous research by Romanian anthropologists and demographers who employed serology as a new methodological tool for indexing blood groups and reexamining the ethnic and racial profile of the Hungarians in Transylvania. Denationalization theories, supported by serological work undertaken by Romanian racial anthropologists, proved useful tools for the recovery of "lost" Romanians.[40]

Around this time, the noted Romanian philologist and classicist Gheorghe Popa-Lisseanu became a prominent exponent of the theories first developed by Chindea and Opreanu. An authoritative figure in academic and public policy circles in Bucharest and a member of the Romanian Academy, Popa-Lisseaunu saw two main problems concerning the Szekler land: the first was his absolute conviction that autochthonous communities of Daco-Romanians predated the arrival of the Hungarian colonists in the region that subsequently became known as the Szekler land; the second was the suspect ethnic origins of the Szeklers themselves. Popa-Lisseanu claimed that the bloc of Szeklers was created through systematic Hungarianization policies directed from Budapest since the eighteenth century. He used as evidence some anomalies he detected in the Hungarian census data of 1910 and purported not to have found any exclusively Szekler villages in the region, suggesting a Romanian ethnic community either coexisted in every Szekler village or else formed a substratum of the Szekler ethnic community itself.[41]

In addition to historical records and ethnographic data, Popa-Lisseanu incorporated into his denationalization thesis the medical and anthropological studies undertaken by racial anthropologists and eugenicists such as Iuliu Moldovan, Gheorghe Popovici, Petru David, and Petru Râmneanțu. Though Popa-Lisseanu was adamant about the Romanian origins of the Szeklers, he nevertheless sought a more patient approach to their renationalization as ethnic Romanians, insisting that Romanians should "talk calmly about [the Szeklers'] past and origin, and show them that as evidenced by the data from ethnological and anthropological science, there is almost no difference between them and us." The Szeklers' brachycephalia,[42] he argued, was identical to that of the Romanians living in the Szekler land, for the blood analysis carried out by Romanian anthropologists on the Hungarians in eastern Transylvania had revealed a blood index identical to the Romanians. The "tall and well-built Szekler" shared a similar anthropometry with the Romanians, "whereas the Hungarian, as we have described from the historical sources, was in general small, with black eyes and protruding cheekbones." The Szekler, it was clear, was simply a "stray Romanian, who is on the wrong path in life." Time and patience were needed to bring these "brothers, lost brothers, but brothers nevertheless," back to the fold: "Those who will come voluntarily back to the bosom of their mother are welcome; for those who will linger in their situation of today, we consider them rightfully consanguineous with us but of Hungarian language and law. We seek to show them in every way their true ethnic origin and to convince them of this. In our work for resurgence of the national sentiment, we do not fear failure, being as we are in the arms of justice, and justice and victory go with those who go the way of the Lord."[43]

To acknowledge the phenomenon of denationalization was the first step toward legitimizing renationalization projects in the new territories. The emphasis on ethnic origins was crucial: Romanian political and scientific elites decried the forced assimilation of ethnic Romanians in the past yet simultaneously introduced a series of homogenization projects targeting the country's ethnic, linguistic, and religious minorities. Rebranding this as a process of "national recovery" avoided the hypocrisy of perpetrating the very same act of coercive denationalization on Romania's national minorities. Furthermore, it mitigated the country's obligation to ensure minority rights, which the Romanian government had agreed to as part of the post–World War I settlement. In other words, the rights of minorities need not be upheld if those communities were, in essence, members of the ethnic Romanian majority, unwittingly and unjustly concealed as national or ethnic minorities. This would have major implications for the ethnic majority-minority dynamic in Greater Romania, such as determining cultural and education policies, redrawing county and regional lines, and categorizing populations in national censuses. Romanianizing the country's institutions and economy could now go hand in hand with Romanianizing its inhabitants.

Works on the Szeklers also showed the potential for recasting the Csangos as ethnic Romanians. Though the reversal of the Csangos' historical narrative—one that posited a Romanian ethnogenesis rather than a Hungarian one—would not be accepted by the Romanian academy until the 1940s, there was by the mid-1930s some indications in this direction.[44] In 1935, Nicolae Iorga published in his journal *Revista Istorică* a letter from one Constantin Lozincă, a schoolteacher from the Csango village of Faraoani in Bacău County. Lozincă had read one of Iorga's articles on the origin of the inhabitants of Bacău and Roman Counties. In the article, Iorga surmised that these inhabitants were originally from the Cuman population, which the Hungarians had impressed into military service in the cities of Transylvania and subsequently used as border guards in Moldavia.[45] As remnants of the Cumans, Iorga concluded, the Csangos were thus "good brothers with the Hungarians, and therefore Hungarians" and, naturally, "agents of Hungarian revisionists."[46] Indignant, Lozincă contested Iorga's insinuation that the Csangos were Hungarian: "Personally, in the three years since I have been a teacher in these parts, as well as another six years in a different village, where they do not know how to speak Hungarian (or the Csango language [*ceangăește*]), I observed the following: The costume, nature (physical and spiritual appearance), customs, and names are, in my opinion, Romanian *par excellence*." According to Lozincă, the garb of the elders was similar to that which the Dacians had worn. The community's "cheerful nature" was "the same cheerful nature of the Romanian. Nothing in this respect betrays their being Hungarian." Furthermore, all of the Csangos' customs—at Christmas, New Year, and Easter as well as at weddings—were Romanian, as were the names. Names that otherwise sounded Hungarian were in fact cognomens from a bygone era.[47] Ultimately, Iorga accepted the new narrative of the Csangos as denationalized Romanians, reversing his previously held conclusions.

Hungarian "Ethnohistory"

Around the same time in Hungary, a number of influential "populist writers," including Dezső Szabó, László Németh, and Zsigmond Móricz, rejected the pre–World War I conceptions of the Hungarian national character and instead proffered neo-Romantic notions of national specificity. These writers celebrated the inborn strength and instinct of the Hungarian peasant and provided new and powerful descriptions of the Hungarian *nép*, or people (in the sense of the ethnonational community). Szabó's epoc-defining novel *Az elsodort falu* (The village that was swept away), published in 1919, shocked Hungarian high society and literary circles, especially with its assault on the culturally alien civilization of the cities—a pointed attack against the Jews and Swabians. It tells the story of a young Hungarian intellectual who renounces life in the economically and culturally corrupted city for one in the impoverished Hungarian countryside, where through genuine and meaningful work he strives to improve the lot of the peasantry in the hope that it will contribute to a national rebirth.[48]

Németh espoused biological and racial interpretations of the ethnic substratum of the Hungarian nation, claiming that there existed but two types of Hungarians: the ethnically pure "deep Magyars," who had upheld the nation and carried eternal Hungarian values, and all the rest—the "diluted Magyars," who had played a limited, if not negative, role in the Hungarian past. He traveled throughout Romania and wrote extensively on the plight of the minorities there, bemoaning the upsurge in ethnic Romanian strength and the withering away of the Hungarians.[49] Németh and writers like him validated the twin fears of the Hungarian political leadership: the Hungarians in the successor states were rapidly being assimilated, and those who were not yet assimilated had become inward looking and thus more distant from Hungary.[50]

These populist writers also inspired a literary and socially conscious youth movement captivated by the peasantry, which drew historical and social parallels to the nineteenth-century *narodniki* movement in Russia. From this milieu the *szociográfia* (sociography) movement appeared in the early 1930s. The sociographers used an approach to examining the life of the peasant and the village that was, while outwardly sociological and ethnographical, an amalgam of disciplinary methods with a bit of literary flair. Though lacking a formal methodology and scholarly institutional support, they cast a bright public light on the dire conditions of the peasantry, the so-called "three million beggars" of Hungary. The Hungarian student and activist movement known as Sarló—formed in Czechoslovakia in 1924 and cofounded by the noted Hungarian Transylvanian writer and activist Edgár Balogh—had a profound influence on the leftist and populist orientation of the sociographers in Hungary and the Hungarian intellectuals in Transylvania (notably those who took part in the Erdélyi Fiatalok [Transylvanian Youth] movement and its eponymous journal). Sarló was the first such Hungarian student movement for village research to help strengthen the national culture of the Hungarian minorities and the intellectual life in the Hungarian villages.[51]

A smaller but quite vocal and radicalized group within the populist youth movement in Hungary eventually split from the mainstream. Led by *népi* poets Jozséf Erdélyi and István Sinka—likewise a countryman who wrote of the mystical, primitive nature of the peasant and of the cult of Turanism[52]—they became converts to *völkisch* ideologies about the purified peasant peoples of Europe and connected the issue of the survival and revitalization of the peasantry to the Jewish question.[53] For them, a rebirth of the Hungarian nation was inextricably linked to the vitality of the peasantry.

Of the major historians in twentieth-century Hungary, Gyula Szekfű—who wrote on the social, political, and moral decay of the Hungarian nation—was most influential. He dislodged the previous generations' historical frameworks, namely, the national Romanticism, historicism, and positivism that had shaped historical thinking and production in Hungary since the nineteenth century. This reorientation of Hungarian historiography was not merely an effort to explain the cataclysmic losses of the Hungarian nation; it was also introspective and forward looking. One of the main tasks of Szekfű and his followers was to lay the groundwork for a reconstituted Hungarian state and a resurrection of an already idealized Hungarian past.

In 1939 Szekfű edited and published the seminal volume *Mi a magyar?* (What is the Hungarian?), which brought together a number of prominent intellectuals in an edited volume to explore the self-consciousness of the Hungarian people's Hungarianness and to counter Nazi-inspired discourses and research on national racial types. The volume included the writings of a wide range of historians, ethnographers, established racial anthropologists such as Lajos Bartucz, and even poets and ethnomusicologists. The aim of this work was to recreate the canon on Hungarian national character within some semblance of historical normativity.[54]

By contrast, Hungarian historian Elemér Mályusz emphasized the bond between the ethnos and the soul, disavowing Szekfű's aim to resituate the Hungarian nation within a broader European context (and more narrowly within the Austrian and German sphere). Mályusz diverged from the Szekfű-led agenda of representing a Hungarian history based on the nation's "transformational" Christian (especially Roman Catholic) heritage and its universal values; he developed his *népiségtörténet* (ethnohistory) as an alternative perspective on the history of the Hungarian nation, a history that was, in all its facets, essentially a history of the Hungarian *nép*.[55] Like Dimitrie Gusti's approach to the "science of social reality" in Romanian villages, which advocated acquiring systematic knowledge of social collectivities in their entirety, the Mályusz approach to historical research and writing promoted a comprehensive understanding of

The Profane

the *nép* through both time and space, unbounded by political frontiers or the various concepts and institutions of statehood. Mályusz rejected notions of the political nation and instead emphasized the *népi nemzet* (ethnic nation), dismissing histories that concentrated on the state, on ideas, and on the great historical personalities.[56]

Mályusz offered important intellectual and theoretical alternatives for Hungarian historians committed to an ethnocentric interpretation of Hungarian national history. Moreover, his ethnocentric and essentialist, eastward-looking perspective on the cultural and historical legacy of the Magyars would heavily influence Hungarian historiography and ethnography on the Hungarian diaspora. He advocated the need to undertake systematic data collection concerning the Hungarian nation, to produce village monographs, and to incorporate subdisciplines such as ethnography, ethnology, anthropology, and sociology.[57] He pushed for the integration of many of these "auxiliary disciplines" into the science of ethnohistory, which could prove crucial in determining the racial origins of ethnic groups such as the Csangos and Szeklers.[58]

"Modern Magyar Narodniks" and the "Orphaned" Csangos

To a certain extent there existed a "narodnicist" spirit and "peasant romanticism" among the young Hungarian intellectuals researching the history and plight of the Hungarian minority in Romania. The philosopher and member of the Romanian Academy Ernő Gáll, who as a young man studied sociology in Cluj and participated in Gusti's school, even characterized these young intellectuals as "modern Magyar narodniks."[59] Disaffected by urban life and purely academic pursuits, many had abandoned the cities for life in the villages, to live among the true *nép*, convinced that "the social and existential role they had to assume was to explore the reality of a minority—the Hungarian one—which corresponded essentially to a rural reality." The collapse of the monarchy, the revolution and counterrevolution in 1918–19, and the economic crisis that marked the beginning of the 1930s all contributed to the sense of disillusionment and inertia of life in Hungary. A number of students simply abandoned their university studies in Hungary, relocated to Transylvania, learned Romanian, and cofounded some of the most influential Hungarian-language journals of the interwar period. For them, the peasantry was not just an object for economic and social reform but also an agent for national rejuvenation.[60]

Mályusz, Gusti, and other sociological and literary movements in Hungary and Transylvania produced new discourses and scientific approaches to understanding the nation that were absorbed by Hungarians living, researching, and writing in interwar Romania. Their overriding aim was to create new pathways toward self-discovery (*önmegismerés*), an honest and critical self-knowledge (*önismeret*), as well as an inventory of "native" or "homeland" knowledge (*honismeret*). However, this self-knowledge was not just an end in itself, for it was also a necessary step toward carrying out social reforms.

The village research of the Transylvanian youth and village movements blended the methods of Hungarian sociography and Gustian sociology, though they did not necessarily regard themselves as direct inheritors of either. Most of the young Hungarian sociologists who studied with Gusti and his teams were from Cluj or elsewhere in Transylvania, though there were also students who came from Hungary and the other successor states of Austria–Hungary. Some of them carried out their research and writing independent of the university system, especially as the main Hungarian university in Cluj/Kolozsvár had been taken over by Romanian authorities in 1919 and renamed the Romanian University of Cluj. While something identifiable as a Transylvanian–Hungarian school of sociology never quite emerged, there was nevertheless a concerted effort in this direction heavily influenced by Gusti. Gusti's methods and scientific orientation—especially his focus on the village—provided an ideal framework for Transylvanian Hungarians to cultivate an understanding of the ethnic Hungarian (or Hungarian-speaking) peasantry in Transylvania and Moldavia.[61]

Research undertaken on the Csangos by Hungarian historians, ethnographers, and sociologists in the late 1930s and during World War II was part of broader research on the biological origins of the Hungarians and Romanians. It can also be seen within the context of other scientific endeavors elsewhere in east-central Europe, especially German accounts of the *Volksdeutsche* in the east. Hungarian research and writing often depicted the Csangos as "more Hungarian" than either their Transylvanian counterparts or even the Hungarians back home in decadent, cosmopolitan Hungary. Fueled by racist-*völkisch* ideologies, especially after the coming of the Third Reich, such undertakings imagined the peripheral ethnic kin or *Volksgruppe*—ethnically self-conscious yet struggling for survival on their "diasporic 'language islands'"—as somehow purer or more authentic than their atrophic cousins living in or near the national homeland.[62] Much could be learned from these ethnically resilient communities. For Hungarian researchers, proper understanding of Hungarians across the border could provide a model for Hungariandom to fend off foreign influences and to develop strategies for cultural, linguistic, and ethnic preservation.

The Profane

The historian, researcher, and advocate Endre Veress, though part of an earlier generation of Hungarians writing on the minority in Romania, influenced the young Hungarian intellectuals living in Romania in the 1930s.[63] Writing on the Csangos in 1920 under the pseudonym John Tatrosi, he anticipated the growing concern over the Hungarian communities left outside the nation, fearful of their assimilation into the surrounding communities of the dominant ethnic nation: "It is most interesting to notice in what measure the Csango-Hungarians differ from the population of the neighboring Romanian villages: in the manner of building their homes, in cleanliness, order, customs and behavior. These Hungarian villages constitute real isles in the Romanian sea, which threatens to devour this assiduous people."[64]

Veress also drew attention to what he saw as legal injustices perpetrated against the "autochthones of Moldavia," the Csangos.[65] He highlighted Romanian state policies responsible for accelerating the Romanianization of the Csangos, specifically the Romanian government's Public Education Act of 1893, which mandated the use of the Romanian language in schools and churches throughout the kingdom. He was critical furthermore of Romania's failure to adhere to the terms of the Paris Peace Treaties and the Romanian Constitution.

Mályusz and Gusti influenced several writers on the Csangos, an influence best exemplified in the life and work of Hungarian ethnographer and folklorist Gábor Lükő, whose contribution to the scholarship on the Csangos was primarily in the field of linguistics, folklore, and material culture. As with Endre Veress, Lükő was integrated within the Romanian scholarly community, having studied in both Budapest and Bucharest. Typical of the lives of these Hungarian authors who were attracted to writing on the Moldavian Csangos, Lükő had formative experiences growing up outside the new Hungarian borders, living and studying in multiethnic and multiconfessional communities in the Czech lands.[66] He was also steeped in Gusti's system and spent a great deal of time with his Romanian village research teams. In Lükő's seminal monograph on the Csangos, *A moldvai csángók* (The Moldavian Csangos), published in 1936, he identified two distinct communities of ethnic Hungarians within the Csango land on the basis of dialect, material culture, and self-identification.[67] The first of these groups, the northern Csangos, referred to themselves as Hungarians and spoke an archaic dialect of Hungarian. Lükő surmised that they hailed from the historic Hungarian region known as the Partium and from the Szamos valley.[68] The second group, the southern Csangos, self-identified as Szeklers. Their language and culture indeed more closely resembled the Szeklers across the Carpathians in eastern Transylvania.

Through their dissertations and research in Mályusz's Institute of Settlement and Ethnohistory, Mályusz's students sought to rediscover the "orphaned" Hungarian diaspora left behind in the successor states. One direct influence from Mályusz was in the research and publications of the noted historian Éva H. Balázs and the less-well-known ethnohistorian László Mikecs. Perhaps more than any other work of the period, Mikecs's ethnohistory on the Csangos exemplified the Mályusz approach. Mikecs saw the Csangos as "orphaned, abandoned, stray Hungarians from the faraway provinces" who were detached not just from Hungarian national politics but also from the Hungarian national consciousness.[69] In his 1941 monograph, *Csángók: a moldvai magyarság története* (Csangos: A history of the Moldavian Hungarians), echoing Romanian geographer Vâlsan from only a few years back, the Hungarian ethnohistorian Mikecs attempted to portray the totality of Csango life, society, and history by examining the Csangos as a social entity.[70] Mikecs sought to usher in not only a new way of writing about the nation but also a new era, as momentous as the Reformation and the Enlightenment: "We need a new attitude, a new course, a new zeal, a new dissemination of knowledge about our nation's past, to show from a detailed, bottom-up examination that which invades the soul. From this motivation, knowledge, and lucidity will grow the will and the knowledge that will enable us to construct and implement a new culture for the lives of the Hungarian people."[71]

By the start of World War II, the notion of *faj* (race) emerged as a more powerful concept in mobilizing Hungary's national elite and policy makers.[72] As in other European countries during this period, race was instrumentalized so as to transcend social, religious, and even territorial divisions, so that national problems became problems for the entire ethnic nation rather than a particular class or rank. Just as in Romania, the term crept into scientific, literary, and popular discourses alike, and with great utility refashioned social, political, and economic concerns into new and more salient cultural and biopolitical ones. These discourses on identity and national belonging reinforced the Hungarian government's population transfer schemes, in which communities such as the Csangos were targeted for relocation to Hungary.

Alexander Baumgartner (also known as Sándor Besenyő, who sometimes published under the pseudonym Siculus) published a number of highly charged works depicting the plight of the Csangos at the hands of the merciless Romanian state. Baumgartner, who taught theology in the seminary in Iași around 1935–36 and worked as a diplomat for the Hungarian government in its effort to relocate the Csangos during World War II, viewed the Csangos and the Szeklers as forming a solid ethnic block or "unit" of Hungarians, over six hundred

The Profane

Csango men in the village of Şumuleu-Ciuc/Csíksomlyó, a famous destination for Transylvanian and Moldavian Catholic pilgrims during Pentecost. Ethnographic photo by Josef Fischer, 1934. (courtesy of the Csángó Ethnographical Museum, Zăbala/Zabola, Romania)

thousand strong, on either side of the Carpathians. The Csangos—"the pride of the Hungarian race"—were engaged in a "life-and-death struggle to return to the greater national body" of the Hungarians.[73] Preventing this were the Romanian state and the Orthodox Church, which persecuted the Csangos in order "to wipe out their Hungarian consciousness—in short, to wage a war of extermination against them."[74] As suggested by the title of one of his books, *Moldva: a magyarság nagy temetője* (Moldavia: The great cemetery of the Hungarians), Baumgartner sought to elevate the Hungarian ethnic and national consciousness of the Csangos while forewarning other Hungarians about the potential annihilation of their fragile nation.

These Hungarian authors became important advocates for minority causes in interwar Romania and, moreover, contributed to the Hungarian historiographical and ethnographical production on the Csangos, including the works discussed above by Veress, Lükő, and Mikecs as well as other writers such as ethnographer Pál Péter Domokos and linguist T. Attila Szabó.[75] Domokos, who was born in the eastern Szekler village of Şumuleu-Ciuc/Csíksomlyó[76] at the turn of the century, produced in 1931 a major ethnography on the Csangos, *A moldvai magyarság* (The Moldavian Hungarians), and was active in the Hitel (Credit) movement in Transylvania. Equally significant was his role in the

Hungarian ethnographer Pál Péter Domokos recording folk songs with phonograph. Surrounding girls in traditional costume from the village of Trunk/Galbeni, Bacău County, 1932. (courtesy of the Ethnographic Museum, Budapest)

Hungarian government's effort to resettle the Moldavian Csangos in Hungary, which will be discussed in a subsequent chapter. The discursive production and political advocacy of these writers would also provide one of the few sources of ideological, political, and historiographical resistance against the Romanianization efforts of the Csango clergy in Moldavia during the early 1940s.

4

Certifiably Romanian
Codifying National Belonging

New ideas about the nature of the state and its relationship to individuals and communities transformed understandings of citizenship across east-central Europe. Hungarians and other minorities in Romania were, in principle, protected under the Minority Treaties signed at the Paris Peace Conference after World War I. Though many of the Csangos spoke Hungarian and some even remained socially and culturally connected to the Hungarians in Transylvania, few if any had ever possessed Hungarian citizenship. The Csangos were never recognized or considered as a Hungarian minority by any international treaty or domestic Romanian law. Consequently, they enjoyed no outside protection as an official ethnic or national minority. The only guarantee of the Csango's religious liberty remained the Romanian-Vatican Concordat of 1927/29.

By the standards of the time, the Romanian Constitution of 1923 could rightly be called liberal. Article 5 proclaimed, "The Romanians, irrespective of ethnic origin, language, or religion, enjoy freedom of conscience, freedom of education, freedom of the press, freedom of assembly, freedom of association and all the freedoms and rights established by law." Article 8 stipulated, "All the Romanians, irrespective of ethnic origin, language or religion, are equal before the law and are obliged to contribute without exception to taxes and public duties." The Constitution also guaranteed universal male suffrage and consecrated in law the provisions of the Minority Treaties of 1919, to which Romania was a signatory. Specifically, the Treaties of Saint Germain and Trianon, signed in 1919 and 1920, respectively, assured Romanian citizenship to all persons of the former Austro-Hungarian Monarchy then residing in Romania. Formally, at any rate, the path was cleared for Jews and other minorities to participate more broadly in Romanian civic and political life, including integration within the professional classes and the state bureaucracy.

Granting Romania's ethnic and religious minorities equality with ethnic Romanians of the Orthodox rite was anathema to the growing numbers of Romanian nationalists who filled the ranks of right-wing organizations and political parties. Right-wing politicians, intellectuals, and the press blamed these "foreign elements" for depriving the Romanian nation of its rightful place among European nations. Having to contend with large numbers of these minorities—particularly Jews—for places in universities, for jobs, and for other national resources was not the post–World War I outcome most Romanians had envisioned. Despite the vocal and increasingly violent opposition to postwar liberalizing measures, the Romanian government extended citizenship and the franchise to most of the inhabitants of the country according to its international obligations. However, the international peace treaties provided little guidance for how and to what extent these liberal principles should be implemented. Consequently, the efforts to codify citizenship and national belonging became embroiled in public debates about the status of ethnic and religious minorities in Greater Romania.

By the mid-1930s, fascist and anti-Semitic movements across Europe were ascendant. In Romania, right-wing movements such as Codreanu's Legion of the Archangel Michael (and its paramilitary wing the Iron Guard) and A. C. Cuza's National-Christian Defense League grew in strength and appeal during the years leading up to World War II. In addition, vocal intellectuals such as Nichifor Crainic and Nae Ionescu gained notoriety and even celebrity through their virulently racist and xenophobic diatribes in some of Romania's most widely read newspapers and journals. These and other nationalist movements and personalities in Romania had broken from the older and more conservative forms of Romanian nationalism. Due in no small part to the influence of Fascist Italy and then Nazi Germany, Romanian nationalists pushed for a more radical political agenda centered on anti-Semitism, racial nationalism, and "ethnocracy." For them, the legally recognized, formal citizenship extended to minorities by the Romanian state was by no means tantamount to national belonging. Not only radical nationalists but also lawmakers and politicians now viewed the nation through the twin prisms of ethnicity and religion. They institutionalized a new social hierarchy, one that legalized majority privilege and minority subordination.

In exchange for security guarantees from Germany, Romania agreed to the Second Vienna Award on August 30, 1940 and ceded Northern Transylvania to Hungary (it also ceded the region of Dobrudja to Bulgaria). Transylvania had long been the most important site of contention between Hungary and

Romania. As Holly Case has noted, the struggle to "win" Transylvania shaped not only the historical and contemporary identities of both Romanians and Hungarians but also the web of relations between the two populations and their respective states. While the terms of the Second Vienna Award protected Hungarians who remained in Romanian-ruled Southern Transylvania, in practice they often had little recourse to Romanian courts and police. Nevertheless, since there remained a sizable Romanian population within Hungarian Northern Transylvania, the treatment of one another's minorities was based in large measure on the politics of "reciprocity."[1] The politics of Transylvania—including contests over territorial belonging and the treatment of one another's minorities—had numerous implications for the Csangos in Moldavia. Might Hungary one day claim parts of Moldavia that were home to Hungarian-speaking Catholics? If the Csangos were part of a population exchange with Hungary, might Hungary resettle them somewhere in Transylvania, tilting the ethnic balance of the region in favor of the Hungarians? The influx of Transylvanian Romanian refugees into Moldavia only exacerbated already fraught tensions between Orthodox Romanians and the Catholic Csangos, who, by guilt of religious and linguistic association to Hungary, were blamed for the humiliating loss of the northern half of Transylvania.

Throughout the 1930s, rhetorical, legislative, and ultimately physical assaults on Romania's minorities targeted primarily the country's Jews and, by the 1940s, its Roma population. During World War II, the Antonescu regime likewise subjected other categories of peoples deemed not ethnically Romanian to various forms of state-sponsored discrimination and violence. The regime stripped the civic rights of the Csangos in Moldavia, Bulgarians in Dobrudja, Ruthenians in Bukovina, and others, most of whom were Romanian citizens, denying these communities access to many public-sector jobs and state services and goods and restricting them from certain economic activities. Minorities in Moldavia and Bukovina, especially, lived under the constant threat of forced relocation to a putative other national homeland or else internment at camps in the Governorate of Transnistria (Guvernământul Transnistriei), the Romanian administered territory between the Dniester and Bug Rivers during World War II.

However, the possession of much-coveted "nationality certificates" or "certificates of ethnic origin" could safeguard some minorities—typically religious minorities or persons with a contested or ambiguous ethnicity—against discriminatory acts by the state, especially after the revision of Romania's citizenship laws and the implementation of coercive relocation policies during the war.

To be certifiably Romanian—that is, to possess a certificate of Romanian ethnic origin—not only helped ensure one's rights as a Romanian citizen but also helped prevent (or at least forestall) deportation.

Nationality and Citizenship in Interwar Romania

After World War I, Romanian lawmakers created a pathway to Romanian citizenship for the country's recognized minorities, albeit a very narrow one via a tedious process of naturalization. In theory, Romanian citizenship was open to all Romanian nationals who legally resided in those territories awarded to Romania and unified with the Old Kingdom. However, citizenship, nationality, and residency in Romania became more narrowly defined, harder to acquire, and easier to lose after the introduction in early 1924 of the "Law on Acquiring and Losing Romanian Nationality," known more commonly as the Mârzescu Law.[2] Over the next two decades, the terms *cetățenie* (citizenship) and *naționalitate* (nationality) would become invested with new meanings that conflated national belonging with ethnicity, religion, and blood.

Nonnaturalized minorities residing in interwar Romania had to acquire Romanian nationality to become full citizens before the law. Only after establishing Romanian nationality, as evidenced by a *certificat de naționalitate* (certificate of Romanian nationality), could one benefit from Romanian citizenship.[3] Beginning in April 1924, a series of statutes under the rubric "The Regulations on Establishing Romanian Nationality" aimed not only to establish the procedure for acquiring Romanian nationality but also to facilitate the recording and cataloging of the various peoples in the new Romanian territories. Within their designated areas, local authorities such as mayors and city councils, county prefects, chiefs of police, commanders of the gendarmes—and even local citizens designated by the Ministry of the Interior—were required to make lists enumerating those who laid claim to Romanian nationality. In every communal district, these lists were to be gathered at the office of the mayor, reviewed, and collated into a register of nationality.[4] In these registers were written the names of the heads of families, spouses, and children. Thus was created an inventory and topology of the Romanian nation using nationality lists, nationality registers, and nationality certificates.

Once certified, nationality lists could not be modified except through court appeal and, ultimately, a decision of the Ministry of Interior. Moreover, anyone who happened not to be home at the time authorities prepared these lists, or who for any other reason was not counted, could not later add their name.

These persons—including their descendants—were subsequently regarded as foreigners before the law. They could not be counted as either Romanian citizens or nationals, a status they could only acquire through an onerous process of naturalization, granted through the Commission for Establishing Conditions for Naturalization and Recognition, which functioned under the Ministry of Justice.⁵

To implement this massive data collection of the population and complete these nationality lists within thirty days of the law's passage, the state devolved considerable powers and responsibilities to local officials, leading to confusion, inaccuracy, and corruption. An illustrative example is the case of Iacob Kerns from Bessarabia, a territory that belonged to the Russian Empire and then the Soviet Union prior its unification with Romania in April 1918. Kerns had been working in Moscow as a lawyer around this time. According to his passport, he had returned home to Bessarabia on September 8, 1918, only five months after unification. Because his temporary absence coincided with a change in borders and law, he was not entitled to Romanian nationality or citizenship except through naturalization. Making matters worse, he only learned of his situation in 1924, some six years after his stint working in Moscow, further complicating his ability to resolve his case in Romania's serpentine legal system. Kerns later acquired his nationality by bribing an official.⁶

Another case was that of Maria Kohn, a law student in Târgu Mureș, a predominantly Hungarian and Jewish city in northeastern Transylvania, which prior to Transylvania's unification with Romania had belonged to Hungary. In 1937, after discovering she was not, in fact, a Romanian citizen, Maria appealed her exclusion from the nationality lists. Her father, since deceased, had been entitled to Romanian citizenship and nationality but for reasons unknown to Maria had not been registered in the nationality lists in 1924. At the time, Maria was a minor, and thus her right to Romanian nationality was contingent upon her father exercising his own right to Romanian nationality. Unfortunately for Maria, the Ministry of Justice ruled against her. Without another nationality or citizenship to opt for, she and thousands like her were rendered stateless persons in interwar Romania, foreigners in their own homeland.⁷

Requirements for nationality certificates changed after 1935, before which a person's ethnicity was not specified.⁸ This change reflected the increasing importance of race and ethnic origin within the newly legislated hierarchy of national belonging. It is no coincidence that the issuance of these types of certificates in Romania came shortly after the Nazi regime began issuing various types of individual certificates attesting to racial origin (*Abstammungsnachweis*) after its passage of the Law for the Restoration of the Professional Civil Service in 1933 and the Nuremberg Laws in 1935. Documents such as the Certificate of Aryanization (*Ariernachweis*), the Ancestor Passport (*Ahnenpass*), and the German Blood Certificate (*Deutschblütigkeitserklärung*) were required for employment in the public sector, including education, and for certain types of commercial activity, land ownership, and membership in the SS. By contrast, Romanian documents attesting to an individual's nationality and ethnic origin were much less specific than in Nazi Germany. Mandated from Bucharest but processed and issued locally, Romanian certificates adhered to no countrywide standard, resulting in discrepancies in acquisition, meaning, and application. Consequently, the Romanian state's practice of certifying nationality and ethnic origin had deleterious effects on individuals, entire families, and even businesses.

The template for legal discrimination against Romania's minorities was created during the short-lived Goga-Cuza government (December 1937 to February 1938), formed at the king's behest. The poet Octavian Goga and the law professor A. C. Cuza, two of Romania's leading anti-Semites and Nazi sympathizers, who served as prime minister and minister of state, respectively, closed down Jewish publishing houses and libraries, expelled Jewish members from professional organizations, and implemented what amounted to a *numerus clausus* (or *numerus vallachicus*, as it was often called in Romania) in universities and certain sectors of the economy.

King Carol and Prime Minister Goga's decree No. 169 "concerning the revision of citizenship," issued in January 1938, was the first in a torrent of anti-Semitic legislation that continued through World War II. The decree required nonethnic Romanians and former nationals of other states to prove they or their parents had resided on Romanian territory prior to the formation of Greater Romania in 1918 and otherwise met an onerous new set of conditions for naturalization. It deprived the citizenship of large numbers of so-called "foreign Romanians," including thousands of Jews and their descendants who had immigrated to Romania in the preceding decades, especially those who were former citizens of the Habsburg Monarchy or the Russian Empire.

In February 1938 the Romanian government passed a new constitution to replace the 1923 constitution. This new one enshrined into law King Carol II's royal dictatorship and a corporatist system of government. Subtle changes in the language of the constitution also signaled profound changes in the law and its application. Mihai Antonescu, who served as vice president of the Council of Ministers, the minister of justice, and the minister of foreign affairs during World War II, described the 1938 constitution as "organized for the advantage of ethnic solidarity." The constitution, he wrote, endeavored "to accentuate the features of the Romanian nation in the Romanian State and to serve the institution of nationality as a veritable instrument of ethnic conservation."[9] By the end of 1939, additional laws passed under Carol II's dictatorship had deprived over two hundred thousand Jews of their Romanian citizenship.[10]

The legal provisions guaranteeing the equality and protection of minorities in Romania rang hollow next to the corpus of legislation passed over the next several years to circumscribe the enumerated rights of the country's ethnic minority citizens. Circumscription of minority rights was typically justified on the basis of *jus sanguinis* (right of blood) or the oft-invoked "principle of the hierarchy of rights," articulated and codified by Romania's powerful minister of justice Ion V. Gruia. One of the first anti-Semitic laws, decreed on 9 July 1940, forbade the marriage between Jews and "Romanians by blood." By autumn 1940 the National Legionary government had imposed yet more antiminority legislation, this time modeled on Nazi Germany's Nuremberg Laws, defining the Jews on racial grounds and discriminating in favor of citizens of Romanian ethnic origin and blood. On this basis, ethnic and religious minorities were largely excluded from participation in the civic and economic life of the nation. Legislation from 5 September 1940, written by Gruia, established guidelines for reorganizing the professions in Romania, effectively instituting *numerus clausus* and "the *right to livelihood*, which is based on the principle of the hierarchy of rights," with ethnic Romanians naturally on top. This "legal solution" for the nationalization of the professions further strengthened and legitimated the continuity between the Romanian state, the Romanian nation, and the ethnic Romanian community: "For new realities, new rules of law. What constitutes the organic reality of the state is the Nation. . . . From an ethical standpoint, this means a spirituality based on origin, i.e., the same ethnic origin. The national state cannot be achieved except through the nationalization of the professions. The inner life of professions—original and autonomous—is contained within the limits of the National State."[11]

For Gruia, "Romanian blood" was a principal element in the formation of the nation, and thus the state had to distinguish between citizens of Romanian blood and citizens of "non-Romanian blood." In his words, the hierarchy of blood corresponded to the hierarchy of citizens, namely "citizens with major rights and citizens with minor rights."[12] This new biopolitical language woven into Romanian legislation had ominous implications for the country's Jews and other minorities.[13] However, even Gruia acknowledged the impossibility of determining with any precision Romanians by blood.

In addition to the "law of Romanian blood," this new legislation included the Christian rite as a basis for national belonging: "These two forces determine, in full, the biological conception of the Nation, shaken of the slag (*zgura*) and the purely physical and material."[14] In other words, blood and religion revealed the true essence of the nation. To realize itself, the nation had to remove the foreign debris or "slag"—a metaphor for Jews and other unwanted impurities—from its physical body. Once purified, the nation could be visible in its most elemental form. Henceforth, civic rights and entitlements flowed not from the legal status of citizenship but from the extralegal abstraction of national belonging, which was now predicated on blood and ethnic origin.

Nationality and Citizenship in Wartime Romania

In the years preceding Romania's entry into World War II, Romania's minorities were suddenly engaged with a series of radical, violent, and exclusionary regimes. In September 1940, King Carol II ended his royal dictatorship, which had lasted less than three years. He suspended the 1938 Constitution, abdicated the throne, and transferred power to General Ion Antonescu, who committed Romania to the Axis powers in November. In January 1941, after a brief and bloody joint rule with the fascist Legion of the Archangel Michael, Antonescu dissolved parliament, abolished all political parties, crushed the Legionary movement, and established a military dictatorship that lasted throughout World War II, with himself as *Conducător*, or "leader." It was amidst the chaos of this last regime change that one of Romania's deadliest pogroms took place in Bucharest. In just three days, rebellious Legionaries and other anti-Semites in the city, including disaffected police, students, and union members, kidnapped and killed one hundred Jews and looted and destroyed over one thousand Jewish businesses, homes, and synagogues, setting many of them ablaze. Six months later, in June 1941 in the Moldavian city of Iași, the Romanian military, the local police and gendarmerie, and many civilians perpetrated the infamous Iași pogrom, murdering over thirteen thousand Jews, many of whom were thrown from the "death trains" deporting Jews from the city.[15] Doubtless that many Csango communities within and around Iași would have witnessed firsthand or heard secondhand about these atrocities perpetrated against the Jews. With Antonescu's grip on power secured, and with the full support of Hitler, he ushered his country into war, joining Germany's invasion of the Soviet Union that same month. Later that year and into 1942, the Antonescu regime began the systematic deportation and elimination of Jews and Roma from its territory, primarily those from Moldavia, Bukovina, and Bessarabia.

As with the certification and documentation of race and genealogy in Nazi Germany, by the start of World War II, certificates of Romanian nationality and ethnic origin were required in Romania for certain types of employment, purchasing certain goods or properties, owning certain businesses, possessing firearms, and obtaining places in universities or receiving state funding. Even the famous Romanian playwright Eugène Ionesco was required to obtain one while working in Romania in the years 1940–42.[16] These certificates, and the rights and privileges they accorded, further complicated the distinction between Romanian citizenship and nationality. A January 1942 report within the newly created State Undersecretariat of Romanianization, Colonization, and Inventory (SSRCI) addressed the confusion over what these nationality certificates communicated: "In doctrine, the concept of the nation is synonymous with the collectivity of individuals of the same race, same blood, same traditions, same customs, same history, and the same conceptions of morals, etc. Being of Romanian nationality means being of ethnic Romanian origin. Nationality is not identical with citizenship. The individual can be of Romanian nationality and still be a foreign citizen, just as the Romanian citizen is not always Romanian by nationality. Confusion has been produced about these notions."[17] But statements like this in no way clarified for local officials who could and could not be issued certificates of nationality.

The nationality certificates issued in the 1920s and 1930s were remnants of the citizenship and naturalization laws passed just after the signing of the post–World War I treaties, which guaranteed citizenship rights to the inhabitants of Romania's newly awarded provinces. The SSRCI report acknowledged that the governmental commissions responsible for creating these certificates in the early 1920s had failed to make clear distinctions between nationality and citizenship. Since then, the naming of these certificates had generated much confusion for both the authorities who issued them and the individuals who sought them. New types of certificates would be required to indicate proof of Romanian ethnic origin rather than mere nationality or citizenship.

A raft of legislation between 1941 and 1943 provided the legal means for accelerating the wartime economic and demographic Romanianization of the country, an enterprise overseen by the SSRCI, headed by Titus Dragoş, the undersecretary of state for Romanianization. The bulk of this legislation targeted Jews, dispossessing them of their property, capital, and civic rights. However, many of the provisions for Romanianization affected non-Jewish Romanian citizens deemed not ethnically Romanian. Outlining the conditions for admission into public service and employment, Article 98 of the regulations on the Organization and Operation of the Romanian Association of Radio Broadcasting stipulated that "only citizens of ethnic Romanian origin can be appointed or employed in the service of society, as civil servants."[18] Article 27 of

Nationality certificate specifying "Romanian ethnic origin" and born of parents of ethnic Romanian origin, Tulcea County, northern Dobrudja, 1942. (courtesy of Romanian National Historical Archives)

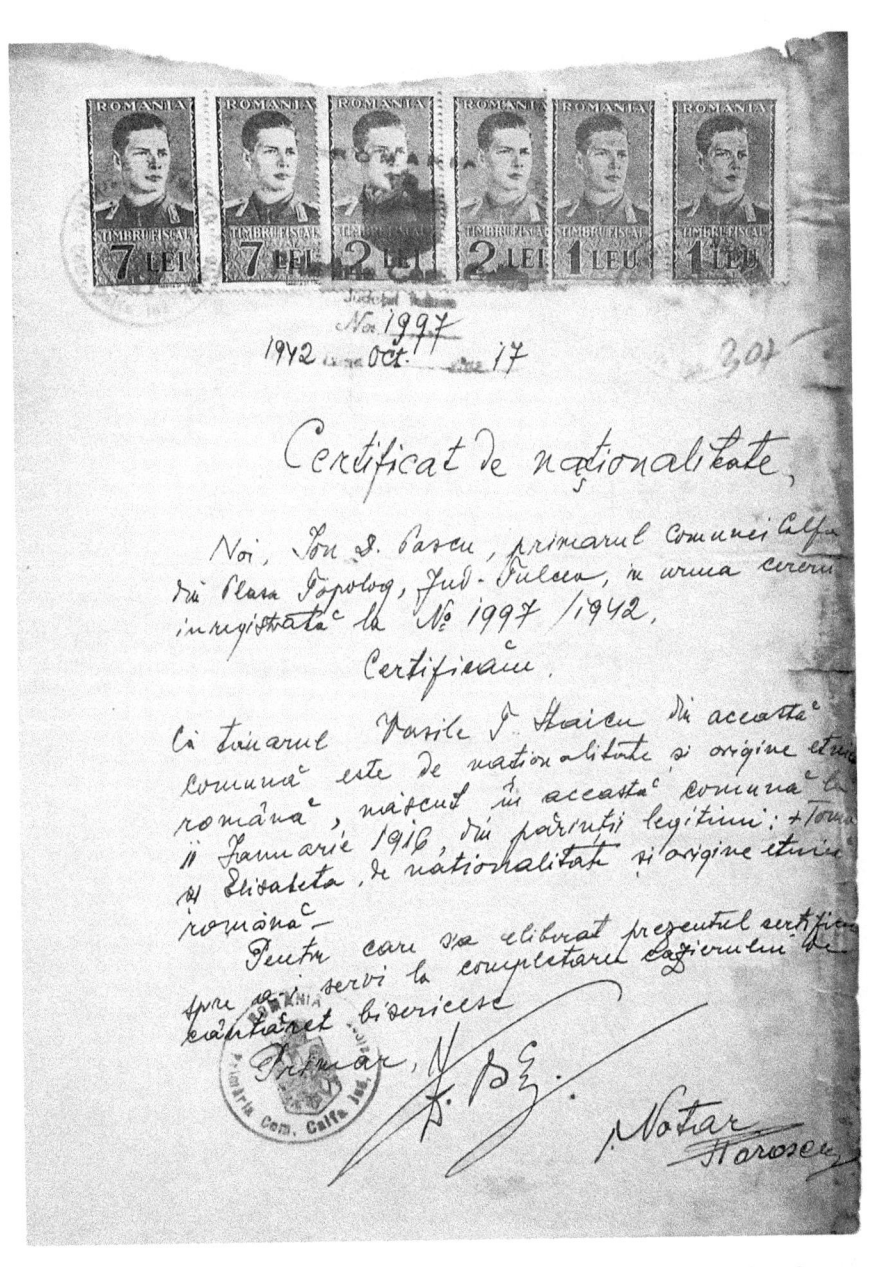

Nationality certificate specifying "Romanian nationality and ethnic origin," Tulcea County, 1942. (courtesy of Romanian National Historical Archives)

ROMÂNIA

PRIMĂRIA MUNICIPIULUI SIBIU

No. 65/3 /1944

CERTIFICAT

Noi, Primarul Municipiului Sibiu, certificăm că Dl.Drăgan Ovidiu născut în comuna Bungard la 1912, domiciliul în Sibiu, Str. Petru Rareș Nr. 7, este de origine etnică română și religie ortodoxă.

Acest certificat se eliberează la cerere, spre a-i servi **la dovedire a originei ariene.**

Sibiu, la 5 Ianuarie 1944.

PRIMAR:
ss Vătășanu

Secretar General:
ss L. Vulcu

Pentru conformitate consiliere

Nationality certificate specifying "ethnic Romanian origin" and "proof of Aryan origin," municipality of Sibiu, Southern Transylvania, 1944. (courtesy of Romanian National Historical Archives) the Law on Bearing and Dealing in Arms, decreed 24 July 1941, also forbade any person who was not "of ethnic Romanian origin" from carrying, buying, or selling arms or munitions. Law 125 of 24 February 1941 concerning the establishment of new commercial and industrial firms effectively nullified applications submitted by nonethnic Romanians, with exceptions for Germans and Italians.[19]

Additional legislation stipulated that only ethnic Romanians could buy expropriated Jewish land, forbidding all "foreign citizens" from buying and selling property without permission from the Ministry of National Economy and later the SSRCI. The legislation aimed foremost to prevent the flight of capital abroad and secondly to redistribute to ethnic Romanians the capital and land of "foreigners"—a term understood not just as foreign noncitizens but also Romanian citizens whose ethnic origin was not demonstrably Romanian. While Romanian ethnicity might very well be self-evident for anyone who spoke Romanian, had a Romanian-sounding name, and was baptized in the Romanian Orthodox rite, actually demonstrating one's Romanian ethnicity before the law was an altogether different matter. Romanian law required buyers at public auctions (of mostly Jewish property) to present certificates of ethnic origin, which could only be issued by local authorities. As Vladimir Solonari rightly observes, the nature of such documents and the criteria used for "certifying" precisely who was and who was not of ethnic Romanian origin was a major dilemma for everyone involved. County prefects, whose responsibility was to issue these documents, inundated the Ministry of Justice with requests for further guidelines on establishing or proving Romanian ethnicity. In addition, the ministry received numerous appeals from putative minorities claiming they had been erroneously categorized as nonethnic Romanians.[20]

Inscribing Ethnic Origin

The legislation that positively discriminated in favor of ethnic Romanians curiously omitted a precise definition of Romanian ethnicity and blood. Gruia's notion of ethnic Romanianness can, in some ways, be inferred from his other writings that portray Romanian blood "as an ethnic and moral element" based on the legal criterion of "origin and rite,"[21] in other words, whoever was not Jewish but Romanian Orthodox. But this hardly qualifies as a legal definition. A second problem was that the issuance of certificates of ethnic origin was left to local, often rural, functionaries. Most of these local officials were unable to discern, for example, the difference in terms of ethnicity between "Csango,"

"Hungarian," and "Catholic." And yet, despite no clear legal guidelines on what constituted "ethnic Romanian origin"—let alone how one was to prove this—these officials could authenticate a constituent's ethnicity and nationality or else strip him or her of the legal recognition thereof. Consequently, they had the power to deprive a person of his or her civic rights as a Romanian citizen.

In his 1941 monograph *Originea etnică* (Ethnic origin), Eugen Dimitrie Petit, a jurist and councilor in Section III of the Court of Cassation in Bucharest (the highest Romanian Court of Appeal, which also reviewed individual citizenship and naturalization cases), detailed the problems at all levels caused by the ambiguity of Romania's "blood laws." Although the real objective of this legislation was to discriminate against Jews and to positively discriminate in favor of ethnic Romanians, the legislation's failure to produce a clear definition of what constituted Romanian ethnic origin generated a bureaucratic nightmare at the most inauspicious time: Romania had just committed to joining the Wehrmacht's invasion of the Soviet Union and had just ceded half of Transylvania back to a staunchly irredentist Hungary, which was committed to taking back the other half.

Petit sketched a scenario of a Romanian peasant attempting to obtain from his mayor's office a certificate of Romanian origin, a document the peasant has no other information about but has been told by the Chamber of Commerce is needed in order to purchase hunting rifles. Petit's vignette could very well have been based on reports by the Csangos in Moldavia as well as the cases he came across as a jurist on the appeals court in Bucharest; and it should come as no surprise that Petit was a Roman Catholic (of French descent) who hailed from Iași. To begin, Petit describes a Romanian peasant who's been told he's required to obtain one of these certificates. At the county hall, the local commissioner takes the peasant's request but informs the poor man, with some frustration of his own:

> LOCAL COMMISSIONER: "Look, sir, I know you, since you live in my district; I know that you are a decent man, who lives a peaceful life and who goes to church on Sunday. But how—for heaven's sake!—am I able to certify your ethnic origin? Do I really know all of your ancestors down to your mother and father? Whether any of them were Greek or Armenian or I don't know what? Do you want to see me taken to jail someday for issuing false public documents?"
>
> PEASANT: "Then what can I do?"
>
> LOCAL COMMISSIONER: "How should I know. Go to the prefect of police, as he has greater authority than I and can do as he pleases."

Certifiably Romanian

Of course, the prefect of police, being a conscientious man but also caring for his own job, is likewise unwilling to take responsibility for resolving the problem:

> PREFECT OF POLICE: "In any case, what do we mean by a law of ethnic Romanian origin? How to prove this? What authority has the right to establish this? And then, how do I, as the Prefect, know what blood flows in the veins from one man to the next?"[22]

Unable to take any kind of decision in these circumstances, the prefect sends the peasant and paperwork to the Interior Ministry. The peasant and all his documents—his birth certificate, baptismal certificate, marriage license, letters from his priest and employer—are subsequently directed to the Ministry of Justice, which then sends the poor man and this superfluity of papers, all stamped and notarized at considerable expense, back to the very same mayor's office to be resubmitted. And so goes the process, back and forth, with no authority willing to risk contravening an ambiguous law.

Widespread noncompliance or misapplication of the law hindered all sorts of local economic transactions, as individuals—be they business owners, shopkeepers, or farmers—who could not secure these certificates were barred from certain activities. These hindrances impacted not only local but also regional economies, which in turn had cumulative effects on the national economy. For example, bank credits specifically set aside for ethnic Romanians could not be distributed because ethnic Romanians could not prove their origin. Consequently, capital flows were disrupted, goods and property taken from Jews were not redistributed, and assets were not plugged back into the economy.[23]

In the early years of the war, the inability of both rural ethnic Romanians as well as urban ethnic Romanian businessmen to obtain these certificates hampered the state's distribution of preferential credits to buy commodities such as cereals, sugar, and other merchandise and equipment needed to implement Antonescu's Romanianization agenda.[24] Thousands of otherwise loyal ethnic Romanians, whose lives were supposed to improve because of the discriminatory legislation passed for their benefit, found their lives even more restricted than when nonethnic Romanians controlled a greater share of capital and other resources. Moreover, the various local governments applied these decisions inconsistently across the country. A prefect in Iași might issue these certificates on the basis of criteria and local factors different from a prefect in Bucharest. As Petit remarked, "Ethnicity varies according to the conception of the functionaries who issue the certificate." From one locality to another, nationality became a question of happenstance, "ceasing to be the real consequence of someone's blood."[25]

In the multiethnic regions of Romania, especially Southern Transylvania and Bukovina, one of Antonescu's primary concerns was to bolster the economic life of the ethnic Romanians vis-à-vis the foreign inhabitants still resident there.[26] The effort was not only to remedy the historical economic backwardness of the Romanians but also to demonstrate to foreign powers—namely Germany and Hungary—that indeed the Romanians could successfully manage and even improve the territories they possessed and thus be stakeholders in the general reordering of Europe.

Antonescu recognized the shortcomings of Romania's administration of Bukovina, in particular. "Not only can we not maintain it at the level we found it, but, continuing this way, it will go into rapid decline," he complained to his cabinet. "If we continue as such, if we regress, then at the [settlement negotiations] the Hungarians will say that the Romanians are an incapable people. The Hungarians will say that in Transylvania they found a miserable situation, which they were forced to redress." Thus, Romania had to demonstrate its ability to manage these contested territories. Again, one of the impediments to administrating the state-controlled, corporatist economy was the inability of citizens to obtain requisite documents and certificates of ethnic origin. Titus Dragoş, head of the SSRCI, reminded Antonescu that no document could be authenticated if a certificate of ethnic origin was not presented at the point of transaction. An exasperated Antonescu admonished his advisors: "What's with this issue? So, one is encountering obstacles because he is the owner of some blocked commodities, and another because he didn't prove he is Romanian. Run to the town hall, run to the gendarmes, the priest, the prefect, and the court so that he can prove he's Romanian. You ask the peasant to bring a certificate that he is Romanian. In this case, we cannot give credit to anyone and therefore in vain we establish institutes of credit. . . . Get yourselves together and clarify all of these issues, so that we can say we are done with them."[27] One of the early problems was that the Ministry of the Interior simply required persons to present their certificates of ethnic origin at the town hall. This was a disaster, as everyone went to the town halls with certificates, overwhelming the understaffed offices with lines of distressed people and endless paper work.[28]

As might be expected, the confusion over definitions, quantifications, and qualifications concerning who could be counted as Romanian (and for that matter, who was authorized to do the counting) was reflected in terminology used to refer to these documents. Such documents were typically labeled "certificates of ethnic origin" or "certificates of nationality," both of which specified or implied *Romanian* origin and nationality. In rural areas, with little instruction as to what these certificates were and how they should be issued, producing them was frequently done ad hoc. Some were even produced in longhand, and some specified race or religion or both.

As a result, in the Csango areas, certificates were granted (or withheld) with little consistency as to what, precisely, constituted the ethnicity and nationality of the Moldavian Catholics there. Did Roman Catholics in Moldavia constitute an ethnically homogeneous group? Were they Romanian or Hungarian, or simply Csango? And what was Csango anyway? Were those in the counties of Roman and Iași any different from those in Bacău County? If they were all Romanian citizens, what was the difference between possessing "Romanian nationality" yet being identified as having some other ethnic origin? Officials wrote on these certificates descriptions such as the following: "Romanian nationality, of Csango Romanian ethnic origin"; "Csango Romanian nationality"; "Romanian-Csango nationality"; "Romanian nationality and ethnic origin, of the Catholic religion"; and "ethnic Romanian origin, being born of Romanian parents."[29]

This ill-conceived system for issuing certificates of ethnic Romanian origin in the Csango-inhabited area was symptomatic of a larger problem of abuse, corruption, and disregard for the implementation of official decrees in Antonescu's Romania, stemming mainly from the fact that laws were issued without the due deliberation of a properly functioning legislature and without taking into account local and regional concerns. Romanian authorities only belatedly acknowledged this problem. Discussions about remedying this situation by providing a clear definition of "ethnic Romanian origin" alongside procedures for determining whether or not one's ethnic origin met this definition did take place in wartime Antonescu's cabinet. Nevertheless, authorities and lawmakers failed to establish such guidelines by the end of the war.[30]

The Catholic Moldavian Milieu at the Start of the War

In 1938, under threat of "severe punishment" and even imprisonment, the prefect of Bacău County forbade church singing and the conducting of any parts of the Catholic liturgy in Hungarian.[31] Romanian authorities further prohibited Csangos from attending Hungarian language schools in Transylvania.[32] In the village of Ferdinand in Bacău County, Judge P. H. Setur decreed the following: "We, in the mayor's office of the district of Ferdinand, Bacău County, on the basis of the order No. 7321 of 3 May 1938 by the prefect of Bacău, bring to the attention of the population of this district that no language other than Romanian is permitted to be spoken in any public place, including the town hall or any other location. In the Catholic churches religious service will be conducted in Latin or Romanian. Priests and church cantors are not allowed to perform religious songs in any language other than Latin or Romanian. Priests and cantors have orders in this regard. All those who contravene this order will be severely punished according to the Law."[33]

The cession of Romanian territory at the end of 1940 only exacerbated the local Romanian Orthodox population's resentment against the Csangos.[34] Antiminority rhetoric and legislation intensified with the militaristic, pro-Nazi orientation of Romanian politics. Romania's territorial concessions triggered a massive influx of Romanian refugees from the ceded provinces, and with them came accounts of abuse and mistreatment, particularly at the hands of the Hungarians in what was now Hungarian-ruled Northern Transylvania. While most Romanian refugees from Northern Transylvania relocated to Romanian-ruled Southern Transylvania, over one hundred Transylvanian families resettled around Iași alone, and nearly all the refugees from northern Bessarabia settled in temporary encampments in and around Bacău, where most Csangos lived.

Hungarians who remained in Southern Transylvania bore the brunt of anti-Hungarian treatment. Thousands of these Hungarians were fired from their jobs and forced to house Romanian refugees. Despite the fact that the Catholic Church in Moldavia was proactive in collecting money and goods for Romanian refugees, much of the local Romanian Orthodox population associated the Csangos with Romania's misfortunes at the hands of the Hungarians. As the commander of the Premilitară (compulsory military training) unit in the Moldavian village of Gherăești rebuked his Catholic cadets, "It is because of those like [you] that we have lost Bessarabia."[35]

The cession of Northern Transylvania to Hungary turned the hilly western region at the foothills of the Carpathians into a new Romanian-Hungarian border zone that stretched eastward from the Szekler land in Transylvania deep into the Ghimeș pass in Moldavia. The loss of Romanian territory at the expense of historic Hungary's reconstitution sparked new fears in Romania about Hungary's territorial ambitions over the Csango-inhabited lands. As one Romanian civil servant wrote at the time: "It is known that Hungarians in general have temerity without limits, and, if in the past, they have carried out the plan of denationalization along the borderlands of St. Stephen, then today . . . they raise their voice more brazenly and have the courage to fix on their irredentist map all the Hungarians of Transylvania as well as a great number of Hungarians in Moldova. It is clearly discernable on this map that Neamț,

Roman, and Bacău Counties and their surroundings form part of the empire they imagine for themselves."[36]

The Csangos made convenient scapegoats for their Orthodox Romanian neighbors, including local government officials, judges, schoolteachers, and commanders in the Premilitară. It should be noted, however, that since the consolidation of Greater Romania in the early 1920s, many police chiefs and educators had been assigned to their respective stations or schools from other parts of the country in an effort to modernize these rural areas, especially the minority-inhabited ones, and to centralize the Romanian administration.[37] For these officials, the Csangos were something of an anomaly in Moldavia that fed existing prejudices and stereotypes or else fostered new ones as tensions escalated with neighboring and increasingly irredentist Hungary.

In the minds and attitudes of local Romanian officials and the Orthodox clergy, the synonymity between Catholic and Hungarian endured despite the efforts of the Csango clergy to Romanianize, in its own way, the population. Some of these officials were relative newcomers to Moldavia and therefore unfamiliar or simply unconcerned with the ethnic, linguistic, and religious composition of the local population over which they governed. Officials who hailed from the area, by contrast, would have known all too well this heterogeneity and in many cases resented it as anathema to the national ideal of "Romania to the Romanians." Moreover, local officials' newfound authority to ascribe specific ethnic identities to their non-Orthodox neighbors could be used to advance the economic interests of one individual or community over another, for example, by restricting who could buy or sell property, own certain types of businesses, or gain employment in the public sector. This power could also be used to settle local, personal scores. Entire communities could be castigated as national enemies and therefore stripped of the civic rights and privileges they had previously exercised as Romanian citizens.

"Enemies in the House"

The situation for minorities further deteriorated after Romania joined the Axis Powers in November 1940. Mihai Merfea launched one of the first attacks against the Csangos in an article published in the autumn of 1940.[38] Merfea was a school principal in the village of Pildești and a regular contributor to *Cuvântul Dăscălesc* (the teacher's word), an official pedagogical journal of the Teachers' Association of Roman County. Merfea's stated mission was to foster a new educational environment in which the schoolteacher could promote the

Romanian national ideal in their classrooms, "with a central interest in the nation, pure Romanian blood, the language, and the border."³⁹

The purity of the Romanian nation and its language was, evidently, central to pedagogy in Roman County, one of the counties comprising the Csango-inhabited area. Writing in the same journal, Vasile Hopu, another educator in the region, wrote of the four main elements that formed the basis of the Romanian nation, which should in turn form the basis of Romanian education: language, religion, race, and territory. According to Hopu, fostering unity of the Romanian language was the only way "to awaken the idea of the nation and to save the nation." The Romanian "community of blood" was morally sustained by Romanian Orthodoxy, "the richest patrimony of the nation." Race, meanwhile, "formed the essence of the nation." It was the "substratum of the ethnos, the physiological prototype and intimate structure" that generated Romania's specific national type.⁴⁰ Such were the guiding voices and ideas in the Roman County school system. Given this learning environment, it is little wonder that school attendance and literacy were extremely low in the Csango region,⁴¹ even by the standards of the day in rural Romania. It is also little wonder that incidents of discrimination and abuse in the classroom increased during the war. In one reported case, the parents of schoolchildren in the village of Gherăești, near Roman, wrote to their parish priest about the local schoolteacher, Ms. Măgăleasa, who told some twenty Csango children in her sixth-grade class that, "by the end of the war, the Catholics will be turned into Orthodox or else sent to Hungary." If they refuse either to convert to Orthodoxy or else leave Romania, she warned, then "they will be shot."⁴² Catholic parents reported that in many schools their children were constantly berated, told they were of "Csango nationality" or were "Hungarians," not Romanians.

Around 1940/41, local officials tasked Merfea with investigating claims by Roman Catholic families that their children experienced abuses in school. Merfea found these claims entirely fabricated. He lambasted the Csangos as "vengeful" and "insincere." "The Csango," observed Merfea, "follows you step by step and wishes upon the Romanian the worst harm by any way or means possible." In a blatant attempt at racial transference from Jew to Csango, he equated the region's closely knit community of Roman Catholics— predominantly peasants and workers—to sinister ingrates who represented an enemy inside the very heart of the nation: "The Csangos are sly. They use any means necessary and do not spare anything from the start, even if they have a significant amount of money; and, in the end, they achieve their aim, earning twofold or threefold. They are closed among themselves, do not cheat one another but rather help one another, as do the Jews. They look for every which way to display their worth, praising themselves on every occasion. Insincerity and pride are prominent aspects of their race. In their interactions with Romanians they are false, without character." Not only were the "Jew-like" Csangos unscrupulous and opportunistic, they were also backward, unclean, lazy, and stubborn. Consequently, he believed the Csangos incapable of progress or assimilation, for "to advise the lot of them to make improvements in schooling, their hygiene in their yards and houses, and their general social education is a lost cause."

Finally, according to Merfea, the Csangos maintained a dangerous, inseparable link not only to the Hungarians of Transylvania but also to Hungary proper. It was clear to him and "other cultural agents" that these "enemies in our house" represented the rebirth of the "Hungarian camp that asked for the head of Horia."[43] The Csangos represented "an invincible force." But when "taken individually, they are weak," after which "you can do what you wish with them." Merfea was convinced that Romanians would prevail over "these enemies from within" and ultimately "purify them of their impulses against the great national ideal."[44]

Elsewhere, in the town of Roman, Iosif Cobzaru, a Roman Catholic, ran both of the town's cinemas. One he owned outright and the other he rented from the state. The county prefect, General Constantin S. Ionescu, had plans to give one of the cinemas to the Comitetul de Patronaje al Operelor Sociale (social works patronage committee), a charitable organization headed by Marshal Antonescu's wife Maria and supported by the wives of other regime elites in Bucharest, in time for Christmas 1941. General Ionescu asked Iosif to hand over one of the cinemas, a request the cinema owner naturally declined, as the businesses were his livelihood. Infuriated, the general attempted to force the transfer of one of the cinemas to the county on the pretense that Iosif was "a Hungarian and therefore has no right to own anything."[45] Iosif was ordered to present his nationality papers within twenty-four hours to prove that he was Romanian. He promptly went to his hometown in Gherăești, retrieved his documents from the mayor's office and had them notarized, then returned to Roman and presented them to an indignant Ionescu. Unwilling to abide the mayor's decision and Iosif's persistence, General Ionescu contested the authenticity of the papers and ordered the mayor of Gherăești to annul them. Fortunately for Iosif this could not be done, as papers that had already been issued and notarized could not be rescinded. Unfortunately for the remaining Catholics in Gherăești, Ionescu thereafter instructed the mayor to deny nationality certificates to the entire community on the basis that they were Hungarians, foreigners.[46]

In February 1942, the Rezident Principal of Moldavia,[47] based in Iași, relayed the above account to Bucharest, detailing the quandary of the mayor's office in Gherăești concerning the legal guidelines for issuing these certificates. The report noted, moreover, that the Cobzarus were a family in good standing in both Gherăești and Roman, and that Iosif and his brothers had fought with distinction in World War I, with Iosif achieving the rank of sergeant. At the time of the report, Iosif was no longer in Roman, as he was being mobilized by the Romanian Army to fight on the Eastern Front.[48]

Between 1942 and 1943, the Romanian secret service compiled for the Antonescu cabinet a series of detailed reports on the Csangos.[49] Most of these anonymous reports betray a level of ignorance about the community's history and current predicament, as well as its attitude toward the Romanian state. Understanding the contexts in which these reports were written is far more important than evaluating whether they were indicative of a broader ethnic-majority perspective: these viewpoints were shared up and down the chain of command and informed major policy decisions in wartime Romania, for instance, whether or not to conclude an agreement with Budapest to resettle the Csangos in Hungary.

One report suggested that, on the basis of the Hungarian language spoken among many in the community, the ethnic origin of the Csangos was obviously Hungarian. The agent remarked, however, that if in fact the Csangos were not of Hungarian ethnic origin then they should be forced to abandon the Hungarian language, since it was not their original tongue. The report drew parallels to the linguistic assimilation of others regarded as lost ethnic Romanians, citing cases in Transylvania, Bessarabia, and the Timoc valley in Serbia, where centuries of foreign domination had led to the "denationalization" of native Romanians.[50]

Another report commented on the attitude of the Csango clergy, depicting them as having "absolute spiritual mastery" over the population, preventing the assimilation of Catholics into the local Romanian Orthodox population. The clergy, contended the report, had instilled a form of "Catholic nationalism" in the community, breeding hostility against the local Orthodox population: "This is extremely dangerous and harmful to the interests of the Romanian State because the Catholic clergy holds the population under their domination, as an isolated community that is quasi-belligerent toward the [Romanian Orthodox] natives."[51]

A third report depicted the Csangos as "a state within a state" owing to the clerical hegemony over the community, a situation enabled by a weak local administration. The clergy had, however, made efforts to "de-Hungarianize" the community. Nevertheless, the clergy's overriding aim was to lock the community within a "Catholic enclosure, controlling it fully, and keeping it within the universal Catholic world."[52] Most of these reports acknowledged the historical loyalty of the Csango community to the Romanian state, for instance through their military service in successive Romanian wars, including conflicts that pitted Romania against Hungary. This recognition only underscores the ethnic majority's exclusivist understanding of the Romanian nation, in that a minority community that had long resided within the nation and demonstrated no hostility to it was now subject to outright expulsion from the country.

The existence of the Csangos raised two major questions for the Antonescu regime at the start of the war: Did the community pose a genuine threat to the ethnic and religious majority in Moldavia? And regardless of its "true" ethnic origin, could the community be Romanianized? If indeed the Csangos could be Romanianized, then it should be done as soon as possible "to remove once and for all from the body of the nation this gangrene that is the Catholic population from Moldova." However, many of the neighboring Orthodox Romanians interviewed in these reports stated that the Csangos could never be Romanianized without first converting them to Orthodoxy. Other intelligence sources reported that the ethnic origin of most Csangos was clearly Hungarian, and "nothing could erase this from their minds." Claims of a Romanian ethnic origin by some publications were therefore regarded as "hypocrisy" and unfounded. From this point of view, the Csangos could never be Romanianized, nor should they: "On the contrary, they should be sent *en bloc* to Hungary. Only through this measure can the gangrene be removed from the body of the nation."[53]

The Csangos Decertified

To participate more fully in the civic and economic life of the Romanian nation, many Csangos were compelled, from 1942, to obtain certificates of ethnic Romanian origin. However, the question over the ethnic origin (or origins) of the Csangos caused a great deal of confusion among the civil authorities in Moldavia responsible for issuing these certificates. Many of these officials withheld the certificates on the pretense that Hungarian-speaking Roman Catholics could not possibly be Romanian.[54] Further complicating matters, the Ministry of Justice revoked the Romanian citizenship of some of the Csangos in 1942 on the apparent misunderstanding that some in the community had settled in

Moldavia only two generations back and therefore should not be counted as naturalized citizens.[55]

What were some of the ramifications of being cast as ethnically non-Romanian? A letter sent from the Catholic bishopric of Iași in 1943 to Antonescu and the Presidential Council of Ministers outlined a number of problems the Moldavian Catholics faced as a result of being denied their certificates of ethnic Romanian origin. It was not simply that the Csangos were looked on as "foreigners, enemies of the country" but also that they were treated as such in legal terms.[56] Moreover, the "atmosphere of hostility" against the community created by their Romanian Orthodox neighbors and lower-level government officials compounded the problem.[57] Local officials regarded as "unjust" the complaints against them registered by the Csangos with higher-level officials in the army, Ministry of Interior, or the Ministry of Religious Denominations. Such complaints led to further accusations of betrayal, which in turn provoked retribution.

The inability to obtain the certificates of Romanian ethnic origin not only prevented the Moldavian Catholics from gaining employment in public offices but also caused many of them to lose their existing state jobs, whether as railway workers or functionaries in local administrations. Catholics in public employment, including military officers, were denied the right to be married by a Catholic priest, while Catholic students were barred from admission into teacher-training colleges simply because of their religion, despite meeting all technical and legal requirements.[58] In the parish of Hălăucești, Catholics were even prevented from voting in the nationwide plebiscites in 1941.[59]

In one reported case of discrimination, a police chief in the village of Bălțați in Iași County banned outright the popular Catholic journal *Lumina Creștinului* and forbade the ringing of morning and evening bells in Catholic churches. Civil and military officials likewise interfered in religious practices. Cadets in the Premilitară reported that their superiors forced them to attend Orthodox churches as part of their military training, being told that these were the "real national churches." Other reports tell of schoolteachers who forced Csango children to attend Orthodox churches and to make the sign of the cross in the Eastern Orthodox way. In some villages, Catholic priests and cantors were forbidden from holding Catholic religious education classes, a privilege supposedly guaranteed by the Vatican-Romanian Concordat since 1929. Also reported were instances of schoolteachers admonishing their pupils for attending Catholic churches and festivals. Elsewhere, near the town of Suceava, a county clerk refused to register as a Catholic the child of a mixed Orthodox-Catholic marriage, despite the parents' insistence the child be listed as Catholic.[60]

Certifiably Romanian

In summer 1942 in the town of Cozmești, north of Roman, a number of Catholic families complained of "daily persecutions and unjust slander" in their communities "on account of the fact that we are of 'Csango' nationality and of 'Hungarian' ethnic origin." Distraught over their predicament, which included delays and difficulties in their attempt to acquire the requisite documents showing their ethnic origin as Romanian, they wrote plaintively to their parish priest in hopes that he could help resolve their situation:

> After we have paid all of our taxes as *good Romanians*, fulfilled our public duties toward the state still as *good Romanians*, supported all state institutions as *good Romanians*, and after we have worked the land of our Romanian country, still as *good Romanians*, fought in wars from 1877, 1913, 1916, and 1941, through the heroic deaths of our grandfathers, our parents, our brothers and our sons, we are repaid for this sacrifice when we go to the mayor's office in our respective districts to be issued some certificate or proof, still as *good Romanians*, as history proves, Mayor Sobariu, helped by Notary Țintilă and Secretary Daj, issues these certificates only after much difficulty, specifying that we are "Csangos" and "Hungarians." ... Please bring this to the attention of those with the authority to clarify our situation.[61]

On 26 November 1942, an order was handed down from the Ministry of Justice to the Ministry of Internal Affairs concerning the Csangos, inclusive of all the Roman Catholics of the region: "Dear Minister, Responding to your address No. 51.704 from 6 November 1942, the advice of this Ministry concerning the origin of the Csango inhabitants in Bacău County is that they cannot be considered of ethnic Romanian origin." Evidently, the initial inquiry was made to the respective ministries by the aforementioned prefect of Bacău, General Ionescu, in the summer or autumn of 1942. After receiving the above decision from the Ministry of Justice, the county prefect promptly issued his own edict, No. 374.484, on 20 December to all the mayors in the districts with Catholic populations: certificates of Romanian ethnic origin could no longer be issued to Catholic citizens in the region.[62]

In February 1943 the Catholics in the village of Săcatura-Mărgineni, outside Bacău, were also denied these certificates. They wrote a letter directly to Marshal Antonescu, pleading with him to resolve the matter:

> Our ancestors, our parents, and even our sons fought for our Romanian Fatherland, even against the Hungarians, and today when we go to the mayor's office we are told that we are of Hungarian nationality and that we are not ethnic

Romanians, that we cannot be given the documents we need to buy and sell land, or to enter into employment. Marshal, we plead with you, with tears in our eyes, to have mercy on us and to give an order that we be considered and treated as true Romanians and not as Hungarians. We know of no other Fatherland than our Romanian one, for which we have shed blood from generation to generation. We know that we are of Romanian nationality and have ethnic Romanian origin, and we do not want to hear insults or to be labeled Hungarians, Magyars, or Csangos. For us these names are shameful. We are Romanians of the Catholic Christian religion. This is how we were born, and this is how we want to die.[63]

They attached to the letter a list of over sixty names and the marks of those villagers who had either served in World War I or else were serving in the current one, as well as the names and marks of many war widows.

The inhabitants of nearby Talpa-Sărata sent a similar letter to Antonescu. The mayors had refused to issue the Catholics certificates of Romanian origin and denied them the right to buy and sell land. The mayor's office had been instructed by the Ministry of Justice to consider them as Hungarians. "Marshal Antonescu," the villagers pleaded, "as our ancestors have fought for the Country, so have we, even against the Hungarians, and not one from our community has been a traitor to this Country." They begged Antonescu to reverse the ministry's decision as soon as possible, as they were "true" Romanians, "belonging to the Romanian Nation and of the Catholic Christian religion, not Hungarians, as some of our Orthodox brothers have labeled us."[64] In support of their cause, they attached a list of fifty-five veterans, war widows, and soldiers currently serving in the war.

Catholics from Oituz-Grozeşti were also denied certificates of ethnic origin despite, as they pointed out, being counted entirely as ethnic Romanians in the 1941 census. Consequently, they could no longer buy and sell land. As most of the Csangos were farmers in rural communities and villages, some of them quite remote, their inability to participate fully in the region's agricultural-based economy took a heavy toll on their livelihoods: "They no longer have the appetite for work, and added to all of this misery is that in every Catholic family there is at least one killed or missing in action, or else a prisoner of war; the remaining care daily for the women who struggle against this black misery," wrote the parish priest to the bishop of Iaşi in May 1943.[65]

In Ploscuţeni, authorities had referred to the Catholics there as *boanghen*,[66] a derogatory term used by Romanians for Hungarians. The police confiscated all the Catholics' hunting weapons, leaving only the Orthodox population the right and the means to hunt.⁶⁷ Only Romanians could possess arms. Unauthorized persons caught with firearms were subject to the death penalty.⁶⁸ "The hour is near in which all Hungarians will be expelled from the country," one Orthodox family was reportedly heard shouting in the streets of the small but mixed Orthodox and Catholic town. In addition, the local notary refused to register Catholic names such as Tereza, Lucia, and Aloiziu into the birth records, forcing Catholic parents to choose Romanian-Orthodox-sounding names. Applications by Catholics in the region for certificates of ethnic Romanian origin were rejected because, they were told, "those born and baptized in the Catholic rite cannot be considered of ethnic Romanian origin."⁶⁹

Catholics inhabiting the Trotuș River valley, which runs west to east from the Ciuc Mountains in the Eastern Carpathians to join the Siret River, were excluded from the Premilitară altogether.⁷⁰ Those from Oituz-Grozești in Bacău County were also prohibited from serving in the border battalions guarding the new Romanian-Hungarian border in the middle of the Ghimeș valley (a trans-Carpathian pass linking Transylvania and Moldavia), as they were considered "dangerous, being that they are Catholics."⁷¹

Mihai Robu, the bishop of Iași, wrote often to Antonescu about the dire situation of the Catholics in Moldavia. Robu attached to his own letters affidavits attesting to the "antipathy" shown by lower-ranking authorities toward the Catholics in the region, "on the motivation that, being Catholic, they cannot be true Romanians, but rather must be Hungarians." The bishop appealed to Antonescu to end the "campaign of abuse and persecution" waged by local officials, Orthodox priests, and schoolteachers in the Catholic-inhabited villages, assuring Antonescu that even those few Catholics in the region who did refer to themselves as "Hungarian" understood this term as meaning only "Catholic," "without any relation to the respective nationality."⁷² They simply used the term out of long-standing custom in the region, by which Romanian or Moldavian implied Orthodox while Hungarian implied Catholic. Robu also wrote to the minister of religious denominations, acknowledging that indeed there were Catholics in the area who did not know Romanian. He insisted, however, that no blame should be placed on the Iași episcopate or on the Catholic priests in Bacău County, "who preach and catechize only in Romanian."⁷³

In light of this purported misunderstanding about the ethnic origin of the Moldavian Catholics, Robu appealed to Antonescu to reverse the decision of the Ministry of Justice and the decree of the prefect of Bacău, in the hope of ending the persecution in Roman, Bacău, and Iași Counties against these "Romanians by blood (in the great majority), all of whom are Romanian by sentiment and aspiration." Robu asked Antonescu to allow the issuance of certificates of Romanian nationality and ethnic origin for all the Catholic Romanian citizens in Moldavian villages, "so that they can participate without restrictions in the public life of the state, occupying public offices just as their Orthodox brothers." In addition, Robu asked that his Catholics be allowed to work again in public offices and to earn the rank of officer in the army on the basis of merit. He begged Antonescu: "Restore the former peace and serenity of mind to the 100,000 Romanian Catholics of Moldavia, so that they can live without fear of being banished to the country across the border, as foreigners, as being dangerous or unsympathetic only because we are Catholic Christians."[74]

Finally, Robu asked that epithets be removed from primary and secondary school textbooks for history, geography, and religion. These textbooks made offensive references to the Romanian Catholics from Moldavia as "Csangos" and "Hungarians," names that implied "enemies of the Country" and fueled speculation that Hungary was using the Catholics of Moldavia to extend its dominion across the Siret River, "if not further."[75]

The threat of deportation loomed large over the Csangos. Already in the autumn and winter of 1940, the Hungarian and Romanian governments resettled in Hungary the entire community of Bukovinan Szeklers, some fourteen thousand strong. To repopulate lands taken after its invasion of Yugoslavia the following spring, Hungary was in need of yet more ethnic kin from abroad. A precedent had therefore been set. If ethnic homogenization was the goal for both states, then forced relocation seemed the quickest and most efficient means to achieve it.

5

Resettlement "Home"
Solving Demographic Crises

By the 1930s, national governments and minorities alike increasingly viewed the Minority Treaties signed after World War I as inadequate for protecting minority populations and ensuring stable national borders. For nationalists and irredentists across east-central Europe, including in Romania and Hungary, population transfers and exchanges offered a way to resolve these issues permanently. This option was particularly attractive to newly created nation-states like Romania that gained territory after the postwar breakup of surrounding multi-ethnic empires and kingdoms as well as for states like Hungary that subsequently regained some of its lost territory: expelling minorities from, and relocating ethnic kin into, newly acquired (or reacquired) territories bolstered long-standing claims over these contested lands, which usually straddled historically contested borders. Precedents for formal population transfers and exchanges had already been set in the Balkans during World War I, including the accords between Bulgaria and Turkey in 1913 and Greece and Turkey in 1914. Under the Treaty of Neuilly in 1919, the Bulgarian inhabitants in and around Thessaloniki were exchanged for Greeks in Bulgaria. A few years later, under the Treaty of Lausanne in 1923, a Greek and Turkish population exchange provided for the transfer of 1.5 million Greeks from Turkey and Bulgaria into Greece and sent most of Greece's Muslim population to Turkey. During the 1920s and 1930s, the Soviet Union implemented a sweeping internal colonization agenda to re-order the country demographically.

Since the late nineteenth century, successive Romanian governments had actively supported Aromanian or Vlach communities living outside Romania's borders, notably in Greek Macedonia and elsewhere in the Balkans, by establishing Romanian schools and maintaining Romanian Orthodox churches.[1] During the 1920s, Romania relocated over two thousand Aromanian families from Macedonia to Romanian Dobrudja, especially in the southern part that was ceded to Romania from Bulgaria in 1913. Southern Dobrudja, also known as the Cadrilater ("Quadrilateral," because of its shape), was populated predominantly by Bulgarians, Greeks, and Turks. To redress this ethnic imbalance, the Romanian government facilitated Aromanian/Vlach migrations into the region. In 1936 a convention between Romania and Turkey provided for a "voluntary" population transfer of Tatars and Turks from Romanian Dobrudja to Turkey.[2]

Between 1918 and 1924, approximately 350,000 ethnic Hungarians were repatriated from the successor states of the Austro-Hungarian Monarchy to the new Hungary, a great many of whom came from the regions of Transylvania, Vojvodina, and Slovakia.[3] The loss of peripheral, multiethnic territories, combined with large inflows of ethnic Hungarians from abroad, transformed Hungary into an ethnically homogeneous "rump" state, with the notable exception of its sizeable, mostly urban, Hungarian-speaking Jewish population. The de-Hungarianization policies in the neighboring successor states (including Yugoslavia, Czechoslovakia, and Romania), combined with the exodus of Hungarians from territories Hungary had ceded to these new states after World War I, diminished the population of Hungarians in the frontier zones on all sides of the Hungarian border.[4] Hungary would reclaim these territories by treaty or by force in 1940–41. In an effort to redress what it viewed as an ethnic imbalance in these contested lands during World War II, especially in Hungary's southern territories retaken from Yugoslavia, the Hungarian government attempted to "restock" these lands through a policy known as *hazatelepítés*, or the "resettlement home." The government targeted ethnic Hungarians living as minorities in neighboring states.

With the onset of war, population transfers became an even more attractive solution to the interrelated problems of demographics, borders, minorities, and international relations. Between 1939 and 1942, Nazi Germany sanctioned the uprooting of hundreds of thousands of ethnic Germans from South Tyrol, the Baltics, Bessarabia, Bukovina, Dobrudja, and occupied Poland. Resettlements were part of a broader *Heim ins Reich* agenda, which aimed to relocate "home" to the Reich large numbers of *Volksdeutsche* in central and eastern Europe. Other German enclaves in eastern Europe, particularly in Ukraine, were kept in place to reinforce the *Volksdeutsche* in the occupied East.[5] These population policies were key to Hitler's *Lebensraum* and *Generalplan Ost* strategies for German expansion and colonization. They also legitimized similar schemes drawn up in Romania and Hungary during the war.

Where assimilationist policies failed, population transfers provided an ideal solution to the minority question and contested border issues, especially after the outbreak of World War II. In this way, putative "foreigners" could be removed from a given nation while ethnic kin could be "returned" to their rightful homeland. Wartime population policies held out the promise that a Europe comprised of ethnically homogeneous states could soon be realized through the orderly mass movement of peoples, and that individual nations—and the continent—could be physically reconfigured along ethnic and racial lines.

Population Transfers and "Regeneration" in Interwar Romania

In the 1920s Romanian governments experimented with a variety of population policies, including internal colonization. The government not only resettled Aromanians from abroad into Dobrudja but also resettled existing Romanian citizens from one part of the country to another. As part of broader agrarian reforms, the Romanian government incentivized Romanians from Moldavia and Wallachia to relocate to minority-inhabited areas, such as Hungarian strongholds in Transylvania, by offering these *colonizatori* (colonizers) lands dispossessed from the former dominant groups, such as the Hungarian aristocracy and the Hungarian churches.

Prior to the mid-1930s, however, the prevailing solution to the minority-related demographic and territorial issues was not total ethnic purification but rather integration, assimilation, and centralization.[6] Still, those states that lost territory after World War I, including Hungary, Bulgaria, and the Soviet Union, continually advocated border revisions with Romania based on the ethnic principle, namely that Hungarians, Bulgarians, and Slavs represented a majority in large parts of the territories ceded to Romania after World War I. Also, the larger proportion of minorities in universities and in professions such as law and journalism proved a major source of grievance for the growing nationalist movements in Romania. These factors contributed to the rise of the radical right in Romania. Over the course of the interwar period, Romanian intellectuals and scientists began to reconceptualize the state along ethnic lines in an effort to confront what they viewed as threats to Romania's territorial integrity and social stability. By the time of the Munich Agreement and the First Vienna Award in September and November 1938, respectively,[7] King Carol II's government saw population exchanges as a way to prevent future territorial losses. In lieu of large-scale territorial concessions to Hungary and Bulgaria, the Romanian government offered Hungary and Bulgaria an exchange of populations alongside modest border revisions, arguing that Hitler himself approved of this policy as a means to ethnic homogenization. However, as long as Bulgaria and Hungary felt they had Hitler's backing for a revision of borders, neither agreed to this proposal.

By the late 1930s and early 1940s, a critical number of Romanian population scientists, intellectuals, and politicians believed the minority question could be settled through a reinvigorated policy of population exchanges, transfers, and internal colonization. Demographer Sabin Manuilă was one of the first to propose a broader national strategy of demographic reordering. As early as 1929, he justified such policies in stark biopolitical terms, writing about population transfers as a "purification" of the national body and as a solution to minorities' "centrifugal tendencies." Many of Romania's public intellectuals began to echo these sentiments.

The results of the 1930 census, which depicted in stark statistical terms the ethnic and religious heterogeneity of Romania's prized territorial acquisitions Transylvania and Bessarabia, made clear to Romania's nation builders that the "cultural offensive" and assimilationist projects undertaken in the 1920s by reformers such as Constantin Angelescu were inadequate to ensure national unification. In any case, most Romanian nationalists now rejected the ideals of unification and integration; instead, ideas about "purification," "regeneration," and "transfiguration" became the order of the day. As symbolist poet and novelist Nicolae Davidescu remarked in 1930: "There are, in our midst, a series of national, religious, and racial susceptibilities. Within the idea of the state, those religions, those races, and those nationalities do not in any way overlap. In this complex situation, they are divergent and centrifugal." In this mindset, the minorities themselves were to blame for what was commonly referred to as the "minority problem." Through their "heterogeneous solidarity" and "provocative" and "chauvinistic" attitudes, minorities undermined the good-faith attempts to build bridges between themselves and "the new majority, the indigenous inhabitants of the Romanian land."[8]

However, it was only at the end of the 1930s that Romanian intellectuals, academics, and politicians discussed the idea of a complete ethnic reorganization and "regeneration" of the country through population policies. In 1937 the public intellectual, writer, and polymath Nicolae Porsenna[9] concluded that *numerus clausus* and other legislative measures to redress the minority problem were merely "palliative." The only viable way to begin the "regeneration" of the Romanian nation was through the "liquidation of minorities" via an exchange and restitution of populations:

> Minorities, especially the Jews, completely avoid menial work, which they leave for the Romanians; and they, through their strong solidarity of race, ensure for

themselves only lofty careers. Thus, they have become a truly privileged caste, in a country that abolished all privileges through the Constitution. This is a vital question for the Romanian nation, namely to restore the political and economic equilibrium of the State, taking control of the levers of power from the hands of the minorities and limiting their access to any career in just, logical, and equitable proportion to their numbers. Surely, this is only a palliative. The solution to the minority problem is but one: *population exchange* with neighbors, i.e., the bringing of Romanians from abroad and the expulsion of foreigners from within.[10]

A year later, Nichifor Crainic famously (or infamously) proposed the "ethnocratic state," which he characterized as the "political will of the autochthonous race to make the state the expression of her character and the vehicle of her mission in the world." Crainic described his ideal state in Nietzschean terms: "The ethnocratic state is the will to power and expansion of the Romanian nation. Its principal factors are: soil, blood, soul, and faith."[11] In his quest for national "regeneration," Crainic promoted a new form of ethnic nationalism that was both spiritual and biological; recognizing this reality, the ethnic state was to play a vital role in shaping the ethnic character of the nation.[12] Within the ethnic state, "ethnocracy" would be an antidote for the deleterious effects of Romania's ethnic diversity and would guide the country into becoming an ethnically homogeneous nation-state. Crainic advocated massive population exchanges, colonization of Romanians along the borders, removal of the Jews from rural areas, and making Romanians a "royal race" in their own country.[13]

Ultimately, Crainic argued, the solution to the minority problem was to expatriate the Hungarians, the Germans, and the "Jewish element," all of whom, he believed, incapable of assimilation. The Jews, who had no other homeland to return to, would be purged from the Romanian nation "by sending them to Madagascar or through their extermination en masse as far away as heaven is to earth."[14] Until such time as these foreigners could be expelled, they were to be *numerus nullus* in the Romanian leadership and *numerus clausus* in the areas of education and industry.[15] Crainic framed the minority question as a matter of state security and territorial integrity: "By granting universal citizenship, in time our existing minorities will refuse to take part in the Romanian nation, and by their centrifugal tendencies many will seek to undermine the existence of the Romanian state. ... The foreign element cannot form a basis of security for the existence of our state, but rather it is through the elimination of these elements that the sustainability of the national state is realized."[16]

Eventually, all ethnic minorities—not just the Jews—came to be seen as magnets for irredentism, characterized as having "centrifugal tendencies" that could tear apart the Romanian nation. The trope of "centrifugal forces" or "tendencies" was also being used in Nazi Germany. Alfred Rosenberg and racial anthropologist and serologist Otto Reche used the same phrase to describe the potentiality of minorities as an agency of state destruction.[17]

Once race laws were implemented across much of German-aligned central and eastern Europe beginning in 1938,[18] and certainly by the onset of the Second World War, biologically racist arguments for "purifying the nation" and excising "cancerous" populations legitimized state policies for expelling large contingents of Romania's ethnic minorities. Many of the scientists, politicians, and intelligentsia who supported this "solution" to the minority problem gained positions of great power and influence, thus their words hinged more readily on deeds. Davidescu, for instance, served as director general of the Romanian National Theater as well as a general secretary in the Ministry of Culture between 1938 and 1939. Crainic served as minister of national propaganda in the Ion Gigurtu government and again during the Antonescu dictatorship.

Like Crainic, both Goga and Cuza endorsed the idea of forcibly relocating Romania's minority populations. In January 1938 Goga smugly told a *Time* magazine correspondent, "I hear that American Jews are appealing in Geneva against me. Well, nothing could suit me better. I propose to ask the League [of Nations] to see that these people are removed from Rumania and sent to their proper homes. How and when is a question for the future."[19] Cuza, no less imperious, seconded the idea: "It is for the world to find a residence for the world's Jews! Madagascar seems a suitable spot."

"An Ethnically Romanian State, between Natural Ethnic Boundaries"

By 1941 the Romanian government had already begun planning for the shape of postwar Romania. During World War II, population "exchange" (*schimb de populație*) often amounted to the unilateral transfer of undesired "elements" and the internal colonization of ethnic Romanians in their stead. As a policy with international precedent, it masked or legitimized the forced deportation of minority populations, especially Jews and Roma. Wartime colonization, particularly in Bessarabia and Bukovina, was key to Antonescu's long-term agenda of ethnic resettlement, mass reeducation, and the reconstruction of Romania as an ethnically homogeneous nation-state. The expulsion of Jews was but the first phase of an all-out ethnic cleansing of Romanian territory. Next to be removed were the Ukrainians, Bulgarians, Russians, Gagauz, Roma, and others, especially in regions contested by the Soviets, namely Bessarabia and Bukovina.[20]

Sabin Manuilă, demographer and director of Romania's Central Institute for Statistics, devised a wartime plan to carry out the ethnic homogenization of Romania by means of population transfers. This idea was predicated on the notion that the Romanian nation was a community based on a common origin, to the exclusion of all nonethnic Romanians.[21] The stated aim of his proposed population transfers was twofold: to prevent war with its equally fanatical neighbors and to homogenize the state along ethnic principles. According to Manuilă's plan, the Romanian government would systematically deport most of Romania's minority populations, which totaled 3,581,618 Hungarians, Slavs, Germans, and others. From outside Romanian territory, the government would systematically import a total of 1,602,359 Romanians (the differential would be a net loss to Romania of 1,979,059). Jews and Roma, however, did not quite figure into this scheme; rather, they would be subjected to "unilateral transfer." Manuilă, in consultation with Romania's military dictator Marshal Ion Antonescu, viewed these population transfers and exchanges in terms of national survival: "Politically, the moment has arrived for executing operations consisting of taking across the borders from Romania all minorities with centrifugal tendencies and bringing back to the country all Romanians in blood from wherever they are."[22]

The ultimate goal of the Antonescu regime was to delineate new borders around the limits of ethnic Romania. "We want an ethnically Romanian state, between natural ethnic boundaries and are not tempted by the insane idea of domination of ethnically foreign territory," wrote Manuilă in a government white paper during the war.[23] Manuilă saw this as the only way to preempt an otherwise certain war between Hungary and Romania. He noted the Hungarians were "just as fanatical" as the Romanians, and that a war between the two would be the costliest in Europe in terms of material destruction and human suffering.[24]

Manuilă's was only the first of several plans. Titus Dragoș, head of the SSRCI, developed another plan between November and December 1942. Sociologist Anton Golopenția completed yet another in March 1943, as did Emil Oprișanu in the Foreign Ministry.[25] These plans were never fully realized. However, some transfers were enacted in the early years of the war. Bulgaria and Romania sought to empty their respective Dobrudjan territories of ethnic minorities after Southern Dobrudja (the Cadrilater) was returned to Bulgaria as a result of the Treaty of Craiova in September 1940. A year later, the two countries negotiated terms for an exchange of populations. Alexandru Cretzianu, a diplomat in the Foreign Ministry who led the Romanian delegation during negotiations over the Treaty of Craiova, first proposed the exchange of all ethnic Bulgarians from Romania and all Romanians from Bulgaria.[26] The final numbers, however, were to be based on the 1930 Romanian census, with estimates to account for growth rates up to 1940.

During World War II, approximately 170,000 persons in the Romanian-Bulgarian border region were relocated to their "appropriate" ethnic nation state. Most of the Romanian colonists in Southern Dobrudja, some 80,000, were relocated to Northern Dobrudja; another 20,000 ethnic Romanians from elsewhere in Bulgaria were sent north to be resettled in Romania. From Romania, 65,000 Bulgarians in Dobrudja were sent to Bulgaria.[27] Beginning in 1940, most of Romania's Germans from Northern and Southern Bukovina, Northern Bessarabia, and Northern Dobrudja—over 200,000 in all—were repatriated to Germany as part of Hitler's *Heim ins Reich* initiative. In a matter of days, the Romanian and German governments rounded up and evacuated from Dobrudja the 16,000 *Dobrudschadeutsche* who had settled the region since the 1840s.[28] Their homes and land were allocated to internal Romanian colonists from Wallachia and Moldavia. In autumn 1941 the Romanian and Hungarian governments also negotiated the resettlement of approximately 13,500 Bukovinan Szeklers into southern Hungary.

Hungary's "Diluted Magyars" and "Race Protectors"

In the 1930s Hungary was dubbed "a nation with three million beggars," an epithet taken from the title of György Oláh's novel that had exposed the sheer misery of the Hungarian peasantry.[29] Nearly half of Hungary's 8.5 million people were agricultural workers. Of these, approximately 3 million were landless or else owned dwarf holdings.[30] Since the late nineteenth century, birthrates among the downtrodden peasantry had fallen in certain regions of Hungary. Across the lands known as Transdanubia (Dunántúl), west of the Danube, particularly in the southern counties such as Baranya, the natural rate of population increase among the Hungarians was lower than anywhere else in the kingdom, while the natural rate of population increase among the Serbs, Croats, and even the Germans was correspondingly higher.[31] Statistically, however, the number of Hungarians, as well as the growth rate of the Hungarian population across the country, had actually increased in proportion to other nationalities since the turn of the century. This suggests much of the "crisis" arose from a collective sense of loss after World War I and Trianon as well as associated, heightened fears about the encroachment of foreigners.[32]

Many Hungarian demographers, social scientists, and politicians characterized the country's demographic situation as a national crisis. The causes were many. One was the self-imposed *egyke* or "one-child" practice among small landholders across rural Hungary, whereby peasant families practiced fertility control. In doing so, these families retained as much property as possible by handing down undivided shares to fewer heirs. As Ildiko Vasary has commented on the one-child system (*egy gyermek rendszer*), which began in the mid-nineteenth century, "The one-child system was a political issue, a national problem, an academic puzzle, a mirror reflecting fears for the future of the nation and an opposition propaganda piece."[33]

During the 1920s and 1930s the demographic crisis attributed to the *egyke* practice was in many respects the creation of those who recorded its existence, including priests and ministers in the countryside, and especially the young village explorers and sociographers of the folk-populist movement.[34] Lajos Fülep, the noted art historian, philosopher, and Calvinist minister, who spent much of his life and career in southern Hungary, linked the demographic crisis to "biological exhaustion" of the Hungarians and even forewarned of racial extinction: "By its very nature, the *egyke* system is attacking and disintegrating the family, and finally destroying it. Killed is the sense of family, the fathers' and mothers' love for their own children, the appreciation of motherhood, brotherly love, and the consciousness of belonging together. The decay begins with the family, and from there it spreads to the nation and every economic, intellectual, and moral field of life, and it will not stop until it reaches its logical end, which is the destruction of the race's will to live, resulting ultimately in the destruction of the race itself."[35]

The wretched poverty and the poor state of health in rural Hungary, combined with massive casualties during World War I and devastation to agricultural and industrial output during the Great Depression, contributed to a general sense of demographic and even biological decline of the nation, a sense that was amplified by nationalist politicians and intellectuals at the time.[36] The perceived demographic crisis in Hungary was exacerbated by large-scale emigration to the United States at the turn of the century and subsequently by fears of being outbred by non-Hungarians, especially the large contingents of Catholic Slavs and Germans in southern Hungary.[37] Many of these and other non-Hungarian populations had been encouraged to settle the region beginning in the latter half of the eighteenth century by Austrian empress Maria Theresa.

As in Romania, racialized tropes in public and literary discourses in Hungary ran parallel to other manifestations of racism in politics and the sciences. It was during the 1920s in Hungary that a number of political parties and societies formed with an explicitly racist platform, including the Ébredő Magyarok

Egyesülete (Awakening Hungarians Association) and the Etelközi Szövetség (Etelköz Association),[38] and by the 1930s, the Magyar Fajvédők Országos Szövetségé (Hungarian National Alliance of Race Protectors), an official subsection of one of the most significant national conservative organizations, the Magyar Országos Védérő Egyesület (Association of Hungarian National Defense).

Groups such as these had their origins in the counterrevolution against the Hungarian Soviet from 1919, and many were led or else nurtured by Gyula Gömbös, the leader of the radical right and the conservative fascist movement in Hungary.[39] The "race protectors" promoted a politics of "national autotelism" (*nemzeti üncélúság*). "There is only one end in itself, the interests of the nation," wrote Gömbös in 1925. In terms of policy, the "race protectors" pursued an agenda centered on territorial revision and national independence, specifically rejecting the third-way ideas about a Danubian Confederation; they were, moreover, as hostile to German *Anschluss* and domination of Europe as they were to the threat of pan-Slavism and the Soviet Union from the east.[40]

The lawyer and politician Miklós Bonczos was another prominent figure whose political career emerged from the ideology and politics of "race protection."[41] Working in the Hungarian Ministry of Interior throughout World War II, Bonczos became a key figure in the development and implementation of Hungary's population policies during World War II. As with many of his contemporaries, he viewed the degeneration of Hungarian villages as symptomatic of the degeneration of the Hungarian race, especially in the south, and believed the continued loss of Hungary's collective racial vitality would prevent the nation's resurgence. During the war, he penned the foreword to a book on the racial anthropology of the Hungarian nation and its connection to the Hungarian homeland.[42] Setting the tenor of the book, Bonczos fused nation and homeland, the two "ancient and eternal pillars" on which the nation and its future rested: "We are the nation of the land, unbreakable and unchangeable, the ancient Hungarian land, watered by blood and sweat, the symbol of our ever-budding racial strength." Bonczos, a major advocate for resettling ethnic Hungarians from abroad, stated unequivocally the nation's "great objective": "to acquire the land, the country, the nation for the Hungarian race."[43]

"Our Bodies Are Degenerating": The Churches' Biological Imperative

Arguments about biological and national degeneration indeed mobilized sentiment in Hungary, both within the Christian churches as well as in the government, and prompted the idea that Hungarians from abroad should be resettled in Hungary to repopulate and rejuvenate the nation. A growing number of intellectuals and social scientists now saw in the peasantry, including those Hungarian peasants across the border, a repository of "authentic" Hungarians. As early as the mid-1930s, the Catholic and Reformed churches in Hungary—as well as the Unitarian, Hungarian Lutheran, and Hungarian Greek Catholic churches—also promoted the idea of resettling foreign Hungarians in areas dominated by Slavs and Germans. The Catholic Prohászka Ottokár Társaság (Bishop Prohászka Society) and a number of other Catholic organizations in Hungary and Transylvania wrote letters to the Hungarian Prime Ministry and Foreign Ministry encouraging this policy.[44]

However, it was the Reformed Church in southern Hungary and in Transylvania that pressed hardest for the transfer of "authentic" Hungarians into Hungary, especially Calvinist ones capable of working the land. Resettling Calvinists into ethnically and confessionally heterogeneous areas along the southern border was, moreover, viewed in terms of national defense.[45] The Calvinist priest Géza Kiss, along with his colleagues in the Upper Baranya County diocesan assembly, championed this cause in 1935: "Reformed institutions—churches and schools—stand ready and wait with joy to welcome within their walls the solely reliable [group] from the national standpoint—the racially pure Hungarian Calvinists, settling here from the great Hungarian Plain."[46]

Kálmán Németh, the medical doctor and parson of Vornicenii Mici/Józseffalva in Bukovina, was an early and ardent supporter of population resettlements. Shortly after Romania's cession of Northern Transylvania to Hungary in the summer of 1940, Németh raised the idea with Prime Minister Pál Teleki and other officials.[47] Teleki agreed and subsequently made plans to resettle the Bukovinan Szeklers and Moldavian Csangos in Northern Transylvania. He gave Németh a verbal commitment regarding the relocation of the Szeklers of Bukovina, but told the parson to wait until a more propitious moment to begin the resettlements. Nevertheless, Németh reported to the villagers that the decision was official and that they should therefore make preparations to pack what belongings they could take and to sell what they could not. No doubt to the dismay of some of these villagers, Németh failed to arrange their resettlement into Hungary as promised. In fact, the Romanian authorities put him on trial in Cernăuți for suspected irredentist activities. Throughout the war, Németh played a key role in relaying to the Hungarian government information about Hungarians in Romania. He spearheaded propaganda seeking to convince the Bukovinan Szeklers and the Moldavian Csangos of the virtue in relocating to Hungary.[48]

In March 1941, in the Transylvanian village of Börvely,[49] a like-minded Calvinist priest urged Teleki to replenish Börvely and the surrounding areas with ethnic Hungarians. "Our bodies are degenerating," he wrote plaintively. This was because of the villagers' practice of endogamy, given that the Hungarian Calvinists were surrounded by Romanians and refused to mix with their only other neighbors, the Swabians (Germans). The priest appealed to Teleki to relocate ethnic Hungarians from Transylvanian villages in the south and east so as "to strengthen the nation and ennoble the race." The Calvinist congregation from Măneuți/Andrásfalva in Bukovina sent a similar letter to Teleki later that year, requesting they be relocated to Hungary so that, among other reasons, they could marry outside their own community. "We are almost all blood relatives," they wrote.[50]

In a report to the Hungarian Foreign Ministry dated 17 July 1941, priest and politician József Bálint[51] demanded Hungary repatriate the Szeklers of Bukovina, whom he described as "true Hungarians," "loyal to their ancient religion and race." He insisted Hungary also repatriate the Hungarians from Croatia and Moldavia, who could be saved "for our own homeland because they are of such outstanding material." Moreover, he enjoined, "We should send twice as many Romanians from Transylvania to take the place of the Moldavian Hungarians." If the Romanian government did not agree to deliver the Csangos to Hungary, then Hungary should simply demand the Csango land as territory already inhabited by Hungarians.[52]

"A Hungariandom, 20 Million Strong": The State's Biological Imperative

Secular and governmental organizations also promoted the reincorporation of all ethnic Hungarians into the territorial nation. On 2 October 1940, the Hungarian National Alliance of Race Protectors—alongside twenty or so other secular, governmental, and religious institutions[53]—sent a letter to Teleki, imploring him to take action on the resettlement issue. They claimed the Hungarian nation could only survive "in quantity and quality" if strengthened by the addition of ethnic Hungarians from neighboring states: "Outside the sensitive borders of the country, many Hungarian brothers hear our calling voice. The question of resettling is not unsolvable. For those brothers living outside the historical homeland, there is a chance to settle them back home, maybe through population exchanges. When we think about the wasted possibility, our hearts break for those living in Southern Bukovina and over the Russian and Romanian borders. . . . We believe that Your Excellency and the Hungarian government will feel and see that we need to do something immediately."[54]

In 1940 the Magyar Nemzetbiológia Intézet (Hungarian National Biological Institute) was established under the aegis of the Egészségpolitikai Társaság (Society of Public Health) to research the means by which a biologically unitary and expansive "Hungariandom, 20 million strong" might be created (the population of Hungary was around 11.5 million at the time). The institute had sections devoted to researching biology and Hungarian history, national nutrition, hereditary biology, racial biology, and eugenics.[55]

A pamphlet published in 1940 by the Hungarian National Biological Institute received much attention from Romanian authorities.[56] Its author, András Korponay, called for an awakening of the "vegetative popular [folk] forces" to solve the country's demographic and border problems. Nothing less than "a ruthless liquidation of the population policy constructed around the chimera of assimilation" was required. In Korponay's view, the Hungarian future, should it last, would be built "on the numerical reinforcement of Hungarians by blood" and an "acceptance of the Hungarian biopolitical idea as a State program." Such were the conditions for a "new ascension of the Hungarian people" and the foundation for the "Hungarian resurrection": "Without numerical strengthening and healthy reproduction, it is impossible to ensure advancement and a better future. Hungarian society has completely misjudged—or rather, not even recognized—the significance of this most important national biological cooperation. This is apparent in the certain one-sidedness to our historical perspective, and is responsible, moreover, for the fact that our irredentism and most of our public opinion has turned the resurrection of Hungary from the disaster of Trianon into a purely geographical question."[57]

Speaking for the institute and its government supporters, Korponay saw the history of nations as being driven by "ethnic forces," and thus small nations—especially those surrounded by larger, more prolific ones—stood little chance of survival. The populations of Russians, Slovaks, Germans, Croatians, and especially the Serbs and Romanians were all on the increase, he warned. Hungarians had permitted "these two powerful races," the Romanians and Serbs, "to impregnate and then fill up for their ethnicums once-undisputed Hungarian territories." In doing so, they had severed these lands from the Hungarian nation.[58] Since World War I, he noted, the Romanian birthrate was nearly double the Hungarian one (a claim he does not substantiate with statistics or references). These putative numbers had not just demographic but also political and territorial ramifications, justifying to European powers the dismemberment of Hungary in the peace settlement after World War I. If Hungary failed to rejuvenate its population, then it would be unable to maintain its territory and sustain its "rebirth" after the war.

Péter Vida, another proponent of large-scale demographic reordering, likewise made the case for "20 million." Stimulating the biological imperative to procreate in order to achieve a statistical majority was insufficient; assimilation and the repatriation of Hungarians from across the border would also be required.[59] To achieve "the rebirth of the idea of St. Stephen," Vida maintained that the "natural assimilation" of the various nationalities in the historical Hungarian Crown lands must continue apace. The small community of South Slavs known as the Bunjevci[60] and many others, he noted, had over time been integrated into the idea of the Hungarian state. Because the reconstruction of the Hungarian state could not rely solely on assimilation, whether natural or by force, the repatriation of foreign Hungarians was absolutely necessary, beginning with the Hungarians of Banovina in southern Croatia and the Hungarian Csangos of Moldavia. Vida was convinced that the numbers of Hungarians living in the east were grossly underestimated or else deliberately miscounted. The true numbers of Roman Catholics in Moldavia, according to Vida, were double the estimated 110,000, closer to 160,000 to 200,000. He argued that all Moldavian Catholics should be counted as Hungarians, even those who no longer spoke Hungarian, and even a number of those who had since converted to Orthodoxy.[61] Vida, however, was not content with repatriating the Hungarians from Yugoslavia and Romania. Rather all Hungarians from the east should be brought "home":

> A certain Hungarian tradition endures in the Caucasus, around Abkhazia. The most powerful tribe of Circassians, the Balkar-Kabardin, consider themselves Hungarians. Likewise, the Ingush are declared as having Hungarian origin. The descendants of the Ossetians, the Digor, pride themselves of their Hungarian origin. In Dagestan remain indisputable traces of the Hungarian people. Altogether this would be a mass of about half a million, and if we add related ethnic groups, one million. And in the same place, on the southwest slope of the Urals, where Brother Julian, the envoy of our King Béla IV,[62] found those consanguines of ours who are the Bashkirs, let us not forget that they are expecting us: they recently abandoned their writing in Cyrillic and replaced it with the Hungarian alphabet, which speaks loudly for the argument of their common origin with us.... If the fortune of war will favor our guns as it has up to now, armies will arrive in the course of their advance in the region of the Hungarians' ancestral homeland and then an opportunity will arise, as favorable as there has ever been, such that we can appropriate for ourselves the plan of Béla IV: to repatriate the Hungarians from the east.[63]

Resettlement "Home"

Meanwhile, Sándor Besenyő (known as Baumgartner before 1940),[64] a key figure in the Hungarian government's effort to relocate the Csangos, published a number of highly charged works depicting the plight of the Csangos at the hands of the merciless Romanian state.[65] Besenyő, who taught theology in the seminary in Iași around 1935–36, viewed the Csangos and the Szeklers as forming a solid ethnic block or "unit" of Hungarians, over six hundred thousand strong, on either side of the Carpathians. The Csangos—"the pride of the Hungarian race"—were engaged in a "life-and-death struggle to return to the greater national body" of the Hungarians.[66] In Besenyő's view, the Romanian state and the Orthodox Church were persecuting the Csangos in order "to wipe out their Hungarian consciousness—in short, to wage a war of extermination against them."[67]

As suggested by the title of one of his books, *Moldva: a magyarság nagy temetője* (Moldavia: great cemetery of the Hungarians), much of Besenyő's work sought to elevate the Hungarian ethnic and national consciousness of the Csangos while forewarning other Hungarians about the attrition of their fragile nation, which if not reversed would lead to its annihilation. His work was, furthermore, an invective against Romania:

> All this oppression, terrorism, and persecution by the Romanian state are in vain! The Moldavian Hungarians living in a mass of hundreds of thousands demand law and justice. They occupied the area before the Romanians, and despite the vicissitudes of history have held onto it for 1,200 years: they have survived the devastation of the Tatar-Cumans and have even survived Romanian oppression, which is still more barbaric and dangerous because of the war of extermination launched against their spiritual existence.... The conscience of Europe cannot allow the Romanian government to deny to the indigenous Hungarians of Moldavia the most basic human and national rights that even the savages receive.[68]

During World War II, Besenyő helped shape the discourse on the national identity of the Csangos and, moreover, was instrumental in relaying information about the status of Csango communities and their readiness to relocate to Hungary in the wake of the Bukovinan Szeklers. Evidently, he was well connected to Hungarian political and intellectual circles in both Hungary and Romania and helped compile a number of studies on the Csango population. In 1940–41, Besenyő worked as a press attaché in the Hungarian Embassy in Moscow, and in 1944 he served as a press secretary in the Hungarian Consulate in Brașov. Officially, his position within the Hungarian government was as a press secretary in the Hungarian Foreign Ministry, and thus he travelled on a diplomatic passport. From what little can be gleaned from archival records about his life story, it appears he worked clandestinely in Moldavia and had ties with Germany.[69]

Targeting Csangos for *Hazatelepítés*

In April 1941 Hungary permitted its territory to be used as a staging ground for the German blitzkrieg on Yugoslavia. Following the German onslaught, Hungarian troops annexed and occupied a portion of the Délvidék (southlands), territory that Hungary had ceded to the newly formed Kingdom of Serbs, Croats, and Slovenes (renamed the Kingdom of Yugoslavia in 1929) as a consequence of the Treaty of Trianon in 1920. The Hungarian Army occupied the southern tip of Baranya County and, to the southeast, the adjacent Bácska County. These territories already had some of the lowest birthrates among Hungarians, due in no small measure to the practice of *egyke* over previous generations.[70] Under Yugoslav rule in the 1920s and 1930s, the Yugoslav government implemented a number of policies aimed at de-Hungarianizing these territories, which in any case had a relative South Slav majority prior to World War I. With these territories back under Hungarian rule, the most pressing need for the Hungarian government was to reinforce this multiethnic border area by repopulating it with ethnic Hungarians.[71] Uprooting and restructuring Hungary's own population would be too difficult, and legislating its way to ethnic homogeneity would require time the country did not have. However, transferring en masse Hungarian kin from across its borders proved an attractive solution, especially given their treatment as undesirables in neighboring states.

Prime Minister László Bárdossy quickly drafted policies to expatriate non-ethnic Hungarians, to expropriate foreign-owned land and property, and to restock ethnically mixed areas with repatriated and presumably loyal Hungarians.[72] Already by the end of 1940, the Hungarian government had appointed the Transylvanian-born ethnographer Pál Péter Domokos (a Szekler) to a six-month assignment as a diplomat in the Hungarian Embassy in Bucharest.[73] Using his own fieldwork and data collected in the Csango-inhabited lands in Moldavia in the 1920s and 1930s, along with information taken from the 1930 Romanian census, Domokos identified Szekler villages in Bukovina and Csango villages in Moldavia that had a preponderance of linguistic and ethnic Hungarians suitable for resettlement into Hungary. Domokos produced several studies and maps for the Hungarian repatriation effort, categorizing the Csango villages according to race (*faj*) and mother tongue (*anyanyelv*).[74]

In a cable to the Hungarian Foreign Ministry written from Bucharest in December 1940, Domokos gave the following update: "I have made a list of the villages that could interest us from a Hungarian point of view ... and I will continue as my next assignment to find people to create a movement to encourage [the Hungarian-speaking Csangos] to opt for Hungarian citizenship." To aid this "movement," Domokos requested he be allowed to retain as his "assistants" a number of Roman Catholic priests from among the Bukovinan Szeklers. These priests, acting in the service of the Hungarian state, would encourage the Hungarian-speaking Csangos to petition the Romanian government for relocation to Hungary. Domokos further proposed exchanging the Greek Catholics of Bihar County for the Romanian Catholics in Moldavia and indicated that he would ask the bishop of Alba Iulia (effectively, the bishop over Transylvania) Áron Márton to inquire with the papal nuncio about transferring these populations.[75]

Domokos argued it was necessary to join the Csango resettlements with those of the Bukovinan Szeklers. Eventually, however, the Hungarian government pursued a strategy to resettle the Szeklers first, presumably because of their smaller numbers and more accessible location. While Domokos supported the resettlement of the Csangos in the 1940s and played a role in the early formulation of these plans, he eventually had a falling out with the leadership in the Hungarian Embassy in Bucharest over the relocation of the Csangos.[76] Domokos resigned his post some months later, just prior to official negotiations with Bucharest.

In February 1941 the Bárdossy government in Hungary formally proposed to the Antonescu regime in Romania the resettlement of the Bukovinan Szeklers into Hungary and even suggested a resettlement of populations modeled on the German-Romanian agreement in 1940, which facilitated the relocation of the German populations of Bukovina and Dobrudja to Germany.[77] The Romanian government was, for the moment, noncommittal, fearing ethnic Hungarians would be resettled in Northern Transylvania, a territory that Romania had every intention of reclaiming after the war. While Antonescu dithered, Hungarian agents worked clandestinely in Bukovina and Moldavia to encourage and mobilize communities there for *hazatelepítés*.[78]

On 19 April 1941, two weeks after the German-Hungarian invasion of Yugoslavia and two days before the Yugoslavs surrendered, Henrik Werth, the Hungarian Army's chief of General Staff, who developed Hungary's attack plans for the invasion of the Soviet Union and Yugoslavia, relayed to Bárdossy news from the Yugoslav front. Serbian troops had fled and civilians had been displaced, and the Hungarian Army had identified those sites emptied of

Yugoslav troops and thus available to resettle Hungarian families, "foremost the thousand-year-old Hungarians living outside the borders."[79] Werth, in fact, advocated a "total resettlement" of ethnic Hungarians inside Hungary and the removal of minorities—a reshuffling of around eight million people, he estimated—so as to reestablish and reinforce St. Stephen's "thousand-year borders" after the war.[80] Though not convinced of the feasibility of the ambitious plan, Bárdossy nevertheless proceeded with a more targeted and immediate plan for resettling the Bácska region, eschewing Teleki's original idea of relocating the community to the Bihar/Bihor and Szatmár/Satu Mare regions of western and northern Transylvania, respectively, or else to the Szekler land in eastern and southeastern Transylvania.[81]

Like many of the late interwar and wartime population policies undertaken in Hungary and Romania, Bárdossy's plan was modeled on and justified by similar undertakings in Nazi Germany. The decision to relocate Hungarians from across the border was made in a classified planning session led by Miklós Bonczos on 9 May 1941, which included the ministers of justice, finance, and agriculture, among others. Plans were made to create the Foreign Hungarians Repatriation Committee, with Bonczos as director. The minutes from the session reveal discussions on how best to move the Bukovinan Szeklers into the Bácska and southern Baranya, into those areas that were "being emptied" as part of the military campaign to clear the Hungarian-occupied part of Yugoslavia.[82]

It was only a few months later, in January 1942, that a series of raids later known as the "Délvidék Massacres" in Bácska took place, in which units from the Hungarian Army, gendarmes, and police executed approximately 2,550 Serbs and 700 Jews.[83] The massacre had come on the heels of a mass deportation of Jews from "newly liberated" Hungarian territories in the Felvidék (northlands or Upper Hungary) and Carpatho-Ruthenia as well as Budapest.[84] Roughly 18,000 Jews on Hungarian territory were rounded up, transferred across the border to German-occupied Poland, and handed over to the SS, after which they were summarily executed. Werth helped devise the plan and Bárdossy persuaded the Council of Ministers to authorize it.[85]

The Bárdossy government had to move quickly to resettle these Hungarians from across the border into the occupied territory, since 80–90 percent of the crops there had already been planted. Moreover, the civilian population in the occupied territory had begun stealing without compunction, making it imperative to begin resettlements immediately.[86] Additional pressure came from Germany, which demanded from Hungary surplus agricultural produce from its occupied corner of the Bácska, particularly wheat, maize, and flax.[87] As nearly 10,000 mainly agricultural South Slavs had been pushed off their land after the

Hungarian invasion, Bonczos recommended settling the first waves of immigrants in the homesteads of these southernmost territories. Thereafter, other Hungarians could resettle Upper Hungary. Similar to Werth's plan in both scope and mission, Bonczos's plan aimed to resettle with "foreign Hungarians" sixty-two different localities across the Hungarian borderlands: first, the Szeklers of Bukovina, 5,000 of whom were already in Hungary; then, the Hungarians from the Burgenland, approximately 18,000 strong; next, the Hungarians in Croatia, another 10,000; and later, the Csangos of Moldavia.[88] There were also plans to resettle some 57,000 Hungarians from Bosnia.[89] Furthermore, Bonczos insisted that the Szeklers be allocated larger plots of land so as to strengthen the Hungarians there, since in the south the remaining Serbs were strongly entrenched. To buttress these newly relocated foreign Hungarians, especially those from Moldavia, Bárdossy suggested settling down other categories of Hungarians, including refugees, the *vitézek* (distinguished World War I veterans), and the families of those men who had died or been injured in the current war.[90] Under mutual agreement between Bucharest and Budapest, the roughly 13,500 Szeklers of Bukovina left for Hungary in the second half of 1941 and were officially granted land and houses in Bácska.[91]

For its part, Romania was happy to oblige Hungary and rid Bukovina of its Hungarian population, provided those Hungarians were settled far away from any territory claimed by Romania. Bukovina, along with Bessarabia and Dobrudja, were three provinces that contained the lowest proportion of ethnic Romanians. A draft memorandum on a proposed law for colonization in the province, delivered to Antonescu's Council of Ministers, stressed the importance of redressing the ethnic imbalance in these eastern territories: "In respect to national and cultural interests, we find that numerous heterogeneous populations remain in these provinces. Ukrainians, Russians, Bulgarians, Gagauz, etc., were brought here in the past as part of the politics of denationalization, pursued methodically and constantly under Russian and Austrian domination. These populations continue to cultivate exclusionary ideologies and maintain hostile sentiments toward our nation. In some regions, these elements of foreign ethnic origin are gathered in compact masses, which exceed the Romanian element and represent a great danger to Romanian culture and to the defense of the country."[92]

The Csangos, however, posed a dilemma for the Antonescu regime. As detailed in the Antonescu government's secret service reports, the national identity and ethnic origin of the Csangos remained a matter of debate if also confusion. However, unlike the Szeklers, the Csangos and their clergy appeared, in the main, to assert a Romanian identity and an allegiance to the Romanian state. Csango villagers, parish priests, and the hierarchy in Iași continued to send letters to the Romanian government, pressing the Antonescu regime not to deprive the Moldavian Catholics of their citizenship rights as ethnic Romanians and not to relocate their community to Hungary.[93]

Contrary to the Romanian government's attitudes toward the Szeklers up to this point, and despite the Romanian Ministry of Justice's instructions to consider the Csangos as Hungarian and thus "foreigners," Antonescu and his close circle of advisors were not so quick to condemn the Csangos as hostile to or incompatible with the regime's new designs for an ethnically homogeneous Romania. Most of the antipathy directed at the Csangos came from the Orthodox Church and from local actors around Bacău, Roman, and Iași. In fact, the central government in Romania had paid little attention to the Csango communities until 1940, when Moldavia once again became a border region with Hungary after the Second Vienna Award. It was only after Romania's entry into the war in 1941 that the Hungarian government approached the Romanians about including the Csangos in a population transfer scheme similar to the one involving the Szeklers of Bukovina.

The Antonescu regime therefore had to weigh a number of factors. Where in Hungary would the Csangos be resettled? If they were resettled in Northern Transylvania, then surely this would increase the Hungarian population there, thereby increasing Hungary's chances of retaining the territory in a future peace settlement. And how would the Vatican view the resettlement of the Csangos outside of Romania? The Csangos represented the second largest contingent of Roman Catholics in Romania, after the Hungarian Catholics in Transylvania. How would moving this community to Hungary affect Romania's international standing, specifically its relations with other Catholic countries in Europe? Finally, the Antonescu government had to consider the broader impact of removing thousands of able-bodied men and their families out of a sensitive border region during a critical juncture of the war. What would this mean for the Csango men currently serving in the Romanian army on the Eastern Front? And what of the impact on industrial and agricultural production after depleting the local labor force in Moldavia? Was it really worth the diplomatic and bureaucratic time and effort, and the mobilization of precious resources, when Romania was following Germany eastward into the Soviet Union en route to Stalingrad?

Meanwhile, a small number of Csangos did opt to relocate to Hungary of their own accord. In September 1941 representatives of two Csango villages inquired at the Hungarian Embassy in Bucharest about relocating their villages to Hungary.[94] László Nagy, the Hungarian ambassador to Romania at the time, reported this to the Ministry of Foreign Affairs in Budapest, and thus began the effort to repatriate the Csangos en bloc. Over the course of the next six months,

Resettlement "Home"

about one hundred families applied for and received repatriation papers from the Hungarian embassy, with many of these individuals renouncing their Romanian citizenship. Historian Gábor Vincze cites evidence from the Hungarian Foreign Ministry archives that many more were willing to relocate.[95]

But in March 1942 the exigencies of war precluded the further resettling of Csangos into Hungary, as Admiral Miklós Horthy, regent of the Kingdom of Hungary, forced the resignation of the pro-Nazi Bárdossy in favor of Miklós Kállay, who promptly pursued a more independent Hungarian domestic and foreign policy by attenuating Hungary's alliance with Hitler, restraining Hungary's fascist Arrow Cross Party, and even making overtures to the Allies.[96] The two-year rule of the Kállay government (March 1942–March 1944) halted Hungary's population policies, cracked down on extreme right-wing groups, and modulated the country's alliance with Germany. More important for those Csangos who did not want to be relocated to Hungary, Kállay ended the business of population transfers, whether forced, negotiated, or otherwise. Kállay's counterpart in Romania, Marshal Antonescu, had likewise halted the deportation of Jews and Roma to Transnistria. Thus, by the end of spring 1942, only a small number of Csangos—around 40 families, some 160 individuals—had been repatriated to southern Hungary.[97]

Attempts to resettle the Csangos would not be retried until early 1944, after the collapse of the Eastern Front, Germany's occupation of Hungary that spring, and a return to a Hitler-backed prime ministership of the country under Döme Sztójay, who promptly recommenced the deportation of Jews from Hungary and restarted talks with Romania about relocating the Csangos. For Bonczos, who was now elevated to minister of interior, as well as other supporters of *hazatelepítés*, the regime change offered the best opportunity since the invasion of Yugoslavia to restart negotiations with Romania on transferring the Csangos. Bonczos had estimated a month earlier that, "with the right propaganda," approximately fifteen thousand Csango families (or seventy-five thousand individuals) could be relocated from Romania, even without the Romanian government's consent. In April, Besenyő and Hungarian Army reconnaissance officials secretly visited some Csango villages around Bacău County to assess the readiness of Csango families to relocate to Hungarian territory. They also established "cells" of "reliable men" in these villages to recruit families for voluntary relocation.[98] On 13 May, however, Besenyő was arrested by the gendarmerie in Bacău, accused of making propaganda in the Csango communities. Two days later he escaped his military escort en route to Bucharest, where he was to be interrogated and tried.[99]

A report from the Hungarian 19th and 22nd Army Administrative Command endorsed this view of returning the Csangos to the Hungarian nation, even if it meant taking the Hungarian nation to the Csangos in Moldavia: "The lives of the Moldavian Hungarians, as the documents show, began before Moldavia was established. In this way, we have historical rights over Moldavia. To claim back Moldavia, or even take it back with the power of the army, this is the Hungarian challenge. [The Csangos] are still worth much more than that of the most educated population from the country of St. Stephen."[100] The Hungarian people, lamented the author of the report, were ignorant of the "Hungarians who are flesh from their flesh, blood from their blood," who were left in a state of humiliation and anguish by man and God alike. Bonczos's new plan, however, was contingent on events, namely an evacuation of Moldavia after the impending Soviet invasion of eastern Romania. In this scenario, much of the Moldavian population was expected to evacuate Moldavia through the Szekler land, which remained part of Hungarian-ruled Northern Transylvania.

Instruments of Policy and the Rise of Clericalism

Hungarian discourse on the *hazatelepítés* schemes and on Romanian persecution of the Csangos found its way into Moldavia. A November 1942 report from the Romanian secret service out of Bacău noted that over the previous year many institutes, associations, journals, and newspapers in Hungary were preoccupied with the Csango question. In particular, the Kisebbségi Intézetének Kiadványai (Institute for Minorities Publications) in Pécs had published several nationalist books on the Csangos. Also, "leading Hungarian circles" were recruiting local Transylvanian villagers, loyal to the Hungarian cause, to propagandize from one Csango village to the next.[101]

Another report in December noted that Antal László and Dénes Elekes, two priests who hailed from a community of Bukovinan Szeklers that had recently resettled in Bácska, were reappointed as vicars to the Catholic parishes in Văleni and in Valea-Seacă in Moldavia. According to this report, László "proved to be in the service of Hungary" and was spreading Hungarian propaganda throughout the Csango villages he served. On the basis of information relayed to the episcopate in Iași by the parish priest Albert Weber, this report claimed that László was "looking to win people over to his side, giving them money and saying that the Csangos are Hungarian and that their country is Hungary." Elsewhere the report mentioned Hungarian actions "led by Budapest agents," notably Hungarian priests, to distribute across Moldavia nationalist prayer books in Hungarian.[102] Yet another report detailed one of

László's sermons in Văleni: "Whoever wants to immigrate to Hungary can go as they will. There they will be given 15 hectares of land and will receive other advantages."[103]

In spring 1941 the Romanian authorities intercepted a dispatch from Budapest to the Hungarian Legation in Bucharest. The dispatch concerned the use of Hungarian clergy in Romania for propaganda and was to be circulated among Romania's Calvinist, Roman Catholic, and Unitarian clerics sympathetic to the Hungarian cause: "The priest is the first and most important agent of national propaganda, because he has the best means to accomplish this work. The church does not need to be an altar only, so long as it can play the role of a secret political tribune, where conationals can exchange information, receive orders, and submit reports."[104]

Documents from the Hungarian Foreign Ministry reveal that in fact some of these Hungarian priests were working in the service of the Hungarian government. Dénes Elekes's mother, who was among those Szeklers resettled in Bácska, wrote plaintively to Prime Minister Bárdossy requesting that her son be allowed to rejoin his family in Bácska. She noted that he had permission and repatriation papers to leave Romania for Hungary, "which in a moment he had to give back at the Hungarian Embassy in Bucharest" because, she writes, of "an order from above." Instead of relocating to Hungary, her son and another priest were instructed to return to Moldavia to "fulfill a mission," namely to encourage the Csangos to renounce their Romanian citizenship and relocate themselves to Hungary.[105] A report from the Office of the Prime Minister acknowledged that Dénes was indeed ordered back to Moldavia. The author of the report surmised that "from the previous documents it can be determined that the continued residence of [these priests] who are living among the Moldavian Csangos is needed." Those priests who had left Moldavia for Hungary did so only "because of the attitude of the Romanian authorities," which subsequently deported them from Romania.[106]

That a number of Catholic priests loyal to Hungary were active in persuading the Hungarians in Bukovina and Moldavia to relocate to Hungary is not disputed. Using priests as agents of national policy to relocate foreign Hungarians presents a more complex historical picture of the events and personalities in Bukovina and Moldavia during this period. While the documentary evidence remains incomplete—and much of it circumstantial—it does dispel any lingering notions that these Csango villagers, as a result of some timely awakening of their Hungarian national consciousness and a desire to reconnect with a Hungarian homeland, themselves initiated or drove the resettlement schemes, as some historians contend.[107] Rather, the Hungarian government, nationalist parties and institutes, and the Hungarian churches were primarily responsible for promoting this "desire to return home."

The motives of those imputing a willingness of the Csangos to be repatriated to Hungary—and, moreover, to regard Hungary as a national homeland—should be viewed in the context of Hungary's post-Trianon and World War II political aims.[108] The Hungarian government endeavored to reclaim lost territories and to repopulate them with ethnic Hungarians from across the border. When led by the likes of Bárdossy, Werth, Bonczos, and Sztójay, the Hungarian state pursued these aims with zeal. They used warfare to cleanse heterogeneous areas such as the Délvidék and then used loyal clergy and Hungarian nationals to encourage "foreign Hungarians" in Bukovina and Moldavia to renounce their Romanian citizenship and colonize Hungarian-occupied Yugoslavia.

By contrast, men such as Domokos, Németh, and Besenyő, who had direct experience in the Szekler and Csango villages, advocated the resettlement of the Szeklers and Csangos on the basis of what they believed to be the genuine welfare and interest of these communities. They were often critical of what they perceived to be the Hungarian government's use of these populations as mere tools or surrogates for the homogenization of Bácska and Baranya Counties.[109] Nevertheless, these activists viewed the Csangos as integrally linked to the Hungarian nation, separated by an age-old border and long trapped inside a hostile Romanian nation not their own.

The resettlement schemes gave rise to a new form of local clericalism that impacted national and even international politics. To be sure, priests in east-central Europe had long played roles as partisans, historians, instruments of national policy, and arbiters of collective national consciousness. Beginning in the 1930s, and certainly by World War II, however, the agency and activism of many clerics became indistinguishable from that of their counterparts in the secular intelligentsia. In the Csango region, the inability to obtain certificates of Romanian ethnic origin combined with the threat of being deported to Hungary would spur a clerical counteraction, one that aimed, first, to thwart the expatriation of the Hungarian-speaking Catholics rom the region and, second, to restore the civic rights of the community as ethnic Romanian citizens.

These two forces—one internal, another external—created the conditions in which a handful of Csango priests would refashion the ethnic identity and historical narrative of the Csangos as "good Romanians." In this endeavor, Father Iosif Petru M. Pal would lead the way.

6

The Cry of Blood
The Csangos Recertified

The infiltration of Hungarian publications and "agents" stoking a Hungarian national consciousness among the Csangos and encouraging them to resettle in Hungarian-occupied territory unnerved the Catholic clergy back in Moldavia. The clerical elite of the Iași diocese perceived these incursions as existential threats to their community. To combat what they viewed as Hungarian propaganda and meddling in their parishes, a group of intellectuals formulated and asserted their own set of historicist claims. In short order, they assailed the Hungarian historical narrative about the Csangos, accusing not only the Hungarians but also many Romanians of denying the reality, as they saw it, about the Romanian origins of the Csangos.

The Great Intercessor: Father Iosif Petru M. Pal

Iosif Petru M. Pal belonged to the Franciscan order and was a parish priest of Luizi-Călugăra, near Bacău. He held a doctorate, spoke many languages, and taught theology and philosophy at Catholic seminaries in Moldavia. As a young man in his twenties, Pal lived and studied in Rome, where he was ordained in 1916.[1] Upon his return to Romania, he became head of the Franciscan order in Moldavia and one of the most influential members in the hierarchy of the Iași diocese. During World War II, Pal regularly wrote to Marshal Antonescu, Mihai Antonescu, and the apostolic nuncio in Bucharest, Andrea Cassulo, enumerating the litany of injustices perpetrated against the Moldavian Catholics since the start of the war. His intent was to change the Romanian government's perception of the Catholics as foreigners—as Hungarians—and thereby reverse the government's policy of discrimination against the community.

Pal's discussion and history of the Csangos sought to negate claims that Orthodoxy was an essential component of Romanianism, bolstering Iosif Frollo's arguments against Nae Ionescu and the Romanian Orthodoxists some ten years earlier. Moreover, he endeavored to portray the majority of Orthodox Romanians, especially those in Moldavia who surrounded the Roman Catholics, as "brothers in blood and arms" with the Csangos and, furthermore, to depict the relations between the two communities as historically fraternal and peaceful. Careful to reject extremist notions of race, he nevertheless emphasized the role of blood as a marker of national belonging by showing consanguinity and shared ancestry among the Catholics and Orthodox in Moldavia, which stemmed from several autochthonous communities in the Transcarpathian space. Finally, Pal asserted that the Csangos' Catholicism was in fact a marker of their "Romanity" (*romanitatea*) and "Latinity" (*latinitatea*)—a testament to the continuity of Romania's historical, religious, and prenational heritage unique to the Csangos. In this respect, the Csangos were not the antithesis of Romanianness but rather a paragon of it. The weight of these arguments, Pal hoped, would demonstrate that the ethnic origin of the Csangos—and hence their nationality—was, and always had been, *Romanian*, and that the strength of their religion was actually a marker of their ethnicity.

Pal employed a range of sources to support his claims about the Romanian ethnic origin of the Csangos, from papal bulls, census data, Propaganda Fide, missionary reports and codices to contemporaneous works such as Popa-Lisseanu's on the denationalization of Transylvanian Romanians.[2] Pal detected an anomaly in Popa-Lisseanu's statistics concerning some Romanian villages in the Szekler land in the mid-eighteenth century, an anomaly that indicated a rapid population decrease in the area and the wholesale disappearance of a number of villages. From his reading of church and other historical records, Pal linked the disappearance of these Romanian Transylvanians to a concomitant influx of Catholics into Moldavia from the mid-eighteenth century. These Catholics bolstered existing Catholic settlements there, which dated from the founding of Catholic bishopric of Cumania in 1227.[3]

Pal concluded that these late-eighteenth-century immigrants into Moldavia were Romanian Greek Catholics from Transylvania, accompanied by a number of Romanian Roman Catholics and even Calvinists, who were actually Hungarianized Romanians. Because of years of Hungarianization by the Szeklers as well as Saxons, the names and mother tongue of these newcomers appeared to be Hungarian. That the vast majority of Moldavian Catholics would subsequently be mistaken for Hungarians or "Csangos" was due to a misunderstanding about the provenance and identity of these newcomers. He recalled that in 1763 even the bishop of Bacău, Raymundus Jezierski, reported to the Vatican that large numbers of Catholics from Transylvania had entered Moldavia. Because these immigrants had long been under Hungarian domination, the locals apparently referred to them as "Hungarians." These immigrants introduced a dialect of the Hungarian language and Hungarian patronyms to the otherwise "authentic" Romanian Catholic community. For Pal, the Hungarian elements among the Moldavian Catholics were therefore superficial and inauthentic: rather, "the ethnology, ethnography and ethnicity of this population is authentically Romanian," and therefore "all Catholics in Moldova are only *Romanian* Catholics."[4]

In 1942 Pal published what would prove to be a seminal work in the dispute over the Csangos' ethnogenealogy. His monograph, *Originea Catolicilor din Moldova* (The origin of the Catholics of Moldavia), was both a historical survey and an ethnonational manifesto.[5] Pal rejected not only the Hungarian ethnogenesis of the Csangos but also the Csango ethnonym itself. "Csango" was an appellation reflecting "the aspirations of Hungarians from Budapest," he contended. Furthermore, "the only true name worthy of the Catholics of Moldavia is *Romanian Catholics*." For Pal, the Catholics of Moldavia were "native, authentic Romanians," whose ethnic origin was Romanian "and in no way Hungarian." Pal also revisited the polemic of Nae Ionescu and Iosif Frollo concerning the individuation of Orthodoxy and Romanianness, declaring the Csangos no less Romanian than the Orthodox Moldavians. Great Orthodox Romanian leaders such as Mihail Kogălniceanu and Costache Negri saw no problem in counting the Csangos as proper Romanians, he noted, yet contemporary Romanian political and church leaders insisted on counting them as Hungarians: "Even today when the laws of the country consider the Catholics to be 'good Romanians,' with rights equal to the Orthodox, there can still be found those who deny them in particular the right to social and public life, in the affairs of the country and army, as well as in education, based solely on the principle that they are Hungarians, that is to say, they are Catholics."[6]

The efforts of Romanian authorities to strip the Catholics of their rights as Romanian citizens, Pal believed, was attributable solely to religious discord, caused by a coterie of Orthodoxist, ultranationalist intellectuals. He was, nevertheless, at pains to absolve the majority of Orthodox believers: "Thank God there are enough Orthodox in this country who realize that the Orthodox faith is not an integral part of the idea of Romanianness." In everyday life, of course, Pal and his fellow Roman Catholics confronted a rising anti-Catholicism and were all too aware that exclusivist sentiments linking Orthodoxy and nationality were indeed widespread, promoted mainly by local Orthodox priests in

Moldavia. Taking the Orthodoxists to task, he wrote of the senselessness of regarding Orthodoxy as an "essential" component of Romanianness:

> Who would admit that the Greek, the Bulgarian, the Russian or the Serb is Romanian because he is Orthodox? Thus, to be Romanian it is insufficient simply to be Orthodox. Thus, logic demands that the rights as *good Romanians*, that is to be good members of the Romanian nation, not be denied the Moldavian Catholics simply because they are not Orthodox, since they meet all of the essential qualifications—both philosophical and juridical—of those required for belonging to the *Romanian nation*. It is not possible to give any credence to the objections of those who contend that Romanianism is solidified through the influx of Orthodoxy. Did the Romanians not exist as a people before the founding of the Romanian Principalities? And who does not know that the Romanian people, until the end of the ninth century, adhered to the pope of Rome and even belonged to the Latin rite, as befitting a Latin people such as ours?[7]

Again, echoing Frollo, Pal lamented the lack of progress and understanding about the issue of religion and nationality, still so heavily influenced by the writings of Ionescu and Nichifor Crainic. Too many Romanians took for granted what he termed the "convertibility" of the words *Romanian* and *Orthodox*, which led to the conclusion that "the Romanian is the Orthodox, and the Orthodox is the Romanian." What, he asked, about the Romanians who for centuries were Orthodox but recently became Adventists, Anabaptists, Evangelicals, and Repenters (*pocăiți*) as well as Freemasons, agnostics, and atheists? Have all of these ceased to be Romanian?[8]

According to Pal, the heightened interest in the Csangos by the Hungarians was a product of the modern Hungarian nationalist movement; before the end of the nineteenth century, the Csangos had largely been absent from Hungarian national consciousness. Frenzied by post-Trianon revisionism and irredentism, Hungarians were now attempting "to stretch their egomania" across the Carpathians and into Moldavia. Hungarian ethnographers walked "uninvited" throughout the region, "seeing only Hungarians on the fields, covetous of our beautiful Moldavia, being that here and there they hear some Hungarian jargon being spoken, largely incomprehensible to the real Hungarians." Hungarian ethnologists, musicologists, and historians had likewise become enamored with the Csangos, "dreaming of the possibility of spreading Hungary across the mighty Carpathians, at least to the Siret [River], if not to the Prut or even the Dniester."

Equally contemptible, in Pal's view, were the few Romanian writers who had even bothered to write about the Csangos. Out of sheer ignorance, they had accepted Hungarian historical and ethnographical narratives about the origin, language, and culture of the community. Consequently, these Romanian authors dismissed the Csangos as a peculiar if not pernicious little community of foreigners: "Too easily they passed judgment on us, considering us as foreigners, as Hungarians; and even when they did not condemn us as such, they frequently suspected us as enemies of the Romanian fatherland."[9] Such historical misinterpretations had "overshadowed the entire physiognomy of the origin of the Moldavian Catholics" and for this reason had led to their being counted as Hungarians simply because they were Catholic.

If Pal was to convince the Orthodox community and the Romanian government that the Csangos were Romanian by origin, then he first had to articulate a definition of nationality in which the Csangos could be included alongside their Orthodox brethren. Pal rejected any exclusivist racial ideas and discourses about a "pure" Romanian racial type. He insisted that "common ancestry" was not the result of an unbroken lineage but rather arose from "the same mixture" of autochthonous peoples: "Neither in civilized Europe nor in the wild regions of Africa is it possible today to find a people who might have come from the same lineage; everywhere we find an ethnic mix of many peoples. Our Romanian nation in principle is a Daco-Romano-Slavic mixture." Pal is relying here on historian Constantin C. Giurescu's and Eugen Petit's hypothesis about the ethnic foundation, composition, and character of the Romanian people as being formed from an admixture of Slav, Dacian, and Roman "elements." Within this autochthonous brew, Pal discerned a mixing with "other, foreign blood," trace elements of which had been added to the autochthonous elements, forming the basis of the Romanian people. However, this infusion of foreign blood was no less a reality for the Orthodox population of Moldavia than it was for the Catholics. What was more important than the precise ethnic or racial composition of the present-day Romanian people was their common historical and ancestral genesis, which existed a priori of any religious sectarianism in the Romanian principalities.

For Pal, nationality was rooted in a common origin of agglomerated autochthonous peoples living together in a shared space: "Thus in our case, affirming that the Catholics of Moldova are *Romanians by origin*, I affirm that in our veins flows in the greatest proportion Romanian blood, i.e., we have the same ancestors as the Orthodox of Moldova." In fact, the Csangos' Catholicism was proof of their "Romanity" and "Latinity," which was, in turn, proof of their continuity with the ancient Romans: "With small interruptions, [the Moldavian Catholics] have maintained true Romanity through both blood and faith; i.e., they are formed from an ethnic basis that is doubly connected to Mother Rome, and since they are Catholics they cannot be stripped of their rights to be counted as true Romanian descendants of the illustrious Roman people, as in fact they are." In this way, Pal linked the Csangos to the foundation myth of the Romanian people and nation, historicized in the Roman conquest of Dacia in the second and third centuries: "Beyond a doubt, we are over seventy percent Romanian by origin—i.e., we are Romanian and in no way Hungarian, as our Orthodox brethren have labeled us." This, despite the fact that the ancient Romans had occupied the Dacian province for less than two centuries while the Hungarians had for a millennium populated and ruled over the Carpathian basin.[10]

How could Pal explain the presence of Hungarians in Moldavia? The answer lay in the answer to another question: "Who settled Transylvania first, Romanians or Hungarians?" The provenance of Hungarians in Transylvania had preoccupied Romanian historians for generations (and in some circles, continues to preoccupy them). As outlined in a previous chapter, denationalization theories—specifically, the Hungarianization and Catholicization of Transylvanian Romanians in the Middle Ages—advanced by Romanian historians and social and biomedical scientists offered the most popular, if also most convenient, explanation of the presence of Hungarian speakers in Transylvania. Pal, therefore, had a ready-made template to explain, in turn, the presence of Hungarian speakers in Moldavia. After the "invasion of the Hungarians" in Transylvania, he contends, many of the Romanians there—"the only indigenous people"—wittingly and unwittingly aided these Hungarian invaders. Much of the Romanian nobility, most notably, appropriated Hungarian customs, "thereby losing their [Romanian] nationality." The Hungarianized Romanians in time lost their Romanian language and customs. Those in the southern Szekler land also adopted Calvinism, while those in the northern Szekler land, at the entryway to the Ghimeş Pass connecting Transylvania to Moldavia, adopted Roman Catholicism. Though the Hungarianized and Catholicized Romanians in the north had lost their ancestral nationality and language, Pal took solace from the fact that they had "at least won spiritually by returning to their ancestral religion," namely, the Christianity of Rome. For it is well known, remarked Pal, "that the ancestors of Romanians received the Christian religion from Rome in the Latin rite—i.e., they were Catholics." Regrettably, the Calvinized Romanians "lost everything," becoming tools of oppression in the hands of the Hungarians, "the fiercest persecutors" of non-Szeklerized Romanians.[11]

As Pal indicated, autochthonous Catholics had resided in Moldavia since at least the thirteenth century. Numerous populations, mostly from Transylvania, streamed through the Csango land over the next five hundred years. These newcomers naturally brought with them different religious practices, customs, and languages, "nearly extinguishing Catholicism." However, if the immigrants who spilled into Moldavia from across the Carpathians, bolstering the Catholic population there, were denationalized Romanians, then their descendants, the present-day Catholics of Moldavia, were therefore "Romanian by blood and not some strays (*pripășiți*), foreigners to the Romanian nation." Moreover, the Romanian Orthodox inhabitants of Moldavia—including populations of Romanians, Cumans, Szeklers, and Saxons—were themselves comprised of assimilated Catholics. Consequently, "in the veins of the Orthodox flows over the centuries the same blood as in the veins of our Catholics."[12]

Reinforcing the Romanian Narrative

In promoting an alternative historical narrative that presupposed a Romanian ethnogenealogy of the Csangos in lieu of a Hungarian one, both clerical and secular advocates for Pal's thesis began to publish articles and monographs of their own.[13] Romanian geographer Victor Tufescu wrote of the "waves of Csangos" that had "infiltrated" the region of Târgul Frumos, whose eastern part overlaps the area inhabited by the so-called "northern Csangos."[14] Tufescu acknowledged that, indeed, waves of Hungarians had settled the region over previous centuries, though Romanians had assimilated most of them by the eighteenth century. Newer but smaller waves of Hungarians and Szeklers arriving in the nineteenth and early twentieth centuries "grafted" themselves onto remnants of older Hungarian settlements. However, Tufescu argued that the communities of Catholics east of the Siret River and west of the Moldavian plain—his geographical area of interest—were denationalized by the Hungarians and Szeklers traversing the Târgul Frumos gateway, en route to the tiny settlements in the Cotnari region on the Moldavian plain: "The result was the estrangement (*înstrăinare*) of all of these villages,[15] which, with total certainty—as confirmed by documents—were purely Romanian up to the seventeenth century. This was only a relative estrangement, however, as in almost none of the cited villages can Hungarian be heard, and the so-called Csangos from there consider it an insult to be called *Hungarian* and not *Romanian*. Today, only their Catholicism distinguishes them from the autochthonous population."[16]

In 1942 the parish priest of Gherăești and former Legionary sector chief who had been imprisoned by Antonescu the previous year, Father Ioan Mărtinaș, published a monograph challenging the long-held assumptions about the Csangos' Hungarian ethnic origin. Mărtinaș's work was in many ways a reformulation of Pal's thesis, affirming the Romanian origin and ethnonational sentiment of the Moldavian Catholics.[17] Accordingly, he concluded, the Catholics of Moldavia were in the main Transylvanian Romanians who emigrated from Transylvania after 1700; they had for centuries been "Hungarianized" and subjected to a policy of "Hungarian chauvinism." Mărtinaș acknowledged, however, that although the ethnic origin of some Catholics was indeed foreign, they had long been "naturalized" as Romanians. How many hundreds of thousands of Romanians today, he asked, were not in some way the product of Hungarians, Szeklers, Germans, and Poles that lived in the region during the time of the great voivodes and princes in the late Middle Ages? Moreover, elsewhere in Romania, those whose ancestors were undoubtedly of Russian, Greek, or Bulgarian ethnic origin—"Have they not all disappeared into the Romanian mass?" After hundreds of years, "are there still pure Hungarians, Germans, and Poles?" To Mărtinaș, the answer to all of these questions was obvious: "They are true Romanians through language and sentiment. Only the names of some of them tell us of their old ethnic origin."[18] Half the nation's boyars were of foreign origin, he observed; the Romanian nation had canonized them as heroes and founders, yet shunned the Catholic multitude as strangers in their own land.

While Mărtinaș acknowledged the ethnic heterogeneity that characterized Moldavia over the centuries, he nevertheless asserted that the great majority of Catholics in Moldavia were not some "Romanianized element" of foreigners but rather "authentic Romanians." Their Catholicism was the product of historical forces and events—invasions, immigrations spurred by epidemics and religious persecutions or heresies, conversions from Orthodoxy, and the influx of Catholics from Transylvania[19]—that replenished the Catholic population of Moldavia over the ages: "The truth is that they are true Romanians through sentiment, language, and ethnic origin, and their Catholic religion connects them to the ancestral religion of the Romanians from the first millennium and to Old Mother Rome, which defended and cultivated yesterday and today Catholic Orthodoxy (*ortodoxia catolică*). . . . It is time to stop neglecting history and reality, to give the Moldavian Catholics the right to be called true Romanians, to no longer be insulted by their love of nation and country, to no longer be shown in speeches and school textbooks as Hungarians and foreigners, to no longer toss around the epithet "Csangos" because *Csangos do not exist.*"[20]

Blood and the Ethnic Unmasking of the "So-Called Csango-Hungarians"

A number of Romania's most enterprising social and biomedical scientists of the interwar period found themselves in important institutional and policy-making positions in Marshal Antonescu's wartime government. Disciplines such as geography, demography, eugenics, and anthropology—including racial anthropology and the study of ethnic origins—were no longer niche sciences, for they became important tools wielded by the state to collect detailed demographic information and exercise state power. Research on populations both at home and on the Eastern Front had diplomatic as well as military applications. It was also essential for the development and implementation of population policies, namely the effort to ethnically homogenize or "purify" certain territories.

Among the most important Romanian scientists writing on minority populations were the aforementioned Petru Râmneanţu, Anton Golopenţia, and Iordache Făcăoaru. In addition to their writings on the Transylvanian populations of Romanians and Hungarians, Râmneanţu, Golopenţia, and others investigated the ethnic basis and demography of the Csangos in Moldavia and other purportedly Romanian communities residing in Moravia and the Timoc valley (in Serbia and part of Bulgaria), known as the *timoceni*.[21] During World War II, Făcăoaru undertook extensive anthropometric research in Transnistria to examine the ethnic makeup of the Romanians living there. Under the auspices of the Central Institute for Statistics, within the division known as Identificarea Românilor de la Est de Bug or IREB (Identification of Romanians East of the Bug River), Golopenţia headed up research teams for expeditions outside the territory of the Romanian-controlled Governorate of Transnistria, all in an effort to identify ethnic Romanians across the border (*românii de peste hotare*).[22]

The serological research and subsequent publications on the Csangos by eugenicist Petru Râmneanţu would have enormous implications for the community. Through the indexing of blood groups, Râmneanţu provided, by the scientific standard of the day, confirmation of the Csangos' Romanian ethnic origin. His research legitimated claims by the Catholic clergy in Iaşi and Bucharest as well as those Romanian historians and politicians who rejected out of hand the presumptions that Hungarians had colonized and continuously inhabited the Romanian Old Kingdom since about the fourteenth century. Râmneanţu's data furthermore supported the Csangos' efforts to obtain the much-coveted certificates of ethnic Romanian origin from the Antonescu government. In turn, the validation of their Romanian ethnic origins would forestall efforts to "repatriate" the community to Hungary.

Râmneanțu had been a student of, and assistant to, Romania's leading eugenicist, the Sibiu-based medical doctor and professor Iuliu Moldovan. Influenced heavily by Moldovan's vision of national eugenics, Râmneanțu produced an enormous body of research and publications on the hereditary background and biological potential of the Romanian population.[23] Beginning in September 1942, he traveled through Tecuci, Bacău, and Neamț Counties in western Moldavia to conduct serological and anthropological research on the populations there, particularly on schoolchildren and young men in the Premilitară.[24] It is evident that the Antonescu regime commissioned Râmneanțu to validate Pal's claims about the Romanian ethnic origins of the Csangos. This kind of research, however, was also part of a broader research agenda and system of teams across Romania, coordinated by Moldovan and the Institute of Hygiene and Public Health.

Through serological work and the indexing of blood groups, Râmneanțu believed he could solve a number of historical dilemmas regarding the multiethnic composition of large parts of Romania.[25] In 1943 Râmneanțu published an article detailing the blood groups of the Csangos and in 1944 a monograph titled *Die Abstammung der Tschangos*. In these two works—the only such works on the Csangos produced by a Romanian racial anthropologist—Râmneanțu deployed the highly specialist and authoritative language of serology and racial anthropology to the narrative of Csango ethnogenesis. He claimed that, considering the history of the Csangos and the recent demographic evolution reflected in the census of 1941—revealing that the vast majority of Csangos had chosen "Romanian" as their ethnicity—the tendency of their ethnic consciousness was to declare themselves Romanian rather than Hungarian. The ethnic consciousness of the Csangos was, therefore, a natural consequence and manifestation of their biological reality.

Râmneanțu contested the long-accepted Hungarian theories on the settlement of the Csangos, namely that they were a group separated from the main body of the Hungarians or else were Hungarianized Cumans. Instead, Râmneanțu developed a biologically grounded theory positing the Romanian ethnic origin of the Csangos, as evidenced by his serological research in the Csango villages of Grozești, Luizi-Călugăra, Lespezi, and Fundu-Răcăciuni in Bacău County; Bârgăoani in Neamț County; and Unguri in Tecuci County. In this way, he extracted the Csangos from Hungary's national body and inserted them into Romania's. After conducting research in the Csango villages, Râmneanțu arrived at the very same conclusion as Pal: "The majority of the Catholics of Moldavia are natives and, as such, are of ethnic Romanian origin with Romanian mother tongue."

Râmneanțu also rejected the Csango ethnonym. Except for trace numbers of Hungarians (around 8,523) in southwestern Moldavia dispersed along the banks of the Siret River, Râmneanțu rejected even the existence of a community of so-called Csangos, or those classified as "non-Romanian Catholics" with a Hungarian mother tongue: "A Csango ethnic space does not exist, nor do there exist any pure Csango villages.... Moreover, there has never existed a village with Hungarians-Csangos."[26] In this respect, it was impossible to speak of a homogeneous area inhabited by Csangos or Hungarians without including the hundreds of thousands of "purely Romanian" communities residing in between. Even these trace numbers of "so-called Csango Hungarians" never imagined themselves living within an enclosed ethnic space, claimed Râmneanțu. Such settlements merely bore the remnants of a more recent Hungarian "infiltration" into areas already densely populated by "native Romanians." In all, according to Râmneanțu, the so-called Csangos ranged from 7 to 9 percent of the Csango region, and just 3.1 percent of all Moldavia.[27]

These were truly radical assertions. Romanians and Hungarians alike had long assumed the Moldavian Catholics represented "a continuity of the same hereditary strain" in the east Carpathian space, from the thirteenth century up to the present. Râmneanțu challenged this assumption, claiming that the original ethnic structure of the Catholics there was replaced with an altogether new one, namely an authentically Romanian one, as further evidenced by alternating periods of rapid population growth and decline in Moldavia. To confirm this thesis, Râmneanțu proposed identifying the ethnic origin of the Moldavian Catholics on the methodological basis of blood-group frequency. For this method to be valid, their "biological material" (blood and other somatic data) had to reveal the community as a homogeneous group and therefore descendent from a common origin.

The results were predictable. Even those eight thousand or so "real Csangos" proved, through the serological data collected and interpreted by Râmneanțu, to be Romanian by ethnic origin, for their blood-group index was closer to the Romanians than to the Hungarians. The results showed that, in fact, the Csangos were none other than Szeklers from Transylvania, "and as we all know, the Szeklers are actually a Romanian population."[28] Since the founding of the Catholic bishopric of Cumania in 1227, there were indeed Romanian Catholics; however, because of repeated invasions and the colonization of Moldavia by Szeklerized Romanians (under Hungarian domination), the Hungarian language had taken hold in some parts of the region. No matter. Even if these "established elements" were Hungarianized and Catholicized, there "can be no question of an identity convergence between 'Hungarian' and 'Catholic.'"

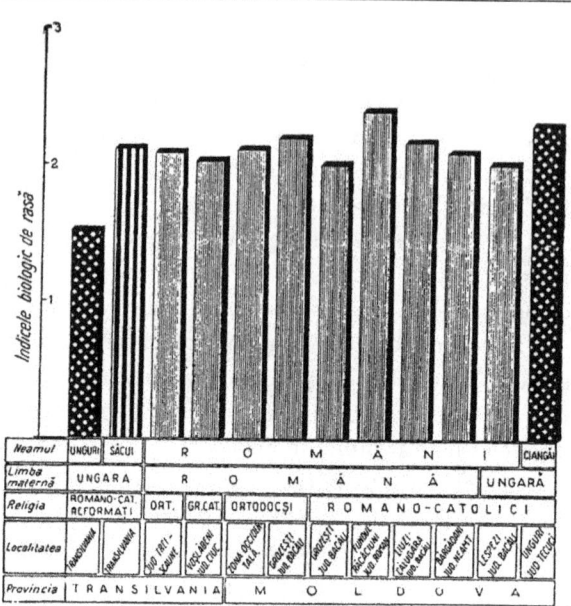

Fig. 1. — *Indicele biologic de rasă*. (Hirszfeld).

Blood-group frequency chart of the Moldavian Csangos, with their "biological index of race," according to Romanian racial anthropologist Petru Râmneanţu, who used the Polish immunologist Ludwig Hirszfeld's method to show that the Csangos were racially much closer to the Romanians than to Hungarians or Szeklers. (Râmneanţu, "Grupele de Sânge la Ciangăii din Moldova")

The bulk of the Catholics living in Moldavia descended from Szeklerized Romanians, who colonized the area between 1741 and 1824, and from Orthodox Romanians of Moldavia, who during this time converted to Catholicism: "They have mistakenly been called Csangos, and now their true Romanian nationality can be proven for the vast majority of them."[29]

Any ambiguity regarding the ethnic origin of the so-called Csangos could now be removed: racially they were Romanians, not Hungarians. According to Râmneanțu's results, the present-day community was never Hungarian in the first place—thus there was no ancestral Hungarian homeland to return to, only a Moldavian one to remain in. Through serology, Râmneanțu dismantled the linkage between religion and nationality used by many Romanian nationalists since the 1930s.[30] The Romanian government, the Orthodox and Catholic churches, and, not least, the community members themselves must reject any affirmations of the so-called Csangos' ethnic identity linked to custom, language, or religion (attributes most prone to assimilation), for the community's identity was now established by the immutability of blood.[31] Through the marvel of modern science, their contested identity and supposed alterity proved surmountable; and in the new biopolitical paradigm of national identification and reorganization, their religion, Catholicism, was irrelevant.

"The Cry of Blood"

It is evident that Pal and Râmneanțu corresponded about the latter's research project (Râmneanțu was, incidentally, a Greek Catholic from the Banat region). In a letter to Pal dated 3 November 1942, Râmneanțu assured the priest that the preliminary results of his serological work indicated proof of the community's ethnic Romanian origin: "Your Reverence, I received your letter. Be assured the problem of the Romanian Csangos will from now on be a subject of our continual preoccupation. Therefore, please be patient until the appearance of our journal, which should not be delayed more than 3–5 weeks. The sero-biological structure of the Romanian Csangos indeed confirms your findings."[32]

Henceforth, Pal could use this scientific confirmation of his thesis to bolster and advance the cause of *Romanian* Roman Catholics—specifically, that they rightfully belonged to the Romanian nation and to their Moldavian homeland. In spring 1943 Pal published a pamphlet titled *Glasul sângelui* (the cry of blood), in which he hailed Râmneanțu's findings. Armed with solid evidence produced by the anthropology of race, Pal could now dispel any lingering suspicions[33] about ethnic authenticity of the Roman Catholics in Moldavia: "Behold, to aid my claims comes the anthropology of race, which today plays a meaningful role in the systemization of peoples. . . . By our blood, it is required we be counted and named as that which in fact we are: *Romanians* by ethnic origin and *Catholic Christians* by religion, fully justified by the isohemaglutination of our blood."[34] This, then, was the allegorical "cry of blood," spilled to the ground by one brother's hatred for the other: Just as Cain had spilled the blood of Abel, so too had the Romanian Orthodox spilled the blood of their Catholic brethren. Through the work of Pal and Râmneanțu—a coming together of the sacred and the profane—the "voice" of the Csangos' blood had been made audible to Romanians and Hungarians, Orthodox and Catholic.[35]

In line with the propaganda campaign ordered by Mihai Antonescu, the lawyer and politician who ran Romania's internal and foreign affairs (while Marshal Antonescu ran the war), several articles and reviews appeared shortly after Pal's and Râmneanțu's publications.[36] The recovery of the Csangos' Romanian ethnic origins through the science of serology and racial biology led one commentator in 1943 to proclaim the following: "Even if sometimes the data presented by the historians can be annulled by the serologists (especially when history is not impartial), the results of serology can never be refuted by historical argument—because serology researches the ever-present reality of a character that neither time nor facts nor anything can transform."[37]

Romanian writers who otherwise had no stake in the identity of the Csangos soon took up their cause. With the precedent now set, Mihai Gârnițeanu, a professor at the University of Bucharest, dug deeper into the ethnogenealogy of the Csangos. He traced the Csangos back to a particular tribe of the Dacians and even disputed that the Csango ethnonym originated in the Hungarian language. Accordingly, Gârnițeanu claimed, the Csangos descended from a Dacian tribe known as the Kaukoensi, supposedly named after the type of earthen vase they produced to retrieve water from local wells. The original Dacian word for this vase, *kaukos*, through Romanian became *cenac*, and this in turn became the ethnonym *Kenagaci* or *Cenagăi*. The Szeklers had it coming, too. Their ethnonym stemmed from the Latin *situla*, the term for a well bucket, which transformed into the Romanian *ciutură* and later became corrupted into *sicula*, and still later into the attributed ethnonym *Săcui*. Selectively conflating the history and ethnic genealogy of groups who had inhabited the east Carpathian space since antiquity, Gârnițeanu pegged the Szeklers and Csangos as descendants of Dacians gingers.[38]

The Csangos Recertified

The protests and petitions sent from the Catholic villagers, priests, and church hierarchy in the Iași episcopate, namely through Pal and Bishop Robu, finally got the attention of Antonescu's Council of Ministers in Bucharest. Simultaneously, Andrea Cassulo and the Vatican had been pushing for a favorable resolution to the Catholics' situation in Moldavia. In July 1943 Mihai Antonescu replied to Bishop Robu acknowledging the problem. He assured Robu that he would raise the issue with the Ministry of Justice and shortly issue orders to resolve "once and for all" the problem concerning this "ethnic group of denationalized Romanians," hitherto classified as having "Csango ethnic origin."[39]

By month's end, Mihai Antonescu had assembled a commission comprised of the Judicial Council of the Foreign Ministry (Consiliul Juridic al Ministerului de Externe) and the State Council of Lawyers (Consiliul Avocaților Statului) to resolve the legal status of the Csangos as ethnic Romanians, using studies produced by Sabin Manuilă, Râmneanțu, Pal, and others. Specifically, the commission was tasked with establishing "an administrative enforcement procedure to determine the political principle to settle once and for all the government's position" on the Csangos, namely that they were denationalized Romanians from Transylvania. In addition, the government was to establish a procedure recognizing the Csangos as ethnic Romanian citizens. Effectively, this mandate would reverse a previous order by the Ministry of Justice excluding the Csangos from Romanian citizenship, provided any such individuals had lived on Romanian territory for at least two generations, so that those without rights to Romanian citizenship could not "illegally slip back into the country" under the pretense of being "Hungarian Csango." Presumably, this referred to the small numbers of Csangos and even Bukovinan Szeklers who, after renouncing their Romanian citizenship and resettling in the Hungarian-occupied Bácska, now sought to reenter Romania.[40]

Finally, certificates of ethnic origin were no longer to read "of Csango-Romanian nationality" but rather "Romanian nationality, of Romanian-Csango ethnic origin." This was, clearly, an ambiguous rephrasing that subsequently raised more problems than it attempted to solve. Nevertheless, the order recognized, formally and for the first time by the Romanian government, the Csangos' Romanian nationality. In any case, the government had less of an interest in knowing who the Csangos really were; rather, they wanted make known who the Csangos most assuredly were not. This was important. The "definitive principle" to be adopted by the Romanian government—based on the scientific and demographic studies produced by researchers in the Central Institute for Statistics—was that the Csangos were not Hungarian.[41]

Why the about-face? Were Ion and Mihai Antonescu and others in the Council of Ministers so convinced of the science behind the anthropological and serological work on the Csangos or the quality of Pal's historical scholarship? Perhaps. Undoubtedly, long-held assumptions about the ethnic-Romanian substrata beneath the mass of Hungarians in Transylvania offered a compelling enough case. Since the late 1920s, Romanian historians and social and biomedical scientists had put forth a number of hypotheses about the denationalization of "lost Romanians." To a public and government that possessed such an excessive belief in the power of scientific knowledge and techniques, the scientism that characterized so much of Romania's racial-anthropological and serological research validated many of these theories already by the mid-1930s and early 1940s. During the war, this type of research took on greater political significance: the government could utilize it not only in the practical application of demographic policies, such as the demographic and ethnic reorganization of Romanian territory, but also in the looming postwar dispute and settlement over national borders, especially between Hungary in the west and the Soviet Union in the east.

The Antonescu government created and directly oversaw institutes and departments whose task was to map nation and territory. These included the Directorate of Minorities (Direcția Minorităților), aptly run within the State Under-Secretariat of Romanianization, Colonization and Inventory (Subsecretariatul de Stat al Romanizării, Colonizării și Inventarului, SSRCI), as well as a number of the research teams that were to survey problematic populations in Transylvania, Moldavia, Bessarabia, and the Timoc valley, all coordinated by Manuilă in the Central Institute for Statistics. In June 1942 the Antonescu government established the Bureau of Peace (Biroul Păcii), which operated out of the Ministry of Foreign Affairs, to deal with issues concerning not only the future settlement of borders but also the minority question. The bureau included statistician and sociologist Manuilă, historians Silviu Dragomir and Gheorghe Brătianu, and geographer Simion Mehedinți, among other luminaries from academia. Within the bureau, Mehedinți and Golopenția helped run Section 3, the Ethnical, Biological and Statistical Section (Secțiunea Etnică, Biologică și Statistică). The special section was to focus on the problem of Transylvania, especially the Romanians in Southern Transylvania, as well as the Romanian populations living outside existing Romanian territory, notably those across the Dniester River to the east and others in the Balkans to the south. These institutes, bureaus, and sections worked together to rationalize Romania's population into the regime's wartime state-building project, whose stated aim was to establish a "definitive ethnic demarcation" between Romania and its neighbors (especially Hungary).[42] Within this vast, state-building bureaucracy and war and "peace" machine, the Csangos—and other minorities whose identities seemed ambiguous or, at any rate, pliable—might actually prove an asset.

That most of Romania's leading population scientists and racial anthropologists hailed from Greek Catholic families from Transylvania certainly did not hinder the Csangos' cause.[43] Manuilă was born the son of a Greek Catholic priest in the village of Sâmbăteni, near the city of Arad, on the Banat-Crişana/Bánság-Körösvidék border (and his uncle was none other than Vasile Goldiş, who negotiated and signed Romania's Concordat with the Vatican in 1927/29). Both Iuliu Moldovan and Petru Râmneanţu were raised Greek Catholic, the former from the Mureş region of Transylvania and the latter from the Banat. Anton Golopenţia, also from the Banat, had Germanized Czech family (likely Catholic) on his mother's side. In the main, these scientists and technocrats eschewed the religious factor in constructing their respective ethnic ontologies of the Romanian people; they favored the more objective bioanthropological criteria discerned through blood, genes, and anthropometry. Most never affiliated themselves with any of the ultranationalist, fascist, and Orthodoxists movements in Romania, such as the Iron Guard, even before Antonescu cracked down on these groups in 1940.

As Transylvanians and Banatians born in the late nineteenth or early twentieth century, these men were former subjects of the Hungarian Crown and, therefore, subject to its Hungarianization policies, especially in the churches and schools. Nearly all of them had studied in Hungarian-language lyceums and universities, and some had even served in the Hungarian army during World War I. It should also come as no surprise that, after the unification of Transylvania with Romania in 1920, they pioneered the research into the ethnogenealogy of supposedly denationalized Romanian populations. Throughout this period, not a single study within their collective body of research into the ethnic origins of the Szeklers and Csangos confirmed the centuries-old assumptions that these populations were, in the main, Hungarian.

This research into the ethnic composition of the Romanian population—one of eastern Europe's largest—must also be seen in the long-standing historical and political context of the relationship between Transylvania and the Old Kingdom and, by extension, the relationship between Romania's Greek Catholics and its Eastern Orthodox population. Romanian eugenics and racial anthropology emerged in the late 1920s and reached its zenith in the 1930s and early 1940s, at a time when Romania aimed for integration and unification. Thus, much of the research and writing from this field investigated the biological basis on which the Romanian ethnic body—spread across a vast landscape, from one side of the Carpathians to the other—could transcend regional, cultural, and religious differences. To be sure, research by the likes of Râmneanțu, Manuilă, and Golopenția also informed Romania's exclusionary legislation and wartime population policies, notably against the Jews and Roma but also Slavs in Dobrudja, Bukovina, and Bessarabia. Nevertheless, Râmneanțu's local research on the Csangos and his emphasis on the exclusion of religion as an aspect of racial (and thus ethnic and national) identity had far-reaching significance, as it demolished walls traditionally erected between the autochthonous Orthodox population and the supposedly alien Catholic populations of Transylvania and Moldavia.[44]

What becomes clear to the Antonescu regime by 1943 is that the settling of this "Csango business" would ultimately rest on political and not ideological considerations. What, in the end, was this "Csango business" but the inability of the state to manage its own citizens—loyal ones, at that? Mihai Antonescu oversaw the investigation into the issues raised by the Csangos themselves and their clergy, on the one hand, and by the state and local agencies paralyzed by indecision or ineffectual decisions as to the status of the Csangos, on the other. Whether Mihai accepted the scientific validity of the claims made by the research teams clustered around Manuilă is a matter of speculation. In any event, Mihai was convinced that the accumulated research and data on "the ethnic situation of the Romanian people, the graphical presentation of ethnic and biological nature of the Romanian people," would be key to any future European peace settlement and border revisions:

> When I say ethnic and biological, I do not limit myself to the ethnographic data or studies and statistics that have been made in the domain of our demographic preoccupations, in which the Institute of Statistics and Dr. Sabin Manuilă have been so useful. When I say that Europe will have to be settled on a biological basis and not a conventional one—such as any treaty, even Westphalia—and that it will have to take into account the purpose and functions of every people, I mean that in this settlement biological data will have great significance. . . . Therefore, I believe this research on the biological nature of the Romanian People, which shows the procreative strength of Romania and the force and vitality of the Romanian Nation, can constitute one of the compelling elements in the present circumstances.[45]

In connection to the activities of the aforementioned Bureau of Peace, Silviu Dragomir set up the Center for Studies and Research on Transylvania (Centrul de Studii și Cercetări privitoare la Transilvania) within the University of Cluj/Sibiu. Historians and other researchers and specialists quickly compiled studies on a range of topics useful for achieving Romania's postwar goals, especially the legitimation of its territorial claims on the whole of Transylvania. As part of a collection titled *Bibliotheca Rerum Transylvaniae*, the center published a series of nineteen works on Romanian history, territory, and demography in the border regions, mainly in German, French, and English (languages of the countries that would determine the postwar settlement). Commissioned at the behest of Mihai Antonescu, these studies highlighted the plight of Romanians across the border, such as the *timoceni* in Serbia and Bulgaria and the Romanians in Southern Transylvania, and the plight of supposedly denationalized Romanians, such as the Csangos, whose identities and localities were contested on the international stage.[46]

By the summer of 1943, internal and external political realities weighed heavily on all these decisions. The Eastern Front had collapsed, with Romania losing over one hundred fifty thousand men and eighteen divisions at the Battle of Stalingrad. King Michael publicly disavowed the Axis Powers, opening a political rift between the Romanian monarchy and the Antonescu dictatorship. Antonescu began making overtures to the Allies in hopes of suing for a separate peace, having come to the realization that its erstwhile ally, Nazi Germany, would not prevail. By summer 1942, Marshal Antonescu had stopped the deportation of Jews and Roma to Transnistria.[47] By January 1943, Antonescu had even permitted Jews from Czechoslovakia and Hungary to escape into Transylvania. By year's end, Antonescu would also order those surviving Romanian Jews in Transnistria, whom his government had deported and interned there, repatriated to their province of origin. Allied governments were already condemning Romania as one of the worst perpetrators of violence against the Jews. It was therefore clear to Antonescu that the Western powers and the Soviets would hold his regime accountable for the atrocities perpetrated in Moldavia, Bessarabia, and Transnistria. Facing these headwinds, Mihai Antonescu came to the following conclusion about the Csangos: "It is not only an attitude of objective principle in front of historical reality, but it is a political measure, inasmuch as the Romanian government has no interest in increasing the number of minorities on its territory, nor to legitimize Hungarian theories that Hungarians can be found in the Old Regat,[48] nor to dispute the historical truth and the realities of blood of this ethnic group by denying that it is of Romanian origin but has been denationalized, when the facts of history and the demographic and anthropo-sociological realities prove this conclusion."[49]

On 17 March 1943, Marshal Antonescu addressed the situation of the Csangos in a meeting with his Council of Ministers. He expressed regret about the treatment of the Csangos, noting that the prefect of Bacău, other local officials, and even the press in Moldavia had indeed treated them unjustly. "These are Romanian Catholics," he stated forthrightly, acknowledging that they had resided in the country for centuries, dating back to the time of Stephen the Great, and had fought in every war alongside their fellow Romanians. "All of them have lived in this environment and are the product of such a society, of this environment. Considering this, we are to proceed, in all respects, in the most perfect manner before the Csangos of Moldavia, and before all minorities in the country."[50]

This from the regime that two years prior sent over two hundred thousand Jews and Roma to their deaths across the Dniester and deprived most other nonethnic Romanians the right to participate in the civic life of the nation. This from the very same leadership that frequently spoke of "cleansing" and "purifying" Romanian soil of foreigners, and in fact did so through the mass murder of Jews and Roma and the deportation of Bukovinan Szeklers and Ruthenians as well as Dobrudjan Turks and Bulgarians, with detailed plans in place to expel many others.

Mihai Antonescu concluded that the Csangos posed two main problems, one that was simultaneously political and administrative/demographic, another that touched on the treatment of the different confessions in Romania generally. The first problem was to be resolved through a communiqué from the Interior minister to the prefect of Bacău, stating, "the advice of the Ministry of the Interior, concerning the origin of the Csango inhabitants in Bacău, is that these inhabitants can be considered of ethnic Romanian origin." This determination, remarked Mihai Antonescu, was based on a number of historical studies, commissioned by the Ministry, which concluded the Csangos were not a population of Hungarians but rather "infiltrations from Transylvania, but denationalized." Antonescu instructed the Interior minister to send the accumulated research on the Csangos over to the Ministry of Propaganda in order to establish publicly and officially the new position of the Romanian government vis-à-vis the Csangos.

The Antonescu regime now saw the Csangos within a much broader context. How, after all these years and amid the welter of world war, did antagonizing these Roman Catholics in the Regat benefit the present and future configuration of the Romanian state? To expel them would be counterproductive. Practical politics and demographic reality had begun to trump ideology. As always, decisions regarding the Hungarian minority in Romania—in this case, a minority with an imputed Hungarian identity in the relatively uncontested region of Moldavia—took into consideration the ramifications on relations with Hungary. Clearly, the Antonescu regime was staking out a position both on historical grounds and with an eye cast to the postwar settlement:

"In no case, however, do we have an interest in considering the Csangos as Hungarian, even if they have become Hungarian through denationalization, nor in increasing the number of Hungarians in our country [by including the Csangos as such], at the very moment when Budapest is saying there are Hungarians in Moldavia. Currently we are reinforcing their claims through our own official actions."[51]

The second problem—also administrative—was the inability of Romania's confessional minorities to obtain certificates of ethnic Romanian origin. The Interior Ministry had denied these certificates not only to the Csangos and to other communities deemed not ethnically Romanian but also anyone born or baptized in the Catholic rite. This synonymy between Romanian Orthodox and Romanian ethnicity was an idea that had persisted into the 1940s, even among the decision makers in the Interior Ministry and other government agencies, including the Romanian National Railways. By virtue of their non-Orthodox confession—and irrespective of their mother tongue or self-declaration in the 1930 and 1941 censuses and on other official documents—Romania's state bureaucracy and law regarded Catholics not ethnically Romanian and, therefore, relegated them to second-class citizenship. Finally, it seemed, Mihai Antonescu would settle the polemic first raised by Nae Ionescu and Dumitru Stăniloae and countered by Iosif Frollo more than a decade earlier: "It is impossible to proclaim the principle that to be Catholic means not to be Romanian." Romania had over one million Catholics spread across the country, not just in Transylvania and Bukovina but also in the historical provinces of the Regat. "We cannot establish a contradiction between [on the one hand] the state for Catholics and [on the other] the ethnic Romanian state."

The Romanian government needed to signal to everyone involved—Hungary, the Vatican, the Romanian bureaucracy from top to bottom, and not least, the Roman Catholic citizens of Romania—that this had all been a mistake, "a simple confusion," to quote Antonescu. This mistake, he confessed, sprung from the dogmatism of much of the Orthodox faithful, "who continue this same confessional impermeability against the Catholic Church." The regime needed to eliminate such behaviors and attitudes, which only complicated Romania's diplomatic relations, especially with Hungary, a predominantly

Catholic country. Mihai lambasted the perpetuation of this sectarianism, acknowledging that even secular political orders—including Germany's national socialism—had recently slid backward into this "Christianism":

> In no case will it be appropriate, considering the circumstances of today, to take such an attitude regarding the confessional terrain [of Romania], which in our country is senseless, given the many Roman Catholics we have. The political aversion [to the Catholic Church] was understandable at the time when the papists were instruments of denationalization. Today, when we [Romanians] are in the great majority and when in Northern Transylvania the Greek Catholic clergy has partnered with the Orthodox clergy in the most Romanian action in defense of our interests and our rights, we have no direct interest, whatsoever, as Romanians, in taking such an antagonistic position toward Catholicism. All the more reason since, in the diplomatic circumstances of today, Hungary is making intense propaganda and a cause on behalf of the Catholics in order to influence the Holy See in its favor. At the very least, we should not take an attitude that gives the impression that we do not respect the Concordat and have a religious mentality of antagonism toward Catholicism.[52]

By early 1943 the Antonescu regime showed little patience for religious nationalism in any guise, especially from the Orthodox clergy and others who complicated the regime's international position vis-à-vis the Vatican and Romania's neighbors, with whom the regime would soon be negotiating. An exasperated Mihai Antonescu even remarked about the unending complaints of the papal nuncio, made worse by the intransigence of the Orthodox Church on an array of religious and political matters. "I never go into political bargaining, not in this [the religious] domain, even if one good day I will be excommunicated from the Orthodox Church, in which I was born and in which I will die," he quipped. Mihai believed that Romania had to rescue itself from decades of "a politics of religious separatism of dogmas of confessions." Going forward, the reconstruction of Europe would require an opposite approach, "a politics of solidarity and cooperation of the churches," albeit one predicated on a specifically Christian order.[53]

Pal's *Coups de Grâce*

By autumn 1944 the Red Army had occupied much of Moldavia and, by March 1945, had established a Soviet Supreme Command in Bucharest. After thwarting attempts to relocate the Csangos to occupied Hungary in the west at the war's beginning, the community and its clergy now faced the specter of deportation to the Soviet Union at war's end under the pretenses that (1) they were "Hungarian-Magyar" and (2) they had given quarter to German soldiers stuck behind enemy lines.[54] According to Pal, the Romanian authorities in Bacău and Roman informed him that the Soviet Command in Bacău planned to deport the Csangos. While there is scant documentary evidence in Romanian archives about such plans, it is nevertheless the case that Pal and others believed this threat was both genuine and imminent. Their fears were not unfounded, as around that time Soviet authorities were interning thousands of Germans across Romania, Hungary, Czechoslovakia, and Yugoslavia and slating them for deportation to Russia to work as forced labor. In the months immediately following the war, Soviets deported an estimated seventy-five to eighty thousand of Romania's ethnic German communities to Russia.[55] The massive deportations and relocations mirrored similar events in Soviet-occupied Czechoslovakia.

Pal and the Catholic clergy could take no chances. They had to convince yet another authority that the Csangos were ethnic Romanians who belonged in Moldavia. In desperation, he wrote to Cassulo, asking him to appeal to both the Romanian government and the Vatican to intervene on behalf of the Moldavian Catholics. Pal's letter encapsulates his entire work and strategy over the previous four years. For that matter, it encapsulates the new, postwar national historical narrative of the Csangos, now merged into the Romanian historical metanarrative. It therefore merits quoting at length:

> Your Excellency, we have proven our Romanity not only with cold reason but also with the warm blood sacrificed from our Moldavian Catholic ancestors over seven centuries. So, too, have our soldiers today, siblings in blood and arms with Orthodox Romanians, shed their blood for the freedom and progress of our beloved Romanian homeland. We are of Romanian origin. Without solid arguments, Hungarian writers and some Romanian writers have denied this truth. But, in recent years, thanks to findings of the Rumanian Advanced School of Rome, which has published four thick volumes with historical documents—*Diplomatarium Italicum*—and also my personal research in the Vatican archives, many documents have been found which prove our Rumanian origin. Based on these new historical documents, I have shed light in my book titled *Originea Catolicilor din Moldova și Franciscanii păstorii lor de veacuri*. In this book, I have proved our Rumanian origin clearly. . . . This book of mine has been elevated to the level of historical debate in the University of Iași, and

the conclusion was that my thesis has been accepted with unanimity; the same conclusion was reached at the University of Bucharest and published in the historical journal, *Preocupări universitare* in 1943. The University of Cluj-Sibiu, through the Historical Commission on Transylvania (Comisiunea Istorică pentru Transilvania), under the guidance of university professor Iuliu Moldovan, has confirmed the same truth, approving of the racial results of Prof. Dr. P. Râmneanţu, who was sent from the Cabinet of the Antonescu Government to the Catholic villages of Moldavia in order to assess my thesis.[56]

Again, Pal is committed to representing the Moldavian Catholics as Romanian—Romanians by blood, nationality, and conviction, distinguished only by their Roman Catholic confession. Despite the backing of a number of Romanian authorities and intellectuals who, Pal noted, "defended our Romanian origin and citizenship, which is in no way Hungarian," this support evidently did not satisfy the Red Army commander in Bacău. Consequently, the commander sent the case to Bucharest for adjudication by the Soviet Supreme Command. In April, Cassulo wrote to Pal again, warning him that, despite the Allied Control Commission's assurances that the Soviets would leave Csangos alone, the Soviets now appeared to be acting in bad faith.[57] The Communist prefect and the chief of the Communists had confirmed to Cassulo that the Russians intended to transport "our Catholics" to Russia.[58] Fortunately for Pal and the Csangos, the plans to deport the community eastward never came to fruition.

Pal's letters and his publications illustrate the penetration, absorption, and utilization of biopolitics in the Catholic region of Moldavia. This was a discourse that emerged innocuously enough in the fields of anthropology and demography but found its way into the lexicon of nationalist ideologies; it was later instrumentalized to advance the goals of ethnic homogenization and to legitimize the exclusion of those minority populations considered dysgenic to the nation. Remarkably, Pal recognized and understood the implications of this discourse, assimilated it to his own narrative of the Csangos, and exploited it to justify the community's inclusion into the Romanian nation—thereby forestalling attempts to expatriate the community from Moldavia. In retrospect, we can rightly view him among the most consequential figures in this milieu.[59]

Pal's writing in defense of the Csangos provides a unique example of one man's ability to filter and synthesize the very ideologies and discourses that were the source of his community's troubles—ethnocentrism, religious sectarianism, and exclusivist notions of national belonging based on religion, race,

The Cry of Blood

and blood. In his embracing of Popa-Lisseanu's theories about the denationalization of the Transylvanian Romanians, as well as Râmneanţu's work on race and serology that sought to establish a definitive Romanian national identity of the community based on indices of their blood type, Pal reconstructed the Csango historical narrative and refashioned their identity as "authentic" Romanians. Through the research and writings of Pal and Râmneanţu, we can witness a culmination and working out of an entire nation's ideas on the sacred and the profane: from Catholic-Orthodox polemics to the impact of interwar-era denationalization theories on wartime renationalization policies, to the forging of alternative historical narratives for contested minorities, and to the efficacy— and sometimes inefficacy—of biopolitical agendas that attempted to solve the nation's demographic problems, especially with regard to ethnic minorities and other populations deemed antithetical to an ethnically homogeneous Romanian nation. Though Pal was at pains to separate the more extremist notions of race from the concept of nationality, he nevertheless championed the results of Râmneanţu's study of six Csango villages that revealed to the nation—and more importantly to the Antonescu government—that the community was, by proof of blood, Romanian.

Conclusion

How are ethnic allegiances formed and why they are challenged? Examining the Csangos through the prisms of religious polemics and the sciences offers new perspectives on minority enclaves and local clergy as active participants in the making of modern Europe. The remarkable story of the Moldavian Csangos, a bilingual community of Roman Catholics at the periphery of the Eastern Carpathians, reveals the often-overlooked roles of religion and science in the crafting of minority and majority populations. It reveals, moreover, how the identity and history of even the smallest communities influenced the creation of European states and borders.

The fact that the Csangos survived largely intact also sheds light on the entangled history of Romania and Hungary, suggesting the history and politics of the two states are as unifying as they are divisive. Though ever on the precipice of confrontation and conflict during the twentieth century, the two states never did engage in all-out war with one another. One reason explored in this book may well be that "mixed" and contested communities such as the Csangos have a little-understood binding effect between nations and states. The existence of such communities, whose impossible "unmixing" certainly makes relations fraught with controversy and complication, nevertheless force states into perpetual dialogue and negotiation, even if mutual agreement is never quite reached.

Even minor histories such as those on ethnic and religious enclaves—or even small bands of priests, historians, scientists, and activists—can offer unique if also peculiar looks into the social, political, and demographic transformations of twentieth-century east-central Europe. Their story, and perhaps the book itself, is a window into how identity is experienced in real life rather than in theory. The story of the Csangos is therefore not so much about

Conclusion

upheaval and distress (though there was plenty of that during the interwar and wartime periods), or even identities lost or found, but rather about the ways in which communities and individuals can utilize their backgrounds to preserve that which they cherish most: their home, their family, their church, one another.

On "Origins" as a Category of Analysis

Who do we think we are, and where do these beliefs come from? And, for that matter, what does it mean to be a Hungarian, or a Romania, or a Csango? As evidenced by the explosion in popularity of genetic ancestry tests (as of 2018) and, especially with the advent of the internet, of genealogical research and societies, the reiteration of origins (personal or communal) and the quest for some kind of foundational myth are not unique to interwar and wartime east-central Europe, much less the specific case of Csangos or any other human grouping. As Lucian Boia observes, to invoke a genesis is, necessarily, to build a bridge between the past and the present, so as to conjure up the facts on which present realities are predicated: "Each human group recognizes itself in its foundation myths that ensure its specificity when compared to others and offer it the warrant of a certain everlastingness. Thus, paradoxically, nothing is more present in the conscience of man than origins—a mythicized, ideologized, politicized domain."[1] Invariably, the historical narratives generated by ethnographers, historians, and specialists of all types projected specific national and ethnic attributes onto the bilingual peasant community known as the Csangos. These attributes, of course, reflected the politics and discourse of newly formed nation states of east-central Europe, states that were grappling with the processes of unification, centralization, and modernization.

By comparison with the twentieth-century consensuses in either Hungarian or Romanian historiographies, my approach to tracing and understanding the genealogy of ethnic groups rejects any notion of "pure" peoples or cultures in favor of a more interdisciplinary understanding of "ethnogenesis," one that stresses the important roles played by different historical and cultural components in the formation of ethnic and national groups.[2] Understood in a contemporary anthropological sense, "ethnogenesis" can refer to the cultural and political struggles by indigenous populations "to create enduring identities at times of often violently imposed radical change," such as demographic collapse or forced relocation.[3] Barbara L. Voss defines ethnogenesis more broadly as "the birthing of new cultural identities" or else the emergence of a new ethnic identity or a reconfiguration of an existing one, especially for marginalized peoples, creating a new cultural space for themselves amidst their desperate struggle to survive. The endeavor of such research into ethnic genealogies should therefore be to trace the changing contours of social life as it has unfolded in the past, to reveal the politics of social difference, and to trace the webs of social discourse and material practices, rather than to discover some root "cause" of ethnicity, as if it were something fixed and essential.[4] Anthropologist John Moore argues for replacing cladistic (branching, treelike) models of ethnogenesis with the rhizotic (root-like) metaphor, according to which "each human language, culture, or population is considered to be derived from or rooted in several different antecedent groups."[5]

As Edwin Ardener asks about "ascribed" or "labeled" populations: "What is meant by the demographic continuity of populations of this sort? Do we assume they are all the rump remnants of larger groups in the past?"[6] In his study of "ascribed populations" along the coast of Cameroon, the evidence for ethnolinguistic continuity for many such groups can suggest the opposite. Many populations become fixed as an "ethnic group." Their labeling as such, over time, has a socially reifying effect on both their self-perception as an ethnic group and on others' perception of them as an ethnic group. In this way, Ardener dissociates ethnicity from demography by showing that carriers of a particular ethnic label do not necessarily share in some timeworn biological continuity.[7] In fact, any number of peoples can be "recruited" into the ethnically reified group. Consequently, writes Ardener: "The dynamics of a 'population' with a certain label over the centuries are not the dynamics of cohorts, and of fertility or mortality rates. They are the dynamics of an economic, social and linguistic situation.... It is essential to make this effort to separate the concept of 'population' from those of language and ethnicity." To be sure, a biological population may very well coincide historically with a given language or culture. Yet, in the historical or ethnographic analysis of supposedly "enigmatic" groups such as the Csangos, we should be careful in viewing them wholly as biologically linked populations: "We are concerned with continuities whose processes are only in part biological. Fulbe, Jews and (as we know) Britons are created by definition as much as by procreation."[8]

Anthony D. Smith likewise shows the potentialities for group identity and collective action when biological filiation and genealogical ancestry are used as the basic principle of ethnic myth construction. Presumed biological links, with a presumed common ancestor, often presupposes a high degree of communal

Conclusion

solidarity and "ties of blood" that form the basis of belonging and identity. Typically, however, this production of myths about descent serves the intellectuals' or elites' vested interest in portraying one or another ethnonational identity of the group or population in question. In the case of the Csangos, these ethnopolitical entrepreneurs are typically the ethnographers, linguists, historians, politicians, and clergy who write about the Csangos in both Hungary and Romania. Through this kind of historicism, "the special preserve of intellectuals," these interpreters of the origin and ethnogenealogy also become the missionaries of the national ideal: "And since myths and memories are capable of infinite interpretation and multiform dissemination, the educator-intellectuals, especially historians and linguists, help to 'recreate' a sense of ethnicity out of the chronicles, traditions, memories and artefacts at their disposal."[9] As I hope I have illustrated in this book, the identification by others is an important feature in the establishment of self-identities.

Likewise, approaches from linguistic archaeology can shed light on the question or issue of origins. Not only do people move, but so too do their languages. As Johanna Nichols notes, the spread of languages (language trajectory) is not necessarily a trajectory of substantial population movement. Unlike peoples, languages can spread in the abstract, with no reference to human migration.[10] Nichols cites a familiar example in the spread of Romance languages in Europe. A Roman governing minority brought Latin into many towns in western and even southeastern Europe (notably in present-day Romania), and gradually the majority indigenous populations adopted Latinate languages. Conquests such as these did not depopulate and then repopulate the countryside with the conquering majorities.

Albeit in less protracted ways, and certainly on a smaller scale, since the fourteenth century the military, political, migratory, and economic activities of Hungarians and the Hungarian Kingdom resulted in the Hungarian language (and for that matter Catholicism) taking root where it did—in outposts, border garrisons, and missions along the banks of the Siret River in Moldavia. Over the centuries, and especially by the twentieth century, that linguistic hegemony shifted to Romanian. I should think it plausible that any number of distinct and not-so-distinct peoples in due course entered and exited this cultural and linguistic contact zone that is eastern Moldavia. Families and individuals possessing their own Slavic, Germanic, Turkic, Armenian "ethnogenesis" were absorbed into the ethnodemographic fabric that was or is the Csango land, as were "Hungarians" from Transylvania and "Romanians" from just about all directions.

Indeed, the formation of many of the villages in Ghimeş/Gyimes and Ciuc/Csik Counties described by ethnographer György Takács tend to support this view.[11] Takács describes not only how big groups migrated intact into these regions but also how individuals and families moved in and out of these villages at different times and rates. Using oral traditions, oral history, interviews, and church records, Takács shows how the village of Coşnea/Kostelek, for example, was founded by families from both Csik in Transylvania and Comaneşti in Moldavia. This has been preserved in local memory when villagers say, "We are from Moldavia and Csik." Over the centuries, the names of these founding families—Bezsán/Bejan, Csilip, Vátá, and Olá (meaning Romanian in Hungarian)—shifted between Hungarian and Romanian forms or else were present in both Transylvania and Moldavia. Moreover, church and other historical records show that multiple parishes—whether Greek Catholic, Orthodox, Protestant, or Roman Catholic—existed in the respective provenances from which these families originally hailed.[12]

Takács describes similar processes in the formation of nearby villages, notably Cădăreşti/Magyarcsükes, whereby the absence or presence of one or another church ultimately determined the putative national identities of the respective villages and its inhabitants. Throughout the region, the same family names can be identified as Roman Catholics, Greek Catholics, and Romanian Orthodox. Moreover, church records indicate that the ancestors of many present-day members of one religion were registered in another religion. Migration, shepherding, the fleeing of military conscription, war, border revisions, and the expropriation or conversion of local churches have all contributed to the drawing and redrawing of ethnic and religious boundaries in the region over the last few centuries.[13] Taking all this into account, the Csango land, like so many other regions in eastern and east-central Europe, can be viewed as a kind of palimpsest, an overlay of religious practices, of languages and dialects, and of various kinship identities, both real and imagined.

In recent years, even geneticists have attempted to unravel the enigma of the Csangos' origin. Most genetic studies acknowledge that what distinguishes Hungarians from most other European populations is their non-Indo-European language. Yet in spite of their linguistic relic from Asia, "the Hungarians *in toto* are genetically close to European populations," primarily the Slavs and Germans.[14] Results of gene frequency comparisons between specific Hungarian groups and other "probable ancestors" are for the most part inconclusive, except to say that Csangos and Szeklers "seem to have a similar genetic pool, which could be composed mainly of Iranian, but also of Turkish and Finnish

Conclusion

genes," and that ethnic groups such as the Csangos "are more related to hypothetical ancestral populations than unspecified Hungarians."[15] I put little credence in such formulations, especially when studies do not include comparisons with known Romanian gene frequencies, if such a thing exists.

Another study analyzing the Szeklers and Csangos states that "both populations claim to be Hungarian, although they live in the Transylvania region of Rumania"; moreover, the data used for the Csangos in the study belonged to the "more or less isolated Szekely and Csango populations who left their homeland and settled in Hungary before and after World War II."[16] The Csangos, of course, live in and hail from Moldavia; and as discussed in the chapter on the resettlement of Csangos during World War II, only about 160 individual Csangos were relocated to Hungary in 1941 and only twenty-two families emigrated in 1947, all from only two Moldavian villages.[17] Moreover, the Szeklers who emigrated were from Bukovina, not Transylvania. Yet another study examines the mitochondrial DNA sequence variation and restriction site polymorphisms among 68 "ethnic Csangos from Hungary and Romania," who are described as "countrymen" with Hungarians "who have lived in Romania in self-sufficient village communities isolated from the main Romanian population."[18] Still another compares the "entire mtDNA control region sequences from 360 individuals of Hungarian ethnicity from two populations (the Csángó and the Székely)." Representing all "Csangos" was a sample taken from 182 individuals in Lunca de Sus/Gyimesfelsőlok, which is in Harghita County, Transylvania, just at the mouth of the Ghimeș Valley (not Moldavia).[19] Contrary to the study cited above, the conclusion of this study found that, despite sharing a similar gene pool, the gene flow between Csangos and Szeklers has in fact been quite poor.

The sampling for many of these studies is hardly representative. Moreover, presumptions about which genes belong to which national or ethnic group hardly comport with other forms of knowledge about the complex histories, demographics, and ethnographies of these peoples and lands. As geneticist Csanád Bálint notes, there are serious methodological objections to many of these studies, as geneticists tend to address seminal historical and linguistic questions without first acquiring sufficient knowledge in these fields: "Their overreach means that conclusions are drawn about the origins of peoples and their interrelatedness, overlooking the fact that only individuals, not groups, can be regarded as biological entities. Groups and peoples are the product of history and are moulded socially. . . . Today's populace is not a living fossil of the ancient one."[20]

Contemporary Relevance

In my story of the Csangos I am reminded of Edward Muir's notion that the makers of history on the European continent are seldom "great men" but rather the little peoples lost to European history.[21] My hope with this book is to contribute to the historiography on the Csangos a more holistic interpretation of "the making of the Csangos" over the greater part of the twentieth century. Moreover, national politics in the twentieth century have imbued much of the history written about the Csangos. In Hungary, the historiography and discourse on the Csangos have often been centered on the plight of the community as ethnolinguistic kin under siege, severed from the Hungarian national body through the forces of Romanianization, which today seem irreversible.[22] By contrast, Romanian perspectives on the Csangos tend to be framed within the context of national unity, ethnic continuity, and the recovery of "lost" or de-nationalized ethnolinguistic kin. Many of these debates persist to this day, informing the national and regional politics of Romania and Hungary, from minority language use to educational and cultural policies and issues over migration and citizenship.

This is not to suggest that my own work can somehow depolarize the debate over the identity of the Csangos. Nevertheless, in my own historicization of the Csangos I have attempted to address what I see as a shortcoming in the historiography on the community, namely the lack of transnational historical, political, and cultural perspectives. For that matter, I would argue these perspectives are also lacking in the historiography on other ethnic and religious enclaves in central and eastern Europe. As Helmut Walser Smith and others have argued, the histories of minority groups in the region all too often focus on their respective subjects as if they existed in isolation, as if collective identity can somehow be reduced to "Hungarian" or "Romanian," as the case may be.[23] Smith contends that it is possible to train our analysis on the "bridges to the other" and thereby to uncover "the stuff of history as happening in the friction-filled margins of cultural groups and at the crossings between them." In this way, we can breathe new life into the tired debates about the contested identities and national belonging of peoples historically situated at the margins.

Glossary

For the most part I have used the Romanian or Hungarian original for important names and terms, with English translations provided in parentheses. When relevant, I provide both the Romanian and Hungarian names; for example, the names of villages in Moldavia and Transylvania. As the timeframe of this book is 1920–45 (the interwar period and World War II), most of the locations I mention were (and are today) in Romanian territory; they are thus listed first in Romanian. The shifting orthography and the official and unofficial changing of personal names throughout these periods pose additional problems for consistency and style. International treaties, war, and internal policies resulted in a number of border revisions that continually redefined (both literally and figuratively) states, regions, counties, towns, and villages in Romania and Hungary. Historiographical debates likewise precipitated changes in group names and ethnonyms, as did the establishment, disestablishment, and renaming of institutions, political parties, schools, church dioceses, and so forth. All of this has necessitated some rather subjective, if at times inconsistent, choices of my own.

The list of selected terms and definitions below is intended not just as a reference guide but also as an informal essay or introduction to the languages, discourses, and concepts used in Romania and Hungary during the period under investigation. I hope this will also be useful for students studying or writing about twentieth-century Romania and Hungary, especially those who are just beginning their research and who have little background with these languages and discourses in their respective national and historical contexts.

Populations

Csango (Hu. *csángó* [sing.]/*csángók* [pl.]; Ro. *ceangău* [sing.]/*ceangăii* [pl.]) is an anglicized form of the ethnonym ascribed to the Hungarian- and

Romanian-speaking Catholic population residing mainly in Bacău and Neamț Counties in the region of Moldavia, eastern Romania. According to *A Magyar nyelv történeti-etimológiai szótára* (The Hungarian historical-etymological dictionary), the standard work on the etymology of Hungarian words, the ethnonym Csángó derives from the verb *csáng*, meaning "to wander away" or "to stray." The similar verb *csángál* or *elcsángál* means to drive livestock from here to there, though it is used in folk speech to denote wandering all over the place. Thus, it has the sense of "to roam" or "to rove," implying the Csangos had long ago separated themselves from the main body of Hungarians. The name first surfaces as a family name in the fifteenth and sixteenth centuries. The first documented use of the term as an ethnonym, referring specifically to the Hungarian-speaking communities of Moldavia, can be traced back to several letters by the Catholic priest Péter Zöld in the 1770s and 1780s. Other groups of so-called Csangos have also been identified and historicized, for example, the *Gyimesi csángók* (Csangos of the Ghimeș/Gyimes valley) in the mountain pass connecting Transylvania and Moldavia as well as the *Hétfalusi Csángók* (Csangos of the seven villages) in a group of villages east of the Transylvanian city of Brașov. In the late nineteenth century some Csangos were resettled around the Transylvanian city of Deva/Déva, and in the 1940s other Csangos were resettled in southern and western Hungary.

Szekler (Hu. *székely* [sing.] / *székelyek* [pl.]; Ro. *secui*) is the anglicized (via German) ethnonym for the Catholic and Protestant ethnolinguistic subgroup of Hungarians in eastern Transylvania, a region historically part of the Kingdom of Hungary but part of Romania since World War I (Northern Transylvania, including the Szekler land, was ceded back to Hungary from 1940 to 1944). It is generally held that the Szeklers colonized the area around the eleventh century, though some theories place them in the Carpathian basin much earlier. Historically, the Szeklers were among the ruling nations of Transylvania, the Unio Trium Nationum (Union of the three nations), alongside the Saxons and Hungarians (and excluding the Romanians, the largest ethnic community in Transylvania). By the modern period, the Szeklers had their own national theater, a number of lyceums, and a near-autonomous local political structure. They participated culturally, politically, and militarily in the Hungarian national movement. Other communities of Szeklers once populated the northern Moldavian region of Bukovina (from the eighteenth century) but were later resettled in southern and western Hungary (from the 1940s) as well as in the historical county of Turda-Arieș/Torda-Aranyos, today in Alba and Cluj Counties (central Transylvania).

Glossary

Geography and Place Names

Csango Land (Hu. *Csángóföld*; Ro. *Pământul Ceangăilor*) is the homeland of the Csangos in eastern Moldavia, Romania. Today the Csango land extends through Bacău and Neamț Counties, and to a lesser extent Iași County. (Inside present-day Neamț County there previously existed Roman County, seated in the town of Roman, which contained most of the so-called Northern Csangos. Roman County was eliminated during the Communist period.) Csango settlements are clustered around the city of Bacău and north of the town of Roman, mainly along the Siret and Trotuș River valleys as well as the Bistrița and Moldova River valleys, and along the foothills of the Outer Eastern Carpathians, around the Culmea Pietricica, Tarcău, and Berzunți ranges.

Délvidék or "Southlands" was historically part of the Kingdom of Hungary's southern region. Precisely which lands and counties are included in the various historical regions of Hungary can be confusing, especially as these borders fluctuated. Chapter 5 of this book deals with the transfer of ethnic Hungarians from Romanian Moldavia and Bukovina into the Hungarian Délvidék during World War II, specifically into Baranya and Bácska (Bačka) Counties, which bordered the Kingdom of Yugoslavia. Baranya County is located in the southern part of the region called the Dunántúl (Transdanubia). The southernmost part of Baranya County extended into the Délvidék. Just to the southeast of Baranya, on the eastern side of the Danube, is Bácska (Bács-Bodrog) County. Bácska is situated primarily in the Délvidék. It is also included in the historical province of Vajdaság, more commonly known as Vojvodina.

Moldavia (Ro. *Moldova*; Hu. *Moldva*) is used in English for the historical and geographical region in present-day eastern Romania. Moldavia is situated between the Carpathian Mountains in the north and west, the Prut River in the east, and the lower Danube and Black Sea in the south. Moldavia existed as a separate principality from about the 1350s until the union of Moldavia and Wallachia in 1859, which formed the United Principalities of Moldavia and Wallachia (Principatele Unite ale Moldovei și Țării Românești), or simply the Romanian United Principalities. In 1881 the principality became part of the Kingdom of Romania (Regatul României). In the region, however, inhabitants have long used the term Moldova. Historically, at its greatest extent, this region included Bessarabia, with its eastern boundary at the Dniester River. Present-day Moldavia or Romanian Moldavia is not to be confused with the present-day Republic of Moldova, formerly the Moldovan Soviet Socialist Republic (1944 to 1991).

Romania in the twentieth century has been redrawn and officially named and renamed a number of times. In 1859, after the election of Alexandru Ioan Cuza as prince of both Moldavia and Wallachia, the two principalities (commonly known as the Danubian Principalities) united to form the United Principalities of Moldavia and Wallachia (Principatele Unite ale Moldovei și Țării Românești). In 1881, after international treaties recognized Romanian independence and the German prince Carol I became the first king of Romania, the united principalities formally became the Romanian Kingdom (Regatul României). After World War I, adjacent territories from Russia, Austria-Hungary, and Bulgaria were awarded and united to the kingdom, forming what became known as Greater Romania (România Mare). Although Greater Romania was a new national state born of the post–World War I peace settlement, it remained a monarchy (hence the pre-1918 Romanian Kingdom is sometimes referred to as the Old Kingdom [Vechiul Regat]). From September 1940 to January 1941 the country was known as the National Legionary State (Statul Național Legionar). From 1947 to 1965 it was known as the Romanian People's Republic (Republica Populară Română) and from 1965 to 1989 the Romanian Socialist Republic (Republica Socialistă România).

Szekler Land (Hu. *Székelyföld*; Ro. *ținutul Secuiesc* or *Secuime*) is the homeland of the Szeklers in eastern Transylvania, Romania. Today the Szekler land extends through Covasna and Harghita Counties and, to a lesser extent, Mureș County. (Within the Hungarian Kingdom and, after 1920, Greater Romania, the Szekler lands were comprised of Trei Scaune/Háromszék, Ciuc/Csik, Odorhei/Udvarhely, and Mureș/Maros-Torda Counties. They were reorganized and renamed during the Communist period.)

Transylvania (Ro. *Ardeal, Transilvania*; Hu. *Erdély*) historically refers to the principality within the Carpathian basin, inhabited mainly by Romanians, Hungarians, and Germans. The Hungarians who conquered central Europe took control over this territory at the beginning of the second millennium, and thus it became a voivodeship of the Hungarian Kingdom until the sixteenth century, when it became a separate principality. In 1699 it was officially added to the Habsburg Monarchy by the terms of the Treaty of Karlowitz; after the Austro-Hungarian Compromise of 1867, it was reincorporated into the Kingdom of Hungary. In 1920, as part of the peace settlement after World War I, Transylvania was awarded to Romania through the Treaty of Trianon. It was the largest and most ethnically and confessionally diverse new territory in what became Greater Romania. It was also the largest and most populous territory lost by Hungary. As a result of the Second Vienna Award, between 1940 and 1944 Transylvania was divided between Hungarian Northern Transylvania and Romanian Southern Transylvania. After World War II, the entire territory was awarded to Romania once again. Historically, Transylvania is just one of the provinces or territories in the Carpathian basin. Since its incorporation into Romania, however, Transylvania has been understood as all the adjacent Hungarian territories annexed by Romania, including Maramureş, Crişana, and part of the Banat.

Some Romanian Terms

boanghină/boanghen—epithet for Hungarians in Transylvania and analogous to the Hungarian term *bozgor*. Both terms are of dubious origin but imply "stateless" or even "homeless" and thus belonging to the Hungarians.

bun român—"good Romanian." This was a phrase coined by King Ferdinand, who on his assumption of the throne in 1914 (during World War I) promised he would rule as "a good Romanian." It was significant because King Ferdinand, who came from the Hohenzollern royal line, which was both German and Catholic, presided over the creation of the Romanian national state at the end of World War I. His presence as a German-Catholic king amidst a newly confident Romanian national movement was fraught with contradiction. During the interwar period, the phrase "A fi bun roman?" (A good Romanian?) became the title of several articles and a religious polemic. As discussed in chapter 2, this polemic pitted the Romanian Orthodox intellectuals against the Romanian Catholic ones, specifically the priests and theologians in Moldavia. Like the phrase *Mi a magyar?* in Hungarian, this Romanian phrase communicates the ideas and debates about what it meant to be Romanian—ethnically, nationally, politically, spiritually.

cult (*culte* [pl.])—generally understood as "denomination" or "confession" within Christianity (though minority religions such as Judaism and Islam were sometimes categorized as *culte*) and therefore should not be equated with modern English usage of the term as an obscure religious sect. The historian C. A. Macartney likens this term to the old Hungarian idea of "received" or "historic" Christian religions in Transylvania—Catholicism,

Calvinism, Lutheranism, and Unitarianism—that were granted special privileges, though the model was supplied by the former French *ministère des cultes* (and German equivalents).

desnaționalizare—literally, "denationalization"; that is, to have lost one's ethnonational identity and consciousness, typically through forced assimilation over the centuries. The terms *maghiarizare* and *secuizare* refer specifically to being "Hungarianized" or "Szeklerized"; in other words, to have lost one's Romanian ethnonational identity or consciousness and assumed a Hungarian or Szekler one in its stead.

etnicul—generally translates as "ethnos" and connotes the meta-quality of *being* Romanian or possessing Romanianness, especially as used in interwar and World War II Romania. It is rather closer to the French *ethnie* for "ethnic community" and thus not quite the same as the Romanian word for ethnicity, *etnicitate*.

înstrăinare—see entry of străin.

latinitatea—Latinity, and was used in Romania to emphasize historical connections to Rome, which signaled historical, linguistic, ethnic, and even territorial continuity in the Romanian space, especially the region that became Transylvania.

naționalitate—translates as "nationality." However, this word took on different meanings during the first half of the twentieth century, from the more civically minded notion of state membership and citizenship to the more ethnically or racially minded notion of belonging to the *neam*. This problem was exemplified by the changing criteria used for requiring and issuing Romanian nationality certificates (*certificate de naționalitate*). During the 1920s and 1930s, these certificates showed proof of meeting the formal criteria for naturalization as a Romanian citizen; during World War II, by contrast, they showed proof of ethnic Romanian origin.

neam—generally translates as "nation" but also has the sense of both "the people" (*popor*) and "nationality" (*naționalitate*), usually, though not exclusively, understood in ethnic terms. It can also be used for extended family or kin.

pământul strămoșesc—ancestral homeland.

popor—"people" in Romanian, understood in both the ethnic sense, akin to the German notion of *Volk*, as well as in the sense of the masses.

rasă—the Romanian word for "race." While in Romania during the interwar period and World War II this term took on different shades of meaning, it usually referred to the different genetic or ancestral groupings of human peoples (whereas the Hungarian word for race, *faj*, had many different literal and figurative meanings). However, for some writers the Romanian

Glossary

race was conflated with the inherent psychology, spirituality, and even the Orthodox religion of the Romanian people. Others, especially the biomedical and social scientists, viewed race in a strictly biological and anthropological way; still others used it in a more exclusionary and racist sense, as did their counterparts in Germany and Hungary.

românii de peste hotare—"Romanians across the border"; that is, those living in neighboring states as ethnic Romanian minorities.

românismul—Romanianism.

romanitatea—Romanity; shares connotations with Latinity.

românizare—the word for "Romanianization," which took on a number of meanings after World War II. During the war it implied the dispossession and nationalization of foreign-owned (especially Jewish) property inside Romania. Calls for *numerus vallachicus*, the Romanian twist on *numerus clausus*, can also be seen in this context. On another level it stood for the policy of expelling foreigners (*străini*) from Romanian territory, that is to say, "cleansing" or "purifying" the nation of ethnic Others. *Romanizare* soon became the organizing principle of the Romanian state. Such policies and principles were embodied in one of the most important Romanian institutions during the war, the Subsecretariatul de Stat al Romanizării, Colonizării și Inventarului (State Undersecretariat of Romanianization, Colonization, and Inventory).

străin—the word for "foreigner" or "stranger." Typically, this refers to those outside the Romanian national community, especially minorities within Romania. In the countryside, this can also be applied to any outsider, even if Romanian (e.g., someone from another region, locality, or village). The term *înstrăinare* is used in a similar way to *desnaționalizare*; in other words, to become "estranged" or "alienated" from one's ethnonational kin, to be banished or exiled, or else "foreignized" by another.

Some Hungarian Terms

faj—a rather loaded word used for "race." Depending on context and usage, *faj* can also be used in a purely taxonomic sense, such as species, genus, pedigree, or else type, kind, sort, as well as ethnicity, blood, tribe, ancestry, or heritage. *Faj* not only has different literal meanings but also different figurative meanings. Though many Hungarian writers during the interwar period and World War II employed the word *faj* when speaking of the Hungarian "race," "blood," or "ethnonational community," for some these notions were used in a more cultural or "psychospiritual" sense, to quote historian Bela Vardy. Others conflated notions of the Hungarian race with the Hungarian "soul" or "spirit" (*lélek*). Still other writers used *faj* in a more exclusionary and racist sense, as did their counterparts in Germany and Romania; for example, *fajvédelem* (racism, racialism, race protection/defense), *fajgyalázás* (racial dishonor), and Magyar Fajvédők Országos Szövetségé (Hungarian National Alliance of Race Protectors).

határon túli magyarok—literally, "Hungarians across the border," a term used especially during the interwar period and World War II to designate the Hungarian diaspora "left behind" in the successor states such as Czechoslovakia, Yugoslavia, and Greater Romania that were created or expanded at the expense of Hungary's territorial losses after World War I. It also referred to putative Hungarian communities, such as the Moldavian Csangos or other Hungarian-speaking enclaves in the Balkans, who had never lived within the borders of the modern Hungarian kingdom and state.

hazatelepítés—literally, "settlement home" (*haza* is home, *telepítés* is settlement). Though resettlement policies in the Habsburg and Hungarian kingdoms date back many centuries, the idea of bringing the *határon túli magyarok* "home" to Hungarian territory took on greater significance during World War II. The Hungarian government's Foreign Hungarians Repatriation Committee (Külföldi Magyarokat Hazatelepítő Kormánybiztosság) targeted populations deemed "good ethnic kin" (such as the Csangos) who could be "returned" to Hungary and resettled along sensitive, multiethnic border regions, especially in the Southlands (Délvidék).

kisebbségek—minorities.

lélek—soul.

magyar—the Hungarian word for Hungarian. It is sometimes used in English instead of "Hungarian."

"Mi a magyar?"—translates as "What is the Hungarian?" This was also the title of a seminal edited volume in interwar Hungary, bringing together a number of prominent intellectuals to explore the self-consciousness of the Hungarian people's Hungarianness and to counter Nazi-inspired discourses and research on national-racial types. The volume included the writings of a wide range of historians, ethnographers, established racial anthropologists such as Lajos Bartucz, and even poets and ethnomusicologists. The aim of this work was to redefine the canon on Hungarian national character within some semblance of historical normativity.

nemzet—generally understood as "nation" in the political and institutional sense but can also convey ethnocultural meanings, as in *nemzetiség* (nationality), *nemzetiségi* (national/ethnic), and *nemzeti kisebbség* (national/ethnic minority).

Glossary

nemzetség—clan, family, kinship.

nép—generally understood as "people" in the sense of the ethnonational community, similar to the German *Volk*; for example, the Magyar Népi Szövetség (Hungarian People's Union) or *népballada* (folk ballad). During the interwar and World War II periods, *nép* often referred to people of the villages, the peasants, as opposed city dwellers. However, *nép/népi-* can also be used for "ethno-/ethnic," as in *néprajz* (ethnography), *népcsoport* (ethnic group), *népiségtörténet* (ethnohistory), and *népi nemzet* (ethnic nation).

The Churches

Greek Catholic Church of Romania, or the Romanian Church United with Rome, constitutes a major archiepiscopate of the worldwide Catholic Church. It is part of the Eastern Catholic churches and known more commonly as the Romanian Greek-Catholic Church or Uniate Church. It recognizes the authority and supremacy of the pope yet maintains the Byzantine liturgical rite as well as some devotional and theological traditions. The term "Uniate" (orig. mid-nineteenth century from the Russian *uniat*, from *uniya*, from Latin *unio*) refers specifically to those Eastern Orthodox churches that subsequently formed a "union" with the Church of Rome. Some Catholics consider the term derogatory. In Transylvania in 1698 the Orthodox bishop Atanasie Anghel, who was the metropolitan of Alba Iulia, led a synod of protopopes to declare union with the Catholic Church. Today, the seven hundred thousand followers of the Romanian Greek-Catholic Church make it the one of the largest Greek Catholic congregations.

In partibus infidelium translates as "in the regions of the nonbelievers" and was used in a bishop's title after the name of a diocese conquered by a power of another faith, which in the case of Moldavia was the autocephalous Eastern Orthodox Church in Romania, or the Romanian Orthodox Church. Since the Middle Ages, Moldavia was an important point of entry for Catholic missionaries in an eastern Europe dominated by the Eastern Orthodox Church, one of many regions designated by the Catholic Church as *partibus infidelium*. Maintaining a Catholic toehold in Orthodox lands was a priority for the Congregation of the Propaganda Fide.

Orthodoxism and its exponents, the so-called *Orthodoxists*, refer to the mystical, traditionalist theologies and theologians of Romanian Orthodoxy that infused both original and borrowed forms of nationalism and ethnocentrism in the understanding of the relationships between God, religion, and nation. To quote historian Lucian Boia's distinction: "'Orthodoxism' (adj.:

'Orthodoxist') is to be understood as referring to a political ideology which makes the Orthodox faith a mark of national identity, and should not be confused with 'Orthodoxy' (adj.: 'Orthodoxist'), the transnational Orthodox faith itself, which resists identification with any modern ideological '-ism.'"[1]

Roman (Latin) Catholic Church in Moldavia is administered by the bishopric of Iaşi, founded 1884, which today covers the Romanian counties of Suceava, Botoşani, Neamţi, Iaşi, Bacău, Vaslui, Vrancea, and Galaţi. The institutional presence of the Roman Catholic Church in Moldavia dates back to the thirteenth century with the founding of the Diocese of Cumania in 1227. The diocese was seated in the town of Milcov and attached to the Hungarian Archdiocese of Esztergom, serving the converted Cumans and the Teutonic Knights before the Mongols laid waste to it in 1241 (Milcov was restored in 1347). Thereafter, episcopal sees or dioceses were established in Siret in 1370, Baia in 1413, and Bacău in 1611. These dioceses were often short lived, as they were either destroyed by invasions from Eurasia or else disestablished following political changes in the voivodship/principality of Moldavia. From the late Middle Ages to the unification of the Wallachian and Moldavian principalities and the formation of the Kingdom of Romania in the mid-nineteenth century, the ethnically and linguistically diverse communities of Moldavian Catholics were administered alternately by Hungarian, Polish, or Austrian bishoprics. To varying proportions, the Catholic communities of Moldavia were comprised of Hungarians, Romanians, Germans (Saxons), Poles, and Armenians, among others. Moldavia was also an important point of entry for Catholic missionaries in eastern Europe, *in partibus infidelium*, seeking to spread the faith and later to care for the faithful (Moldavia became a vassal state of the Ottoman Empire from the sixteenth century). It was thus an important field of activity for the Congregation of the Propaganda Fide from the seventeenth century. Most of the missionaries were Franciscans, Dominicans, and Jesuits who hailed from Italy, Poland, Hungary, and the Balkans (including Bosnians, Bulgarians, and Greeks). The Apostolic Vicariate of Moldavia was established in Iaşi in 1818 and raised to the Iaşi diocese in 1884; the Vicarate of Bucharest was elevated to the rank of archdiocese in 1883 and metropolitan in 1930. It was only after the First World War and the unification of Greater Romania in 1920 that Romanian-born bishops and archbishops were appointed in Iaşi and Bucharest, respectively. In addition to the Greek- and Latin-rite Catholics, there also existed Armenian-rite Catholics and Ruthenians of the Ancient Slavonic rite, both of which had vicarages in Romania up to the late 1920s. This

Glossary

book deals more in-depth with the history of the church in Romania—and more specifically Catholicism in Moldavia—from the interwar period through World War II. I should like the reader to note that when I refer simply to the "Catholics," "Catholicism," or "the Roman Catholic Church," I am referring to the Roman Catholic (Latin rite) faithful, religion, or church.

Romanian Orthodox Church and *Romanian Orthodoxy* refer to the autocephalous Eastern Orthodox Christian Church in Romania. It was around the thirteenth and fourteenth centuries that "Schismatics" among the natives in the principalities of Wallachia and Moldavia were first mentioned in correspondence to the pope. The Metropolis of Ungro-Wallachia was founded in 1359, and the Metropolis of Moldavia, in 1401. After the formation of the Romanian kingdom and state in the nineteenth century, the two churches joined to form the Romanian Orthodox Church. In 1925 the Romanian Orthodox Church was finally elevated to the rank of Patriarchy, a recognition that successive Romanian governments and church leaders had solicited from the Patriarchate of Constantinople since the Romanian Constitution of 1866 declared the church independent of any foreign hierarchy. It continues to be the majority religion in Romania, practiced mainly by ethnic Romanians. Today the nearly twenty million followers of the Romanian Orthodox Church (including seven hundred thousand in the Republic of Moldova) make it one of the largest Eastern Orthodox congregations in the world. I should like the reader to note that when I refer simply to the "Orthodox," "Orthodoxy," or "the Orthodox Church," I am referring to the Romanian Orthodox faithful, religion, or church.

Notes

Introduction

1. See Pozsony, *The Hungarian Csango of Moldova*, 202–224; and Benda, "The Hungarians of Moldavia (Csángós) in the 16th–17th Centuries," 27–31.
2. As Robin Baker has acknowledged, the "Hungarian-speaking Csángós of Moldavia are one of Europe's most enigmatic and least known ethnic minorities. . . . Of all the enigmas surrounding the Csangos it is their origin that has attracted the most attention, debate and, increasingly over the last fifty years, rancor." Baker, "On the Origin of the Moldavian Csángós," 658–60.
3. Isohookana-Asunmaa, "Csángó Minority Culture in Romania," 81.
4. Kontra, "Prefatory Note to the Csángó Issues," 9.
5. Tánczos, "About the Demography of the Moldavian Csángós," 117–47. Supporting this view is Baker, who notes "the weight of opinion favours a Magyar origin for the Csángós." Baker concludes it is to those Magyars who resettled in Moldavia in the fourteenth century "that the Moldavian Csángós who live today in the Siret valley owe their origin." Baker, "On the Origin of the Moldavian Csángós," 664, 680. Some Hungarian authors writing in the early 1940s even counted as Csangos or Hungarians many of the region's Protestant and Romanian Orthodox population, believing them to be ethnically Hungarian by origin but subsequently "denationalized." Thus, their number was 160,000–200,000. See Péter Vida, "Magyar Kárpát-medencét," *Kárpátmedence*, 1/5 (Sept. 1941).
6. The authors of the study claim furthermore that "the Csángó consider themselves Hungarian." See Andrásfalvy and Kelemen, "Ethnic Groups in Hungary," 59.
7. While the study acknowledges that the origin of the Csangos is disputed, it nevertheless states that the Csangos, 120,000 strong, "are regarded as ethnic Hungarians." Lahermo et al., "MtDNA Polymorphism in the Hungarians," 35–36.
8. For a historiographical discussion of the numerous theories on the earliest possible settlements of the Csangos into Moldavia, see Baker, "On the Origin of the Moldavian Csángós"; and Davis, "The Csángós of Moldavia: Historical Narratives," 9–14.

9. I use here the most recent estimation of the demographer and ethnographer Vilmos Tánczos, who suggests about 250,000 Moldavian Catholics on the basis of data from the Romanian census of 2002 combined with his own fieldwork in 1994–96 and 2008–10 (the census identified exactly 232,045). See Tánczos, "Hungarian Language Command among the Moldavian Csángós, 2008–10," 269–381 (table 11, 369).

10. As Sándor Ilyés noted about the symbolic value of the term Csango that has emerged in the last fifteen years or so, "Wherever and whenever we hear the term Csángó, we automatically make some associations: Hungarian, of Hungarian origin, Hungarian speaker and keeper of ancient values." Ilyés, "The Image of the Csángós in the Hungarian Press of Transylvania," 335–54.

11. See Brubaker, *Nationalism Reframed*, 55–56.

12. The phrase translates as "in the regions of the nonbelievers" and was used in a bishop's title after the name of a diocese conquered by a power of another faith, in this instance the autocephalous Eastern Orthodox Church in Romania, or the Romanian Orthodox Church. The Metropolis of Moldavia was set up in 1386 and recognized in 1401. In 1227 the Catholic Church created the Diocese of Cumania—so named because of its mission to the converted pagans known as the Cumans, who had settled the region after arriving from central Asia—with its main see in the town of Milcov along the Milcov River. It was destroyed by the Tatars in 1241 but subsequently recreated, if only in name, around 1350.

13. Tánczos estimated around 62,000 in 1992 but claims that in recent years this number has dropped to around 43,000. The 2001 Committee on Culture, Science and Education report to the Parliamentary Assembly of the Council of Europe by Tytti Isohookana-Asunmaa estimated 60,000–70,000. Ferenc Pozsony writing in 2006 estimated 100,000; Kálmán Benda in 1990 estimated 80,000; and Bernard Le Callóch, also in 1990, suggested 40,000–60,000. See Tánczos, "Hungarian Language Command among the Moldavian Csángós," 271; Peti and Tánczos, *Language Use, Attitudes, Strategies*; Pozsony, *The Hungarian Csango of Moldova*, 5; Benda, "Les Hongrois de Moldavie (les Tchangos) aux XVIe–XVIIe siècles"; Le Callóch, "Un peuple oublié: Les Csángós," 39; and Isohookana-Asunmaa, "Csángó Minority Culture in Romania," 81.

14. The Romanian census of 1930 recorded 23,894 Hungarian-speaking Catholics in Moldavia, of whom 20,964 were recorded as having "Hungarian nationality." The 1941 Romanian census, which for the first time introduced ethnic origin as a category, recorded 9,352 "Hungarians" among the Moldavian Catholics. These numbers dwindled during the Communist period. For the counties of Bacău, Neamț (which includes the former Roman County), and Iași, the 1992 Romanian census recorded only 5,270 who self-identified as ethnically "Hungarian" and only 2,165 (throughout the country) who self-identified as "Csango." In 2002 the number of self-identified ethnic Hungarians in the above counties totaled 4,934, with 1,266 self-identified as "Csango." I cite these numbers only to give a general picture of the official count of Moldavian Hungarians and Csangos according to Romanian census data. Many (mostly Hungarian) ethnographers and demographers, as well as cultural and political activists supporting one or

another agenda in support of the Hungarian-speaking Csangos, dispute these numbers. Moreover, different figures can be arrived at when employing other categories, such as mother tongue, religion, and region. For instance, among those who self-identified as "Csango" in the 2002 Romanian census, 127 were recorded as Romanian Orthodox by religion, 11 as Greek Catholic, and still smaller numbers as Protestant, neo-Protestant, and "without religion." Evidently, somewhere in Romania there is even a self-identified Csango who is Muslim and 3 self-identified Csangos whose mother tongue is Romani (Gypsy). See the Romanian census data online, specifically tables 1, 4, and 5 in vol. 4, "Structura etnică și confesională," http://www.insse.ro/cms/files/RPL2002INS/vol4/titluriv4.htm, accessed 22 Apr. 2012. I take no position on any of these numbers, though I do, generally, rely on the demographic data produced by the demographer Vilmos Tánczos. In English, see Tánczos, "About the Demography of the Moldavian Csángós"; Tánczos, "Hungarian Language Command among the Moldavian Csángós, 2008–10"; and Peti and Tánczos, *Language Use, Attitudes, Strategies.*

15. As Joseph Rothschild has observed, "ethnicity is a plastic, variegated, and originally ascriptive trait" that is readily politicized in certain fertile historical circumstances. See Rothschild, *Ethnopolitics*, 1.

16. Even those Romanian authors who rejected the Hungarian ethnic origin and nationality of the Csangos, in part or in whole, still employed the term in their writings. See, for example, Râmneanțu, *Die Abstammung der Tschangos*; D. Mărtinaș, *Originea ceangăilor din Moldova*; and Dumitriu-Snagov, "Ceangăii—Dincolo de enigmă," 33–38. By contrast, the clerical and laic historians whose works are supported by the Catholic Church in Moldavia (and typically bear the imprimatur of the bishop of Iași) have consistently rejected or avoided the term Csango, especially in the titles of their articles and books. In recent years, this includes the group of village monographers and historians who write on the Catholic Church and the Catholic communities in Moldavia. See for example Coșa, *Catolicii din Moldova în izvoarele Sfântului Scaun.*

17. Rothschild, *Ethnopolitics*, 2–3.

18. Brubaker acknowledges that we must take vernacular categories and participants' understandings seriously, "for they are partly constitutive of our objects of study." Nevertheless, "we should not uncritically adopt *categories of ethnopolitical practice* as our *categories of social analysis.*" Brubaker, "Ethnicity without Groups," 166 (emphasis in original). I have endeavored to keep this in mind while writing this book and acknowledge that my uses of the term Csango, for instance, can often reify or reconstitute the very "group" I aim to describe and deconstruct.

19. I reference here Anthony D. Smith's distinction between, on the one hand, "ethnie" or "ethnic community" and, on the other, "ethnic category." Smith defines the former as a named population with myths of common ancestry, shared historical memories, and one or more common elements of culture, including an association with a homeland, and some degree of solidarity, at least among elites. These traits are recognized by both members of the *ethnie* and by outsiders. He defines the latter as populations distinguished specifically by outsiders as possessing the attributes of a common

name or emblem, a shared cultural element (usually language or religion), and a link with a particular territory. Smith, "Ethno-symbolism and the Study of Nationalism," 25.

20. Cotoi, "The Politics of Ethnography: Figures of Csangoness in Fin-de-siècle and Twentieth-Century Hungary and Romania"; Cotoi, "New Technologies for Ethno-nationalist Imaging: The Case of Moldavian Csangos." Cotoi has proposed, for example, the "figures" of the "ethnographic Csango," the "confessional Csango," and the "statistical Csango," to name but a few possibilities.

21. See Ilyés, "The Image of the Csángós in the Hungarian Press of Transylvania."

22. See Turda, "The Nation as Object"; and Trencsényi, "'Imposed Authenticity.'"

23. Kapalo's work on the Gagauz examines the dichotomy between the community's Orthodox religious faith and their Turkish linguistic identity as well as the role of the Gagauz clergy in processes of identity formation and the development of a Gagauz national consciousness embracing both Russian Orthodoxy and "Turkishness." See Kapalo, *Text, Context and Performance: Gagauz Folk Religion in Discourse and Practice*; Kapalo, "Clerical Agency and the Politics of Scriptural Translation: The 'Canonization' of the Gagauz Language in Southern Bessarabia."

24. On "representative biography," see Muller, *The Other God That Failed*.

25. Verdery, "The Production and Defense of 'the Romanian Nation,'" 107 (emphasis in original).

26. Ibid., 91 (emphasis in original).

27. Important discussions about this debate are dealt with in Hitchins, *Rumania 1866–1947*, 315–17; Ornea, *Anii treizeci: Extrema dreaptă românească*, 91–94; Boia, *History and Myth in Romanian Consciousness*, 146–47; and, especially, Biliuță, "The Philosopher and Orthodoxism: An Inquiry into the 'Ethnic Ontology' of Nae Ionescu," 191–95. According to Biliuță, Ionescu's polemic represented a landmark in the construction of Romanian nationalism, further differentiating his radical brand of ethnocentrism from those of his contemporaries, including Nichifor Crainic and the leaders of the Iron Guard.

28. Turda, "The Nation as Object," 415.

29. See Antohi, "Romania and the Balkans: From Geocultural Bovarism to Ethnic Ontology."

30. See, for example, Bryant, "Either German or Czech"; Slezkine, *Arctic Mirrors*; Chu, "'*Volksgemeinschaften unter sich*'"; Brock, "Florjan Cenôva and the Kashub Question"; Kiril Feferman, "Nazi Germany and the Karaites in 1938–1944"; and Mikhail Kizilov, *The Karaites of Galicia*.

31. Hirsch, *Empire of Nations*, 14. See also Slezkine, "The USSR as a Communal Apartment, or How a Socialist State Promoted Ethnic Particularism"; and Martin, *The Affirmative Action Empire*; and Polian, *Against Their Will*.

32. Jeremy King and James Bjork have produced important works on the various ways in which specific communities in east-central Europe reacted to competing claims on their identities and loyalties, showing how these communities with such convoluted pasts and presents were able to accommodate (or not) the impositions of national states and nation-building elites. See King, *Budwiesers into Czechs and Germans*; and Bjork, *Neither German nor Pole*. In many ways, my own work on the Csangos offers a similar type of case

study, one situated much farther east, in a Hungarian-Romanian and Catholic-Orthodox historical border zone.

33. Burleigh, *Germany Turns Eastwards*, 4.
34. Chu, "'*Volksgemeinschaften unter sich*,'" 105. On "amphibious" communities, see Bryant, "Either German or Czech."
35. Bryant, "Either German or Czech," 701.
36. Ibid., 691.
37. Caplan and Torpey, "Introduction," 1–2; and Scott, *Seeing Like a State*, 65, 78–79.
38. Hirsch, *Empire of Nations*, 12–14.
39. Bryant, "Either German or Czech," 684.

Chapter 1. Demography Is Destiny

1. Iordachi, "Citizenship and National Identity in Romania," 18–19.
2. This was a rather stunning turn of events for most Csangos, for as C. A. Macartney noted at the time, "The Csángós have clung to their old customs, yet they have never been overtly nationalist, much less irredentist, nor have they lived on bad terms with their Romanian Orthodox neighbors." Macartney, "The Csángós of Roumania," 1.
3. Population figures taken from Manuilă, *Recensământul general al populaţiei României*, 24, 26, and 50. Additional population data taken from Auner, *A romániai magyar telepek történeti vázlata*; Rothschild, *East Central Europe between the Two World Wars*, 284 and 289; Svart-Kara, *Obştea evreiască din Bacău*, 50–51; Ioanid, "The Holocaust in Romania," 121–22; and Tánczos, "About the Demography of the Moldavian Csángós," 123–36.
4. Population figures taken from Tánczos, "About the Demography of the Moldavian Csángós," 123–36; Manuilă, *Recensământul general al populaţiei României*, 24, 26, and 50; Auner, *A romániai magyar telepek történeti vázlata*; and Râmneanţu, *Die Abstammung der Tschangos*, 21–24.
5. Pozsony, *The Hungarian Csango of Moldova*, 58–59.
6. See AN Bacău, fond Comunitatea Evreilor din Bacău, dosar 5/1939, 8. Cited in Svart-Kara, *Obştea evreiască din Bacău*, 153; and Rothschild, *East Central Europe between the Two World Wars*, 285.
7. The name of Codreanu's fascist political organization—at once a political movement, paramilitary group, and political party—changed a number of times.
8. Approximately two hundred thousand of the country's Jews were killed, in addition to nearly twenty-five thousand Roma and the one hundred thousand Ukrainian Jews killed in Romanian controlled territory in the east. However, estimates vary as to Jewish and Roma death tolls under the Antonescu regime. See Ioanid, "The Holocaust in Romania," 121–22; Frilling, Ioanid, and Ionescu, *Final Report: International Commission on the Holocaust in Romania*, 175–79 and 381–82; Deletant, *Hitler's Forgotten Ally*, 127; and Ioanid, "Studiu introductiv: Tragedia deportării romilor în Transnistria," 43–44, 51–53.
9. See Jelavich, *Russia and the Formation of the Romanian National State*; Cristina Petrescu, "Contrasting/Conflicting Identities," 157–61; and Nagy-Talavera, *The Green*

Shirts and the Others, 17. For a more sustained discussion on how modern Romania was "Romanianized," see Boia, *Cum s-a românizat România*, 13–50. Neagu Djuvara also explores the multiethnic character of the Romanian peoples, and specifically the Romanian voivodes, from the Middle Ages. See Djuvara, *Thocomerius–Negru Vodă*.

10. Weber, *Peasants into Frenchmen*, xii.

11. I find Kate Brown's description of the peasantry in multiethnic Polish-Ukrainain lands an apt comparison for much of rural Romania prior to World War II. See Brown, *A Biography of No Place*, 40. Anastasia N. Karakasidou's description of Greek Macedonia paints a similar portrait in the Balkans. See the introduction in Karakasidou's *Fields of Wheat, Hills of Blood*, 1–27.

12. Liulevicius, *War Land on the Eastern Front*, 185. Silviu Miloiu suggests applying Liulevicius's notion of "elective ethnicity" to the case of the Csangos. See Miloiu, "The Csangos of Romanian Moldavia," 125–26. Antonina Kłoskowska's insights into borderline situations characterized as "bivalence" (in which individuals can oscillate between two national communities and their culture) or even "ambivalence" (understood here as uncertain national identification) can likewise provide apt frameworks for understanding identic positioning of many Csangos in recent history. See Kłoskowska, *National Cultures at the Grass-Root Level*.

13. Social scientists, psychologists, philosophers, and historians have applied the term Other (capitalized, as a pronoun) as a means of exploring identity-building processes and examining the processes of symbolic exclusion, especially of the so-called "internal Other." Such individuals and communities exist not only around the contested, crooked borders in far off lands between newly created states or else old ones with historical enmities but also at the margins or peripheries of cultural systems. It is when these cultural differences—most commonly linguistic and religious—are recognized and sharpened that the image and stigma of their marginality arises. See Wingfield, "Introduction," 1. See also Stråth, *Europe and the Other and Europe as the Other*.

14. What is more, Carol I's wife, Elizabeth, was Protestant. Ferdinand's wife, Marie, belonged to the Church of England (and later in life was recognized as a convert to the Baha'i faith). Carol II's longtime mistress and third and final wife, Elena Magda Lupescu, was born a Roman Catholic. Her father was a Jewish apothecary before he converted to Catholicism.

15. Vladimir Ghika, referred to by Pope Pius XI as "the great apostolic vagabond," converted to Catholicism in 1902 while in France, famously stating that he did so "in order to become more Orthodox." Ghika became an ordained Catholic priest in 1923 and over the course of his life set up a number of hospitals and charities in Romania and elsewhere in Europe. He also converted the noted Romanian writer and former communist Panait Istrati on the latter's deathbed in 1935. In 1952 the Romanian Communist government arrested him. He died in prison two years later. See Vasile, "Monseniorul Vladimir Ghica în atenția serviciilor de informație, 1945–1948."

16. The leader of the Iron Guard was born Cornelius Zeliński in the small Moldavian town of Huși. At his trial in 1938, much was made of his supposed foreign ancestry.

His mother, Elisa (née Brauner), was of German heritage, and his father, Iohan Antec Zeliński, was born with a Polish name. Of course, the Slavicization of Romanian names (and the Romanianization of Slavic names) in the region was not uncommon, depending on the period and the rule. The Polonization of names was prevalent in Bukovina after its annexation to the Habsburg Monarchy in 1775. As with the case of the Csangos, it would be remiss to draw conclusions as to the ethnic and national sentiments of generations of peoples whose names were constantly being transformed by the dominant national community or institutions (such as the church) in a given area.

17. On the SSRCI, the policy of Romanianization, and the grand designs for population exchanges, I am again indebted to the works of Viorel Achim and Vladimir Solonari. Much of my own research on the plight of the Csangos during World War II can be seen as a case study that fits within the broader framework and themes laid out in their scholarship. See Achim, "Romanian-German Collaboration in Ethnopolitics," 139–54; and Solonari, *Purifying the Nation*.

18. Burleigh, *Germany Turns Eastwards*, 9. As Liulevicius has noted, the fluidity of national identifications was further proof of the east's essential disorder. After World War I, a semantic shift occurred from the notion of "lands and peoples" to "spaces and races." By World War II, this perception of the east fueled Nazi ambitions for a systematic cleansing of eastern territories. See Liulevicius, *War Land on the Eastern Front*, 279.

19. The meaning of the term "diaspora" has proliferated in recent years, both in the social sciences and in the media. According to Rogers Brubaker, a diasporic community need not be treated simply as a bounded entity but as an idiom, stance, and claim. I use the term here in a basic sense, one described by Brubaker as "ethnonational communities separated by a political frontier from their *putative* national homeland" (emphasis in original). See Brubaker, "The 'Diaspora' Diaspora." The Hungarian term for diaspora, *szórvány*, became more widely used after the post–World War I settlement and redrawing of borders in 1920, which left a third of the pre-war Hungarian population in neighboring states. See also Bárdi, "Hungary and the Hungarians Living Abroad," 124–25.

20. Nagy, "Szórvány és beolvadás." Quoted in Barna, "Internal Diaspora—Assimilation—Formation of the Internal Diaspora," 64. Nagy cited as a case in point the linguistic assimilation of the Moldavian Csangos to the Romanians.

21. See Hitchins, "Erdélyi Fiatalok."

22. See Erős, *A Szekfű—Mályusz vita*.

23. On Christian nationalism in Hungary, see Hanebrink, *In Defense of Christian Hungary*; for the Romanian case, Keith Hitchins, "Orthodoxism: Polemics over Ethnicity and Religion in Interwar Romania," 135–56. Comparatively, Brian Porter's work on nineteenth-century Polish nationalism is illuminating for the Romanian and Hungarian cases. Poland's struggles for territorial reintegration and security were often justified through the use of heterodox religious terminology, for example, Poland as the "Christ of Nations." Like most of its neighbors, conceptions of the nation underwent a dramatic shift from the abstractions of romantic idealism, which defined the nation according to the

"national spirit" or "ideal," to the "modern," positivist sociological and ethnographic definitions. See Porter, *When Nationalism Began to Hate*, chapters 1–2.

24. Boia, *History and Myth in Romanian Consciousness*, 34. On the distinctions between French and German traditions of nationhood, see Brubaker, *Citizenship and Nationhood in France and Germany*, 1–3; and Fahrmeir, *Citizenship: The Rise and Fall of a Modern Concept*, 5–6. Both Brubaker and Fahrmeir caution against seeing the French and German cases as a "bipolar comparison" or "ready-made conceptual pairs." They note furthermore that the distinctions between them were not always the dominant tradition in either country.

25. Iordachi, "Citizenship and National Identity in Romania," 19.

26. See Burleigh, *The Third Reich: A New History*, 95.

27. Trencsényi, "'Imposed Authenticity,'" 21. See also Hofer, "The 'Hungarian Soul.'" In Hungary, the landmark volume *Mi a magyar?*, edited by Gyula Szekfű and published in 1939, brought together a number of prominent intellectuals to address the self-consciousness of the Hungarianness of the Hungarian people. The volume included the writings of a wide range of historians, ethnographers, established racial anthropologists such as Bartucz, and even poets and ethnomusicologists. The aim of this work was to redefine the canon on national characterology within some semblance of historical normativity. For a critical look at the volume, see Trencsényi, "'Imposed Authenticity,'" 39; and Miskolczy, "Mi a magyar?"

28. Várdy, *Modern Hungarian Historiography*, 68.

29. Deák, "Historiography of the Countries of Eastern Europe: Hungary," 1049–50. As Szekfű's colleague and coauthor Bálint Hóman once remarked, "Hungarian history is nothing but the history of the Hungarian soul." The two coauthored the monumental, multivolume historical synthesis of the history of Hungary, *Magyar történet*, vols. 1–8.

30. Hofer, "The 'Hungarian Soul' and the 'Historic Layers of National Heritage,'" 78.

31. Even between the young historians there were diverging views as to whether the ethnic formation was a Daco-Roman or a Daco-Romano-Slav mix and, moreover, which entity colonized the other. See, for example, Panaitescu, *Istoria românilor*; Gh. I. Brătianu, *Une énigme et un miracle historique: Le peuple roumain*; and C.C. Giurescu, *Istoria românilor*, vols. 1–5.

32. See Trencsényi, "'Imposed Authenticity,'" 25; Zub, *Istorie și istorici în România interbelică*, 173–74; Turda, "National Historiographies in the Balkans, 1830–1989," 483–84; and Kellogg, *A History of Romanian Historical Writing*, 45.

33. Rădulescu-Motru, *Românismul. Catehismul unei noi spiritualități*; Rădulescu-Motru, *Psihologia poporului român*; and Rădulescu-Motru, *Etnicul românesc. Comunitate de origine, limbă și destin*; Blaga, *Spațiul mioritic*. See also Georgescu, *The Romanians: A History*, 205.

Chapter 2. The Sacred

1. On Transylvania, see Puttkamer, "Framework of Modernization," 22. On the confessional schools and school system in Transylvania, see Nóda, "The Roman Catholic Denominational Education between the World Wars."

2. Mitu, *National Identity of Romanians in Transylvania*, 244; and Macartney, *Hungary and Her Successors*, 302.

3. H. Smith, "Prussia at the Margins," 78.

4. Macartney, *Hungary and Her Successors*, 285.

5. Lutheran churches in the Regat were regulated from Germany. From the late Middle Ages to the unification of the Romanian principalities in the mid-nineteenth century, the Catholics of Moldavia were under Hungarian, Polish, or Austrian bishoprics (the Bacău and Iași dioceses were alternately disestablished, reestablished, and moved). The Apostolic Vicariate of Moldavia was established in Iași in 1818, which was subsequently raised to the Iași Diocese in 1884. The Catholic communities of Wallachia and Bucharest dated from around the eighteenth century and were comprised mainly of Italians, Hungarians, and the French. These communities were under the authority of the Bulgarian bishopric of Nikopol and of the archbishop of Constantinople. The vicarate of Bucharest was elevated to an archdiocese in 1883 and metropolitan in 1930.

6. See Hitchins, *Rumania 1866–1947*, 292–334; and Verdery, "The Production and Defense of 'the Romanian Nation,'" 85–91.

7. See Clark, *Holy Legionary Youth: Fascist Activism in Interwar Romania*; Clark, *Nationalism, Ethnotheology, and Mysticism in Interwar Romania*; Ornea, *Anii treizeci*; Hitchins, "Orthodoxism"; and Neamțu, "Between the Gospel and the Nation."

8. Mitu, "'Rămășițele zilei,'" 210.

9. Marmaggi was reappointed as the nuncio to Czechoslovakia in 1923, less than three years after arriving in Romania. Netzhammer was forced by the Vatican to retire in 1924.

10. Prior to Cisar and Robu, the previous bishops of the Iași and Bucharest dioceses had hailed from Switzerland, Germany, Austria, or Italy. Robu held the position of bishop of Iași until his death.

11. Historically, the northern Csango villages were linguistically mixed. Săbăoani/Szabófalva was one of the few northern Csango villages in Neamț County where Hungarian functioned as a communal language up until the 1930s. Since then, there has been a sharp decline in the use of Hungarian. See Pozsony, "Church Life in Moldavian Hungarian Communities," 100–104. Though a "Csango in origin," Robu was "in sentiment and culture entirely Romanian," according to Bálint Csűry, a prominent twentieth-century Hungarian linguist who worked in the region studying the northern Csango dialects. See Csűry's 1934 letter, "Részletek Csűry Bálint nyelvész moldvai útibeszámolójából," in Vincze, *Asszimiláció vagy kivándorlás?*, 204. Csűry's account is dated June 1934, from Debrecen, Hungary.

12. *Memoriu și scrisoarea lui Vasile Goldiș*, 16 May 1927. Cited in Gojinescu, "Concordatul din 1929 și organizarea cultului catolic în România," 32.

13. Bălan, *Biserica neamului și drepturile ei*, 36, 57.

14. Netzhammer in Netzhammer and Zach, *Episcop în România*, 1290.

15. King Ferdinand of Romania (1865–1927, r. 1914–27) was from the Hohenzollern-Sigmaringen dynasty, the Catholic branch of the Prussian ruling family. He ardently

supported the Concordat despite much opposition within Romanian society, especially from the Orthodox Church.

16. Nóda, "The Historical, Political and Ecclesiastical Background of the 1927 Concordat between the Vatican and Romania," 289.

17. This would come to pass after 1948, when the Romanian communist state renounced the Concordat and broke off relations with the Vatican, forced Greek Catholic priests to convert to Romanian Orthodoxy, and for a period of time disbanded the Greek Catholic Church in Romania.

18. All primates and Orthodox and Greek Catholic bishops in Romania were *ex officio* members of the senate, while only the heads of the other "recognized" denominations of at least two hundred thousand adherents enjoyed this privilege. Hossu had opposed the etatization of the Transylvanian Greek-Catholic confessional schools as part of Minister of Education Constantin Angelescu's school reforms of 1925.

19. Bălan, *Biserica neamului și drepturile ei*, 53, 57.

20. Bălan, *Biserica împotriva Concordatului*, 48–49.

21. Botoșăneanu, "Biserica Ortodoxă Română și celelalte confesiuni," 485–88. Cited in Leustean, "'For the Glory of Romanians,'" 729.

22. Ghibu, *Nulitatea Concordatului*, 45–46, 61.

23. Ghibu, *Politica religioasă și minoritară a României*, 512–13.

24. Ionescu, "Concordatul."

25. Livezeanu, *Cultural Politics in Greater Romania*, 48.

26. See Neamțu, "Between the Gospel and the Nation"; Clark, *Nationalism, Ethnotheology, and Mysticism in Interwar Romania*; and Biliuță, "The Philosopher and Orthodoxism," 191.

27. Stăniloae, "Ortodoxie și latinitate," 199, 202.

28. Stăniloae, *Ortodoxie și românism*, 94–95.

29. Crainic, "Sensul tradiției," 3.

30. See Livezeanu, "After the Great Union: Generational Tensions, Intellectuals, Modernism, and Ethnicity in Interwar Romania," 118.

31. Durcovici, who was born in Austria and completed most of his seminary training and higher education in Italy, was rector of the Catholic seminary in Bucharest from 1924 to 1948. In 1948 he was appointed bishop of Iași, but shortly thereafter was imprisoned, tortured, and killed by the Romanian communists. The Orthodox priest Grigorie Pișculescu, better known as Gala Galaction, was a well-known writer, journalist, translator, theologian, and leftist.

32. As part of his courses on mysticism, he taught the sixth-century theologian and philosopher Pseudo-Dionysius the Areopagite as well as the medieval German mystics such as Meister Eckhart and his followers, Heinrich Seuse, Johannes Tauler, and the Flemish mystic, John of Ruysbroeck. See Crainic's *Cursurile de mistică: Teologie mistică, Mistică germană*, 215–40 and 409–556.

33. Crainic, *Ortodoxie și etnocrație. Cu o anexă: Programul statului etnocratic*, 260. See especially the chapter titled "Catolicismul și fascismul," 256–71.

34. Crainic, "Roma universală," republished in *Puncte cardinale în haos*, 298–99.
35. Biliuță, "The Philosopher and Orthodoxism," 194.
36. Vanhaelemeersch, *A Generation without Beliefs*, 205–6.
37. Clark, *Nationalism, Ethnotheology, and Mysticism in Interwar Romania*, 6; and Hitchins, *Rumania*, 299.
38. Leustean, "For the Glory of Romanians," 717.
39. Notably, the Roman Catholic priests such as Iosif Malinovski, Iosif Petru M. Pal, Ion Ferenț, and Iosif Ghiuzan; Greek Catholics such as Nicolae Popa and Augustin Popa; and lay theologians and intellectuals such as Iosif Frollo.
40. Again, the discussion here centers on the diocese in Moldavia and the archdiocese in Bucharest, not on the Catholic Church in Transylvania. In Moldavia, the most important of these journals were *Lumina creștinului*, *Viața*, *Almanahul Presa Bună*, *Sentinela catolică*, and *Aurora franciscană*. In Bucharest, there was also the aforementioned ecumenical journal *Farul nou*, which Iosif Frollo edited and frequently contributed to. A number of supplements also appeared within these sheets, including *Dacia creștină*. See Dumea, *Cărți și reviste catolice românești în Moldova*.
41. Anon., "Spre o 'internațională' catolică," *Farul nou* 44 (5 May 1935).
42. *Dacia creștină* (c. 1934). Cited in Dumea, *Cărți și reviste catolice românești în Moldova*, 91, fn. 5. See also Ghiuzan, "Deopotrivă libertate și protecțiune," 1–2.
43. Ghiuzan died tragically in a car wreck in 1932. Undoubtedly, he would have remained a strident voice among the Csango's clergy who spoke out publicly in defense of the community, especially as the situation worsened in the late 1930s and during the war.
44. Ghiuzan, "Român catolic," 1.
45. Ibid., 2. There is no incontrovertible evidence of Christianity in Roman Dacia. The practice of Christianity in Dacia and Dobrudja, areas south of the Danube, can be shown from the fourth century CE. See Boia, *History and Myth in Romanian Consciousness*, 11.
46. Anon., "Stiință și religie," 25–26.
47. Iosif Meriea Marin Frollo was born in Bucharest, where he remained for most of his life. He was the son of Gian Luigi Frollo, a nineteenth-century Italian linguist who, after moving to Brăila and then Bucharest, contributed greatly to the development of Romanian language and literature. For a brief description of Frollo and his wife Mia, a noted writer and translator in her own right, see Nastasă, *"Suveranii" Universităților Românești*, 153; and Doboș, "File de istorie: Iosif Frollo," 19.
48. ACNSAS, Iosif Frollo, P.016016, 113.
49. The modern version of Catholic Action had its roots in Article 43 of Pope Pius XI's pact with Mussolini, the Lateran Treaty in 1929. Cardinal Eugenio Pacelli, the future Pope Pius XII, had promoted Catholic Action in Germany in the late 1920s with the aim to stymie political and social Catholicism and to insulate the clergy from the radicalizing right-wing politics in fascist Italy and Nazi Germany. He thereby hoped to secure better terms for the Vatican in any future *Reichskondordat* (finally agreed to in 1933). See Cornwell, *Hitler's Pope*, 114–16.

50. Frollo, "Patriotism și creștinism," 2.

51. Frollo, "Biserică națională."

52. Ungureanu, "Note și comentarii," 133, n. 49. Ștefania Petrescu became a teacher of French at an institute of the Congregation of Notre Dame de Sion in Iași. The Roman Catholic Congregation of Our Lady of Sion (Zion) was a French religious order of women founded in 1843. Its founding mission was to hasten the conversion of Jews to Christianity.

53. Scriban, "Călugărițele catolice nu-și lasă năravul," 1–2. See also Gheorghe Racoveanu's attack on Ms. Petrescu in his entry under "Dumineca," *Cuvântul* 6/1989 (3 Nov. 1930).

54. See also Frollo's response to Scriban in "Scrisoare deschisă cătră S.S. Arhimandritul Scriban," 1–2; and Frollo, "În jurul unei conversiuni la catolicism," 2–3. For Scriban's reply to Frollo, see "Trecerile la catolicism: Răspuns d-lui profesor Iosif Frollo," 1–2; and Scriban, "Dacă d. Frollo vrea dovezi," 1–2.

55. Ionescu, "A fi 'bun român,'" 1.

56. Biliuță, "The Philosopher and Orthodoxism," 192.

57. Frollo, *Romînism și catolicism*, 10–11.

58. Ibid., 20–21, 26.

59. See Biliuță, "The Philosopher and Orthodoxism," 182, 188–95; Vanhaelemeersch, *A Generation without Beliefs*, 231; and Fischer-Galați, "The Interwar Period," 307.

60. See Hitchins, *Rumania*, 385–86.

61. Clark, "Nationalism and Orthodoxy."

62. See Iordachi, "God's Chosen Warriors," 348–54. The term "national ecumenicity" was coined by the Legionary and Orthodox theologian, Ilie Imbrescu. See Imbrescu, *Biserica și mișcarea legionară*, 171. Cited in Iordachi, "God's Chosen Warriors," 349. For the more conventional view that Eastern Orthodox Christianity was intrinsic to the Legion's political structure and message, see, for example, Ioanid, *The Sword of the Archangel*; Weber, "Romania"; and Rebecca Haynes, "Work Camps, Commerce, and the Education of the 'New Man' in the Romanian Legionary Movement."

63. Iordachi, "God's Chosen Warriors," 346–53.

64. Codreanu, *For My Legionaries*, n.p.

65. Săndulescu, "Revolutionizing Romania from the Right," 51–52. See also Săndulescu, "'Taming the Spirit': Notes on the Shaping of the Legionary 'New Man.'"

66. Codreanu, *For My Legionaries*, n.p.

67. ACNSAS, fond Iosif Frollo, I.261389, 1–2 and 66–67; and ACNSAS, fond Iosif Frollo, I.261389, P.016016, 8–20. As Roland Clark has detailed, right-wing movements both large and small flourished in 1930s Europe, and Romania was no exception. Ultranationalist groups regularly appeared and then disappeared, and adherents frequently moved from one to the other. By 1937 Romania had almost ten different "colored shirts" representing one or another radical, outlawed political organization. See Clark, "Nationalism and Orthodoxy."

68. Ion Zelea (Zieliński) Codreanu was a high-school teacher in the northern Moldavian town of Huşi. Born in Austrian Bukovina, he moved to Huşi (in Romanian Moldavia) shortly before the birth of his son Corneliu. Once in Romania, the elder Codreanu Romanianized his Polish surname Zielińsky (from *zieleń* for "green" in Polish) to Zelea and even added a new Romanian surname, Codreanu ("forester," from *codru*, meaning forest in Romanian). He named all his children after Romanian or Dacian heroes. See Nagy-Talavera, *The Green Shirts and the Others*, 73, 350–52.

69. Frollo acknowledges this in his testimony at Codreanu's trial in 1938 and in his later interviews with the Securitate. See ACNSAS, fond Iosif Frollo, I.261389, 1.

70. ACNSAS, fond Iosif Frollo, P.016016, 8–20.

71. In his testimony at Codreanu's trial as well as in his later interviews with the Securitate, Frollo acknowledges his run for Senate under the TPŢ banner in the 1937 elections. He is also listed in the files of the USHMM, SRI reel nos. 105–859, dosar 859, Problema Legionară: Candidaţi Legionari în Alegerile pentru Senat din 22 Dec. 1937, 189.

72. The TPŢ won about 15 percent of the vote nationwide but received only 8.5 percent in Bacău County, 4.5 percent in Iaşi County, and 2.63 percent in Roman County. Statistical data for the 1937 election results taken from the table in Heinen, *Legiunea "Arhanghelul Mihail,"* 466–67.

73. Codreanu, *Circulări şi manifeste 1927–1938*, 238.

74. The deposition of Iosif Frollo took place on 24 May 1938. See excerpts of his testimony in Sfinţescu, *Din luptele tineretului român 1919–1939: Corneliu Zelea Codreanu (culegere de texte)*; and http://foaienationala.ro/depoziia-avocatului-iosif-frollo-din-cadrul-pro cesului-mpotriva-lui-corneliu-zelea-codreanu.html, accessed 24 March 2018.

75. ACNSAS, fond Iosif Frollo, P.016016, 96, 99, and 114.

76. Ioan Mărtinaş (in some files recorded as being born Tamas [or Ianos] Martinas Gabur) was the younger brother of Dumitru Mărtinaş, author of *Originea ceangăilor din Moldova* (Bucharest, 1985). Since its publication, Dumitru's book has had an enormous impact on the debate over the ethnic origins of the Csangos. From the Csango area the only other Roman Catholic priests identified in the Securitate files as linked to the Iron Guard are Fathers Petru Cadaru (or Cadar) and Dumitru Herghelegiu. Mărtinaş, Cadaru, and Herghelegiu all spent time in Italy either in the 1930s or during the war. See ACNSAS, fond Herghelegiu Dumitru, I.141286, vol. 3, 46; and ibid., vol. 4, 122. Additional references to Cadaru's Legionary activities are found in ACNSAS, fond Tocanel Petru, I.234406, vol. 4, 433. According to one of Mărtinaş's files, he is reported to have joined the Legionary movement as early as 1929.

77. AN Bacău, fond Parohia Romano-Catolică Luizi-Călugăra, dosar 1/1940, 38. The letter, sent from Gherăeşti, is dated 20 Dec. 1940.

78. Ibid., 31. This letter, also sent from Gherăeşti, is dated 6 Jan. 1941.

79. "Ajutorul Legionar," *Cuvântul* 17/11, 24 Oct. 1940. One of the founding members of the Legionary movement, Ilie Gârneaţă, established the charity organization on 26

September 1940, two weeks after the proclamation of the National Legionary State. It set up canteens and restaurants around the country to provide for the poor. This charity and social work was also a way to counter any influence from the Communists; simultaneously, it was a means of increasing visibility and support for the Party, as by January 1941 it was clear the regime was divided. Political battle lines were already being drawn between, on the one hand, Sima and the Legionaries and, on the other, Antonescu and the Romanian military establishment.

80. Otu, "Septembrie 1940–ianuarie 1941. Armata in 'Statul Național Legionar': Preliminarii," 37. On the battle between Sima and Antonescu for the military's allegiance during these tumultuous months, see Heinen, *Legiunea "Arhanghelul Mihail,"* 412–14.

81. ACNSAS, fond Ioan Mărtinaș, I.141282, vol. 1, 50–51, 72–73.

Chapter 3. The Profane

1. Brown, *A Biography of No Place*, 195.
2. See Boia, *History and Myth in Romanian Consciousness*, 34.
3. Trencsényi, "Imposed Authenticity," 25.
4. Hettling, "Volk und Volksgeschichten in Europa," 34.
5. Trencsényi, "Imposed Authenticity," 21; Hofer, "The 'Hungarian Soul' and the 'Historic Layers of National Heritage.'"
6. Key to the development of population policies and colonization projects was research undertaken by the Ostforscher on populations such as the Kashubs (or Cassubians), Masures, and the so-called Lodzer Mensch (the ethnic Germans of the cosmopolitan city of Łódź)in Poland, the Sorbs in Germany, and the Karaite Jews in Ukraine.
7. Burleigh, *Germany Turns Eastward*, 4; Lower, *Nazi Empire Building in Ukraine*, 20–24.
8. Other minority communities in central and eastern Europe were likewise subject to these questions and dilemmas, from the Lusatian Serbs, Bunjevci, or Aromanians in the Balkans to Slovincians and Masures in north-central Europe and Csangos, Gagauz, and Karaites farther east.
9. See Chu, "'*Volksgemeinschaften unter sich*,'" 105; Bryant, "Either German or Czech."
10. Szekler(s) (Hu. *székely* [sing.]/*székelyek* [pl.]; Ro. *secui*) is the Anglicized (via German) ethnonym for the Catholic and Protestant ethnolinguistic subgroup of Hungarians in eastern Transylvania, a region historically part of the Kingdom of Hungary but part of Romania since World War I (Northern Transylvania, including the Szekler-inhabited region, was ceded back to Hungary from 1940 to 1944). It is generally held that the Szeklers colonized the area around the eleventh century, though some theories place them in the Carpathian basin much earlier. Historically, the Szeklers were among the ruling nations of Transylvania, the Unio trium nationum, alongside the Saxons and Hungarians (and excluding the Romanians).
11. Bryant, "Either German or Czech," 701.
12. Chu, "'Volksgemeinschaften unter sich,'" 115.

13. Livezeanu, *Cultural Politics in Greater Romania*, 139–40. See also Bucur's discussion of Romanian eugenicists' research on the Szeklers in the interwar period in *Eugenics and Modernization*, 145–46.

14. Porsenna, *Regenerarea neamului romanesc*; Cioran, *Schimbarea la față a României*.

15. The most prominent right-winger in Gusti's circle was Train Herseni, a member of the Legionary movement. See Săndulescu, "Academic Elites and Their Trajectories in Troubled Times," 86–94. Notable Hungarian sociologists and ethnographers who worked with Gusti included Péter Bakk, József Venczel, and Gábor Lükő. Other Hungarians engaged with Gusti's system indirectly. Americans who came into contact with the Gusti School in Bucharest included scholars Robert J. Kerner and Philip E. Mosely.

16. Solonari, "An Important New Document," 271.

17. Cotoi, "Reactionary Modernism in Interwar Romania," 125.

18. Golopenția, "Cronologie," 24.

19. Antohi, "Romania and the Balkans."

20. Bucur, *Eugenics and Modernization*, 49.

21. In Romania, the German communities were the exception to this phenomenon. The Saxons and Swabians had long been held up as model ethnic and national communities. Moreover, unlike Hungary, Germany's role as a "nationalizing homeland" was mitigated by the fact that it had never shared a border with Romania. Even Romanian royalty was German. Thus, Romania's Germans were valued culturally, economically, and politically, especially after the coming of the Third Reich.

22. Turda, "The Nation as Object," 435. See for example Moldovan, *Biopolitica*; Moldovan, *Statul etnic*; Moldovan, *Introducere în etnobiologie și biopolitică*; and Stan, *Rasă și religiune*.

23. Livezeanu, *Cultural Politics in Greater Romania*, 139.

24. Macartney, *Hungary and Her Successors*, 306.

25. Livezeanu, *Cultural Politics in Greater Romania*, 139.

26. Macartney, *Hungary and Her Successors*, 286–87.

27. Vâlsan, in the foreword to Opreanu, *Săcuizarea Românilor prin religie*, ii–iii.

28. Chindea was a native of the village of Valea Strâmbă/Tekerőpatak, located in Harghita County, northern Szekler land. He was educated in Bucharest and Cluj before returning to his native region to become a schoolmaster and to establish local, Romanian-language journals. Chindea published a number of monographs detailing the denationalization or Szeklerization of Romanians (as well as Armenians, Saxons, and Jews) in eastern Transylvania. He founded and wrote for the periodical *Gazeta Ciucului*, which ran from 1929 to 1939.

29. Chindea, *Contribuții la istoria Românilor din Giurgeul-Ciucului*, 118, 25–26.

30. Ibid., 102.

31. "Imnul românilor secuizați," lyrics by Horațiu Comaniciu and music by Ion Mânzatu, date unknown. ACNSAS, Corneliu Zelea Codreanu, P.011784, vol. 21, 42–50. The Nicadors were one of three Iron Guard death squads—the Nicadori, the Decemviri, and the Răzbunători—that assassinated various high-level Romanian political leaders in the 1930s. The Nicadori team (the name is derived from the first letters of the

names of the three assassins) murdered Prime Minister Ion G. Duca on 30 December 1933. Of the three men, two were Greek-born Aromanians. I am grateful to Roland Clark for sharing this source.

32. See Opreanu, *Săcuizarea Românilor prin religie*; Opreanu, *Ţinutul săcuilor*; and Opreanu, *Transilvania: Centrul pămîntului*. Opreanu was from a tiny village in Hunedoara County, in southwestern Transylvania. He taught economic geography in Cluj and Braşov and served on the steering committee (with Constantin Daicoviciu, Silviu Dragomir, Ionel Pop, and Petru Râmneanţu) of ASTRA's journal, *Transilvania: Revistă lunară de cultură*.

33. Opreanu, *Săcuizarea Românilor prin religie*, 16–17.

34. Ibid., 36–39.

35. Opreanu, *Die Szekler. Eine völkische Minderheit inmitten des Rumänientums*, 188.

36. The two Romanian-language dailies in the Szekler region were *Secuimea* and *Glas Românesc în Regiunea Secuizată*.

37. Dobrotă, *Români secuizaţi şi regiune secuizată*, 24. Dobrotă wrote these lines in 1939 and included them in his dedication. See also Dobrotă, *Momente de viaţă românească în Odorheiu*.

38. See Nistor, *Problema românească din ţinuturile secuizate şi Biserica ortodoxă*; and Meteş, *Le problème des sicules en Roumanie*. For an overview of the position of the Romanian Orthodox Church in the Szekler land, see Fola, "Biserica ortodoxă română în perioada dintre cele două războaie mondiale," 173–80.

39. Quoted in Dobrotă, *Români secuizaţi şi regiune secuizată*, 14–15.

40. For the anthropological and serological research done on the Szeklers, see Râmneanţu and David, "Cercetări asupra originii etnice a populaţiei din Sud-Estul Transilvaniei pe baza compoziţiei serologice a sângelui"; and Făcăoaru, "Compoziţia rasială la români, săcui şi unguri."

41. See Popa-Lisseanu, *Originea secuilor şi secuizarea Românilor*; Popa-Lisseanu, *Secuii şi secuizarea românilor*; Popa-Lisseanu, *Date privitoare la maghiarizarea românilor*; and Popa-Lisseanu, *Continuitatea românilor în Dacia*. See also Livezeanu, *Cultural Politics in Greater Romania*, 139–42.

42. A medical term describing short or broad headed, wherein the length of the cranium is shorter than the width.

43. Popa-Lisseanu, *Secuii şi secuizarea românilor*, 62.

44. In 1937 the historian Aurel A. Mureşianu published a monograph on the Romanian origins of the Hétfalusi csángók (Csangos of the seven villages) in Braşov County, just east of the city of Braşov. See Mureşianu, *Originea Ciangăilor din Săcelele Braşovului*.

45. Indeed, Cumans had inhabited Moldavia during the thirteenth century, in a territory known as Cumania. Cumania even had its own bishopric, founded and seated in Milcov in 1227 and attached to the Hungarian Archdiocese of Esztergom. It served the converted Cumans and the Teutonic Knights before the Mongols destroyed the region in 1241, forcing the Cumans to seek asylum in Hungary. After the Mongol wave

receded, Hungarian King Lajos annexed Moldavia in 1352, likely using some of the Cumans as sentinels along the Hungarian kingdom's eastern border. See Baker, "Magyars, Mongols, Romanians and Saxons"; Spinei, *Moldavia in the 11th–14th Centuries*; and Rădvan, *At Europe's Borders*, 312–14, 515.

46. "Primim aceste rinduri, care destăinuiesc originea românească a multor Ceangăi," *Revista Istorică*, 11/10–12 (Oct.–Dec. 1935): 402–3 (402). This was sent as a letter to the editor (Iorga) from Constantin Lozincă, published in the "Notițe" section at the back of the issue.

47. Ibid., 403. For example, the Romanian surname Roca, from the Hungarian *róka*, meaning fox, was originally phonetically similar to the Romanian Roșu, meaning red. The same held true for other Hungarian-sounding surnames such as Boldog (orig. the Romanian *fericit*, for happy) and Labău (orig. the Romanian *croitor*, for tailor).

48. Janos, *The Politics of Backwardness in Hungary*, 236.

49. Várdy, *Modern Hungarian Historiography*, 133; Hofer, "The 'Hungarian Soul,'" 77–78; Németh, *Magyarok Romániában*; Weaver, "More Hungarian Hungarians," 48.

50. Weaver, "More Hungarian Hungarians," 40.

51. Cornelius, *In Search of the Nation*, 1998.

52. Turanizmusz, or Turanism, a nineteenth- and early twentieth-century Orientalist idea about the ethnocultural relationship between the Finno-Ugric and Turkic peoples, which spawned a number of cultural and political organizations promoting the link between Hungarians, Turks, and other Central Asian peoples. Taken to its extreme, Turanism was used to bolster arguments about the racial origins and purity of the Hungarians. See Hanebrink "Islam, Anti-Communism, and Christian Civilization," 116–18.

53. Czigány, *The Oxford History of Hungarian Literature*, 397.

54. Trencsényi, "'Imposed Authenticity,'" 39; and Miskolczy, "Mi a magyar?"

55. Hanebrink, *In Defense of Christian Hungary*, 118; Deák, "Historiography of the Countries of Eastern Europe: Hungary," 1049–50; Várdy, *Modern Hungarian Historiography*, 48; Erős, *A Szekfű–Mályusz vita*.

56. Várdy, *Modern Hungarian Historiography*, 103–5; Erős, "Mályusz's Ethnohistory," 179.

57. Várdy, *Modern Hungarian Historiography*, 109.

58. Erős, "Mályusz's Ethnohistory," 182–83.

59. See Rostás, *Parcurs întrerupt*; Rostás, *O istorie orală a Școlii Sociologice de la București*; and Gáll, "Hungarian Sociologists from Romania and the School of Bucharest." Though Gáll characterized his generation as such, they were not directly influenced by narodnicism (nor were they influenced by its Romanian variant, *poporanism*), especially as they lacked a truly revolutionary program.

60. Gáll, "Hungarian Sociologists from Romania and the School of Bucharest," 67–68; and Némedi, "Remarks on the Role of Peasants in Hungarian Ideology," 68.

61. See also Török, "Planning the National Minority"; Hitchins, "Erdélyi Fiatalok," 85–87; and Borbándi, *A magyar népi mozgalom*, 116–17.

62. Chu, "Volksgemeinschaften unter sich," 115.

63. Raised in Bucharest and educated at the university in Kolozsvár/Cluj in the latter half of the nineteenth century, Veress began writing on the Hungarian minority in Romania at the turn of the century. As a historian, archivist, teacher, and professional translator, he was a product of the positivism that dominated Hungarian historical and ethnographic scholarship prior to the subsequent generation that upturned Hungarian historiography in the interwar period. See Benda, "The Hungarians of Moldavia (Csángós) in the 16th–17th Centuries," 12.

64. Veress, *The Hungarians of Moldavia*, 14. John (János) Tatrosi was the pseudonym for Endre (Andrei) Veress.

65. Veress, "A moldvai csángók származása és neve." Veress and later Mikecs were among the few who persisted in the belief that the origins of the Csangos were Cuman or else from some other tribe of proto-Magyars who had arrived and settled into Moldavia from the east, alongside the first Magyars to settle permanently into Europe beginning in the ninth century. By the 1920s, however, most linguists, archaeologists, and historians agreed that the Csango communities had arrived in western Moldavia from the Pannonian plain in the late Middle Ages, well after the first Magyar settlements.

66. At university in Budapest, he studied under ethnographer István Györffy and composer and ethnomusicologist Zoltán Kodály, where he was first exposed to Romanian folk music. On a scholarship provided by the Hungarian government to undertake research on the Csangos, Lükő left for Romania in 1931. He enrolled in the University of Bucharest and studied Romanian at Nicolae Iorga's summer school in Vălenii de Munte. When not in the Csango land doing research, he lived and studied in Bucharest, working under Gusti. See "Interview with Gábor Lükő," in Rostás, *Parcurs întrerupt*, 174–79.

67. Lükő, *A moldvai csángók*, 344–45.

68. Benda, "The Hungarians of Moldavia (Csángós) in the 16th–17th Centuries," 12.

69. Mikecs, *Csángók*, 5.

70. Várdy, *Modern Hungarian Historiography*, 115.

71. Mikecs, *Csángók*, 7.

72. Hanebrink, *In Defense of Christian Hungary*, 166; Juhász, *Uralkodó eszmék Magyarországon*, 173; and Turda, "Entangled Traditions of Race," 43.

73. Baumgartner [Siculus], *A moldvai magyarok őstelepülése, története és mai helyzete*, 5.

74. Baumgartner, *Moldva: A magyarság nagy temetője*, 5.

75. T. Attila Szabó was a linguist, historian, and ethnographer, who also edited a number of journals in Transylvania. In 1929 he conducted major research on Csango dialects with noted Hungarian linguist Bálint Csüri. In the 1930s and 1940s, he wrote mainly on the history of Hungarian settlements, demography, and toponomy. Living and working in Cluj from the 1950s onward, he took a greater interest in the Csangos and published numerous articles on their history, folk traditions, and dialect.

76. Șumuleu-Ciuc/Csíksomlyó is a famous destination for Transylvanian and Moldavian Catholic pilgrims during Pentecost.

Chapter 4. Certifiably Romanian

1. Case, *Between States*, 115, 121–23.
2. Named after Minister of Justice Gheorghe G. Mârzescu, who wrote much of the legislation.
3. Certificates of nationality or family origin, known as *Heimatscheine*, were issued by German states in the nineteenth century. See Fahrmeir, "Governments and Forgers," 225.
4. Hamangiu, *Codul general al României. Legi noui de Unificare*, 1922–1926, vols. 11–12, 292.
5. Butaru, "The Citizenship Issue in the Great Romania," 86.
6. Juvara, *Pandectele române*, Partea II-a (1939): 33–38.
7. Ibid.
8. Solonari, *Purifying the Nation*, 28.
9. Antonesco (Antonescu), *Nation et nationalité*, 19–20.
10. Pârâianu, "'Romania to the Romanians' and the First Romanian Anti-Semitic Legislation of 1938"; Starr, "Jewish Citizenship in Rumania," 58.
11. Gruia, *Monitorul Oficial*, Partea I, no. 205, 5 Sept. 1940, 5091–94. The announcement is titled, "Referatul d-lui Ministru al Justiției către Consiliul de Miniștri," written by Minister of Justice Ion V. Gruia and dated 4 Sept. 1940.
12. Gruia, *Curs de Drept Constituțional*, 488.
13. Solonari, *Purifying the Nation*, 55.
14. Gruia, quoted in Petit, *Originea etnică*, 25. *Zgura* in Romanian can also refer to the leftover coffee grinds or dregs at the bottom of the cup resulting from the method of preparing unfiltered coffee, so common in the Balkans.
15. Ioanid, "The Holocaust in Romania."
16. Ionesco, *Portretul scriitorului în secol. Eugène Ionesco, 1909–1994*, 32. Eugène Ionescu was granted a certificate of Romanian nationality and ethnic origin despite having Jewish ancestry on his mother's side. Either he concealed this when he applied for his certificate in Bucharest or else the Romanian authorities disregarded this, perhaps because of his celebrity. His certificate, issued in Bucharest on 20 August 1941, stated the following: "Eugen Dimitrie Ionescu, based on the documents submitted and on the opinion of the legal department, possesses Romanian nationality and is of ethnic Romanian origin."
17. ANIC, fond PCM Civil, dosar 420, Corespondență cu SSRCI, 160. The report, drafted by a Dr. Ioan Popescu, is dated 16 Jan. 1942.
18. Gruia, *Monitorul Oficial*, Partea I, no. 206, 6 Sept. 1940, 5266.
19. Solonari, *Purifying the Nation*, 252.
20. Ibid., 244–56.
21. Gruia, quoted in Petit, *Originea etnică*, 24–25.
22. Petit, *Originea etnică*, 9–11.
23. For an incisive account of the Romanianization legislation and the headaches it

caused the Antonescu regime, including a brief discussion of the Csangos, see Ionescu, *Jewish Resistance to "Romanianization," 1940-44*, 37-55.

24. As Lya Benjamin has noted, the Romanian National Bank extended lines of credit totaling about 1.5 billion lei as part of the Romanianization effort. It oversaw all other credit institutions participating in the Romanianization of the economy. The goal was to facilitate a takeover by "native Romanians" and to help solve the socioeconomic problems of the lower classes by creating a new Romanian bourgeoisie. See Benjamin, "Introductory Study," lxxxii-lxxxiv.

25. Petit, *Originea etnică*, 14.

26. Though Romania ceded Northern Transylvania to Hungary in 1940, there nevertheless remained large, important cities in Romanian-ruled Southern Transylvania with a high percentage if not a majority of ethnic minorities, for example, in Braşov, Sibiu, and Alba Iulia as well as Arad and Timişoara in the Crişana and Banat. In Bukovina, the Ukrainians, Jews, and Germans dominated many of the larger towns, including Cernăuţi, Storojineţ, Siret, and Rădăuţi. After the start of the war, however, most of the Bukovinan Germans were repatriated to Germany, the Hungarians to Hungary, and the Jews to Transnistria.

27. Ciucă, Teodorescu, and Popovici, *Stenogramele*, vol. 6, 194-95.

28. Ibid., vol. 5, 465.

29. ACNSAS, Dosar relativ la Ceangăii, 1. See also ASSC, fond Ministerul Cultelor şi Artelor 1933-1944, dosar 131/1943, Declaraţii, referate, şi corespondenţă cu Episcopia Catolică de Iaşi, 164-65; and ibid., dosar 91/1944, Episcopia Catolică Iaşi-Bassarabia, 85.

30. Solonari, *Purifying the Nation*, 254.

31. Use of Hungarian in church services, for instance in prayers and sermons, had long been a rarity in these parts (Latin was the language in which Mass was officiated until after the Second Vatican Council). However, many of the cantors, especially in the predominantly Hungarian-speaking villages, were allowed to lead the singing of some hymns in Hungarian. See Pozsony, *The Hungarian Csango of Moldova*, 58-59.

32. Vincze, "Egy magyar etnikai csoport a román nemzetépítés árnyékában," 24-28.

33. "Részletek Domokos Pál Péternek a moldvai csángómagyarok közt tett útjairól készült beszámolójából," in Vincze, *Asszimiláció vagy kivándorlás?*, 183. Taken from Domokos's accounts of his fieldwork in the Csango region between 1929 and 1938.

34. The Soviet Union invaded and occupied Bukovina, Bessarabia, and the Hertza region in late June/early July 1940. Over the next two months, Romania formally ceded Northern Transylvania to Hungary and Southern Dobrudja to Bulgaria.

35. AN Bacău, fond Parohia Romano-Catolică Luizi-Călugăra, dosar 1/1940, 31 (hereafter PR-C/L-C, 1/1940).

36. Merfea, "Aspecte din viaţa satelor de ciangăi din România Veche," 4-5.

37. Education reforms in the 1920s provided higher salaries and benefits for teachers willing to work in designated "cultural zones" in Romania's multilingual regions. See Livezeanu, *Cultural Politics in Greater Romania*, 44-48.

38. Merfea would change his opinion about the Csangos some fifty years later, in communist Romania, championing their cause as ethnic Romanians and not Hungarians. See Merfea, "Ceangăii despre ei înşişi."
39. Merfea, "Preocuparea învăţătorului de azi," 1.
40. Hopu, "Statul şi naţiunea," 7–10.
41. Pozsony, *The Hungarian Csango of Moldova*, 214; and Vincze, "An Overview of the Modern History of the Moldavian Csángó-Hungarians," 56. Vincze claims illiteracy was 60–65 percent among the Csangos in the interwar period.
42. AN Bacău, PR-C/L-C, 1/1940, 40.
43. Merfea, "Aspecte din viaţa satelor de ciangăi din România Veche," 6–7. Horia (or Horea) was Vasile Ursu Nicola, the Romanian leader of the 1784 peasant revolt in Transylvania waged against the nobility in an effort to abolish serfdom and the feudal order and to put an end to the forced conversion of Greek Catholics. A year after his capture, the Habsburgs publicly executed him in Alba Iulia. Horea's body was dismembered and the pieces put on pikes to be displayed in the major towns across Transylvania.
44. Ibid., 9.
45. ANIC, PCM/SSI, 63/1942, 1.
46. Gen. Ionescu's antipathy for the Jews was even greater. In November 1942, as the prefect of Bacău County, Ionescu issued Decree No. 1097, which among other things strictly forbade the county's Jews from making any contact with Romanians except in the most narrowly defined circumstances. He furthermore forbade Jews from participating in the commerce of cattle, grains, "or any other goods" and from entering any market, with the exception of authorized butchers. Anyone who failed to obey the order would be "sent immediately to concentration camps." This was the very same general who oversaw the roundup of Jews and Gypsies from Bacău County and sent many of them to their deaths in Transnistria. AN Bacău, fond Comunitatea Evreilor din Bacău, dosar 20/1942, 106. See also Svart-Kara, *Obştea evreiască din Bacău*, 106.
47. The Rezident Principal was a holdover of the Rezident Regal from Carol II's regime. It was an administrative unit comprised of ten governorships of the main regions across the country, each headed by an army general.
48. ANIC, PCM/SSI, 63/1942, 1–2.
49. Reports were made by the Bacău and Bucharest sections of the Centrul Contrainformaţii (Center for Counter-Information), a subsection of the Serviciul Special de Informaţii (Special Service for Information), as the Romanian secret service was known under the Antonescu regime.
50. ANIC, PCM/SSI, 63/1942, 12–20 (13). Report titled "Dare de seamă asupra minorităţii etnice din Moldova denumite Ciangăi," dated 17 Nov. 1942.
51. Ibid., 22. Report titled "Problema catolicilor din Moldova: Chestiunea originii etnice în preocuparea populaţiei respective," dated 17 Nov. 1942.
52. Ibid., 25–27. Report titled "Propaganda iredentei ungare faţă de problema 'ceangăilor' din Moldova," dated 18 Nov. 1942.

53. Ibid. The reports referred to recent publications by Csango priests attempting to demonstrate a purely Romanian ethnogenealogy.

54. Ibid., 1–2. The report is from the Bacău section of the Centrul Contrainformații.

55. ACNSAS, Dosar relativ la Ceangăii, 5–6, 27–29.

56. ACNSAS, Dosar relativ la Ceangăii, 1.

57. Coşa, *Cleja*, 35.

58. Ibid., 60.

59. AN Bacău, PR-C/L-C, 1/1940, 30. In 1941 the rubber stamp Adunarea Obştească Plebiscitară a Naţiunii Române (General Plebiscitary Assembly of the Romanian Nation) held a couple of plebiscites to register public approval of Antonescu's governance, giving the regime a patina of legitimacy and popular support.

60. Diaconescu, "The Identity Crisis of the Moldavian Catholics," 84–86; and Pozsony, *The Hungarian Csango of Moldova*, 57–59.

61. AN Bacău, PR-C/L-C, 1/1940, 44–45 (emphasis in original).

62. ACNSAS, Dosar relativ la Ceangăii, 43–44 and 58. See also Coşa, *Cleja*, 35.

63. ACNSAS, Dosar relativ la Ceangăii, 53.

64. Ibid., 17–18.

65. Ibid., 41.

66. The term is analogous to another epithet for Hungarians in Transylvania, *bozgor*. Both terms are of dubious origin but likewise imply "stateless" or even "homeless" and thus belonging to the Hungarians. Ethnographer Péter Halász recorded the following explanation of a Csango man from the village of Frumoasa/Frumosza: "'Banghins' is what we are. That means we still belong to the Hungarians, so we cannot be right, as they [the Romanians] are. When they become angry, they would even say 'Bozgor.'" Halász, "About the Regional and Ethnic Division of the Moldavian Hungarians," 144. See also Szilágyi, *Mi-Egy-Más. Közéleti írások*, 503–6.

67. ACNSAS, Dosar relativ la Ceangăii, 42.

68. Deletant, *Hitler's Forgotten Ally*, 71.

69. ACNSAS, Dosar relativ la Ceangăii, 42, 58.

70. The border of Northern Transylvania (Hungary) followed the pre-Trianon one along the eastern Szekler land down to Braşov. From either Miercurea Ciuc/Csikszereda or Gheorgheni/Gyergyószentmiklós in the eastern part of Szekler land, the border actually stretched farther east some 50 km, midway into the Ghimeş region, a serpentine pass linking Transylvania and Moldavia (and historically the route used by the Tatars to attack Hungary). The actual border crossing was located just beneath the ruins of Rákóczi Castle, near the Hungarian Railways (MÁV) Guardhouse no. 30, between the villages of Ghimeş/Gyimes and Palanca/Palánka. This area is today located within Bacău County and considered part of Moldavia.

71. ACNSAS, Dosar relativ la Ceangăii, 57.

72. Ibid., 58–59.

73. ASSC, fond Ministerul Cultelor şi Artelor 1933–1944, dosar 91/1944, Episcopia Catolică Iaşi-Bassarabia, 93. This letter is dated 29 July 1944.

74. ACNSAS, Dosar relativ la Ceangăii, 60.
75. Ibid.

Chapter 5. Resettlement "Home"

1. Also known as Macedo-Romanians or Romanophile Vlachs, these were disparate communities of highlanders from around the Pindus Mountains in historical Macedonia. They spoke a Romance language akin to Romanian. Aromanian populations remain today in the Balkans and in southeastern Romania.

2. See Kontogiorgi, *Population Exchange in Greek Macedonia*, 240; Gherasim, *Schimbul de populații între state*, 69–71; and S. Golopenția, "Introducere," xiii–xv.

3. Kocsis and Hodosi, *Ethnic Geography of the Hungarian Minorities in the Carpathian Basin*, 19. Approximately 200,000 ethnic Hungarians came from territories ceded to Greater Romania, 107,000 from Czechoslovakia, and another 45,000 from the Kingdom of Serbs, Croats, and Slovenes. Figures based on data from the National Office for Refugees.

4. In Bácska, for example, the 1931 Yugoslav census recorded a total of 784,896 inhabitants: 284,865 Yugoslavs (Serbs, Croats, Bunjevci, Šokci); 268,711 Hungarians; and 169,858 Germans, among smaller nationalities. According to the 1910 Hungarian census, which counted national groups by mother tongue, Slavs numbered less than 30 percent, while Hungarians constituting nearly 45 percent. See Kocsis and Hodosi, *Ethnic Geography of the Hungarian Minorities in the Carpathian Basin*, 22, 137–61.

5. See Lumans, *Himmler's Auxiliaries*; and Lumans, "A Reassessment of *Volksdeutsche* and Jews in the Volhynia-Galicia-Narew Resettlement," 81–100.

6. Achim, "The Romanian Population Exchange Project," 596.

7. The Munich Agreement, signed 29 September 1938, allowed for Nazi Germany's annexation of the Sudetenland in Czechoslovakia. The First Vienna Award (or Arbitration), signed days later, allowed for Hungary's annexation of southern Slovakia and southern Carpathian Rus. In March 1939 Germany established the Protectorate of Bohemia and Moravia, while Hungary annexed the remainder of Carpathian Rus (up to the Polish border), thereby dismantling Czechoslovakia.

8. Davidescu, "Minoritățile provocatoare."

9. Nicolae (Nicu) Porsenna was the pseudonym of Nicolae Gh. Ionescu, a novelist, translator, playwright, screenwriter, film producer, lawyer, and inventor. He was also a sympathizer of the Legionary movement. After World War II, Communist authorities imprisoned him for much of the remainder of his life.

10. Porsenna, *Regenerarea neamului românesc* (Bucharest, 1937), 157 (emphasis in original). See also Porsenna, "Schimbul de populație," 3.

11. Crainic, *Ortodoxie și etnocrație*, 188, 284.

12. See Turda, "Conservative Palingenesis and Cultural Modernism in Early Twentieth-Century Romania," 437–53.

13. Solonari, "An Important New Document," 288, n. 7.

14. ACNSAS, Nichifor Crainic, P.013206, vol. 2, 521. The "Madagascar Plan," i.e., sending all the Jews to the island of Madagascar, was an idea discussed in a number of European countries during the late 1920s and 1930s, including Poland and especially Nazi Germany. See Browning's entry, "The Madagascar Plan," 407–9.

15. ACNSAS, Nichifor Crainic, P.013206, vol. 3, 128. Report dated 2 June 1935, surveilling Crainic at a conference in Chișinău. Crainic was surveilled by the state security service, Direcția Generală a Poliției de Siguranță (DGPS), during the 1930s. Reports in his penal files contain summaries and transcripts from his lectures and speeches across the country.

16. ACNSAS, Nichifor Crainic, P. 013206, vol. 3, 197–98. Dated 5 Apr. 1936, from the town of Roman.

17. In fact, the Nazis sought to harness these very forces in order to accelerate the demise of the territories the Reich aimed to conquer, namely the USSR. See Burleigh, *Germany Turns Eastwards*, 225.

18. For instance, Hungary's First Anti-Jewish Law (no. XV/1938), Second Anti-Jewish Law (no. IV/1939), and Third Anti-Jewish Law (XV/1941); and Italy's so-called Manifesto of Race, passed on 18 Nov. 1938. The governments of Slovakia, Croatia, and Bulgaria also passed race laws in one form or another.

19. "Rumania: Bloodsucker of the Villages."

20. Solonari, "An Important New Document," 274, 281.

21. Ibid., 269. See also Achim, "The Romanian Population Exchange Project."

22. ANIC, fond Sabin Manuilă, dosar 12/211, Audiența lui Sabin Manuilă la Tighina, la Ion Antonescu pentru proiectul schimbului de populație din Ardeal, 1941, 1–10 (1). Memorandum dated 15 Oct. 1941.

23. ANIC, fond Manuilă, 12/194, Posibilitatea unei demarcațiuni etnice în vederea soluționării conflictului etnic româno-maghiar, post-1940, 1–3 (3). Report titled, "Soluționarea conflictului etnic Româno-Maghiar: Posibilitatea unei demarcațiuni etnice definitive." Undated.

24. ANIC, fond Manuilă, 12/211, 1.

25. For a more in-depth look at the plans of Dragoș and Golopenția, see Solonari, "An Important New Document," 282–87. For Oprișanu's plan, see AMAE, fond Conferința de pace de la Paris din 1946, Ciangăi din Moldova, vol. 131, 10–15. Report titled, "Rezolvarea Problemei Minoritare: Punctul de vedere românesc."

26. Solonari, *Purifying the Nation*, 97.

27. Ibid., 106–7; Gherasim, *Schimbul de populații între state*, 114–15.

28. Solonari, *Purifying the Nation*, 256; Gherasim, *Schimbul de populații între state*, 79–86.

29. Oláh, *Hárommillió koldus*.

30. Pamlényi, *A History of Hungary*, 460.

31. Wallis, "The South Slavs of Southern Hungary," 345–46.

32. Wallis, "The Rumanians in Hungary," 158–59; Rothschild, *East Central Europe between the Two World Wars*, 192–99; Braun, "Nemzetiségi statisztika," 187–91; and Braun, "Pusztul-e a magyarság," 252–56.

33. Vasary, "The Sin of Transdanubia," 430.

34. Ibid., 431–34. Gyula Illyés discusses the causes and consequences of the *egyke* practice in the publication of his sociographical journal notes, recorded during his exploration of rural Hungary in 1933–8. See Illyés, *Magyarok—Naplójegyzetek*; and Illyés, *A puszták népe*. In addition to Illyés, the sociographers János Kodolányi and Péter Veres, and the clergymen Géza Kiss and László Fülep, wrote extensively (almost obsessively) on the matter. See also Péter Elek et al., *Elsüllyedt falu a Dunántúlon*.

35. Fülep, *A magyarság pusztulása*, 33.

36. Rothschild, *East Central Europe between the Two World Wars*, 138, 170. See also Kovács, *A néma forradalom*; and Bonczos, *Az Alföld szociális problémái*. The politician Endre Bajcsy-Zsilinszky likewise influenced public opinion on the *egyke* crisis.

37. Over 1.5 million Hungarian citizens emigrated from Hungary to the United States between 1880 and 1913. However, as Julianna Puskás and Tibor Frank note, Slovaks and Ruthenians comprised the bulk of this "Hungarian" emigration. See Puskás, *From Hungary to the United States (1880–1914)*; and Frank, "From Austria-Hungary to the United States," 409–23.

38. Etelköz was the name of the first known territory settled by the Magyars c. 830 CE, prior to their entry into the Carpathian basin (after being pushed out by the Pechenegs). Etelköz was located on the steppe around the Dnieper River basin and possibly extended as far west as the Carpathians and lower Danube.

39. Pritz, "A fajvédők külpolitikai nézetei (1918–1936)," 617–21. See also Nagy-Talavera, *The Green Shirts and the Others*, 77–78 and 104–5.

40. Quoted in Pritz, "A fajvédők külpolitikai nézetei," 634–45.

41. Born in the town of Nagyszalonta/Salonta—which was placed on the Romanian side of the border after Trianon—Bonczos completed his higher-level education in Budapest and worked as a prosecutor in Hungary during much of the 1920s and 1930s. In 1926 he joined the Fajvédő Párt and from 1928 became a sympathizer and confidant of Gyula Gömbös. Bonczos was also a founding member of the Országos Nemzeti Családvédelmi Alap (National Foundation for the Protection of the Family). In December 1938 he became state secretary in the Ministry of the Interior, where he stayed until 1944, when he was then elevated to minister of interior in the pro-Nazi government of General Döme Sztójay. He was therefore involved in the deportation of Hungarian Jews to Nazi concentration camps, which started in May 1944. Bonczos escaped to Argentina after the war.

42. Bonczos, "Előszó," 7. The volume included contributions from a number of government ministers and academics, including the most important Hungarian racial anthropologist of the day, Lajos Bartucz, and prominent sociologist Ferenc Erdei. See also Bonczos's *Az Alföld szociális problémái*.

43. Bonczos, "Előszó," 7.

44. Sajti, *Hungarians in the Voivodina*, 255.

45. Hanebrink, *In Defense of Christian Hungary*, 132–33.

46. Minutes of the General Assembly of the Upper Baranya Reformed diocese,

point 20b. Held in Siklós, 26 Sept. 1935. Quoted and cited in Hanebrink, *In Defense of Christian Hungary*, 133.

47. On this episode involving Kálmán Németh, see Seres, "Németh Kálmán missziója a bukovinai székelyek és a moldvai csángók között I."; Sajti, *Hungarians in the Voivodina*, 253; Rónai, *Térképezett történelem*, 194–95; and Vincze, "A bukovinai székelyek és kisebb moldvai Csángó-magyar."

48. Vincze, "A bukovinai székelyek és kisebb moldvai Csángó-magyar," 147, 163.

49. Börvely/Berveni was located in Szatmár/Satu Mare County, in far western Transylvania. In March 1941 this area belonged to Hungarian-ruled Northern Transylvania.

50. MOL, K28 ME-Nemzetiségi és kisebbségi osztály, cs. 163, t. 271, Bukovinai magyarok támogatási-Magyarországra történő áttelepítésének ügyei, 1941–44, 5–6 (hereafter MOL, K28/ME, 163/271). Letter dated 3 Mar. 1941.

51. Bálint was a member of Hungarian Parliament for the Erdélyi Párt (Transylvanian Party), an advisor to the Holy See, and was involved with a number of Catholic organizations.

52. MOL, K28/ME, 163/271, 227.

53. Including the Arrow-Cross-affiliated National Work Center, the Prohászka Ottokár Society, the Organization of Catholic Students of Budapest, and the National Organization of Catholic Young Workers and Industry, to name but a few.

54. MOL, K28/ME, 163/271, 31–32.

55. MOL, K148, Egészségpolitikai Társaság-Magyar Nemzetbiologai Intézet, 1940-17-3689 (1075), 3. See also Juhász, *Uralkodó eszmék Magyarországon 1939–1944*, 173–74; Hanebrink, *In Defense of Christian Hungary*, 168; and Turda, "'If our race did not exist, it would have to be created,'" 237–58.

56. See Golopenția, "A fost Transilvania în veacul al XVIII-lea țintă sau punct de plecare de migrațiuni Românești? O teorie Ungară combătută de Unguri"; and Golopenția, "Preocupări biopolitice ungurești."

57. Korponay, *Húszmillió magyart*, 38.

58. Ibid., 41.

59. Vida, "Magyar Kárpát-medencét." Sections of Vida's article were translated into Romanian and commented on by Anton Golopenția, "Preocupări biopolitice ungurești." See also Tamás Stark's discussion of Vida and others who proposed such schemes, in Stark, "Migrations during WWII," 184.

60. The Bunjevci are a community of predominantly Roman Catholics who speak a South Slav dialect. Historically they straddled the border region between Hungary and Serbia. See Weaver, "Hungarian Views of the Bunjevci in Habsburg Times and the Inter-War Period," 77–115.

61. Vida, "Magyar Kárpát-medencét," 284–85.

62. King Béla IV (1206–70; r. 1235–70) has been regarded as "the second founder of Hungary" for his efforts to rebuild the kingdom after the Mongol invasions decimated it in 1241. Béla reclaimed lost territory and recolonized the kingdom with Cumans and other tribes from the east. Brother Julian (Julianus barát) was one of a group of

Dominican friars sent eastward across the Eurasian steppe by Béla in 1235 to locate Magyars in the east, those believed to have been left behind after the Hungarian conquest of Pannonia. Indeed, Julian found linguistic kin as far as Volga Bulgaria, a historic Bulgar state at the confluence of the Volga and Kama rivers, located around the present-day city of Kazan in European Russia. Since Julian's time, Hungarian authors have referred to this ancestral territory of the Hungarians as *Magna Hungaria*, i.e., "Great Hungary."

63. Vida, "Magyar Kárpát-medencét," 285–86.

64. Besenyő was presumably born in Romania and had a career in the Catholic Church as a priest or lay theologian. He was known by the surname Baumgartner until he changed it in 1940, after becoming a Hungarian citizen. The name Besenyő is actually the Hungarian word for Pecheneg, a Turkic-speaking Ural-Altic people akin to the Avars and Magyars. In the view of some historians at the time, the Csangos descended from the Pechenegs, who had entered Moldavia at the end of the tenth century. Besenyő also published under the pseudonym Siculus, presumably taken from the Greek historian Diodorus Siculus of the first century BCE, who wrote on the history and culture of the non-Hellenic tribes in Eurasia.

65. See Baumgartner, *Moldva: A magyarság nagy temetője*; Baumgartner, "A moldvai magyarok," 301–7; and Baumgartner [Siculus], *A moldvai magyarok őstelepülése*.

66. Baumgartner [Siculus], *A moldvai magyarok őstelepülése*, 5.

67. Baumgartner, *Moldva: A magyarság nagy temetője*, 5.

68. Ibid., 27–28.

69. On what little is known about Besenyő's life and political activities, see Seres, "Adalékok a moldvai csángók"; Vincze, "An Overview of the Modern History of the Moldavian Csángó-Hungarians," 60–61; and Arens and Bein, "Die Moldauer Ungarn (Tschangos)," 289. There is also a communiqué about Besenyő's arrest in Romania in 1944. See AMAE, fond România, vol. 196, 180.

70. Borbándi, *A magyar népi mozgalom*, 65.

71. Hanebrink, *In Defense of Christian Hungary*, 133; Vincze, "A bukovinai székelyek és kisebb moldvai Csángó-magyar," 152–53; and Arens and Bein, "Die Moldauer Ungarn (Tschangos)," 277–78.

72. See Davis, "Restocking the Ethnic Homeland," 155–74. It was Bárdossy who had introduced Hungary's Third Jewish Law in August 1941, amending the previous anti-Semitic legislation with "racial protection provisions" (*fajvédelmi rendelkezések*), including the prohibition of interracial copulation in order to prevent miscegenation and "racial dishonor" (*fajgyalázás*).

73. MOL, K28/ME, 163/271, 7. Memo from Pál Bella from Bucharest, dated 10 Dec. 1940. On Domokos's mission, see Attila Seres, "Domokos Pál Péter missziója"; and Vincze, "A bukovinai székelyek és kisebb moldvai Csángó-magyar," passim.

74. MOL, K28/ME, 163/271, 9–16. Report by Pál Péter Domokos from Bucharest, dated 28 Nov. 1940.

75. Ibid., 19–20. Report by Pál Péter Domokos from Bucharest, dated 8 Dec. 1940. See also MOL, K28/ME, 162/270, 34–35.

76. Seres, "Domokos Pál Péter missziója," 281–83.

77. Sajti, *Hungarians in the Voivodina*, 256. A number of political and military leaders influenced Bárdossy's decision to undertake this policy, including Viktor Rényei, senior official in the Hungarian Legation in Belgrade; Döme Sztójay, the former army general, the current ambassador in Berlin, and the future prime minister of Hungary; the aforementioned state secretary Miklós Bonczos, who would later become minister of the interior under Sztójay's prime ministership; and Henrik Werth, the Hungarian Army's chief of general staff. Bárdossy and Werth would have an uneasy relationship throughout the war, with the latter resigning in September 1941. The staunchly pro-German Werth—who, as his name suggests, was of German heritage and national sentiment—was among the most committed proponents of massive population transfers. See Pritz, *The War Crimes Trial of Hungarian Prime Minister László Bárdossy*, 43–45.

78. Sajti, *Hungarians in the Voivodina*, 256–57.

79. Quoted and cited in Vincze, "A bukovinai székelyek és kisebb moldvai Csángó-magyar," 152–53. The information and quote was reconstructed using a memorandum from Werth to Bonczos on 11 July 1941. See Vincze, "A bukovinai székelyek és kisebb moldvai Csángó-magyar," 179, fn. 80.

80. Sajti, *Hungarians in the Voivodina*, 258–60.

81. Vincze, "A bukovinai székelyek és kisebb moldvai Csángó-magyar," 153. Teleki had opposed the alliance with Germany and the invasion of Yugoslavia. Under his government, Hungary had maintained a "nonbelligerent" status since 1939 and had even signed a nonaggression treaty with Yugoslavia in December 1940, just months before the Hungarian-German invasion of Yugoslavia in April 1941. Teleki committed suicide over the affair.

82. See anonymous report in MOL, K28/ME, 163/271, 149–57, 230.

83. See Braham, *The Politics of Genocide*, 34–37.

84. Most were transient Jews who had fled south and east from Austria, Czechoslovakia, and Poland after the Nazi occupation in 1938–39. See Braham, *The Politics of Genocide*, 32–34.

85. Braham, *The Politics of Genocide*, 32.

86. MOL, K28/ME, 163/271, 150.

87. Sajti, *Hungarians in the Voivodina*, 262.

88. MOL, K28/ME, 163/271, 150.

89. On the plans to resettle Hungarians from Bosnia and Croatia, see Sajti, *Hungarians in the Voivodina*, 280–90.

90. MOL, K28/ME, 163/271, 150–53. The *vitézek* belonged to the Vitézi Rend (order of heroes), which was established by Regent Miklós Horthy and open to those (non-Jews) who served with distinction in World War I. It was furthermore determined that none of these resettled populations should be placed next to any German settlements—which were to be left untouched, in deference to Germany—lest these Hungarian populations risk German assimilation.

91. Vincze, "An Overview of the Modern History of the Moldavian Csángó-Hungarians," 60.

92. ANIC, fond PCM Civil, dosar 244/1942, Anteproiect de lege asupra colonizărilor, 6. Report titled, "Memoriu cu privire la anteproectul de lege asupra colonizărilor."

93. See AN Bacău, PR-C/L-C, 1/1940, 44–53; ACNSAS, Dosar relativ la Ceangăii, 17–18 and 42–58; and Coşa, *Cleja*, 35–37.

94. Vincze, "An Overview of the Modern History of the Moldavian Csángó-Hungarians," 59–60. The villages were Vladnic/Lábnik and Găiceana-Unguri/Gajcsána-Magyarfalu (today known as Arini in Romanian). These villages were fairly remote and almost exclusively Hungarian-speaking Roman Catholic villages in southeastern Bacău County.

95. Ibid., 60–61.

96. Deak, "Hungary," 364–407 (398).

97. Vincze, "An Overview of the Modern History of the Moldavian Csángó-Hungarians," 60.

98. Ibid., 61–2.

99. AMAE, fond România 71-1939, e. 9, vol. 196, 180.

100. MOL, K28/ME, 163/271, 232. The report is undated. Likely it was written in spring 1944, before the Red Army overran Moldavia.

101. ANIC, PCM/SSI, 63/1942, 26. Report from the Bacău section of the Centrul de Contrainformaţii, titled, "Propaganda iredentei ungare faţă de problema 'ceangăilor' din Moldova" (Hungarian irredentist propaganda regarding the problem of the Csangos from Moldova), dated 18 Nov. 1942.

102. Ibid., 35. Report no. 750, dated 16 Dec. 1942.

103. ACNSAS, fond Documentar, MAE DGP, D.11324, Dosar ref. la situaţia românilor expulzaţi şi refugiaţi din Ardeal . . . Situaţia minoritarilor turci, tătari, ceangăi, lipoveni, ucrainieni. Iredentism maghiar şi tătar, 118.

104. AMAE, fond România, vol. 232, Buletin Informativ: Despre Acţiunea Iridentei Maghiare în România, 5 feb.–5 martie 1941, 110.

105. MOL, K28/ME, 162/270, 43. The letter itself is not dated; however, it is in a Foreign Ministry folder dated 13 Dec. 1941. The mother was Lőrincné Elekes from the village of Fogadjisten/Iacobeşti, about twenty kilometers northwest of Suceava.

106. Ibid., 44. The report is a *nota bene* dated 26 Mar. 1942. The "previous documents" mentioned in the report were not located in this MOL K28 file. The priests who remained in Moldavia up to this point were Dénes Elekes and Jakab Ferenc, while Antal László and Péter Demsa had already been expelled from Romania for spreading Hungarian propaganda within the Csango communities and agitating for their relocation to Hungary.

107. For this point of view, see, especially, Vincze, "An Overview of the Modern History of the Moldavian Csángó-Hungarians," 59–60.

108. See Arens, "An Ethnic Group on the Pressure Field of Totalitarian Population Policies," 113–31.

109. Seres, "Domokos Pál Péter missziója," 282–84.

Chapter 6. The Cry of Blood

1. Iosif Petru Maria Pal was born in the tiny village of Nisiporești in Neamț County in 1889. Upon returning from his studies in Rome, he served as the administrator of a war orphanage and taught in the Catholic gymnasium in the Moldavian town of Hălăucești. From 1923 until his death he served as parish priest in Luizi-Călugăra and taught theology at the seminary there. See Gabor and Simon, *Necrolog 1600–2000*, 135–36; and Dumitru Lucaciu, "Omagiul 'Vieții' P. Dr. Iosif Petru M. Pal," 68.

2. Pal, "Catolicii din Moldova sunt români neaoși," 56–60.

3. On the Catholics and Hungarians in medieval Moldavia, see Rădvan, *At Europe's Borders*, 312–14 and 515; Baker, "Magyars, Mongols, Romanians and Saxons"; and Spinei, *Moldavia in the 11th–14th Centuries*, 52–54, 141, and 221–23. The bishopric of Cumania was seated in the Moldavian town of Milcov. It served the converted Cumans and the Teutonic Knights before the Mongols destroyed the bishopric (and most everyone in it) in 1241.

4. Pal, "Catolicii din Moldova sunt români neaoși," 60.

5. In 1942 Pal published a two-part monograph, part 1 being *Originea Catolicilor din Moldova* and part 2 *Franciscanii păstorii de veacuri ai Catolicilor din Moldova*, the latter of which historicized the role of the Franciscan order as "shepherds" of the Moldavian Catholics throughout the centuries. Both were published by a Roman Catholic press in the towns of Săbăoani-Roman, in Moldavia.

6. Pal, *Originea Catolicilor din Moldova*, 20. On Kogălniceanu and Negri's acceptance of the country's Catholic population as Romanian nationals, see Coșa, *Cleja*, 33–34.

7. Pal, *Originea Catolicilor din Moldova*, 21 (emphasis in original).

8. Ibid., 82. The term *pocăiți* (Repenters) was used to describe many neo-Protestant sects, including the ones listed here by Pal as well as Pentecostals and Jehovah's Witnesses. See Catherine Wanner, *Communities of the Converted*, especially chapter 1, 21–54.

9. Pal, *Originea Catolicilor din Moldova*, 13. Pal is most likely referring to Rosetti, *Despre unguri și episcopiile catolice din Moldova*; and Năstase, *Ungurii din Moldova la 1646 după "Codex Bandinus."*

10. Pal, *Originea Catolicilor din Moldova*, 22 (emphasis in original). Hungarian tribes arrived in and settled central Europe from central Asia at the end of the ninth century; the Hungarians broadly converted to Christianity as Roman Catholics in the eleventh, under the reign of Stephen I.

11. Pal, *Originea Catolicilor din Moldova*, 39–40.

12. Ibid., 50. Hussitism and Calvinism were also practiced in Moldavia. See Baker, "The Hungarian-Speaking Hussites of Moldavia and Two English Episodes in Their History," 3–24.

13. In addition to the works of the clerics Iosif Petru M. Pal and Ioan Mărtinaș discussed in this chapter, see works by the following Catholic priests, Moisescu, *Catolicismul în Moldova până la sfârșitul secolului al XIV*; Morariu, *Series cronologica Praefectorum Apostolicorum Missionis Fr. Min. Conv. in Moldavia et Valachia*; and Morariu, *Series cronologica episcoporum ac praefectorum apostolicorum missionis Fr. Minorum Conventualium in Moldavia durante saeculo XIX*.

14. Tufescu, *O regiune de vie circulație*, 368–71. The region forms a three-hundred-meter-high "gateway" or "saddle" between two massive ranges of hills to the north and south, and between the Siret River valley in the east and the Moldavian plain in the west.

15. The villages Tufescu writes about are located to the north and northeast of the town of Roman, about fifty kilometers east of Iași: Butea/Miklósfalva, Buruenești/Burjánfalva, Oțeleni/Acélfalva, Sagna/Szágna, Fărcășeni/Farkasfalva, Rotunda/Rotunda, Șcheia/Skéja, Slobozia/Szlobozia, Buhanca/Pohánka, Boghicea/Bogicse, and Oboroceni.

16. Tufescu, *O regiune de vie circulație*, 370–71 (emphasis in original).

17. Diaconescu, "The Identity Crisis of the Moldavian Catholics," 83.

18. Mărtinaș, *Cine sunt catolicii moldoveni?*, 8.

19. Various diseases—plague, pleurisy, smallpox, and laryngitis—indeed decimated populations in Transylvania. The Szekler land was one of the regions hit hardest. See Köpeczi, *History of Transylvania*, 529.

20. Mărtinaș, *Cine sunt catolicii moldoveni?*, 33–35 (emphasis in original).

21. See Râmneanțu, "Românii dintre Morava și Timoc și continuitatea spațiului lor etnic cu al Românilor din Banat și din Timocul bulgar"; Golopenția, *Românii din Timoc*; and Marin-Dunăre, "Grupul etnic Românesc din Iugoslavia."

22. See S. Golopenția, "Introducere"; Rațiu, *Românii de la est de Bug*; and Turda, "In Search of Racial Types."

23. See Bucur, *Eugenics and Modernization*, 36–37; and Butaru, *Rasism românesc*, 48–51.

24. AN Cluj, fond Institutul de Igienă și Sănătate Publică Cluj 1920–1966, dosar 98/1942, Coresp. cu încadrarea personalului, 274, 291, and 403.

25. Turda, "The Nation as Object," 435.

26. Râmneanțu, "Grupele de sânge la Ciangăii din Moldova," 51–52. The figure of 8,523 Csangos is based on the number of those who self-identified as Csango in the 1941 Romanian census. In the previous census, conducted in 1930, the Romanian census takers categorized these Csangos as Hungarian.

27. Râmneanțu, *Die Abstammung der Tschangos*, 9–13. In his 1943 article, Râmneanțu uses the Romanian *neam* (nationality) alongside *limbă* (language) and *religie* (religion) when typologizing the inhabitants of the region. In his 1944 book, which he wrote in German, Râmneanțu uses the German *Blutsrumänen/Blutsmadjaren* to refer to Romanians/Hungarians by blood.

28. Râmneanțu is referring to earlier research on this problem by himself and others. See Râmneanțu and David, "Cercetări asupra originii etnice a populației din Sud-Estul Transilvaniei pe baza compoziției serologice a sângelui."

29. Râmneanțu, *Die Abstammung der Tschangos*, 15–18, 27.

30. Turda, "The Nation as Object," 436.

31. Râmneanțu, *Die Abstammung der Tschangos*, 54.

32. ACNSAS, Dosar relativ la Ceangăii, 21. Râmneanțu sent the letter from the Institute of Hygiene and Public Health in Sibiu to Pal at his residence in Luizi-Călugăra.

33. See for example Naghiu, "Istorie 'nepărtinitoare,'" 644–46.

34. Pal, "Glasul sângelui," 14 Mar. 1943. Republished in Pal, *Originea Catolicilor din Moldova* (emphasis in original).

35. The title of Pal's pamphlet is taken from Genesis 4:11 in the story of Cain and Abel: "And the LORD said, 'What have you done? The voice of your brother's blood is crying to me from the ground.'"

36. See Mareş, "Sunt Ciangăii Români?," 104–5; review by Z. S., "Die Abstammung der Tschangos, sau Originea Ciangăilor; de Petru Râmneanţu"; and anon., "Dovada sângelui," 653–54.

37. Mareş, "Sunt Ciangăii Români?," 104.

38. Gârniţeanu, "Catolicii Ciangăi din Moldova sunt Daci."

39. ACNSAS, Dosar relativ la Ceangăii, 5. Communiqué of 28 July 1943.

40. Many of the relocated Csangos grew disillusioned by the hardship they found there, particularly because of the unfulfilled promises of the Hungarian government regarding the amount and type of compensation they would receive. Moreover, many of the local Hungarians of Bácska, who had survived the difficult years and mistreatment under Yugoslav rule, resented the Hungarian government's willingness to provide financial and material assistance only to the Szekler and Csango colonizers, and therefore they treated their new neighbors as interlopers and foreigners.

41. ACNSAS, Dosar relativ la Ceangăii, 5–6.

42. See ANIC, fond Manuilă, 12/194, Posibilitatea unei demarcaţiuni etnice în vederea soluţionării conflictului etnic româno-maghiar, post-1940, 1–3 (3). Report titled, "Soluţionarea conflictului etnic Romano-Maghiar: Posibilitatea unei demarcaţiuni etnice definitive." Undated.

43. On Manuilă, see Solonari, *Purifying the Nation*, 75–76; on Moldovan, see Bucur, *Eugenics and Modernization*, 76 and 242, n. 6.

44. Turda, "'To End the Degeneration of a Nation,'" 103; Turda, "The Nation as Object," 435–36; Bucur, *Eugenics and Modernization*, 211; and Solonari, *Purifying the Nation*, 70.

45. Antonescu, *"Dacă vrei să câştigi războiul, trebuie să pregăteşti pacea."* 33. The text is a publication of Mihai Antonescu's "directives and guidelines" for the newly established Bureau of Peace, which was put together in the summer of 1942 to prepare for a future peace conference and settlement.

46. See Ardeleanu, "Concluding Note," 54. Among the works published in the series were Râmneanţu's *Die Abstammung der Tschangos* and Sabin Opreanu's *The Economical and Political Functions of the Western Frontier*. See also Râmneanţu's English-language publication in the same series, *The Biological Grounds and the Vitality of the Transilvanian Rumanians*; and Tiberiu Morariu's *The Western Frontier of Rumania from the Physical and Biogeographical Points of View*.

47. See Deletant, *Hitler's Forgotten Ally*, 206–8; and Solonari, *Purifying the Nation*, 291–302. The reasons why Antonescu halted the deportation of Jews were not humanitarian but political or self-serving. See Ancel, "The German-Romanian Relationship and the Final Solution," 263–64.

48. That is, the Romanian Old Kingdom, comprised of the Danubian Principalities of Moldavia and Wallachia.

49. ACNSAS, Dosar relativ la Ceangăii, 6.

50. Ciucă, Teodorescu, and Popovici, *Stenogramele*, vol. 9, 142. "Problema catolicilor din Moldova din punctual de vedere al naționalității de origină." Meeting on 17 Mar. 1943.

51. Ibid.

52. Ibid., 143.

53. Ciucă, Teodorescu, and Popovici, *Stenogramele*, vol. 9, 24.

54. AN Bacău, PR-C/L-C, 1/1940, 72–74. Evidence that the Csangos faced deportation to the Soviet Union in 1945 is taken from Pal's letters to Andrea Cassulo, the apostolic nuncio in Bucharest, and to the Romanian minister of interior in Bucharest. See the full account in Coșa, *Cleja*, 37–38.

55. See Polian, *Against Their Will*, 249–58; Reichling, *Die deutschen Vertriebenen in Zahlen*, 33; and Wein, "The Germans in Romania—the Ambiguous Fate of a Minority," 65.

56. AN Bacău, PR-C/L-C, 1/1940, 72–74 and 79–80. The letter to Cassulo is in Italian and dated 18 January 1945. Pal addressed and sent to the Romanian minister of interior a version of this letter in Romanian two days later. On 10 April 1945, Pal sent Cassulo another letter expressing continued fears about deportation to Russia.

57. Allied Control Commissions were comprised of Allied military and civil representatives and established in defeated Axis countries. The Allied Control Commission in Romania was set up in Bucharest following the Armistice Agreement signed on 12 September 1944. It was placed under the nominal leadership of Russian military officers and dominated by the Red Army.

58. Coșa, *Cleja*, 38.

59. The name Iosif Petru M. Pal is ubiquitous in the Romanian archival material on the Csangos during World War II. His letters, published works, and political agenda are discussed in nearly every major report and dossier compiled on the Csangos by the Antonescu government. In 1947 Pal died of exanthematic typhus while caring for patients in his parish of Luizi-Călugăra, where he was buried. It was around this time that the Soviet-backed Romanian Communists began to solidify their power in Romania. Had Pal lived much longer, he likely would have faced imprisonment alongside his fellow Catholic priests and witnessed the destruction of the Greek Catholic Church in Romania. On the destruction of the church in Romania, see Vasile, "The Suppression of the Romanian Greek Catholic (Uniate) Church."

Conclusion

1. Boia, *Explorations into the Imaginary*, 33.
2. See Victor Shnirelman's discussion in "Linguoarchaeology," 158.
3. Matsuda, "Ethnogenesis in Anthropology," 4854.

4. Voss, *The Archaeology of Ethnogenesis*, 36.
5. See Moore, "Ethnogenetic Theory," 10–23.
6. Ardener, "Language, Ethnicity and Population," 69.
7. See Thomas Hylland Eriksen's discussion of Ardener in Eriksen, *Ethnicity and Nationalism*, 89.
8. Ardener, "Language, Ethnicity and Population," 69–70.
9. A. Smith, "National Identity and Myths of Ethnic Descent," 57–58, 84–85. See also Fishman, "Social Theory and Ethnography."
10. Nichols, "The Eurasian Spread Zone and the Indo-European Dispersal," 228.
11. See Takács, *Aranykertbe' aranyfa*. The villages below the Ghimeş pass, between Harghita and Bacău Counties, typify this process, notably Coşnea/Kostelek, Cădăreşti/Magyarcsüges, and Pajeştea/Gyepece.
12. Takács, *Aranykertbe' aranyfa*, 38–47.
13. Ibid., 38–39, 46–47, 81.
14. Guglielmino et al., "Probable Ancestors of Hungarian Ethnic Groups," 156. See also Cavalli-Sforza et al., "Reconstruction of Human Evolution."
15. Guglielmino et al., "Probable Ancestors of Hungarian Ethnic Groups," 156–57.
16. Beres and Guglielmino, "Genetic Structure in Relation to the History of Hungarian Ethnic Groups."
17. See Vincze, "An Overview of the Modern History of the Moldavian Csángó-Hungarians," 59–65.
18. Lahermo et al., "MtDNA Polymorphism in the Hungarians," 39.
19. Brandstätter et al., "Migration Rates and Genetic Structure of two Hungarian Ethnic Groups in Transylvania, Romania," 800.
20. "The Ethnogenesis of Hungarians and Archaeogenetics," 46–47.
21. Muir, "Introduction: Observing Trifles," x.
22. Recent scholarship by Transylvanian academics has, however, taken a critical position against the efforts to "save" or "rescue" the Csangos. As Kontra notes, "the rescuers' arrogance, their 'infallible' views on saving the Hungarian nation, and their irresponsible acts have in some cases led to tragedy for those they have targeted for rescue." Kontra, "Prefatory Note to the Csángó Issues," 11. See also Peti, "'Wearied Respondents,'" 243–67.
23. H. Smith, "Prussia at the Margins," 69–70.

Glossary

1. Lucian Boia, *History and Myth in Romanian Consciousness*, 11.

Bibliography

Archival Sources

Arhivele Naționale Istorice Centrale (ANIC)
Fond Președinția Consiliului de Miniștri
   Serviciul Special de Informații, 1920-49
   Cabinet Civil Mihai Antonescu, 1940-44
   Cabinet Militar Ion Antonescu, 1940-44
Fond Sabin Manuilă 1853-1947

Direcția Județeană Bacău a Arhivelor Naționale (AN Bacău)
Fond Comunitatea Evreilor din Bacău, 1907-50
Fond Parohia Romano-Catolică, Luizi-Călugăra, 1832-1946

Direcția Județeană Cluj a Arhivelor Naționale (AN Cluj)
Fond Institutul de Igienă și Sănătate Publică Cluj, 1920-1966

Arhivele Secretariatului de Stat pentru Culte (ASCC)
Fond Ministerul Cultelor și Artelor, 1933-1944

Arhiva Consiliului Național pentru Studierea Arhivelor Securității (ACNSAS)
Fond Documentar
   Biserica Catolică, D.69
   Ministerul Afacerilor Interne, Direcția Generală a Poliției, D.11325
   Ministerul de Interne, D.10777
Fond Informativ
   Dumitru Herghelegiu, I.141286
   Ioan Mărtinaș, I.141282
   Iosif Gabor, I.207056
Fond Penal
   Corneliu Zelea Codreanu, P.011784

Iosif Frollo, P.016016
Nichifor Crainic, P.013206

Arhivele Ministerului Afacerilor Externe (AMAE)
Fond Conferinţa de Pace de la Paris din 1946-47
Fond 71/1920-44, România Minorităţi

Magyar Országos Levéltár (MOL)
Külügyminisztérium Levéltára 148, Egészségpolitikai Társaság-Magyar Nemzetbiologai Intézet, 1940-47
Külügyminisztérium Levéltára 28, Miniszterelnökségi iratok, Nemzetiségi és kisebbségi osztály
  csomó 162, tétel 270, Moldvai Csángók ügyei 1940-41, 1943-44
  csomó 163, tétel 271, Bukovinai magyarok támogatási-Magyarországra történő áttelepítésének ügyei, 1941-44

Manuscripts

Gabor, Iosif. "Clerul indigen catolic din Moldova." AN Bacău, Colecţie de manuscrise, Manuscris no. 50, written in Nisiporeşti, 1967.
Macartney, C. A. "The Csángós of Roumania." Macartney Papers, Bodleian Library, MSS.Eng C. 3288, box 9, doc. 24, 19 November 1941.
Mărtinaş, Dumitru. "Contribuţii cu privire la Problema Originii Ceangăilor." AN Bacău, Colecţie de manuscrise, Manuscris no. 55, written in Buzău, 1973.

Primary Sources

Anon. "Dovada sângelui." *Cultura Creştină* 10-11 (1943): 653-54.
———. "Spre o 'internaţională' catolică." *Farul nou* 44 (5 May 1935).
———. "Stiinţă şi religie." *Lumina creştinului* 1 (1937): 25-26.
Antonesco, Michel A. [Mihai Antonescu]. *Nation et nationalité: Dans la nouvelle Constitution Roumaine*. Bucharest, 1939.
Antonescu, Mihai. *"Dacă vrei să câştigi războiul, trebuie să pregăteşti pacea." Discursul ţinut la 16 iunie 1942 de Mihai Antonescu pentru constituirea Biroului Păcii*, ed. Ion Ardeleanu. Cluj, 1991.
Auner, Károly. *A romániai magyar telepek történeti vázlata*. Temesvár, 1908.
Bălan, Nicolae. *Biserica împotriva Concordatului, discurs în Senat la 23 mai 1929*. Sibiu, 1929.
———. *Biserica neamului şi drepturile ei—discurs rostit la discuţia generală asupra proiectului de lege al cultelor*. Sibiu, 1928.
———. "Nichifor Crainic şi timpul nostru." *Gândirea* 19/4 (Apr. 1940): 196. Article reprinted in Nichifor Crainic, *Cursurile de mistică*. Sibiu, 2010.
Baumgartner, Sándor [Alexander Baumgartner, Sándor Besenyő, Siculus]. *Moldva: A magyarság nagy temetője*. Budapest, 1940.

Bibliography

———. "A moldvai magyarok." *Kárpátmedence* 1/5 (Sept. 1941): 301–7.
———. *A moldvai magyarok őstelepülése, története és mai helyzete*. Pécs, 1942.
Blaga, Lucian. *Spațiul mioritic*. Bucharest, 1936.
Bonczos, Miklós. *Az Alföld szociális problémái*. Budapest, 1939.
———. "Előszó." In Zoltán Csuka and János Ölvedi, eds., *Magyar föld—magyar nép (a megnagyobbodott Magyarország községeinek adattára)*. Budapest, 1942.
Borbándi, Gyula. *A magyar népi mozgalom: A harmadik reformnemzedék*. New York, 1983.
Botoșăneanu, Grigore. "Biserica Ortodoxă Română și celelalte confesiuni." *Biserica Ortodoxă Română* 6 (1928): 485–88.
Brătianu, Gheorghe I. *Une énigme et un miracle historique: Le peuple roumain*. Bucharest, 1937.
Braun, Róbert. "Nemzetiségi statisztika." *Századunk* 8/6–7 (July–Aug. 1933): 187–91.
———. "Pusztul-e a magyarság." *Századunk* 8 (1933): 252–56.
Chindea, Teodor. *Contribuții la istoria Românilor din Giurgeul-Ciucului*. Târgu-Mureș, 1995; Gheorgheni, 1930.
———. *Geografia județului Ciuc*. Miercurea-Ciuc, 1928.
———. *Monumente istorice în Ciuc*. Gheorgheni, 1933.
Ciobanu, Radu-Ștefan. "Puncte de vedere asupra originii ceangăilor." *Flacăra* 31/1 (7 Jan. 1982): 10.
Cioran, Emil. *Schimbarea la față a României*. Bucharest, 1936.
Ciucă, Marcel-Dumitru, Aurelian Teodorescu, and Bogdan Florin Popovici, eds. *Stenogramele ședințelor Consiliului de Miniștri: Guvernarea Ion Antonescu*, vols. 5, 6, and 9. Bucharest, 1997–2006.
Codreanu, Corneliu Zelea. *Circulări și manifeste 1927–1938*, 5th ed. Munich, 1981.
———. *For My Legionaries*. Madrid, 1976; Sibiu, 1936.
Crainic, Nichifor. *Cursurile de mistică: Teologie mistică, Mistică germană*. Sibiu, 2010.
———. *Ortodoxie și etnocrație. Cu o anexă: Programul statului etnocratic*. Bucharest, 1938.
———. "Roma universală." Republished in *Puncte cardinale în haos*. Bucharest, 1936.
———. "Sensul tradiției." *Gândirea* 10/1–2 (1929): 3.
Cristea, Miron. *Note ascunse. Însemnări personale (1859–1937)*. Cluj, 1999.
Dávid, Zoltán. "Magyarok határaink mentén." *Mozgó Világ* 7 (1982): 38–50.
Davidescu, Nicolae. "Minoritățile provocatoare." *Cuvântul* 6/1984 (30 Oct. 1930).
Dobrotă, Octavian M. *Momente de viață românească în Odorheiu*. Odorheiu, 1932.
———. *Români secuizați și regiune secuizată*. Sighișoara, 1940.
Domokos, Pál Péter. *A moldvai magyarság*. Csíksomlyó/Șumuleu Ciuc, 1931.
Elek, Péter, et al. *Elsüllyedt falu a Dunántúlon: Kemse község élete*. Budapest, 1936.
Eliade, Mircea. *Autobiography, Volume 1: 1907–1937, Journey East, Journey West*. Chicago, 1990.
Făcăoaru, Iordache. "Compoziția rasială la români, săcui și unguri." *Buletin eugenic și biopolitic* 7/4–5 (1937): 124–42.
Frollo, Iosif. "Biserică națională." *Farul nou* 24 (11 Nov. 1934).
———. "În jurul unei conversiuni la catolicism." *Sentinela catolică* 10/11 (Nov. 1930): 2–3.
———. "Patriotism și creștinism." *Farul nou* 2 (14 Jan. 1934).

———. *Romînism şi catolicism*. Bucharest, 1931.
———. "Scrisoare deschisă cătră S.S. Arhimandritul Scriban." *Cuvântul* 6/1985 (30 Oct. 1930): 1–2.
———. "Şeful străin." *Farul nou* 25 (25 Nov. 1934).
Fülep, Lajos. *A magyarság pusztulása: Gondolkodó magyarok*. Budapest, 2003. Originally serialized in *Pesti Napló* (10, 16, and 17 Nov. and 4 and 15 Dec. 1929).
Gálffy, Mózes, Gyula Márton, and T. Attila Szabó. *A moldvai csángó nyelvjárás atlasza*. Budapest, 1981.
Gârniţeanu, Mihai. "Catolicii Ciangăi din Moldova sunt Daci." *Moldova* (26 Jan. 1944). Reprinted in *Lumina Creştinului* (Feb. 1944): f.v. 48.
Gherasim, Dimitrie. *Schimbul de populaţii între state*. Bucharest, 1943.
Ghibu, Onisifor. *Acţiunea catolicismului unguresc şi a Sf. Scaun în România*. Cluj, 1936.
———. *Nulitatea Concordatului*. Cluj, 1935.
———. *Politica religioasă şi minoritară a României*. Bucharest, 2003; 1940.
Ghiuzan, Iosif. "Deopotrivă libertate şi protecţiune." *Sentinela catolică* 6/11 (Nov. 1928): 1–2.
———. "Român catolic." *Sentinela catolică* 6/10 (Oct. 1928): 1–2.
Giurescu, Constantin C. *Istoria românilor*, vols. 1–5. Bucharest, 1935–37.
Goldiş, Vasile. *Memoriu în chestia Concordatului*. Bucharest, 1927.
Golopenţia, Anton. "Cronologie." In Golopenţia, *Opere complete*, vol. 1. Bucharest, 2002.
———. "A fost Transilvania în veacul al XVIII-lea ţintă sau punct de plecare de migraţiuni Româneşti? O teorie Ungară combătută de Unguri." *Geopolitica şi geoistoria* 2 (Jan.–Feb. 1942): 90–97.
———. "Preocupări biopolitice ungureşti." *Geopolitica şi geoistoria* 2 (Jan.–Feb. 1942): 24–35.
———. *Românii din Timoc*. Bucharest, 1943–44.
Golopenţia, Anton, and Ştefania Golopenţia. *Ceasul misiunilor reale. Scrisori către Petru Comarescu, Ştefania Cristescu (Golopenţia), Dimitrie Gusti, Sabin Manuilă, Iacob Mihăilă, H. H. Stahl şi Tudor Vianu*. Bucharest, 1999.
Gruia, Ion V. *Curs de Drept Constituţional*. Bucharest, 1940–41. Revised 2nd ed. Bucharest, 1942.
———. "Referatul d-lui Ministru al Justiţiei către Consiliul de Miniştri." *Monitorul Oficial*, Partea I, no. 205 (5 Sept. 1940): 5091–94.
Hamangiu, Constantin, ed. *Codul general al României. Legi noui de Unificare, 1922–1926*, vols. 11–12. Bucharest, 1926.
———. *Codul general al României (Codurile, Legi şi Regulamentele în vigoare) 1856–1938, Legi Uzuale 1938*, Partea II. Bucharest, 1938.
Hóman, Bálint, and Gyula Szekfű. *Magyar történet*, vols. 1–8. Budapest, 1929–34.
Hopu, Vasile. "Statul şi naţiunea." *Cuvântul Dăscălesc* 11/1 (Sept. 1940): 7–10.
Illyés, Gyula. *A puszták népe*. Budapest, 1937.
———. *Ki a magyar?* Budapest, 1939.
———. *Magyarok—Naplójegyzetek*. Budapest, 1938.

Bibliography

Imbrescu, Ilie. *Biserica și mișcarea legionară*. Bucharest, 1940.
Ionescu, Nae. "A fi 'bun român.'" *Cuvântul* 6/1987 (1 Nov. 1930). Reprinted in Nae Ionescu, *Roza vînturilor, 1926–1933*, 194–98. Chișinău, 1993; Bucharest, 1937.
———. "Concordatul." *Cuvântul* (8 Mar. 1928). Reprinted in Nae Ionescu, *Roza vînturilor, 1926–1933*, 49–51. Chișinău, 1993; Bucharest, 1937.
———. "Între imperialism și democrație țărănească." *Cuvântul* 5/1628 (1 Nov. 1929): 1.
Iorga, Nicolae. "Acte românești din Ardeal privitoare în cea mai mare parte la legăturile secuilor cu Moldova." In *Extras din Buletinul Comisiei Istorice a României II*. Bucharest, 1916.
———. "Începuturile și motivele desnaționalizării în săcuime." *Academia Română—Memoriile Secțiunii Istorice* 3/18 (1936): 217–31.
———. "O carte de rugăciuni catolică." *Revista Istorică* 17/1–3 (1931): 26–27.
Isohookana-Asunmaa, Tytti. "Csángó Minority Culture in Romania." Doc. 9078, 4 May 2001, published in *Parliamentary Assembly Documents*, Working papers 2001 Ordinary Session (part 3), 25–29 June, vol. 7. Strasbourg, 2001, 81–89.
Juvara, Alfred. "Legea privitoare la dobândirea și pierderea naționalității române." *Pandectele române*, Partea IV-a (1939): 81–102.
———. *Pandectele române*, Partea II-a (1939): 33–38.
Köpeczi, Béla, et al. *Erdély története*. Budapest, 1986–88.
———. *History of Transylvania*. New York, 2002.
Korponay, András. *Húszmillió magyart*. Budapest, 1941.
Kovács, Imre. *A néma forradalom*. Budapest, 1937.
Lozincă, Constantin. "Primim aceste rînduri, care destăinuiesc originea românească a multor Ceangăi." *Revista Istorică* 11/10–12 (Oct.–Dec. 1935): 402–3.
Lucaciu, Dumitru. "Omagiul 'Vieții' P. Dr. Iosif Petru M. Pal." *Viața* 27/5–6 (May–June 1941): 66–69.
Lükő, Gábor. *A moldvai csángók*. Budapest, 2002; 1936.
Macartney, C. A. *Hungary and Her Successors: The Treaty of Trianon and Its Consequences, 1919–1937*. London, 1937.
Mályusz, Elemér. *A magyar történettudomány*. Budapest, 2008; 1942.
Manuilă, Sabin. "Acțiunea eugenică ca factor de politică de populație." *Buletin eugenic și biopolitic* 12/1–2 (Jan.–Apr. 1941): 1–4.
———. *Recensământul general al populației României din 29 Decemvrie 1930*, vol. 2. *Neam, limbă maternă, religie*. Bucharest, 1938.
———. *Studiu etnografic asupra populației României*. Bucharest, 1940.
Mareș, Crista. "Sunt Ciangăii Români?" *Preocupări Universitare* 1 (1943): 104–5.
Marin-Dunăre, Nicolae. "Grupul etnic Românesc din Iugoslavia." *Geopolitica și geoistoria* 1 (Sept.–Oct. 1941): 75–79.
Mărtinaș, Dumitru. *L'origine dei cattolici di Moldavia*. Padua, 1987.
———. *Originea ceangăilor din Moldova*. Edited by Ion Coja and Vasile M. Ungureanu, with notes, commentary, bibliography, and index by Vasile M. Ungureanu. Bucharest, 1985.

———. *Origins of the Moldavian Csangos from Moldova*. Iaşi, 1999.
Mărtinaş, Ioan. *Cine sunt catolicii moldoveni?* Iaşi, 1942.
———. "Din istoria Bisericii catolice în Moldova." *Lumina Creştinului*, serialized from March 1942 to April 1943.
———. *Mitropolitul Petru Movilă şi Catolicismul*. Iaşi, 1943.
Merfea, Mihai. "Aspecte din viaţa satelor de ciangăi din România Veche." *Cuvântul Dăscălesc* 11/2-3 (Oct.-Nov. 1940): 4-9.
———. "Ceangăii despre ei înşişi." *Sociologie Românească* n.s. 6/5-6 (1995): 421-38.
———. "Preocuparea învăţătorului de azi." *Cuvântul Dăscălesc. Revista Asociaţiei Învăţătorilor Romaşcani* 11/6 (Feb. 1941): 1.
Meteş, Ştefan. *Emigrări româneşti din Transilvania în secolele XIII-XX*. Bucharest, 1971.
———. *Le problème des sicules en Roumanie*. Bucharest, 1939.
Mikecs, László. "A Kárpátokon túli magyaság." In József Deér and László Gáldi, eds., *Magyarok és románok*, vol. 1, 441-507. Budapest, 1943.
———. *Csángók*. Budapest, 1989; 1941.
Mitrany, David. "The New Rumanian Constitution." *Journal of Comparative Legislation and International Law*, ser. 3, 6/1 (1924): 110-19.
Moisescu, Gheorghe I. *Catolicismul în Moldova până la sfârşitul secolului al XIV*. Bucharest, 1942.
Moldovan, Iuliu. *Biopolitica*. Cluj, 1926.
———. *Introducere în etnobiologie şi biopolitică*. Sibiu, 1944.
———. *Statul etnic*. Sibiu, 1943.
Morariu, Bonaventura. *Series cronologica episcoporum ac praefectorum apostolicorum missionis Fr. Minorum Conventualium in Moldavia durante saeculo XIX*. Rome, 1942.
———. *Series cronologica Praefectorum Apostolicorum Missionis Fr. Min. Conv. in Moldavia et Valachia duratae saec. XVII et XVIII, cui accedit series chronologica Episcoporum Bacoviensium*. Rome, 1940.
Morariu, Tiberiu. *The Western Frontier of Rumania from the Physical and Biogeographical Points of View*. Cluj, 1946.
Mureşianu, Aurel A. *Originea Ciangăilor din Săcelele Braşovului*. Satulung-Săcele, 1937.
Naghiu, Iosif E. "Istorie 'nepărtinitoare.'" *Cultura Creştină* 10-11 (1943): 644-46.
Nagy, Ödön. "Szórvány és beolvadás." *Hitel* 3/4 (1938): 257-76.
Năstase, Gheorghe I. *Ungurii din Moldova la 1646 după "Codex Bandinus."* Chişinău, 1934.
Neculăeş, Dominic. *Latinitatea Bisericii Româneşti*. Săbăoani-Roman, 1940.
Németh, László. "Magyarok Romániában." *Tanú* 3/4 (1935): 113-82.
———. *Magyarok Romániában*. Budapest, 1935.
Netzhammer, Raymund. *Episcop în România: Într-o epocă a conflictelor naţionale şi religioase*, vols. 1-2. Edited by Nikolaus Netzhammer and Krista Zach. Bucharest, 2005.
Nistor, Aurel. *Problema românească din ţinuturile secuizate şi Biserica ortodoxă*. Sibiu, 1930.
Oláh, György. *Hárommillió koldus*. Budapest, 1929.
Opreanu, Sabin. *Die Szekler. Eine völkische Minderheit inmitten des Rumänientums*. Sibiu, 1939.
———. *The Economical and Political Functions of the Western Frontier*. Cluj, 1946.

Bibliography

———. *Săcuizarea Românilor prin religie.* Cluj, 1927.
———. *Terra Siculorum.* Cluj, 1925.
———. *Ținutul săcuilor: Contribuțiuni de geografie umană și de etnografie.* Cluj, 1928.
———. *Transilvania: Centrul pămîntului.* Sibiu, 1944.
Pal, Iosif Petru M. "Catolicii din Moldova sunt români neaoși." *Almanahul Revistei Populare Catolice* (1941): 56–60.
———. *Originea Catolicilor din Moldova și Franciscanii păstorii lor de veacuri.* Bacău, 1997; Săbăoani-Roman, 1942.
Pálóczy-Horváth, György. *In Darkest Hungary.* London, 1944.
Panaitescu, Petre P. *Istoria românilor.* Craiova, 1942.
Petit, Eugen. "Legiferarea în regimurile totalitare." *Universul* (6 June 1941): 1–2.
———. *Originea etnică.* Bucharest, 1941.
Popa-Lisseanu, Gheorghe. *Continuitatea românilor în Dacia.* Bucharest, 1941.
———. *Date privitoare la maghiarizarea românilor.* Bucharest, 1937.
———. *Originea secuilor și secuizarea românilor.* Cluj, 1927.
———. *Secuii și secuizarea românilor.* Bucharest, 1932.
Popovici, Gheorghe. "Diferențe și asemănări în structura biologică de rasă a popoarelor României." *Cultura* 3 (1924): 224–34.
Porsenna, Nicolae. *Regenerarea neamului românesc.* Bucharest, 1937.
———. "Schimbul de populație." *Parlamentul românesc* 10/305 (20 Aug. 1939): 3.
Racoveanu, Gheorghe. "Dumineca." *Cuvântul* 6/1989 (3 Nov. 1930).
Rădulescu-Motru, Constantin. *Etnicul românesc. Comunitate de origine, limbă și destin.* Bucharest, 1942.
———. *Psihologia poporului român.* Bucharest, 1937.
———. *Românismul. Catehismul unei noi spiritualități.* Bucharest, 1936.
———. *Timp și destin.* Bucharest, 1940.
Râmneanțu, Petru. *Die Abstammung der Tschangos.* Sibiu, 1944.
———. "Grupele de Sânge la Ciangăii din Moldova." *Buletin eugenic și biopolitic* 14/1–2 (1943): 51–65.
———. "Românii dintre Morava și Timoc și continuitatea spațiului lor etnic cu al Românilor din Banat și din Timocul bulgar." *Buletin eugenic și biopolitic* 12/1–4 (1941): 40–62.
———. *The Biological Grounds and the Vitality of the Transilvanian Rumanians.* Cluj, 1946.
Râmneanțu, Petru, and Petru David. "Cercetări asupra originii etnice a populației din Sud-Estul Transilvaniei pe baza compoziției serologice a sângelui." *Buletin eugenic și biopolitic* 6/1–3 (1935): 36–66.
———. "Origine éthnique des Széklers de Transylvanie." *Revue de Transylvanie* 2/1 (1935–36): 45–59.
Rațiu, Anton. *Românii de la est de Bug: Cercetări etno-sociologice și culegere de folclor.* Bucharest, 1994.
Rosetti, Radu. *Despre unguri și episcopiile catolice din Moldova.* Bucharest, 1905.
Rubinyi, Mózes. *A moldvai csángók múltja és jelene.* Budapest, 1901.

"Rumania: Bloodsucker of the Villages." *Time*, 31 Jan. 1938.
Scriban, Iuliu. "Călugărițele catolice nu-și lasă năravul." *Cuvântul* 6/1972 (17 Oct. 1930): 1-2.
———. "Dacă d. Frollo vrea dovezi." *Cuvântul* 7/2004 (18 Nov. 1930): 1-2.
———. "Trecerile la catolicism: Răspuns d-lui profesor Iosif Frollo." *Cuvântul* 7/1994 (8 Nov. 1930): 1-2.
Stan, Liviu. *Rasă și religiune*. Sibiu, 1942.
Stăniloae, Dumitru. *Catolicismul de după război*. Sibiu, 1931.
———. "Între ortodoxie și catolicism." *Telegraful român* 78/88 (6 Dec. 1930): 1-2.
———. "Între românism și catolicism." *Telegraful român* 78/86 (29 Nov. 1930): 1-2.
———. "Opera teologică a lui Nichifor Crainic." *Gândirea* 19/4 (Apr. 1940): 269.
———. "Ortodoxie și latinitate." *Gândirea* 18/4 (1939): 197-202.
———. *Ortodoxie și românism*. Sibiu, 1939.
Starr, Joshua. "Jewish Citizenship in Rumania." *Jewish Social Studies* 3/1 (Jan. 1941): 57-80.
Szabó, T. Attila. *Anyanyelvünk életéből*. Bucharest, 1970.
———. *A szó és az ember*. Bucharest, 1971.
———. "Az erdélyi, bukovinai és moldvai népballadagyűjtés történetéhez." In Zoltán Kallós, ed., *Balladák könyve. Élő hazai magyar népballadák*, 5-42. Bucharest, 1970.
———. *Erdélyi Magyar szótörténeti tár*, vols. 1-4. Bucharest, 1975-84.
———. "Kik és hol élnek a Csángók?" In *Nyelv és Múlt. Válogatott tanulmányok és cikkek*, 121-31. Bucharest, 1972.
———. *Nyelv és múlt*. Bucharest, 1972.
———. "Széljegyzetek egy újabb csángó kiadványhoz." *Korunk* 16/12 (1957): 1761-65.
Szekfű, Gyula, ed. *Mi a magyar?* Budapest, 1939.
Tufescu, Victor. *O regiune de vie circulație: Poarta Târgului-Frumos*. Bucharest, 1941.
Ungureanu, Vasile M. "Note și comentarii." In Dumitru Mărtinaș, *Originea ceangăilor din Moldova*. Bucharest, 1985.
Vâlsan, Gheorghe. Foreword to Sabin Opreanu, *Săcuizarea Românilor prin religie*, i-v. Cluj, 1927.
Veres, Péter. *Az Alföld parasztsága*. Budapest, 1936; 1934.
———. "Az író politikája." *Magyar Csillag* 4/1 (Jan. 1944): 8.
Veress, Endre [Andrei Veress, John/János Tatrosi]. "A moldvai csángók származása és neve." *Erdélyi Múzeum* 39 (1934): 29-64.
———. *The Hungarians of Moldavia*. East-European Problems, no. 8. London, 1920.
Vida, Péter. "Magyar Kárpát-medencét." *Kárpátmedence* 1/5 (Sept. 1941).
Wallis, B. C. "The Rumanians in Hungary." *Geographical Review* 6/2 (Aug. 1918): 156-71.
———. "The South Slavs of Southern Hungary." *Geographical Review* 6/4 (Oct. 1918): 341-53.
Z. S. "Die Abstammung der Tschangos, sau Originea Ciangăilor; de Petru Râmneanțu." *Universul* (11 Feb. 1944).

Bibliography

Secondary Sources

Achim, Viorel. "Romanian-German Collaboration in Ethnopolitics." In Ingo Haar and Michael Fahlbusch, eds., *German Scholars and Ethnic Cleansing 1919–1945*, 139–54. New York, 2005.

———. "The Romanian Population Exchange Project Elaborated by Sabin Manuilă in October 1941." *Annali/Jahrbuch* 27 (2001): 593–617.

Ancel, Jean. "The German-Romanian Relationship and the Final Solution." *Holocaust and Genocide Studies* 19/2 (Fall 2005): 252–75.

Andrásfalvy, B., and A. Kelemen. "Ethnic Groups in Hungary: The Csángó Group." In Endre Czeizel, Heide G. Benkmann, and H. Werner Goedde, eds., *Genetics of the Hungarian Population: Ethnic Aspects, Genetic Markers, Ecogenetics and Disease Spectrum*, 59–64. Budapest, 1991.

Antohi, Sorin. "Romania and the Balkans: From Geocultural Bovarism to Ethnic Ontology." Tr@nsit online (*Europäische Revue*) 21 (2002).

Ardeleanu, Ion. "Concluding Note." In Mihai Antonescu, "*Dacă vrei să câştigi războiul, trebuie să pregăteşti pacea.*" *Discursul ţinut la 16 iunie 1942 de Mihai Antonescu pentru constituirea Biroului Păcii*. Cluj, 1991.

Ardener, Edwin. "Language, Ethnicity and Population." In Edwin Ardener and Malcolm Chapman, *The Voice of Prophecy and Other Essays*. New York, 2007; 1972.

Arens, Meinolf. "An Ethnic Group on the Pressure Field of Totalitarian Population Policies." In Sándor Ilyés, Lehel Peti, and Ferenc Pozsony, eds., *Local and Transnational Csángó Lifeworlds*, 113–31. Cluj, 2008.

Arens, Meinolf, and Daniel Bein. "Die Moldauer Ungarn (Tschangos) im Rahmen der rumänisch-ungarisch-deutschen Beziehungen zwischen 1940 und 1944: Eine vornational strukturierte ethnische Gruppe im Spannungsfeld totalitärer Volkstumspolitik." In Mariana Hausleitner and Harald Roth, eds., *Der Einfluss von Faschismus und Nationalsozialismus auf Minderheiten in Ostmittel- und Südosteuropa*, 265–315. Munich, 2006.

———. "Katolikus magyarok Moldvában." In Ambrus Miskolczy, ed., *Rendhagyó nézetek a Csángókról*, 99–141. Budapest, 2004.

Baker, Robin. "The Hungarian-Speaking Hussites of Moldavia and Two English Episodes in Their History." *Central Europe* 4/1 (May 2006): 3–24.

———. "Magyars, Mongols, Romanians and Saxons: Population Mix and Density in Moldavia, from 1230 to 1365." *Balkan Studies* 37/1 (1996): 4–66.

———. "On the Origin of the Moldavian Csángós." *The Slavonic and East European Review* 75/4 (Oct. 1997): 658–80.

Bárdi, Nándor. "'A Keleti Akció': A romániai magyar intézmények anyaországi támogatása az 1920-as években." In László Diószegi and Zoltán Fejős, eds., *Magyarságkutatás 1995–1996*, 143–90. Budapest, 1996.

———. "Hungary and the Hungarians Living Abroad: A Historical Outline." *Regio* (2003): 121–38.

———. "Keleti Akció." *Regio* 3 (1997): 89–134.
Barna, Bodó. "Internal Diaspora—Assimilation—Formation of the Internal Diaspora." *Acata Universitatis Sapientiae—European and Regional Studies* 1/1 (2010): 59–82.
Barszczewska, Agnieszka, and Lehel Peti, eds. *Integrating Minorities: Traditional Communities and Modernization.* Cluj, 2011.
Benda, Kálmán. "Les Hongrois de Moldavie (les Tchangos) aux XVIe–XVIIe siècles." In Ferenc Glatz, ed., *Ethnicity and Society in Hungary*, 59–75. Budapest, 1990.
———. "The Hungarians of Moldavia (Csángós) in the 16th–17th Centuries." In László Diószegi, ed., *Hungarian Csángós of Moldavia: Essays on the Past and Present of the Hungarian Csángós in Moldavia*, 7–50. Budapest, 2002.
Benjamin, Lya. *Evreii din România între anii 1940–1944, Legislaţia antievreiască*, vol. 1. Bucharest, 1993.
———. "Introductory Study." In Lya Benjamin, ed., *Evreii din România între anii 1940–1944, Legislaţia antievreiască*, vol. 1, lix–xcvi. Bucharest, 1993.
Benkő, Loránd. *A magyar nyelv történeti-etimológiai szótára*, vol. 1. Budapest, 1967.
Beres, Judit, and C. R. Guglielmino. "Genetic Structure in Relation to the History of Hungarian Ethnic Groups." *Human Biology* 68/3 (June 1996): 335–55.
Biliuţă, Ionuţ Florin. "The Philosopher and Orthodoxism. An Inquiry into the 'Ethnic Ontology' of Nae Ionescu." *Studia Universitatis Petru Maior. Historia* 7 (2007): 175–200.
Bjork, James. *Neither German nor Pole: Catholicism and National Indifference in a Central European Borderland.* Ann Arbor, 2008.
Boia, Lucian. *Explorations into the Imaginary.* Bucharest, 1999.
———. *History and Myth in Romanian Consciousness.* Budapest, 2001.
———. *Romania: Borderland of Europe.* London, 2001.
———. *Cum s-a românizat România.* Bucharest, 2015.
Bolovan, Ioan, and Sorina Bolovan. "Iniţiative româneşti privind problema schimbului de populaţie în primii ani ai celui de-al doilea război mondial (1931–1941)." In Liviu Ţârău and Virgiliu Ţârău, eds., *România şi relaţiile internaţionale în secolul XX*, 90–116. Cluj, 2000.
Bottoni, Stefano. "The Creation of the Hungarian Autonomous Region of Romania (1952): Premises and Consequences." *Regio* (2003): 71–93.
———. "The Purest Hungarians? National Representation versus Social Development in the Szeklerland (1919–40)." Conference paper at Greater Romania's National Projects: Ideological Dilemmas, Ethnic Classification, and Political Instrumentalisation of Ethnic Identities, Oxford Brookes University, 10–13 Apr. 2008.
———. *Transilvania roşie: Comunismul român şi problema naţională 1944–1965.* Cluj, 2010.
Braham, Randolph L. *The Politics of Genocide: The Holocaust in Hungary.* New York, 1981.
Brandstätter, A., et al. "Migration Rates and Genetic Structure of Two Hungarian Ethnic Groups in Transylvania, Romania." *Annals of Human Genetics* 71 (2007): 791–803.
Brock, Peter. "Florjan Cenôva and the Kashub Question." *East European Quarterly* 2/3 (Sept. 1968): 259–94.

———, ed. *Folk Cultures and Little Peoples: Aspects of National Awakening in East Central Europe*. Boulder, 1992.
Brown, Kate. *A Biography of No Place: From Ethnic Borderland to Soviet Heartland*. Cambridge, MA, 2003.
Browning, Christopher R. "The Madagascar Plan." In Walter Laqueur, ed., *The Holocaust Encyclopedia*, 407–9. New Haven, CT, 2001.
Brubaker, Rogers. *Citizenship and Nationhood in France and Germany*. Cambridge, MA, 1994.
———. "The 'Diaspora' Diaspora." *Ethnic and Racial Studies* 28/1 (2005): 1–19.
———. "Ethnicity without Groups." *European Journal of Sociology* 43/2 (2002): 163–89.
———. *Nationalism Reframed: Nationhood and the National Question in the New Europe*. Cambridge, 2000.
Bryant, Chad. "Either German or Czech: Fixing Nationality in Bohemia and Moravia, 1939–1946." *Slavic Review* 61/4 (Winter 2002): 683–706.
Bucur, Maria. *Eugenics and Modernization in Interwar Romania*. Pittsburgh, 2002.
Burleigh, Michael. *Germany Turns Eastwards: A Study of "Ostforschung" in the Third Reich*. Cambridge, 1998.
———. *The Third Reich: A New History*. New York, 2000.
Butaru, Lucian. "The Citizenship Issue in the Great Romania (1918–1940)." *Studia Universitatis Babeş-Bolyai—Studia Europaea* 2 (2006): 81–89.
———. *Rasism românesc*. Cluj, 2010.
Caplan, Jane, and John Torpey. "Introduction." In Jane Caplan and John Torpey, eds., *Documenting Individual Identity: The Development of State Practices in the Modern World*, 1–12. Princeton, NJ, 2001.
Case, Holly. *Between States: The Transylvanian Question and the European Idea during World War II*. Stanford, CA, 2009.
Cavalli-Sforza, L. L., A. Piazza, and P. Menozzi. "Reconstruction of Human Evolution: Bringing Together Genetic, Archeological, and Linguistic Data." *Proceedings of the National Academy of Sciences of the USA* 85/16 (Aug. 1998): 6002–6.
Chu, Winson. "'*Volksgemeinschaften unter sich*': German Minorities and Regionalism in Poland, 1918–39." In Neil Gregor, Nils Roemer, and Mark Roseman, eds., *German History from the Margins*, 104–26. Bloomington, IN, 2006.
Ciubotaru, Ion H. *Catolicii din Moldova. Universul culturii populare*, vol. 3. Iaşi, 1998.
Clark, Roland. *Holy Legionary Youth: Fascist Activism in Interwar Romania*. Ithaca, 2015.
———. "Nationalism and Orthodoxy: Nichifor Crainic and the Political Culture of the Extreme Right in 1930s Romania." *Nationalities Papers* 40/1 (2012): 107–26.
———. *Nationalism, Ethnotheology, and Mysticism in Interwar Romania*. The Carl Beck Papers in Russian and East European Studies. Pittsburgh, 2009.
Cornelius, Deborah S. *In Search of the Nation: The New Generation of Hungarian Youth in Czechoslovakia, 1925–1934*. Boulder, 1998.
Cornwell, John. *Hitler's Pope: The Secret History of Pius XII*. New York, 1993.

Coşa, Anton. *Catolicii din Moldova în izvoarele Sfântului Scaun (Secolele XVII–XVIII)*. Iaşi, 2007.

———. *Cleja: Monografie etnografică*. Bucharest, 2001.

Cotoi, Călin. "New Technologies for Ethno-Nationalist Imaging: The Case of Moldavian Csangos." *Sociologie Romaneasca* 6/3 (2008): 163–70.

———. "The Politics of Ethnography: Figures of Csangoness in Fin-de-siècle and Twentieth-Century Hungary and Romania." *History and Anthropology* 24/2 (2013): 433–52.

———. "Reactionary Modernism in Interwar Romania: Anton Golopenţia and the Geopolitization of Sociology." In Tomasz Kamusella and Krzysztof Jaskułowski, eds., *Nationalisms Today*, 125–53. Oxford, 2009.

Czigány, Lóránt. *The Oxford History of Hungarian Literature from the Earliest Times to the Present.* Oxford, 1984.

Davis, R. Chris. "Clericalism and Ethnic Mobilization in Twentieth-Century Romania and Hungary." In Robert Pyrah and Marius Turda, eds., *Re-Contextualising East Central European History: Nation, Culture and Minority Groups*, 74–88. London, 2010.

———. "Rescue and Recovery: The Biopolitics and Ethnogenealogy of Moldavian Catholics in 1940s Romania." In Sándor Ilyés, Lehel Peti, and Ferenc Pozsony, eds., *Local and Transnational Csángó Lifeworlds*, 95–111. Cluj, 2008.

———. "Restocking the Ethnic Homeland: Ideological and Strategic Motives behind Hungary's 'Hazatelepítés' Schemes during WWII (and the Unintended Consequences)." *Regio* 10 (2007): 155–74.

Deák, Istvan. "Historiography of the Countries of Eastern Europe: Hungary." *American Historical Review* 97/4 (Oct. 1992): 1041–63.

———. "Hungary." In Hans Rogger and Eugen Weber, eds., *The European Right: A Historical Profile*, 364–407. Berkeley, CA, 1965.

Deletant, Dennis. *Hitler's Forgotten Ally: Ion Antonescu and His Regime, Romania 1940–1944*. Basingstoke, 2006.

Diaconescu, Marius. "The Identity Crisis of the Moldavian Catholics—Between Politics and Historic Myth. A Case Study: The Myth of Romanian Origin." In Sándor Ilyés, Lehel Peti, and Ferenc Pozsony, eds., *Local and Transnational Csángó Lifeworlds*, 81–93. Cluj, 2008.

Diószegi, László, ed. *Hungarian Csángós in Moldavia: Essays on the Past and Present of the Hungarian Csángós in Moldavia*. Budapest, 2002.

Djuvara, Neagu. *Thocomerius–Negru Vodă, un voivod de origine cumană la începuturile Ţării Româneşti*. Bucharest, 2007.

Doboş, Dănuţ. "File de istorie: Iosif Frollo." *Actualitatea Creştină* 20/10 (2009): 19.

Dumea, Emil. *Cărţi şi reviste catolice româneşti în Moldova*. Iaşi, 2002.

———. *Istoria bisericii catolice din Moldova*. Iaşi, 2006.

Dumitriu-Snagov, Ion. "Ceangăii—Dincolo de enigmă." *Magazin istoric: Revistă de cultură istorică* n.s. 24/12 (Dec. 1990): 33–38.

Eriksen, Thomas Hylland. *Ethnicity and Nationalism*. New York, 2002; 1993.

Bibliography

Erős, Vilmos. *A Szekfű–Mályusz vita*. Debrecen, 2000.

———. "Mályusz's Ethnohistory." *Budapest Review of Books* 4 (1995): 179–85.

"The Ethnogenesis of Hungarians and Archaeogenetics." Interview with Csanád Bálint, director of the Archaeological Institute, Hungarian Academy of Sciences. *The Hungarian Quarterly* 50/196 (Winter 2009): 46–49.

Fahrmeir, Andreas. *Citizenship: The Rise and Fall of a Modern Concept*. New Haven, CT, 2007.

———. "Governments and Forgers: Passports in Nineteenth-Century Europe." In Jane Caplan and John Torpey, eds., *Documenting Individual Identity: The Development of State Practices in the Modern World*, 218–34. Princeton, NJ, 2001.

Feferman, Kiril. "Nazi Germany and the Karaites in 1938–1944: Between Racial Theory and *Realpolitik*." *Nationalities Papers* 39/2 (Mar. 2011): 277–94.

Fischer-Galați, Stephen. "The Interwar Period." In Dinu C. Giurescu and Stephen Fischer-Galați, eds., *Romania: A Historical Perspective*. Boulder, CO, 1998.

Fishman, Joshua A. "Social Theory and Ethnography: Neglected Perspectives on Language and Ethnicity in Eastern Europe." In Peter Sugar, ed., *Ethnic Conflict and Diversity in Eastern Europe*, 69–99. Santa Barbara, CA, 1980.

Fola, Nicolae Victor. "Biserica ortodoxă română în perioada dintre cele două războaie mondiale." *Angvista* 8 (2004): 173–80.

Frank, Tibor. "From Austria-Hungary to the United States: National Minorities and Emigration 1880–1914." *Nationalities Papers* 24/3 (1996): 409–23.

Frilling, Tuvia, Radu Ioanid, and Mihail E. Ionescu, eds. *Final Report: International Commission on the Holocaust in Romania*. Iași, 2004.

Gabor, Iosif, and Iosif Simon. *Necrolog 1600–2000: Misionari și preoți autohtoni: Diecezani și franciscani, clerici și frați călugări care au lucrat în Moldova pe teritoriul actual al Diecezei de Iași 1600–2000*. Iași, 2001.

Gáll, Ernő. "Hungarian Sociologists from Romania and the School of Bucharest." An interview by Corina Iosif. *Martor* 3 (1998): 67–72.

Gazda, László. "A moldvai csángók a román törtenetírás tükrében." *Krónika* (8–9 Dec. 2001): 13.

Georgescu, Tudor. "Ethnic Minorities and the Eugenic Promise: The Transylvanian Saxon Experiment with National Renewal in Inter-War Romania." *European Review of History—Revue européenne d'histoire* 17/6 (2010): 861–80.

Georgescu, Vlad. *The Romanians: A History*. Columbus, OH, 1984.

Ghișa, Ciprian. "Întărind vechi alterități, ridicând noi frontiere: Concordatul dintre România și Vatican—1929." *Studia Universitatis Babeș-Bolyai: Theologia Catholica* 55/4 (2010): 43–56.

Glantz, David M. *Red Storm Over the Balkans: The Failed Soviet Invasion of Romania, Spring 1944*. Lawrence, KS, 2006.

Gojinescu, Cristian. "Concordatul din 1929 și organizarea cultului catolic în România." *Etnosfera: Revistă dedicată studiului problemelor de natură etnică în spațiul UE* 1 (July 2008): 25–37.

Golopenția, Sanda. "Introducere." In Anton Golopenția, *Românii de la est de Bug*, vol. 1, v–lxxvii. Bucharest, 2006.

Graham, Hugh F. "Peter Mogila—Metropolitan of Kiev." *Russian Review* 14/4 (Oct. 1955): 345–56.

Griffin, Roger. *Modernism and Fascism: The Sense of a Beginning under Mussolini and Hitler.* Houndmills, UK, 2007.

Guglielmino, Carmela R., A. De Silveestri, and J. Beres. "Probable Ancestors of Hungarian Ethnic Groups: An Admixture Analysis." *Annals of Human Genetics* 64 (2000): 145–59.

Halász, Péter. "About the Regional and Ethnic Division of the Moldavian Hungarians." In Sándor Ilyés, Lehel Peti, and Ferenc Pozsony, eds., *Local and Transnational Csángó Lifeworlds*, 141–69. Cluj, 2008.

Hanebrink, Paul A. *In Defense of Christian Hungary: Religion, Nationalism, and Antisemitism, 1890–1944*. New York, 2006.

———. "Islam, Anti-Communism, and Christian Civilization: The Ottoman Menace in Interwar Hungary." *Austrian History Yearbook* 40 (2009): 114–24.

Haynes, Rebecca. *Romanian Policy towards Germany, 1936–40*. London, 2000.

———. "Work Camps, Commerce, and the Education of the 'New Man' in the Romanian Legionary Movement." *The Historical Journal* 51/4 (2008): 943–67.

Heinen, Armin. *Legiunea "Arhanghelul Mihail": Mișcare Socială și Organizație Politică*. Bucharest, 2006. Originally published as *Die Legion "Erzengel Michael" in Rumänien: Soziale Bewegung und politische Organisation*. Oldenbourg, 1986.

Hettling, Manfred. "Volk und Volksgeschicten in Europa." In Manfred Hettling, ed., *Volksgeschichten im Europa der Zwischenkriegszeit*, 7–37. Göttingen, 2003.

Hirsch, Francine. *Empire of Nations: Ethnographic Knowledge and the Making of the Soviet Union*. Ithaca, NY, 2005.

Hitchins, Keith. "Erdélyi Fiatalok: The Hungarian Village and Hungarian Identity in Transylvania in the 1930s." *Hungarian Studies* 21/1–2 (2007): 85–99.

———. "*Gîndirea*: Nationalism in a Spiritual Guise." In Kenneth Jowitt, ed., *Social Change in Romania, 1860–1940: A Debate on Development in a European Nation*, 140–73. Berkeley, 1978.

———. "Orthodoxism: Polemics over Ethnicity and Religion in Interwar Romania." In Ivo Banac and Katherine Verdery, eds., *National Character and National Ideology in Interwar Eastern Europe*, 135–56. New Haven, CT, 1995.

———. *Orthodoxy and Nationality: Andreiu Șaguna and the Rumanians of Transylvania 1846–1873*. Cambridge, MA, 1977.

———. *Rumania 1866–1947*. Oxford, 1994.

Hofer, Tamás. "The 'Hungarian Soul' and the 'Historic Layers of National Heritage': Conceptualizations of the Hungarian Folk Culture, 1880–1944." In Ivo Banac and Katherine Verdery, eds., *National Character and National Ideology in Interwar Eastern Europe*, 65–81. New Haven, CT, 1995.

Ilyés, Sándor. "The Image of the Csángós in the Hungarian Press of Transylvania." In Sándor Ilyés, Lehel Peti, and Ferenc Pozsony, eds., *Local and Transnational Csángó Lifeworlds*, 335–54. Cluj, 2008.

Ilyés, Sándor, Lehel Peti, and Ferenc Pozsony, eds. *Local and Transnational Csángó Lifeworlds*. Cluj, 2008.

Ioanid, Radu. *The Holocaust in Romania: The Destruction of Jews and Gypsies under the Antonescu Regime, 1940–1944*. Chicago, 2000.

———. "The Holocaust in Romania: The Iași Pogrom of June 1941." *Contemporary European History* 2/2 (1993): 119–48.

———. "Studiu introductiv: Tragedia deportării romilor în Transnistria." In Radu Ioanid, Michelle Kelso, and Luminița Mihai Cioabă, eds., *Tragedia romilor deportați în Transnistria 1942–1945: Mărturii și documente*, 33–53. Bucharest, 2009.

———. *The Sword of the Archangel: Fascist Ideology in Romania*. Boulder, 1990.

Ionesco, Marie-France. *Portretul scriitorului în secol. Eugène Ionesco, 1909–1994*. Bucharest, 2003.

Ionescu, Ștefan Cristian. *Jewish Resistance to "Romanianization," 1940–44*. New York, 2015.

Iordachi, Constantin. "Citizenship and National Identity in Romania: A Historical Overview." *Regio* 1 (2002): 3–34.

———. "God's Chosen Warriors: Romantic Palingenesis, Militarism and Fascism in Modern Romania." In Constantin Iordachi, ed., *Comparative Fascist Studies: New Perspectives*, 316–57. London and New York, 2010.

Isohookana-Asunmaa, Tytti. "Csángó Minority Culture in Romania." Doc. 9078, 4 May 2001, published in *Parliamentary Assembly Documents*, Working papers 2001 Ordinary Session (part 3), 25–29 June, vol. 7, 81–89. Strasbourg, 2001.

Janos, Andrew C. *The Politics of Backwardness in Hungary (1825–1945)*. Princeton, NJ, 1982.

Jelavich, Barbara. *Russia and the Formation of the Romanian National State, 1821–1878*. Cambridge, 1984.

Juhász, Gyula. *Uralkodó eszmék Magyarországon, 1939–1944*. Budapest, 1983.

Kapalo, James. "Clerical Agency and the Politics of Scriptural Translation: The 'Canonization' of the Gagauz Language in Southern Bessarabia." In Marius Turda and Robert Pyrah, eds., *Re-Contextualizing East Central European History: Nation, Culture, and Minority Groups*, 2–20. London, 2010.

———. "Gagauz 'Orthodoxism' in Interwar Romania: Mihail Cakir and the Gagauz National Movement." *Romanian Academy Historical Yearbook* (2011): 103–20.

———. *Text, Context and Performance: Gagauz Folk Religion in Discourse and Practice*. Leiden, 2011.

Karakasidou, Anastasia N. *Fields of Wheat, Hills of Blood: Passages to Nationhood in Greek Macedonia, 1870–1990*. Chicago, 1997.

Kellogg, Frederick. *A History of Romanian Historical Writing*. Bakersfield, CA, 1990.

King, Jeremy. *Budweisers into Czechs and Germans: A Local History of Bohemian Politics, 1848–1948*. Princeton, 2005.

Kizilov, Mikhail. *The Karaites of Galicia: An Ethnoreligious Minority among the Ashkenazim, the Turks, and the Slavs, 1772–1945*. Leiden, 2009.

Kłoskowska, Antonina. *National Cultures at the Grass-Root Level*. Budapest, 2001.

Kocsis, Károly, and Eszter Kocsisné Hodosi. *Ethnic Geography of the Hungarian Minorities in the Carpathian Basin*. Budapest, 1998.

Kontogiorgi, Elisabeth. *Population Exchange in Greek Macedonia: The Rural Settlement of Refugees, 1922–1930*. Oxford, 2006.

Kontra, Miklós. "Prefatory Note to the Csángó Issues." In Lehel Peti and Vilmos Tánczos, eds., *Language Use, Attitudes, Strategies. Linguistic Identity and Ethnicity in the Moldavian Csángó Villages*, 9–12. Cluj, 2012.

Köpeczi, Béla, et al. *History of Transylvania*, vol. 2. New York, 2002. Originally published as *Erdély története*. Budapest, 1986.

Kósa, László. "Mikecs László élete és munkássága." In László Mikecs, *Csángók*, i–xviii. Budapest, 1989.

Kovács, Éva, and Attila Melegh. "Az identitás játékai. Kísérlet Erdei Ferenc a magyar társadalom a két világháború között című tanulmányának tartalmi kibontására." In László Á. Varga, ed., *Vera (nem csak) a városban. Tanulmányok a 65 éves Bácskai Vera tiszteletére*, 487–505. Salgótarján, 1995.

Kürti, László. *The Remote Borderland: Transylvania in the Hungarian Imagination*. Albany, NY, 2001.

Lahermo, Päivi, et al. "MtDNA Polymorphism in the Hungarians: Comparison to Three Other Dinno-Ugric-Speaking Populations." *Hereditas* 132 (2000): 35–42.

Laihonen, Petteri, Magdolna Kovács, and Hanna Snellman. "In Search of New Perspectives on the Moldavian Csángós." In Magdolna Kovács, Petteri Laihonen, and Hanna Snellman, eds., *Culture, Language and Globalization among the Moldavian Csángós Today*, 7–24. Helsinki, 2015.

Le Callóch, Bernard. "Un peuple oublié: Les Csángós." In *Bulletin de l'Association des Anciens Élèves* (Oct. 1992): 36–42.

Leustean, Lucian N. "'For the Glory of Romanians': Orthodoxy and Nationalism in Greater Romania, 1918–1945." *Nationalities Papers* 35/4 (Sept. 2007): 717–42.

Liulevicius, Vejas Gabriel. *War Land on the Eastern Front: Culture, National Identity and German Occupation in World War I*. Cambridge, 2000.

Livezeanu, Irina. "After the Great Union: Generational Tensions, Intellectuals, Modernism, and Ethnicity in Interwar Romania." In *Nation and National Ideology: Past, Present and Prospects*, 110–24. Proceedings of the International Symposium held at the New Europe College. Bucharest, 2002.

———. *Cultural Politics in Greater Romania: Regionalism, Nation Building, and Ethnic Struggle, 1918–1930*. Ithaca, NY, 1995.

Lower, Wendy. *Nazi Empire Building in Ukraine*. Chapel Hill, NC, 2005.

Lumans, Valdis O. "A Reassessment of *Volksdeutsche* and Jews in the Volhynia-Galicia-Narew Resettlement." In Alan E. Steinweis and Daniel E. Rogers, eds., *The Impact of Nazism: New Perspectives on the Third Reich and Its Legacy*, 81–100. Lincoln, 2003.

Bibliography

———. *Himmler's Auxiliaries: The "Volksdeutsche Mittelstelle" and the German National Minorities of Europe, 1933–1945.* Chapel Hill, NC, 1993.
Markó, László, ed. *Új Magyar Életrajzi Lexikon I, A–Cs.* Budapest, 2001.
Martin, Terry. *The Affirmative Action Empire: Nations and Nationalism in the Soviet Union, 1923–1939.* Ithaca, NY, 2001.
Matsuda, Motoji. "Ethnogenesis in Anthropology." In Neil J. Smelser and Paul B. Baltes, eds., *International Encyclopedia of the Social and Behavioral Sciences*, vol. 7, 4854–57. Amsterdam, 2001.
McMahon, Richard. "On the Margins of International Science and National Discourse: National Identity Narratives in Romanian Race Anthropology." *European Review of History—Revue européenne d'histoire* 16/1 (Feb. 1990): 101–23.
Melegh, Attila. *On the East-West Slope: Globalization, Nationalism, Racism and Discourses on Eastern Europe.* Budapest, 2006.
Miloiu, Silviu. "The Csangos of Romanian Moldavia: Between the Cold War Logics and Appeasement." In Arno Tanner, ed., *The Forgotten Minorities of Eastern Europe: The History and Today of Selected Ethnic Groups in Five Countries*, 123–62. Helsinki, 2004.
Miskolczy, Ambrus. "Mi a magyar?" *Századok* 132/6 (1998): 1263–305.
Mitu, Sorin. *National Identity of Romanians in Transylvania.* Budapest, 1997.
———. "'Rămăşiţele zilei': Universalism catolic *versus* particularism naţional în opera lui Raymund Netzhammer." *Studia Universitatis "Babeş-Bolyai." Historia* 50/2 (2005): 200–211.
Moore, John H. "Ethnogenetic Theory." *Research and Exploration* 10 (1994): 10–23.
Muir, Edward. "Introduction: Observing Trifles." In Edward Muir and Guido Ruggiero, eds., *Microhistory and the Lost Peoples of Europe.* Baltimore, 1991.
Muller, Jerry Z. *The Other God That Failed: Hans Freyer and the Deradicalization of German Conservatism.* Princeton, NJ, 1987.
Nagy-Talavera, Nicholas M. *The Green Shirts and the Others: A History of Fascism in Hungary and Romania.* Iaşi, 2001; Stanford, CA, 1970.
Nastasă, Lucian. *Generaţie şi schimbare în istoriografia română: Sfârşitul secolului XIX şi începutul secolului XX.* Cluj, 1999.
———. *"Suveranii" Universităţilor Româneşti. Mecanisme de selecţie şi promovare a élitei intelectuale.* Vol. 1, *Profesorii Facultăţilor de Filosofie şi Litere (1864–1948).* Cluj, 2007.
Neamţu, Mihail. "Between the Gospel and the Nation: Dumitru Stăniloae's Ethno-Theology." *Arhaevs* 10 (2006): 7–44.
Némedi, Dénes. *A népi szociográfia 1930–1938.* Budapest, 1985.
———. "Remarks on the Role of Peasants in Hungarian Ideology." *The Journal of Popular Culture* 19/2 (Fall 1995): 67–75.
Nichols, Johanna. "The Eurasian Spread Zone and the Indo-European Dispersal." In Roger Blench and Matthew Spriggs, eds., *Archaeology and Language II: Archaeological Data and Linguistic Hypotheses*, 220–66. London and New York, 1998.
Nóda, Mózes. "The Historical, Political and Ecclesiastical Background of the 1927

Concordat between the Vatican and Romania." *Journal for the Study of Religions and Ideologie* 9/27 (Winter 2010): 281–301.

———. "The Roman Catholic Denominational Education between the World Wars." *Journal for the Study of Religions and Ideologies* 3 (Winter 2002): 115–30.

Ornea, Zigu. *Anii treizeci: Extrema dreaptă românească*. Bucharest, 1995.

Otu, Petre. "Septembrie 1940–ianuarie 1941. Armata in 'Statul Naţional Legionar': Preliminarii." *Magazin Istoric* 31/6 (June 1997): 37–41.

Păcurariu, Mircea. *Istoria bisericii ortodoxe române*. Sibiu, 1973.

Pamlényi, Ervin. *A History of Hungary*. Budapest, 1973.

Pârâianu, Răzvan. "'Romania to the Romanians' and the First Romanian Anti-Semitic Legislation of 1938." Conference paper at Greater Romania's National Projects: Ideological Dilemmas, Ethnic Classification, and Political Instrumentalisation of Ethnic Identities, Oxford Brookes University, 10–13 Apr. 2008.

Peti, Lehel. "'Wearied Respondents.' The Structure of Saving the Csangos and Its Effects on Their Identity Building Strategies." In Agnieszka Barszczewska and Lehel Peti, eds., *Integrating Minorities: Traditional Communities and Modernization*, 243–67. Cluj, 2011.

Peti, Lehel, and Vilmos Tánczos, eds. *Language Use, Attitudes, Strategies: Linguistic Identity and Ethnicity in the Moldavian Csángó Villages*. Cluj, 2012.

Petrescu, Cristina. "Contrasting/Conflicting Identities: Bessarabians, Romanians, Moldovans." In Balázs Trencsényi, Dragoş Petrescu, Cristina Petrescu, and Constantin Iordachi, eds., *Nation Building and Contested Identities: Romanian and Hungarian Case Studies*, 153–76. Budapest and Iaşi, 2000.

Polian, Pavel. *Against Their Will: The History and Geography of Forced Migrations in the USSR*. Budapest, 2004.

Porter, Brian. *When Nationalism Began to Hate: Imagining Modern Politics in Nineteenth-Century Poland*. Oxford, 2000.

Pozsony, Ferenc. "Church Life in Moldavian Hungarian Communities." In László Diószegi, ed., *Hungarian Csángós of Moldavia: Essays on the Past and Present of the Hungarian Csángós in Moldavia*, 83–115. Budapest, 2002.

———. *The Hungarian Csango of Moldova*. Buffalo, 2006.

Pritz, Pál. "A fajvédők külpolitikai nézetei (1918–1936)." *Századok* 124/5–6 (1990): 617–99.

———. *The War Crimes Trial of Hungarian Prime Minister László Bárdossy*. Boulder, 2004.

Promitzer, Christian, Klaus-Jürgen Hermanik, and Eduard Staudinger, eds. *(Hidden) Minorities: Language and Ethnic Identity between Central Europe and the Balkans*. London, 2009.

Puskás, Julianna. *From Hungary to the United States (1880–1914)*. Budapest, 1982.

Puttkamer, Joachim von. "Framework of Modernization: Government Legislation and Regulations on Schooling in Transylvania, 1780–1914." In Victor Karady and Borbála Zsuzsanna Török, eds., *Cultural Dimensions of Elite Formation in Transylvania (1770–1950)*, 15–23. Cluj, 2008.

Pyrah, Robert, and Marius Turda, eds. *Re-Contextualising East Central European History: Nation, Culture and Minority Groups*. London, 2010.
Rădvan, Laurenţiu. *At Europe's Borders: Medieval Towns in the Romanian Principalities*. Leiden, 2010.
Reichling, Gerhard. *Die deutschen Vertriebenen in Zahlen*. Bonn, 1995.
Rónai, András. *Térképezett történelem*. Budapest, 1993.
Rostás, Zoltán. *O istorie orală a Şcolii Sociologice de la Bucureşti*. Bucharest, 2007.
———. *Parcurs întrerupt. Discipoli din anii '30 ai Şcolii gustiene*. Bucharest, 2006.
Rothschild, Joseph. *East Central Europe between the Two World Wars*. Seattle and London, 1998.
———. *Ethnopolitics: A Conceptual Framework*. New York, 1981.
Sajti, Enikő A. *Hungarians in the Voivodina, 1918–1947*. Boulder, 2003.
———. "The Former 'Southlands' in Serbia: 1918–1947." *The Hungarian Quarterly* 47/181 (Spring 2006): 111–24.
Săndulescu, Valentin. "Academic Elites and Their Trajectories in Troubled Times: The Case of Traian Herseni." *Studii şi Materiale de Istorie Contemporană* 16 (2017): 84–101.
———. "Revolutionizing Romania from the Right: The Regenerative Project of the Romanian Legionary Movement and Its Failure (1927–1937)." PhD dissertation, Central European University. Budapest, 2010.
———. "'Taming the Spirit': Notes on the Shaping of the Legionary 'New Man.'" In Traian Sandu, ed., *Vers un profil convergent des fascimes? "Nouveau consensus" et religion politique en Europe centrale*, 207–16. Paris, 2010.
Scott, James C. *Seeing Like a State: How Certain Schemes to Improve the Human Condition Have Failed*. New Haven, CT, 1998.
Seres, Attila. "Adalékok a moldvai csángók lélekszámának vizsgálatához az 1930-as és 1940-es évek fordulóján." *Székelyföld kulturális folyóirat* 12 (Feb. 2008): 93–113.
———. "Domokos Pál Péter missziója a bukaresti magyar követségen (1940–1941)." *Magyar kisebbség: Nemzetpolitikai szemle* 14/3–4 (2009): 276–321.
———. "Németh Kálmán missziója a bukovinai székelyek és a moldvai csángók között I." *Moldvai Magyarság* (Aug. 2007): 10–16.
———. "Németh Kálmán missziója a bukovinai székelyek és a moldvai csángók között II." *Moldvai Magyarság* (Sept. 2007): 11–14.
Sfinţescu, Duiliu, ed. *Din luptele tineretului român 1919–1939: Corneliu Zelea Codreanu (culegere de texte)*. Bucharest, 1993.
Shafir, Michael. *Romania, Politics, Economy and Society*. Boulder, 1985.
Shipiro, Paul A. "Prelude to Dictatorship in Romania: The National Christian Party in Power, December 1937–February 1938." *Canadian-American Slavic Studies* 8/1 (Spring 1974): 45–88.
Shnirelman, Victor. "Linguoarchaeology: Goals, Advances and Limits." In Roger Blench and Matthew Spriggs, eds., *Archaeology and Language I: Theoretical and Methodological Orientations*, 158–65. London and New York, 1997.
Slezkine, Yuri. *Arctic Mirrors: Russia and the Small Peoples of the North*. Ithaca, NY, 1994.

———. "The USSR as a Communal Apartment, or How a Socialist State Promoted Ethnic Particularism." *Slavic Review* 53/2 (Summer 1994): 414–53.

Smith, Anthony D. "Ethno-Symbolism and the Study of Nationalism." In Philip Spencer and Howard Wollman, eds., *Nations and Nationalism: A Reader*, 23–31. New Brunswick, CT, 2005.

———. "National Identity and Myths of Ethnic Descent." Republished in *Myths and Memories of the Nation*, 57–95. Oxford, 1999.

Smith, Helmut Walser. "Prussia at the Margins, or The World That Nationalism Lost." In Neil Gregor, Nils Roemer, and Mark Roseman, eds., *German History from the Margins*, 69–83. Bloomington, IN, 2006.

Solonari, Vladimir. "An Important New Document on the Romanian Policy of Ethnic Cleansing during World War II." *Holocaust and Genocide Studies* 21/2 (Fall 2007): 268–97.

———. "'Model Province': Explaining the Holocaust of Bessarabian and Bukovinian Jewry." *Nationalities Papers* 34/4 (Sept. 2006): 471–500.

———. *Purifying the Nation: Population Exchange and Ethnic Cleansing in Nazi-Allied Romania*. Washington, DC, 2010.

Spinei, Victor. *Moldavia in the 11th–14th Centuries*. Bucharest, 1986.

Stark, Tamás. "Migrations during WWII." In *Minorities Research: A Collection of Studies by Hungarian Authors*, vol. 4, 182–96. Budapest, 2002.

Ştirban, Aurelia, and Marcel Ştirban. *Din istoria bisericii române unite de la 1918 la 1941*. Cluj, 2005.

Stråth, Bo, ed. *Europe and the Other and Europe as the Other*. Brussels, 2000.

Suciu, Mihai. "Prefaţă." In Teodor Chindea, *Contribuţii la istoria Românilor din Giurgeul-Ciucului*, 5–7. Târgu-Mureş, 1995; Gheorgheni, 1930.

Svart-Kara, Itic. *Obştea evreiască din Bacău*. Bucharest, 1995.

Szilágyi, Sándor. *Mi-Egy-Más. Közéleti írások*. Cluj, 2003.

Takács, György. *Aranykertbe' aranyfa. Gyimesi, hárompataki, úz-vülgyi csángó imák és ráolvasók*. Budapest, 2001.

Tánczos, Vilmos. "About the Demography of the Moldavian Csángós." In László Diószegi, ed., *Hungarian Csángós in Moldavia: Essays on the Past and Present of the Hungarian Csángós in Moldavia*, 117–47. Budapest, 2002.

———. "'Deákok' (parasztkántorok) moldvai magyar falvakban." *Erdélyi Múzeum* 57/3–4 (1995): 82–98.

———. "Hungarian Language Command among the Moldavian Csángós, 2008–10." In Agnieszka Barszczewska and Lehel Peti, eds., *Integrating Minorities: Traditional Communities and Modernization*, 269–381. Cluj, 2011.

Tanner, Arno, ed. *The Forgotten Minorities of Eastern Europe: The History and Today of Selected Ethnic Groups in Five Countries*. Helsinki, 2004.

Török, Zsuzsanna. "Planning the National Minority: Strategies of the Journal *Hitel* in Romania, 1935–44." *Nationalism and Ethnic Politics* 7/2 (2001): 57–74.

Trencsényi, Balázs. "Conceptualizarea caracterului naţional în tradiţia intelectuală românească." In Victor Neumann and Armin Heinen, eds., *Istoria României prin concepte: Perspective alternative asupra limbajelor social-politice*, 339–78. Iași, 2010.

———. "'Imposed Authenticity': Approaching Eastern European National Characterologies in the Inter-War Period." *Central Europe* 8/1 (May 2010): 20–47.

Turcescu, Lucian, ed. *Dumitru Stăniloae: Tradition and Modernity in Theology*. Oxford, 2002.

Turda, Marius. "Conservative Palingenesis and Cultural Modernism in Early Twentieth-Century Romania." *Totalitarian Movements and Political Religions* 9/4 (Dec. 2008): 437–53.

———. "Entangled Traditions of Race: Physical Anthropology in Hungary and Romania, 1900–1940." *Focaal* 58/3 (2010): 32–46.

———. "'If our race did not exist, it would have to be created': Racial Sciences in Hungary 1940–1944." In Anton Weiss-Wendt and Rory Yeomans, eds., *Racial Sciences in Hitler's Europe, 1939–1945*, 237–58. Lincoln, NE, 2013.

———. "In Search of Racial Types: Soldiers and the Anthropological Mapping of the Romanian Nation, 1914–44." *Patterns of Prejudice* 47/1 (2013).

———. "National Historiographies in the Balkans, 1830–1989." In Stefan Berger and Chris Lorenz, eds., *The Contested Nation: Ethnicity, Class, Religion and Gender in National Histories*, 463–89. New York, 2008.

———. "The Nation as Object: Race, Blood, and Biopolitics in Interwar Romania." *Slavic Review* 66/3 (Fall 2007): 413–41.

———. "'To End the Degeneration of a Nation': Debates on Eugenic Sterilization in Inter-War Romania." *Medical History* 53 (2009): 77–104.

Vanhaelemeersch, Philip. *A Generation without Beliefs and the Idea of Experience in Romania (1927–1934)*. Boulder, CO, 2006.

Várdy, Steven Béla. *Modern Hungarian Historiography*. Boulder, CO, 1976.

Vasary, Ildiko. "'The Sin of Transdanubia': The One-Child System in Rural Hungary." *Continuity and Change* 4/3 (1989): 429–68.

Vasile, Cristian. *Între Vatican și Kremlin: Biserica Greco-Catolică în timpul regimului comunist*. Bucharest, 2003.

———. "Monseniorul Vladimir Ghica în atenția serviciilor de informație, 1945–1948." *Arhivele totalitarismului* 9/30–31 (2001): 46–51.

———. "The Suppression of the Romanian Greek Catholic (Uniate) Church." *East European Quarterly* 36/3 (2002): 313–22.

Verdery, Katherine. "Internal Colonialism in Austria-Hungary." *Ethnic and Racial Studies* 2/3 (1979): 378–99.

———. *National Ideology under Socialism*. Berkeley, CA, 1991.

———. "The Production and Defense of 'the Romanian Nation,' 1900 to World War II." In Richard G. Fox, ed., *Nationalist Ideologies and the Production of National Cultures*, 81–111. Washington, DC, 1990.

Vincze, Gábor. "A bukovinai székelyek és kisebb moldvai Csángó-magyar csoportok áttelepedése Magyarországra (1940–1944)." *Pro Minoritate* 3 (2001): 141–87.

———. "An Overview of the Modern History of the Moldavian Csángó-Hungarians." In László Diószegi, ed., *Hungarian Csángós in Moldavia: Essays on the Past and Present of the Hungarian Csángós in Moldavia*, 51–82. Budapest, 2002.

———, ed. *Asszimiláció vagy kivándorlás? Források a moldvai magyar etnikai csoport, a csángók modern kori történelmének tanulmányozásához (1860–1989)*. Budapest, 2004.

———. "Csángósors a II. világháború után." In Ferenc Pozsony, ed., *Csángósors: Moldvai csángók a változó időkben*, 203–49. Budapest, 1999.

———. "Egy magyar etnikai csoport a román nemzetépítés árnyékában." In Sándor Ilyés, Lehel Peti, and Ferenc Pozsony, eds., *Lokális és transznacionális csángó életvilágok*, 9–74. Cluj, 2008.

Voss, Barbara L. *The Archaeology of Ethnogenesis: Race and Sexuality in Colonial San Francisco*. Berkeley, CA, 2008.

Wanner, Catherine. *Communities of the Converted: Ukrainians and Global Evangelism*. Ithaca, NY, 2007.

Weaver, Eric Beckett. "Hungarian Views of the Bunjevci in Habsburg Times and the Inter-War Period." *Balcanica* 42 (2011): 77–115.

———. "More Hungarian Hungarians, More Human Humans: Social and National Discourse on Hungarian Minorities in the Interwar Period." In Robert Pyrah and Marius Turda, eds., *Re-Contextualising East Central European History: Nation, Culture and Minority Groups*, 36–54. London, 2010.

Weber, Eugen. *Peasants into Frenchmen: The Modernization of Rural France, 1870–1918*. Stanford, CA, 1976.

———. "Romania." In Hans Rogger and Eugen Weber, eds., *The European Right: A Historical Profile*. London, 1965.

Wein, Markus. "The Germans in Romania—the Ambiguous Fate of a Minority." In Steffen Prauser and Arfon Rees, *The Expulsion of the "German" Communities from Eastern Europe at the End of the Second World War*, 57–69. EUI Working Paper HEC, no. 2004/1. Badia Fiesolana–San Domenico, 2004.

Wingfield, Nancy M. "Introduction." In Nancy M. Wingfield, ed., *Creating the Other: Ethnic Conflict and Nationalism in Habsburg Central Europe*. New York, 2005.

Zub, Alexandru. *Istorie și istorici în România interbelică*. Iași, 1989.

Index

"A fi bun român" (To be a good Romanian), 17, 54–56, 111, 138, 141, 175
Alba Iulia, 131, 179, 202n26, 203n43
All for the fatherland. *See* Totul pentru Țară
Angelescu, Constantin, 118
Annales School, 34
Anschluss, 124
anthropologists, xiii, 4, 16, 19, 24, 29, 67, 70, 76–77, 80, 120, 148–50, 166, 207n42. *See also* anthropology
anthropology, 4, 17, 30, 69–71, 81, 124, 147–51, 162. *See also* race science
Antonescu, Ion, xx, 25, 62–63, 89, 94, 101–3, 109–14, 121, 131, 134–35, 139, 146–48, 153–54, 158–60, 187n8, 204n59
Antonescu, Mihai, xx, 92, 139, 152–54, 156–60, 214n45
archdiocese: of Hungary (Roman Catholic Archdiocese of Esztergom-Budapest), 9, 180, 198n45; of Romania (Roman Catholic Archdiocese of Bucharest), 39, 41–42, 191n5, 193n40
Armenian Rite Catholic Church, 41
Armenians, 26, 167, 180, 197n28
Aromanians (Vlachs), 59, 115–17, 196n8, 198n31, 205n1
Arrow Cross Party, 135, 208n53
autochthonism, in Romania, 27, 49, 76, 83, 119, 140, 143–45, 156
Axis Powers, 3, 94, 105, 157, 164, 215
Az elsodort falu (The village that was swept away), 79

Bacău (city and county), 3, 7, 11, 23–24, 51, 60–62, 78, 86, 103–5, 111, 113, 134–36, 139, 141, 148, 157–58, 160, 162, 172–73, 180, 184n14, 191n5, 195n72, 203n46, 211n94, 216n11
Bácska County, 130, 132–33, 136–38, 153, 173
Bălan, Nicolae, xix, 42–44, 75–76
Balázs, Éva H., 84
Bálint, Csűry, 191n11, 200n75
Bálint, József, 126
Banat, 22, 151, 155, 175, 202n26; Banat-Crișana/Bánság-Körösvidék, 155
Banovina, 128
Baranya County, 122, 125, 130, 132, 138, 173
Bárdossy, László, 130–33, 135, 137–38, 209n72, 210n77
Bărgăoani, 148
Bartók, Béla, 10
Bartucz, Lajos, 80, 178, 190n27, 207n42
Baumgartner, Alexander (Sándor Besenyő), 84–85, 129, 135, 138, 209n64, 209n69
Bessarabia, 18, 22–24, 30, 59, 72, 91, 94, 104, 108, 116, 118, 120
Bibliotheca Rerum Transylvaniae, 157
Bihar/Bihor County, 131–32
biopolitics, 27–29, 59, 68–70, 76, 84, 93, 118, 127, 151, 162–63
biserica dominantă (dominant church), 8, 37, 42
Blaga, Lucian, 32, 45
blitzkrieg, xii, 3, 130
blood laws, 19–20, 29, 65, 100, 120. *See also* race laws
boanghen, boanghină, 112, 175. See also *bozgor*

Boia, Lucian, 165, 179
Bonczos, Miklós, 124, 132–36, 138, 207n41, 210n77, 210n79
Börvely/Berveni, 126, 208n49
Bosnia, 133, 180, 210n89
bozgor, 204n66
Brașov, 129, 172, 198n32, 202n26, 204n70
Brătianu, Gheorghe I., 34
Brătianu, Ion C., 27, 55
Brown, Kate, 65
Brubaker, Rogers, 11, 13
Bryant, Chad, 20
Bucharest, 23–24, 39–41, 44, 47, 49, 51, 52, 57, 61–62, 72, 76, 83, 92, 94, 100–101, 107–8, 130–31, 135, 137, 152–53, 160–62, 180, 191n5, 193n40, 197n15, 200n63, 200n66, 201n16, 203n49, 215n4, 215n57
Bucur, Maria, 71
Budapest, 43, 83, 132, 134, 141, 200n66, 207n41, 208n53
Bukovina, 18, 22–24, 28, 72, 89, 94, 102, 116, 120, 122, 125–26, 130–38, 156, 159, 169, 172–73, 189n16, 195n68; Northern Bukovina, Soviet invasion of, 23; population transfers, 122; and Southern Bukovina, 122, 126–27
Bulgarians, 56, 89, 115–17, 120–22, 133, 142, 146, 158, 180
Bunjevci, 128, 196n8, 205n4, 208n60
Bureau of Peace (Biroul Păcii), 154, 157, 214n45
Burgenland, 133
Burleigh, Michael, 30

Cădărești/Magyarcsükes, 168, 216n11
Cadrilater, 116, 121
Calvinism (Calvinist or Reformed Church), in Hungary and Transylvania, 23, 32, 36, 45–46, 66, 72–73, 75, 123, 125–26, 137, 140, 144, 175–76, 212n12
Caplan, Jane, 20
Carol I, King of Romania, xx, 39, 54, 174
Carol II, King of Romania, xx, 29, 57, 62, 92–94, 117, 188n14, 203n47
Carpatho-Ruthenia, 23, 132; Ruthenians, 24, 41, 89, 158, 180, 207n37
Cărticica șefului de cuib (The nest leader's manual), 61

Case, Holly, 89
Cassulo, Andrea, xviii, 15, 63, 139, 153, 161–62, 215n54
Catholic Action (Acțiunea Catolică), 52–53, 193n49
Catholicism in Moldavia. *See* Roman Catholicism in Moldavia
Catholicization, 24, 41–42, 144
Catholic Prohászka Ottokár Társaság (Bishop Prohászka Society), 125, 208n53
census(es): Hungarian census (1910), 76, 205n4; and nation-building, 20, 77–78, 140; Romanian census (1930), 24, 48, 118, 122, 130, 159, 213n26; Romanian census (1941), 112, 148, 159, 213n26; Romanian census (2002), 184n9, 185n14; Romanian censuses and declared identity of Csangos, 12, 159, 185n14, 213n26; Yugoslav census (1931), 205n4
Center for Studies and Research on Transylvania (Centrul de Studii și Cercetări privitoare la Transilvania), 157
Central Institute for Statistics (Romanian), 121, 147, 153–54, 156
certificat de naționalitate. *See* nationality certificates
certificates of ethnic origin, 5, 13, 20, 67, 89–97, 99–103, 109–14, 138, 153, 164, 201n16. *See also* nationality certificates
Chindea, Teodor, xxii, 73–74, 76, 197n28
Chu, Winson, 19, 67
Cisar, Alexandru, xviii, 39, 52
citizenship, in Romania, 3, 7–11, 14, 19–22, 29–33, 37–41, 48, 51, 55–56, 59, 65–66, 71, 87–111, 113–14, 117–19, 131, 133–38, 141–42, 153, 156, 159–64, 170, 176. *See also* certificates of ethnic origin; citizenship laws; nationality certificates; nationality laws; naturalization
citizenship laws, 29, 33, 90–95, 99–103, 159. *See also* certificates of ethnic origin; citizenship, in Romania; nationality certificates; nationality laws; naturalization
Ciuc/Csík County, 168, 174; town of Miercurea Ciuc/Csíkszereda, 204n70l. *See also* Șumuleu-Ciuc/Csíksomlyó

Index

Cobzaru, Iosif, 107–8
Codreanu, Corneliu Zelea, 25, 27, 40, 58–64, 88, 187n7, 195n71
Codreanu, Ion Zelea (Zieliński), 61, 195n68
colonization: *colonizatori*, 117; internal colonization in Hungary, 138; internal colonization in Romania, 115–20, 133; of Moldavia and the Regat, 147, 149–51, 190n31; of the Szekler land, 172. *See also* State Undersecretariat of Romanianization, Colonization, and Inventory
colonizatori. *See* colonizers, Romanian
colonizers, Romanian (*colonizatori*), 117
Comănești, 168
Commission for Establishing Conditions for Naturalization and Recognition, 91. *See also* citizenship, in Romania; citizenship laws; nationality certificates; nationality laws; naturalization
Concordat. *See* Romanian-Vatican Concordat
Conea, Ion, 70
Coșnea/Kostelek, 168, 216n11
Cotnari region, 145
Cotoi, Călin, 15
Crainic, Nichifor, xix, 35, 45–47, 57–59, 88, 119–20, 142, 186n27, 192n32, 206nn14–15
Craiova, Treaty of, 121
Cretzianu, Alexandru, 121
Cristea, Miron, 42
Croatia, Croatians, 47, 122, 126–27, 130, 133, 205n4, 206n18, 210n89
Cruciada Românismul (Crusade of Romanianism), 61
Csango land, 2, 11, 24, 83, 126, 145, 167–68, 173, 200n66
Cultul Patriei (Cult of the fatherland), 61
Cumans, Cumania, 51, 78, 129, 145, 148–49, 180, 184n12, 198–99n45, 200n65, 208n62; bishopric of Cumania, 140, 149, 180, 184n12, 212n3
Cuvântul (The word), 54, 57
Cuvântul Dăscălesc (The teacher's word), 105
Cuza, A. C., 25, 54, 61, 88, 92, 120; Goga-Cuza government, 92
Cuza, A. I., 174
Czechs, Czech lands, Czechoslovakia, 19, 23, 39, 79, 83, 116, 155, 157, 161, 178, 191n9, 205n3, 205n7, 210n84

Dacia, Dacians, 47, 78, 143–44, 152, 193n45, 195n68; and Roman conquest, province of, 47, 144
Danubian Confederation, 124
Danubian Principalities, 174, 215n48
Davidescu, Nicolae, 118, 120
Délvidék (southlands or Southern Hungary), 130, 138, 173, 178; and Délvidék Massacres, 132
denationalization, xiii, 15, 27, 56, 68, 71–78, 104, 108, 133, 140, 144–46, 153–62, 176, 183n5
deportation: and Hungarian authorities, 68, 132, 135, 207n41; and Romanian authorities, 13, 25, 68, 90, 94, 109, 114, 120–21, 135, 137–38, 157–58, 160–62, 164, 214n47, 215n54, 215n56; and Soviet authorities, 23, 160–62, 215n54, 215n56. *See also* population exchanges; population transfers
diocese: of Bacău, 180, 191n5; of Cumania, 180, 184n12; of Iași, 139, 191n5, 193n40; of Transylvania (Roman Catholic Diocese of Alba Iulia), 41. *See also* archdiocese
Diplomatarium Italicum, 161
Directorate of Minorities (Direcția Minorităților), 154. *See also* State Undersecretariat of Romanianization, Colonization, and Inventory
Dniester River, 89, 142, 154, 158, 173
Dobrotă, Octavian M., 75, 198n37
Dobrudja, 59, 88, 89, 96, 115–17, 121–22, 131, 133, 156, 158, 193n45, 202n34; population transfers, 115–16, 121–22. *See also* Dobrudschadeutsche
Dobrudschadeutsche, 122
Domokos, Pál Péter, xxv, 31, 85, 86, 130–31, 138, 202n33, 209nn73–75
Dorohoi, 25
Dragomir, Silviu, 154, 157, 198n32
Dragoș, Titus, 95, 102, 121, 206n25

Ébredő Magyarok Egyesülete (Awakening Hungarians Association), 124

education. *See* schools, schooling
Egészségpolitikai Társaság (Society of Public Health), 127
egyke (one-child practice), 123, 130, 207n34, 207n36
Elekes, Dénes, 136
Eliade, Mircea, 35, 40, 45, 52, 69
Enlightenment, 27, 32–33, 55, 84
Episcopate of Iași, xiv, 8, 39–40, 64, 113, 136, 152–53
Erdélyi Fiatalok (Transylvanian Youth), 31, 79
Etelközi Szövetség (Etelköz Association), 124, 207n38
Ethnical, Biological, and Statistical Section (Secțiunea Etnică, Biologică și Statistică), 154. *See also* State Undersecretariat of Romanianization, Colonization, and Inventory
ethnic origins, xi, 3–5, 18, 20, 27–29, 35, 55, 66–69, 71, 82, 89, 91–103, 121, 128, 133, 165–70, 176, 199n52, 201n16; and certificates of ethnic origin, 89–90, 94–103, 109–14, 138, 152–53, 158–60, 164, 201n3, 201n16; of the Csangos, 3–5, 10–14, 32, 45, 51, 64, 78, 81, 103, 108–14, 133–34, 138–64, 167–69, 183n2, 183n5, 183n7, 184n10, 184n14, 185n16, 195n76, 198n44, 200n65; of the Szeklers, 72–77, 81. *See also* ethnogenealogy; ethnogenesis; ethnography; national belonging; nationality certificates
ethnobiology, 70
ethnogenealogy, 13, 72, 141, 145, 152, 155, 167, 204n53
ethnogenesis, 70, 74, 78, 148, 165–67, 215
ethnographers: Hungarian, 6, 10, 12, 31, 67–68, 80, 83–86, 130, 142, 168, 178, 190n27, 197n15, 200n66, 204n66; Romanian, 70, 72
ethnography: in Hungary, 15, 30, 79, 81, 85–86, 179, 200n63; and identity of the Csangos, xi, 10, 67, 85, 143, 156, 166–67, 186n20; as a nation-building science in east-central Europe, 18–19, 35, 67–68, 167, 190n23; in Romania, 31–32, 70, 141, 71, 76, 143. *See also* sociology
ethnohistory. *See népiségtörténet*

eugenics, eugenicists, 17, 70–71, 77, 127, 147–48, 155, 197n13

falukutatók (village explorers), 31, 123
Farul Nou, 47, 61, 193n40
Felvidék (northlands or Upper Hungary), 132–33
Ferdinand I, King of Romania, xxi, 54, 175, 188n14, 191n15
First Vienna Award (1938), 23, 117, 205n7
Foreign Hungarians Repatriation Committee, 132, 178
France, 8, 26, 32, 34, 47, 176, 188n15, 190n24; French Catholics in Romania, 6, 100, 191n5; French language, 26, 52, 157, 176, 194n52; Romanians studying abroad in, 70
Franciscan Order, Franciscans, 6, 50, 139, 180
Frollo, Iosif, xviii, 17, 47, 52–56, 61–64, 140–42, 159, 193nn39–40, 193n47, 195nn69–74
Frollo, Vladimir Anton, 62
Frumoasa/Frumosza, 204n66
Fülep, Lajos, 123, 207n34
Fundu-Răcăciuni, 148

Gagauz, 15, 58–59, 120, 133, 186n23, 196n8
Gârnițeanu, Mihai, 152
Geistesgeschichte, 31, 33, 80
Generalplan Ost, 116
geohistory, 68–69
geopolitics, 68, 70–71
German minority: in Bessarabia, 22–23, 122, 131; in Bukovina, 22–23, 122, 131, 202n26; in Czechoslovakia, 161; in Dobruja (*Dobrudschadeutsche*), 122, 131; in Hungary, 123, 125, 161; in Moldavia, 10, 24, 180; in Poland, 18; in Romania broadly, 36, 51, 99, 119, 121, 161; in Transylvania (Saxons and Swabians), 126, 197n21; in Yugoslavia, 161, 205n4
Germany, Germans, 47, 127, 140; Catholic missionaries from, 39; German Army, xii, 3, 25, 94, 130–31, 134, 160; German Catholicism, 47–48, 56, 192n32, 193n49; German Jews, 60; German language, 157, 172, 196n10, 213n27; nationalism, 66–68, 120,

Index

179, 190n24; Nazism and Nazis, 59, 60, 159; population policies, 116, 120, 132, 202n26; race (blood) laws and documents, 91–92; relations with Hungary, 131, 135; relations with Romania, 62, 88, 102, 120, 131, 135; race, 94, 177–78; Romanian royalty, 27, 54, 174–75, 191n15; Romanians studying in, 69–70

Gherăești, 62–63, 104, 107–8, 146, 195nn77–78

Ghibu, Onisifor, xxi, 43–44

Ghika, Vladimir, 27, 48, 188n15

Ghimeș/Gyimes, 9, 104, 113, 144, 168–69, 172, 204n70, 216n11

Ghiuzan, Iosif, xviii, 51–52, 193n39, 193n43

Gigurtu, Ion, 120

Goga-Cuza government, 92, 120

Goga, Octavian, xxi, 92, 120

Goldiș, Vasile, 41, 155

Golopenția, Anton, xxii, 30, 70, 121, 147, 154–56, 206n25, 208n59

Gömbös, Gyula, 124, 207n41

Governorate of Transnistria (Guvernământul Transnistriei), 89, 147

Greater Romania (România Mare), 8, 11, 22–24, 27–29, 37–41, 72, 77, 88–94, 105, 174–75, 180, 205n3

Greek Catholicism, Greek Catholics (Uniates), 27, 36–38, 41–44, 55, 57, 59, 72, 125, 131, 140, 151, 155, 160, 168, 179–80, 185n14, 192nn17–18, 203n43, 215n59

Greeks, 26, 115–16, 142, 146, 180, 198n38; Greek language, 26. *See also* Phanariot rule

Grozești (Oituz-Grozești), 112–13, 148

Gruia, Ion V., xxi, 93, 99

Gusti, Dimitrie, xxii, 31, 69–70, 80–83, 197n15, 200n66; and Gusti School, 31, 81, 197n15, 199nn59–60

Gypsies. *See* Roma

Habsburgs, Habsburg Monarchy, 9, 11, 68–69, 71–72, 92, 174, 178, 189n16, 203n43

Harom nemzedék: Egy hanyatló kor története (Three generations: The history of a declining age), 33

határon túli magyarok (Hungarians across the border), 30–32, 178

hazatelepítés (resettlement home), 23, 116, 130–36, 178

Heim ins Reich (back home to the Reich), 116, 122

Herseni, Traian, 69, 197n15

Hettling, Manfred, 66

Hirsch, Francine, 19

Hirszfeld, Ludwig, 150

historians: and the Csangos, 6–7, 10, 12–15, 30, 51, 82–86, 138, 142–44, 147, 152–57, 165–67, 185n16, 198n44, 200n65, 200n75, 209n64; German, 19, 30, 67; Hungarian, 6, 10, 12, 30–35, 80–86, 142, 195n27, 200n63, 200n65, 200n75, 209n64; Romanian, 7, 15, 30–35, 70–75, 138, 143–44, 146, 154–57, 178, 185n16, 190n31

Historical Commission on Transylvania (Comisiunea Istorică pentru Transilvania), 161

historiography: French, 34; German, 19, 30–33; Hungarian, 30–35, 68, 80–86, 170, 178, 190n27; and nation-building in east-central Europe, 4, 19, 21, 67, 189n13; Romanian, 15, 31–35, 51, 55, 70–75, 143–44, 154–57, 185n16, 190n31

Hitel (Credit), 31, 85

Hohenzollern-Sigmaringen dynastic line, 27, 54, 175, 191n15

Hóman, Bálint, 190n29

Horia/Horea, 107, 203n43

Horthy, Miklós, xii, 135, 210n90

Hossu, Iuliu, 42, 192n18

Hungarian Army, 3, 130–32, 135, 210n77

Hungarianization, xiii, 15, 41–42, 74–76, 140–49, 155, 176

Hungarian Legation in Bucharest, 137

Hussitism, 212n12

Iași (city and county), 7, 23, 25, 39, 49, 61, 64, 94, 100–101, 108, 134, 147, 161, 173, 184n14, 191n5, 194n52, 195n72, 213n15. *See also* diocese; Episcopate of Iași; seminary, Roman-Catholic

Identification of Romanians East of the Bug River (Identificarea Românilor de la Est de Bug), 147

Ilyés, Sándor, 15

Institute of Settlement and Ethnohistory, 84
înstrăinare (ethnic estrangement), 76, 145, 176–77
Ionescu, Constantin S., xxi, 60, 107, 111
Ionescu, Eugen (Eugène Ionesco), 95, 201n16
Ionescu, Nae, xix, 17, 27, 35, 44–49, 54–58, 61, 88, 140–42, 159, 186n27
Ionescu, Nicolae Gh. (Nocolae Porsenna), 118, 205n9
Iordachi, Constantin, 58
Iorga, Nicolae, xxii, 32, 34, 61–62, 78, 199n46, 200n66
Iron Guard (Garda de fier), 25, 34, 40, 58–64, 74, 88, 155, 186n27, 188n16, 195n76, 197n31. *See also* Legion of the Archangel Michael
Italy, 47, 193n49, 206n18; influence of Italian fascism in Romania, 47, 58–59, 60, 88; Italian Catholics in Romania, 8, 39, 180, 191n10; Romanian priests in Italy, 51, 192n31, 195n76

Jews: in Hungary, 132, 135, 164, 206n18, 207n41, 209n72, 210n84, 210n90; in Romania, 3, 5, 18, 22–25, 28, 33, 36–37, 48–49, 55, 58, 60, 62, 67, 71, 79–80, 87–95, 99–101, 107, 116–21, 156–58, 164, 177, 187n8, 188n14, 194n52, 197n28, 202n26, 203n46, 206n14, 214n47; in Russia, Soviet Union, and Ukraine, 18, 23–24, 196n6
Jezierski, Raymundus (Bishop of Bacău), 141
jus sanguinis, 93

Kállay, Miklós, 135
Kapalo, James, 15
Karaite Jews, 18, 196n6, 196n8
Karlowitz, Treaty of, 174
Kashubs/Cassubians, 36, 196n6
Kaukoensi, 152
Kerns, Iacob, 91
Kiss, Géza, 125, 207n34
Kodály, Zoltán, 10, 200n66
Kogălniceanu, Mihail, 141, 212n6
Kontra, Miklós, 10
Korponay, András, 127
Kulturgeschichte, 34
Kulturkampf, 36, 43–44, 57–58

László, Antal, 136
Lateran, Treaty of, 193n49
latinitatea (Latinity), 140, 176
Lausanne, Treaty of, 115
Law on Religious Denominations (Romania), 53
Law on Acquiring and Losing Romanian Nationality (1924). *See* Mârzescu Law
League of Nations, 120
Lebensraum, 19, 116
Legion of the Archangel Michael (Legiunea Arhanghelului Mihail), 15, 25, 34, 40, 53, 58–64, 74, 88, 93–94, 146, 155, 174, 186n27, 188n16, 194n62, 195n76, 195–96n79, 197n15, 197n31; Legionary Aid, 63, 195n79; Legionnaires' rebellion (1941), 62–63, 94, 155; Romanian Roman Catholics in, 15, 53, 58–64, 195n76. *See also* Iron Guard
Lespezi, 148
Livezeanu, Irina, 68
Lodzer Mensch, 18–19, 67, 196n6
Luizi-Călugăra/Lujzikalagor, 139, 148, 212n1, 213n32, 215n59
Lükő, Gábor, xxv, 31, 33, 83, 85, 197n15, 200n66
Lunca de Sus/Gyimesfelsők, 169
Lutheranism, in Hungary and Transylvania, 36, 43, 45–46, 125, 175–76, 191n5

Macartney, C. A., 36, 175
Madagascar Plan, 119–20, 206n14
Magyar Fajvédők Országos Szövetségé (Hungarian National Alliance of Race Protectors), 124, 178
Magyar Nemzetbiológia Intézet (Hungarian National Biological Institute), 127
Magyar Országos Véderő Egyesület (Association of Hungarian National Defense), 124
Mályusz, Elemér, xxv, 31, 80–84
Măneuți/Andrásfalva, 126
Manuilă, Sabin, xxii, 30, 118, 121, 153–56, 187n3
Marin, Vasile, 61
Marmaggi, Francesco, 39, 41, 191n9
Mărtinaș, Dumitru, 195n76

Index

Mărtinaş, Ioan, xviii, 62–64, 146, 195n76, 212n13
Márton, Áron, 131
Mârzescu Law (Law on Acquiring and Losing Romanian Nationality, 1924), 90, 201n2. *See also* Commission for Establishing Conditions for Naturalization and Recognition
Masures, 18, 67, 196n6, 196n8
Mehedinţi, Simion, 69, 154
Merfea, Mihai, 105–7, 203n38
Meteş, Ştefan, 75
Michael (Mihai) I, 62, 157
Micu-Klein, Samuel, 27, 55
Mikecs, László, xxv, 31, 84–85, 200n65
Milcov, 180, 198n45, 212n3
minorities, ethnic: and the Csangos, 11–16, 18, 23–24, 28, 33, 40–41, 49–56, 65–69, 82–87, 89, 104–14, 125–26, 128–37, 140–58, 162–72; Hungarians living outside territorial Hungary, 11–12, 22, 30–33, 66–69, 71–73, 79–86, 115–17, 124–36, 158–59, 178, 200n63, 205nn3–4, 208n60; in Hungary, 3, 122, 127, 131–33, 178; and the "minority question" in east-central Europe, xii, 4–6, 13–19, 37, 59, 65–68, 93, 115–18, 162, 164–65, 170, 196n8; in Romania, 5, 11–13, 15–17, 22–24, 27–30, 33, 35–36, 45–46, 48–51, 57, 65–68, 71–73, 77–78, 81–83, 87–94, 99, 104–5, 109, 117–21, 147–48, 154, 157–59, 162–63, 177, 202n26; Romanians living outside territorial Romania, 108, 147, 157, 177. *See also* Aromanians; Bunjevci; Gagauz; Germans, Germany; Jews; Karaite Jews; Kashubs; Masures; Minority Treaties; Serbs, Serbia; Slavs; Szeklers
minorities, religious or confessional, 11, 14–16, 22, 27–28, 33, 36–45, 47–51, 71–77, 83, 87–89, 93–94, 125, 175, 186n20, 190n1, 192n18
Minority Treaties, 22, 29, 32, 37, 87–88, 115
Moldavia, 24–26, 32, 36, 49, 67, 72, 82–86, 89, 94, 100, 104–5, 108–10, 113–14, 117, 122, 125–26, 128–54, 156–62, 167–69, 171–74, 179–81, 184n14, 195n68, 198n45, 200n65, 204n70, 209n64, 212n12, 213nn14–15, 215n48. *See also* Roman Catholicism in Moldavia

Moldovan, Iuliu, 59, 70, 77, 148, 155, 161
Moravia, 147, 205n7
Móricz, Zsigmond, 78
Moţa, Ion, 61
Muir, Edward, 170
Munich Agreement (1938), 117, 205n7

Nagy, László, 134
Nagy, Ödön, 30
narodnicism (*narodniki*), 79, 81, 199n59
national autotelism (*nemzeti üncélúság*), 124
national belonging, xi, 4–6, 12–18, 26–28, 32–33, 38–39, 44–46, 51–53, 58–59, 65–68, 70–71, 84, 87–94, 112–14, 140–42, 166–67, 170, 175–76, 204n66; and the Csangos, 12–14, 16–18, 45–46, 51–53, 58–60, 67, 83–86, 89, 112–14, 140–63, 168–70; and the Iron Guard, 59–60; and the Szeklers, 72–78, 81–84, 129, 140–41, 149–52, 155, 168–69, 172, 176, 196n10
National-Christian Defense League, 25, 54, 88
nationalism, xii, 14, 60, 65, 71, 88, 165; in Hungary, 30–33, 35, 65–66, 135–38, 142; in Romania, 8, 15–18, 25–28, 35, 38, 41–49, 53, 57–61, 64, 72, 88, 119, 141–42, 151, 155, 162, 179–80, 194n67; religious, 8, 15–16, 27–28, 38, 41–49, 53, 57–64, 108, 141–42, 160, 189n23, 59. *See also* Orthodoxism, Orthodoxists
nationality certificates (*certificat de naţionalitate*), in Romania, 5, 20, 29, 66–67, 89–92, 94–114, 138, 147, 153, 159, 164, 176, 201n3, 201n16. *See also* certificates of ethnic origin; Mârzescu Law; national belonging
nationality laws, in Romania: influence of Nazi Germany, 91–92. *See also* certificates of ethnic origin; Mârzescu Law; national belonging; nationality certificates
nationality lists, in Romania, 90–91
nationality registers, in Romania, 65, 90
naturalization (laws), in Romania, 33, 90–95, 100, 176. *See also* Commission for Establishing Conditions for Naturalization and Recognition; Mârzescu Law
Neamţ County, 8–9, 104, 148, 172–73, 180, 184n14, 191n11, 212n1

Negri, Costache, 141, 212n6
Németh, Kálmán, xxv, 125, 138
Németh, László, 35, 78–79
népiségtörténet (ethnohistory, Hungarian), 31, 79–84, 179
Netzhammer, Raymund, 39–41, 191n9
Neuilly, Treaty of, 115
Nichols, Johanna, 167
Nistor, Aurel, 75
Northern Bukovina. *See* Bukovina
Northern Transylvania. *See* Transylvania
numerus clausus, 49, 92–93, 118–19, 177; and *numerus nullus*, 119; and *numerus vallachicus*, 92, 177
Nuremberg Laws, 93

Old Church Slavonic, 26
Opreanu, Sabin, 74–76, 198n32
Oprișanu, Emil, 121, 206n25
Originea Catolicilor din Moldova (The origin of the Catholics in Moldavia), 141, 161, 212n5
Originea etnică (Ethnic origin), 100
Orthodoxism, Orthodoxists, xiii, 17, 38–39, 41–49, 51–58, 76, 140–42, 155, 179–80, 186n27, 189n23
Ostforschung, Ostforscher, 18–19, 29–30, 67, 196n6

Pal, Iosif M. Petru, xix, 138–48, 151–54, 161–63, 193n39, 212n1, 212n5, 213n32, 214n35, 215n56, 215n59
pan-Slavism, 124
Paris Peace Conference (1919), 87; and treaties, 22, 29, 32, 65, 83, 95. *See also* Minority Treaties
Pentru legionari (For the legionaries), 60–61
Petit, Eugen Dimitrie, xxi, 100–102, 143
Petrescu, Cezar, 54
Petrescu, Ștefania, 54, 194nn52–53
Phanariot rule, 25
Pius XI, Pope, 52, 188n15, 193n49
Pius XII, Pope, 48, 193n49
Poles, 23–24, 51, 146, 180; Poland, 18, 24, 29, 36, 39, 67, 116, 132, 180, 189n23, 196n6, 206n14, 210n84; Polish-Soviet War, 24
Popa-Lisseanu, Gheorghe, 28, 76–77, 140, 163

popes, papacy, 42–43, 46, 48, 52, 142, 179, 181, 188n15, 193n49. *See also* Pius XI, Pope; Pius XII, Pope; Rome; Vatican
poporanism, 199n59. *See also* narodnicism
population exchanges, 70, 89, 115, 117–19, 126, 189n17. *See also* population transfers
population transfers, 29, 65, 68, 84, 89–90, 114–18, 121, 125, 131, 134–35, 161, 210n77. *See also* population exchanges
Porsenna, Nocolae. *See* Ionescu, Nicolae Gh.
Premilitară (Pregătirea Premilitară), 62–63, 104–5, 110, 113
Public Education Act of 1893 (Romania), 83

race laws, 20–21, 88, 91–93. *See also* blood laws; citizenship laws; nationality certificates
race science, xiii, 3–4, 16–20, 23, 27–32, 60, 66–67, 70–71, 74–81, 88–92, 123–27, 143, 147–56, 161, 178, 190n27, 199n52, 207n42
Reche, Otto, 120
refugees, World War II: Romanian, 63, 89, 104; Hungarian, 133, 205n3
Regat (Vechiul Regat, Old Regat), 37, 57, 72, 157–59, 173–74, 191n5
relocation. *See* population exchanges; population transfers
repatriation, 23, 31, 116, 126, 128–38, 147, 157, 178, 202n26
Rezident Principal of Moldavia, 108, 203n47
Rilke, Rainer Maria, 47
Robu, Mihai, xix, 39–40, 113–14, 153, 191nn10–11
Roma (Gypsies), 10, 185n14
Roman (Romanian town, province), 11, 107, 173, 206n16, 212n5, 213n15
Roman Catholicism in Moldavia, xiii, 3–16, 24–25, 28, 31–32, 36, 39–40, 49, 51, 60–64, 103–5, 139, 141–46, 159, 162, 179–81, 184n13, 185n15, 191n5, 191n11, 193n40, 212n1, 212n3, 212n5
Roman Empire, 47, 52, 146
Romanian Advanced School of Rome, 161
Romanian Army, 7, 22, 108
Romanian Constitution: of 1866, 38, 181; of 1923, 8, 22, 29, 33, 37, 42, 87, 92; of 1938, 29, 92–94

Romanianization (*românizare*), xiii, 15, 28–29, 31, 37, 72, 83, 95, 101, 154, 170, 177, 189n16, 189n17, 201n23, 202n24

Romanian-Vatican Concordat (1927/29), 40–48, 53, 87, 110, 155, 160, 192n15, 192n17

românii de peste hotare (Romanians across the border), 147, 177

Români Secuizați și Regiune Secuizată (Szeklerized Romanians and Szeklerized region), 7

românismul (Romanianism), 34, 38, 48–49, 53–56, 140–42. *See also* Cruciada Românismul

Romanity (*romanitatea*), 140, 143–44, 161, 177

Romans, 144

Rome: Iosif Petru Pal studying in, 139, 176, 212n1; Mussolini's March on, 60; and the Vatican, 41, 43, 142, 179

Rosenberg, Alfred, 120

Rothschild, Joseph, 13

Royal Dictatorship (of King Carol II), 29, 92, 94

Russia, Russians, 24, 79, 142, 146, 161–62, 174, 209n62, 215nn56–57; Russian Empire, 91–92, 133; Russian language, 26, 179; Russian Orthodox Church, 47, 186n23

Ruthenians, 23–24, 41, 89, 132, 158, 180, 207n37

Săbăoani/Szabófalva, 8–9, 40, 191n11, 212n5

Saint Germain, Treaty of, 22

Sarló, 79

Satu Mare/Szatmár, 132, 208n49

schools, schooling, 7, 23, 36, 39, 71–73, 78, 83, 103, 105–7, 110, 113–15, 125, 146, 148, 155, 171, 192n18, 195n68

Școala Ardeleană. *See* Transylvanian School

Școala Nouă (New School), 27

Scott, James C., 20

Scriban, Iuliu, xx, 54–56, 194nn53–54

Second Vienna Award (1940), 22, 88–89, 134, 175

secuizare. *See* Szeklerization

seminary, Roman-Catholic: of Bucharest, 192n31; of Iași, 7, 40, 51, 62, 64, 84, 129; of Luizi-Călugăgura, 212n1

Serbs, Serbia, xii, xiii, 3, 56, 108, 122, 127, 130–33, 142, 147, 157, 205nn3–4, 208n60; Lusatian Serbs, 196n8

serology (in Romania), 17, 76, 148–52, 162

Sibiu, 98, 148, 156, 161, 202n26, 213n32

Sima, Horia, 62

Siret (town), 180, 202n26

Siret River, Siret River Valley, 11, 25, 60, 113–14, 142, 145, 149, 167, 173, 183n5, 213n14

Slavs, 5, 22, 29, 59, 71, 117, 121, 123, 125, 156, 164, 168, 205n4; and South Slavs, 128, 132

Slovaks, Slovakia, Slovak lands, 29, 116, 127, 205n7, 206n18, 207n37

Smith, Anthony D., 31, 166, 185n19

Smith, Helmut Walser, 170

Social Works Patronage Committee (Comitetul de Patronaje al Operelor Sociale), 107

Society of Saint Ladislas (Szent László Társulat), 9

sociologists: Hungarian, 4, 67, 82, 197n15, 199n59, 207n42; Romanian, 4, 30, 67, 70, 121, 154

sociology: Hungarian, 4, 35, 67–68, 79–82; as a nation-building science in east-central Europe, 19, 67; Romanian, xii, 4, 29–31, 35, 67–71, 82, 121, 154

Solonari, Vladimir, 99

Sorbs, 18, 67, 196n6

Southern Bukovina. *See* Bukovina

Southern Transylvania. *See* Transylvania

Soviets, Soviet Union, 18–19, 22–25, 28, 62, 91, 94, 100, 115, 117, 120, 124, 131, 134, 136, 154, 157, 160–62, 174, 202n34, 215n54, 215n59; Polish-Soviet War, 24; Soviet Ukraine, 28

Spain, 47, 58

Spengler, Oswald, 69

SS (*Schutzstaffel*), 30, 92, 132

Stăniloae, Dumitru, xx, 45–46, 49, 54, 159

State Undersecretariat of Romanianization, Colonization, and Inventory (Subsecretariatul de Stat al Romanizării, Colonizării și Inventarului, SSRCI), 29, 95, 154, 177. *See also* Directorate of Minorities; Ethnical, Biological, and Statistical Section

Șumuleu-Ciuc/Csíksomlyó, 85, 200n76

Szabó, T. Attila, 31, 85, 200n75

Szabó, Dezső, 35, 78–79

Szekfű, Gyula, 31, 33, 80, 190n27, 190n29
Szeklerization, 68, 73–76, 144, 149, 151, 176, 197n28
Szekler land, 9, 68, 71–74, 76–77, 85, 104, 132, 136, 138, 140, 144, 172, 174, 197n28, 198n38, 204n70, 213n19
Szeklers, 9, 23–24, 67–68, 71–78, 81–84, 114, 122, 125–26, 129–40, 145–46, 149–55, 158, 168–69, 172, 174, 196n10, 197n13, 198n40; Szekler dialect, 11; "Szekler problem," 72
szociográfia (sociography), 10, 31, 79, 82, 123, 207n34
Sztójay, Döme, xxiv, 135, 138, 207n41, 210n77

Takács, György, 168
Tánczos, Vilmos, 10, 184n9, 184n13, 185n14
Târgul Frumos, 145
Tatars, 28, 116, 129, 184n12, 204n70
Teachers' Association of Roman County, 105
Tecuci County, 148
Teleki, Pál, xxiv, 125–26, 132, 210n81
Theresa, Empress Maria, 123
Timoc, Timoc Valley, 27–28, 72, 108, 147, 154. See also *timoceni*
timoceni, 147, 157
Torpey, John, 20
Totul pentru Țară (All for the fatherland), 61–62
Transnistria, 25, 28, 71, 135, 147, 157, 202n26, 203n46; Romanian Governorate of Transnistria, 89, 135, 147, 157, 202n26, 203n46
Transylvania: retrocession of, refugees from, and resettlements in, 23, 88, 104, 125, 131, 134–36, 172, 196n10, 202n26, 202n34; Northern Transylvania, 160, 175, 204n70, 208n49; Southern Transylvania, 89, 98, 102, 104, 154, 157, 175, 202n26
Transylvanian School, 34, 55
Trencsényi, Balázs, 15
Trianon, Treaty of, 10, 30, 43, 72, 130, 174–75
Trotuș River, Trotuș River Valley, 11, 113, 173
Tufescu, Victor, 145, 213n15
Turanism (*Turanizmusz*), 80, 199n52
Turda, Marius, 15–17, 71
Turks, Turkey, 33, 115–16, 158, 167–69, 186n23, 199n52, 209n64; Ottoman suzerainty, 7, 25, 180. See also Gagauz

Ukrainians, Ukraine, 18, 24, 28, 67, 70, 116, 120, 133, 187n8, 188n11, 196n6, 202n26
Unguri (Găiceana-Unguri, Arini, Ungureni/Gajcsána-Magyarfalu), 148, 211n94
Uniate Church, Uniates. See Greek Catholicism
Unitarianism, in Transylvania and Hungary, 36, 125, 137, 175–76
university: of Bucharest, 57, 152, 161, 200n66; of Budapest, 200n66; of Cluj-Sibiu, 156, 161; of Cluj/Kolozsvár, 82; of Iași, 161
Ustaše, 47

Valea-Seacă, 136
Văleni, 136
Vâlsan, Gheorghe, 69–70, 73–74, 84
Várdy, Steven Béla, 178
Vasary, Ildiko, 123
Vatican, xiii, 3, 9–12, 15, 39–43, 48, 53, 87, 110, 134, 141, 153, 155, 159–61, 191n9, 192n17, 193n49, 202n31. See also popes, papacy; Romanian-Vatican Concordat; Rome
Verdery, Katherine, 16
Veress, Endre (Andrei Veress, John/János Tatrosi), xxv, 83, 85, 200n63, 200n65
Viața (The life), 50
Vida, Péter, 128, 208n59
Vincze, Gábor, 135, 203n41
vitézek, *Vitézi Rend* (Order of Vitéz), 133, 210n90
voivodes, voivodeships, 146, 174, 180, 188n9
Vojvodina, xi, xiii, 3, 23, 116, 173
Völkerpsychologie, 34
Volksdeutsche, 82, 116
Volksgemeinschaft, 17, 19, 67–68
Volksgeschichte, 33–34, 66
Volksgruppe, 82
Vornicenii Mici/Józseffalva, 125

Weber, Albert, 136
Weber, Eugen, 26
Werth, Henrik, xxiv, 131–33, 138, 210n77, 210n79
Westphalia, Treaty of, 156

Young Generation (interwar Romanian intellectuals), 40, 44, 52, 70
Yugoslavia, Yugoslavs (Kingdom of Yugoslavia, Kingdom of Serbs, Croats, and Slovenes), 3, 23, 28, 114, 116, 128, 130–32, 135, 138, 161, 173, 178, 205n4, 210n81, 214n40

www.ingramcontent.com/pod-product-compliance
Lightning Source LLC
Chambersburg PA
CBHW070838160426
43192CB00012B/2235